The Use of the Polygraph in Assessing, Treating and Supervising Sex Offenders

Wiley Series in

The Psychology of Crime, Policing and Law

Series Editors

Graham Davies and **Ray Bull**

University of Leicester, UK

The Wiley Series in the Psychology of Crime, Policing and Law publishes concise and integrative reviews on important emerging areas of contemporary research. The purpose of the series is not merely to present research findings in a clear and readable form, but also to bring out their implications for both practice and policy. In this way, it is hoped the series will not only be useful to psychologists but also to all those concerned with crime detection and prevention, policing, and the judicial process.

For other titles in this series please see `www.wiley.com/go/pcpl`

The Use of the Polygraph in Assessing, Treating and Supervising Sex Offenders

A Practitioner's Guide

Edited by

Daniel T. Wilcox

Wilcox Psychological Associates, UK and School of Psychology, University of Birmingham, UK

WILEY-BLACKWELL

A John Wiley & Sons, Ltd, Publication

This edition first published 2009.

Wiley-Blackwell is an imprint of John Wiley & Sons, formed by the merger of Wiley's global Scientific, Technical, and Medical business with Blackwell Publishing.

Registered Office
John Wiley & Sons Ltd, The Atrium, Southern Gate, Chichester, West Sussex, PO19 8SQ, UK

Editorial Offices
The Atrium, Southern Gate, Chichester, West Sussex, PO19 8SQ, UK
9600 Garsington Road, Oxford, OX4 2DQ, UK
350 Main Street, Malden, MA 02148-5020, USA

For details of our global editorial offices, for customer services, and for information about how to apply for permission to reuse the copyright material in this book please see our website at www.wiley.com/wiley-blackwell

Library of Congress Cataloging-in-Publication Data has been applied for

A catalogue record for this book is available from the British Library.

ISBN 978-0-470-74224-2 (hbk) 978-0-470-74223-5 (pbk)

Typeset in 10/12pt Century Schoolbook by Aptara Inc., New Delhi, India
Printed and bound in Singapore by Fabulous Printers Pte Ltd.

For my wife, Helen, and my daughters, Tara and Roz.

Contents

About the Editor ix

List of Contributors xi

Series Preface xv

Preface xix

Foreword xxiii

1 Overview: Opportunities and Responsibilities 1
Daniel T. Wilcox

2 The Clinical Use of the Polygraph with Sex Offenders: Caveats and Considerations 9
David Whittingham

3 Pre-Conviction and Post-Conviction Polygraph Testing: A Brief History 31
Daniel T. Wilcox and Lars Madsen

4 The Empirical Evidence for the Value of Post-Conviction Polygraph in the Treatment and Supervision of Sex Offenders 49
Lars Madsen and Daniel T. Wilcox

5 Basics of Post-Conviction Sex Offender Polygraph Testing 65
Daniel E. Sosnowski and Daniel T. Wilcox

6 Case Studies in the Utility of the Polygraph 97
Daniel T. Wilcox, Zerine O'Keeffe and Caroline Oliver

7 Polygraph Testing Internet Offenders 113
Jos Buschman and Stefan Bogaerts

8 Risk Assessment and the Polygraph 129
Theresa A. Gannon, Anthony R. Beech and Tony Ward

9 The Accuracy of Polygraphy in the Treatment and Supervision of Sex Offenders 155
Lars Madsen

10 Sex Offender Polygraph Testing in the United States: Trends and Controversies 181
Peggy Heil and Kim English

11 Other Post-Conviction Applications of Polygraphy 217
Shay Addison and Lou Crisilla

12 Interviewing and Interrogation 243
J.P. Blair

13 Alternate Technologies for the Detection of Deception 267
Jennifer M.C. Vendemia, Michael J. Schillaci, Robert F. Buzan, Eric P. Green and Scott W. Meek

14 Forensic Assessment of Sexual Interest: A Review 297
E. Kalmus, Anthony R. Beech and B. Warberg

Index 323

About the Editor

Dr Daniel T. Wilcox is a Chartered Clinical and Forensic Psychologist with the British Psychological Society. He grew up in Up-State New York obtaining a BA and an MA from the State University of New York, College at Geneseo and worked as a Psychologist in Rochester, New York for a number of years before moving to the UK. Dr Wilcox holds a Doctorate in Clinical Psychology from the University of Surrey and is an Honorary Research Fellow with the University of Birmingham, Centre for Forensic and Family Psychology. He is an active member of the National Organization for the Treatment of Abusers. Dr Wilcox is also on the International Advisory Board for the *Journal of Sexual Aggression* and the Editorial Board of the *Child Abuse Review*. Dr Wilcox has frequently presented at conferences and published papers in areas such as risk assessment; offender management, assessment and treatment; working with intellectually disabled sex offenders; resilience and risk factors associated with child sexual abuse; applications of psychometric measures to care and family proceedings and the employment of the polygraph with sex offenders. Dr Wilcox is Managing Director of Wilcox Psychological Associates (WPA), an independent practice that provides psychological reports for Court purposes and he is frequently called upon to give testimony as an expert witness. WPA has delivered assessment, treatment and consultancy to a range of adult and children's services for many years. Dan also contributed to the development of the first Home Office accredited, Community Sex Offender Groupwork Program, through WPA's partnership arrangement with the National Probation Service in the West Midlands, UK.

List of Contributors

Shay Addison

APA Accredited Polygrapher and Psychologist, 4-Life Psychology Centre, Fortitude Valley, Mt Gravatt, City, Wishart, Australia
e-mail: info@4life.com.au

Anthony R. Beech

Professor of Criminological Psychology, Centre for Forensic and Family Psychology, University of Birmingham, Edgbaston, Birmingham, B15 2TT, United Kingdom
e-mail: a.r.beech@bham.ac.uk

J.P. Blair

Assistant Professor, Department of Criminal Justice at Texas State University also Assistant Director of the Center of Geospatial Intelligence and Investigation; The University of Texas at San Antonio, 501 W. Durango, San Antonio, TX 78207, USA
e-mail: pete-blair@txstate.edu

Stefan Bogaerts

Professor of Forensic Psychology (also Deputy Director of the Research Center of the Ministry of Justice in the Netherlands), School of Forensic Psychology, Tilburg University, PO Box 90153, NL-5000 LE Tilburg, the Netherlands
e-mail: s.bogaerts@uvt.nl

Jos Buschman

APA Accredited Polygrapher and Forensic Psychologist, Faculty of Medical Science, Disciplinary Group Biological Psychiatry, University of Groningen, the Netherlands
e-mail: fjg.buschman@dji.minjus.nl

Robert F. Buzan

Department of Psychology, University of South Carolina, Columbia, SC 29208, USA
e-mail: rbuzan@sc.edu

Lou Crisilla III

APA Accredited Polygrapher and Vice President of the Florida Polygraph Association, 5150 Oakwood Trail, Mulberry, FL 33860, USA
e-mail: lou@deception.com

Kim English

Director of Research, Colorado Division of Criminal Justice, 700 Kipling, Suite 3000, Denver, CO 80215-5865, USA
e-mail: kim.english@cdps.state.co.us

Theresa A. Gannon

Lecturer in Forensic Psychology and Director of M.Sc in Forensic Psychology, Keynes College, University of Kent, Canterbury, Kent, CT2 7NP, United Kingdom
e-mail: T.A.Gannon@kent.ac.uk

Eric P. Green

Department of Psychology, University of South Carolina, Columbia, SC 29208, USA
e-mail: epgreen@sc.edu

Peggy Heil

Colorado Department of Corrections, Colorado Springs, CO 81212, USA
e-mail: pegheil@aol.com

Ellis Kalmus

Chartered Clinical Psychologist and Senior Associate with Phoenix Psychological Services, Senior Associate, Phoenix Psychological Services, 73 Priory Road, Kenilworth, CV8 1LQ, United Kingdom
e-mail: ellisk@blueyonder.co.uk

Lars Madsen

Clinical Psychologist, 4-Life Psychology Centre, Fortitude Valley, Mt Gravatt, City, Wishart, Australia
e-mail: info@4life.com.au

Scott Meek

Department of Psychology, University of South Carolina, Columbia, SC 29208, USA
e-mail: smeek@sc.edu

Zerine O'Keeffe

APA Accredited Polygrapher, Wilcox Psychological Associates, 55 Raddlebarn Road, Selly Oak, Birmingham, B29 6HQ, United Kingdom
e-mail: wpa55@btconnect.com

Caroline Oliver

APA Accredited Polygrapher and Chartered Forensic Psychologist, Centre for Forensic and Family Psychology, University of Birmingham, Edgbaston, Birmingham, B15 2TT, United Kingdom
e-mail: c.j.oliver@bham.ac.uk

Michael J. Schillaci

Managing Director of the McCausland Center and Assistant Research Professor in Psychology, University of South Carolina, Columbia, SC 29208, USA
e-mail: mjs@sc.edu

Daniel E. Sosnowski

APA Accredited Polygrapher, President (Elect) of the American Polygraph Association and President of S.O.S. Services Inc., 1069 Jamerson Road, Marietta, GA 30066, USA
e-mail: SOS4911@aol

Jennifer M.C. Vendemia

Research Associate Professor, Department of Psychology, University of South Carolina, Columbia, SC 29208, USA
e-mail: vendemia@mindspring.com

Brent Warberg

APA Accredited Polygrapher and Licensed Clinical Social Worker, 13 Ruby Gulch, Morganton, Georgia 30560 USA
e-mail: bwarberg@tds.net

Tony Ward

Professor of Clinical Psychology and Clinical Director at Victoria University of Wellington, PO Box 600, Wellington, New Zealand
e-mail: tony.ward@vuw.ac.nz

David Whittingham

Clinical and Forensic Psychologist, Psycare, Suite 1, Level 1, 201 Wickham Terrace, Springhill, QLD 4000, Australia
e-mail: davidw@psycare.co.au

Daniel T. Wilcox

Clinical and Forensic Psychologist, Director of Wilcox Psychological Associates, 55 Raddlebarn Road, Selly Oak, Birmingham, B29 6HQ, United Kingdom
e-mail: daniel-wilcox@btconnect.com

Series Preface

The Wiley Series in the Psychology of Crime, Policing and the Law publishes both single and multi-authored monographs and edited reviews of emerging areas of contemporary research. The purpose of this series is not merely to present research findings in a clear and readable form, but also to bring out their implications for both practice and policy. Books in this series are useful not only to psychologists, but also to all those involved in crime detection and prevention, child protection, policing and judicial processes.

The original idea for a device to measure bodily changes such as heart rate and respiration as indices of deception is usually credited to the pioneering Italian criminologist, Cesare Lombroso in 1895, but it was the Americans, particularly John Larson and Leonarde Keeler, who developed the polygraph as a working tool for law enforcement (Alder, 2007). The subsequent history of the use of the polygraph is a controversial one. The conventional polygraph machine in itself does not register lying, but requires the operator to interpret the output as reflecting concealment by the testee. The lack of requirement in the United States for any formal training and accreditation of operators led to a mushrooming of unlicensed operatives in the last century. Polygraphs were used not merely on criminal suspects in the US, but also on applicants and existing staff employed in the public and private sectors as a test of their honesty. A belief in the infallibility of the machine combined with unskilled interpretation of output led to many injustices which were only curtailed by the Employee Polygraph Protection Act of 1988, which limited the commercial applications of the machine. However, the polygraph continues to be widely used by the Secret Service and law enforcement agencies in North America as well as by police in other countries, particularly Israel and Japan. Today, the use of the machine as the ultimate arbiter of a defendant's guilt or innocence is discouraged, particularly in the light of the negative assessments of professional bodies such as the US National Academy of Sciences (2003) and the British Psychological Society (2004). Instead, it is increasingly seen as a screening tool to identify from a potential range of suspects, those on whom greatest investigative attention should be focused.

This book describes a range of work on a new and potentially valuable application of the polygraph, which is summarised in its title: *The Use of the Polygraph in Assessing, Treating and Supervising Sex Offenders*. Concern over the activities of such offenders subsequent to their release into the community is a matter of great public concern, both in Britain and the United States. Society places a heavy burden of responsibility on those who are required to monitor the movements and behavior of sex offenders post-conviction to ensure that they do not reoffend. Any procedure which can improve the quality and reliability of information supplied by offenders is of considerable practical importance. As the editor, Daniel Wilcox, makes clear, the results both from the pioneering studies in the US and the later national pilot scheme in the UK have produced promising results which have paved the way for polygraph testing to now become a routine feature in the post-conviction management of sex offenders in Britain.

Dr Daniel Wilcox is a forensic and clinical psychologist in private practice, with considerable practical experience of treating sex offenders. He was one of the first in the UK to appreciate the potential of the polygraph for monitoring offenders' post-release behavior and this in turn brought him into contact with other pioneers of the field, such as Daniel Sosnowski, Don Grubin and Tony Beech. This book has brought together their contributions and that of other leading researchers in the field from Britain, continental Europe, Australia, New Zealand, and the United States to outline their latest findings and to describe the practical applications and potential of this new and controversial technique. *The Use of the Polygraph in Assessing, Treating and Supervising Sex Offenders: A Practitioners' Guide* will be of interest not just to researchers and practitioners whose work brings them into contact with sexual offenders, but to all those who wish for an informed and informative account of a new weapon in the struggle to regulate and control the behavior of some of society's most feared and reviled offenders.

GRAHAM DAVIES
University of Leicester

REFERENCES

Alder, K. (2007). The Lie Detectors: *The History of an American Obsession*. New York: The Free Press.

British Psychological Society (2004). *A Review of the Current Scientific Status and Fields of Application of Polygraphic Deception Detection*. Leicester: British Psychological Society.

National Research Council of the National Academies (2003). *The Polygraph and Lie Detection*. Washington, DC: The National Academies Press.

Preface

Over the years professionals have become more aware of the impact of polygraphy on sex offender work. However, these developments have generally been in quite discreet areas including the North West of the United States, Texas and Colorado. Its wider spread use has been a much more gradual process. In Great Britain, for example, the application of polygraphy to this field began to emerge during the current decade, while in the Netherlands there has been some support over the past few years following research by Jos Buschman and colleagues, (Buschman, Wilcox, Foulger, Sosnowski, Bogaerts, & Mulder, 2008) though the political determination to employ this technology there still remains somewhat uncertain. In contrast to these recent developments Stan Abrams' early research and professional practice in this area has spanned over a quarter of a century (Abrams, 1991; Abrams & Abrams, 1993; Abrams, Hoyt & Jewell, 1991; Abrams & Ogard, 1986) and in his book, the US Judges who pioneered the earliest post conviction use of the polygraph in the late 60s and early 70s (Partee, 1975; Schmidt, Soloman & Johnson, 1973; Tuttle, 1969).

Even so, the field of polygraphy remains a subject of controversy though my particular interest in this tool has perhaps a stronger, evolving base of support relating to the assessment, treatment and supervision of convicted sex offenders.

My pursuit of polygraph development in Britain was directly influenced by Anna Salter in 1997 at a conference in San Diego. In fact her comments and references to her friend and polygraph trained colleague, Eric Holden, prompted me to contact him and the American Polygraph Association. I wanted to find out whether there was some potential for adding polygraphy to the range of techniques and intervention strategies that we had consolidated at that time to create the first Home Office Accredited Community Sex Offender Treatment Program in the

UK (West Midlands Probation Service, Sex Offender Unit; 1996–2000). In 1999 I subsequently met with Eric in Orlando, Florida at the Annual Police Polygraph Association Conference though due to scheduling difficulties he was unable to assist us with the UK trials. I also contacted Stan Abrams on a couple of occasions. He had generously sent me a range of materials explaining PCSOT early in my investigations and at this stage he gave me helpful guidance about how to design our study. From this point a combination of determination and good fortune followed, with Dave Middleton, Manager of the West Midlands Probation Services' Sex Offender Unit offering great support and encouragement to develop research in this area. Further, Dan Sosnowski, a senior member of the American Polygraph Association (now President incumbent), generously offered his time and considerable expertise to help move the plan forward and conduct two initial, small UK based polygraph trials (Wilcox, Middleton & Sosnowski, 1999; Wilcox & Sosnowski, 2002).

Don Grubin's subsequent involvement was pivotal and within a short time he and Dave Middleton were to play key roles in getting agreement for a large-scale, national pilot study to be undertaken in selected probation areas in England with convicted sex offenders. After the conclusion of Grubin's extensive research (with voluntarily polygraphed British sex offenders) spanning more than five years, the Offender Management Act (2007) was passed and included a provision for mandatory polygraph testing of convicted sex offenders in the UK who were on parole/license having received custodial sentences of a year or more. As such, the further acceptance of polygraphy as a tool in sex offender work has, in Great Britain, now taken a great step forward. The assessment, treatment and public protection implications for using polygraphy, in combination with other tools at our disposal are, in my opinion, very substantial and it is my hope that this book will provide professionals in this very challenging field, a better understanding of how polygraphy can be integrated into their work successfully to augment and further improve the effectiveness of their practice. I would in particular like to recognize these professionals for the important work they do and commend those men convicted of sexual offences whose willingness to voluntarily be polygraphed was critical to the formal establishment of polygraphy as an accepted tool in sex offender work in Britain today.

A wide range of acknowledged experts have made essential contributions to the production of this book and I am enormously grateful for their support. At the outset Tanya Garrett's encouragement and typically pro-active attitude provided the necessary catalyst for me to begin this project. Thanks also to Bill Marshall who quite unknowingly has had a tremendous impact on the approach I have taken to working in this field. A special thanks to my friend and colleague, Lars Madsen, who was extensively involved in developing and conceptualizing the book as well as writing and reviewing early draft chapters. In addition, Zerine O'Keeffe deserves a special mention for assisting me in editing chapters relating to polygraph administration. Thanks to Rita Donathy for her ongoing, steadfast support in typing and amending the chapters. Many other individuals have also contributed to this book including Sally Harley, Carrie-Ann Pash, Sandra Callander, Sarah Foulger, Helena Markall, Roz Wilcox and Tony Axford. Very special thanks to Kathryn Law who helped proof the final manuscript before submission to the publishers. The encouragement of Gillian Leslie, Ally Dunnett, Andrew Peart and Karen Shield from Wiley-Blackwell and Suresh Kumar and Seema Koul from Aptara Inc. was immensely helpful through the latter stages, as was the supportive guidance from the series editors, Ray Bull and Graham Davies. Further, unreserved appreciation and praise is extended to my wife, Helen, and my daughters, Tara, and Roz. Helen, in particular has given me moral support and practical help throughout, as well as being understanding about my frequent lack of availability while I have been involved in this project. Lastly, everything we do starts somewhere so I would like to thank the rest of my family including my brothers Tim, Don, Mike and Tom who, like my parents before them, continue to provide another dimension of support, meaning and enthusiasm that enriches my work and my life.

DANIEL T. WILCOX

REFERENCES

Abrams, S., "The Directed Lie Control Question," Polygraph 20 (1991): 26–31.

Abrams, S., & Abrams J.B. (1993). *Polygraph Testing of the Pedophile*. Portland, Oregon: Ryan Gwinner Press.

Abrams, S., Hoyt, D., & Jewell, C. (1991). The effectiveness of the disclosure test with sex abusers of children. *Polygraph*, 20(3), 204–213.

Abrams S., & Ogard E., (1986). Polygraph surveillance of probationers. *Polygraph*, 15, 174–182.

Buschman, J., Wilcox, D.T., Foulger, S., Sosnowski, D., Bogaerts, S., & Mulder, J. (2008). Sexual history disclosure polygraph examinations among a group of 25 Dutch men who downloaded child pornography. *Panopticon*, 2008.2, 36–47.

Partee, C.E. (1975). Probation and the polygraph. *Legal Admissibility of the Polygraph* Springfield, Illinois: C.C. Thomas.

Schmidt, H.K., Soloman, G.F., and Johnson, H., "The Artificial Conscience," Corrective and Social Psychiatry 23 (1973): 93–100.

Teuscher, T., "The Polygraph and Probation," Polygraph 7 (1978): 1–4.

Tuttle J.C. (1969). Personal Communication. In *Polygraph Testing of the Pedophile*, Abrams, S., and Abrams J.B. (1993), Portland, Oregon: Ryan Gwinner Press.

West Midlands Probation Service, Sex Offender Unit. (1996–2000). *Community sex offender groupwork programme – Manual*. West Midlands Probation Service. Birmingham (Subsequently accredited by the Home Office).

Wilcox, D.T., & Sosnowski, D. (2002). Polygraph testing sex offenders. *Probation in Europe, Conférence Permanente Européenne de la Probation*, No. 26.

Foreword

I am honored to have been given the opportunity to write this foreword. Dan Wilcox has coordinated and edited this outstanding work and I have no doubt that it will significantly contribute to the professional understanding of *polygraph post-conviction sex offender testing* (PCSOT).

This publication will likely become a standard reference. It is a wonderful compilation of information for those who want a clear and concise explanation of PCSOT and a glimpse at the role polygraph may have in the future world of post-conviction oversight. This edited work will have a broader appeal because the authors, for the most part, are not polygraph examiners writing about polygraph and many are noted experts in other professional fields.

Less than twenty years ago, PCSOT was an "experimental" procedure at best and infrequently mentioned among polygraph examiners. At that time terms like post-conviction polygraph, pre-conviction polygraph, maintenance testing, monitoring testing, sexual history verifications, instant offense testing, and confronting denial were not familiar to most practicing examiners.

Today PCSOT represents the fastest growing segment of polygraph practice in the United States and internationally. In fact, as a result of this, perceptions about polygraph are changing. In the United States PCSOT is mandated in many cases as a requirement for probation/parole. Frequently, subsequent decisions about a sex offender's movement and activities are influenced by polygraph examinations. Polygraph is now identified by many as one important element in society's fight to protect its citizens from sexual assault. Pre-conviction, investigative polygraph is generally viewed by its users as a valuable tool; *PCSOT is now increasingly viewed by its users as an invaluable tool.*

A 2007 American Polygraph Association survey revealed that 46 states in the United States employ PCSOT for the treatment and oversight of sexual offenders. The other four states are reviewing its applicability in their communities. In the history of the polygraph profession, no other application has expanded so much while simultaneously gaining the support of associated professions, as well as the judiciary and elected representatives.

Against this backdrop I am reminded of how PCSOT actually started as a discipline distinct from its pre-conviction applications. While in an APA board meeting in the early 1980s, a highly respected APA member and forensic psychologist, Stan Abrams, requested that the Board fund $10,000 for initial research in a newly developing polygraph specialty – "clinical polygraph" which was the term that preceded PCSOT. I remember the curious expressions and blank looks of many Board members, myself included. Dr. Abrams explained the significant potentials and development in this emerging area and suggested that Clinical Polygraph might, in time, alter the direction of polygraph and change peoples' perspectives about its usefulness. At that time testing was ongoing in the northwest United States, primarily with sex offenders. Describing his work there, Dr Abrams discussed the scope of sexual offending in the US and internationally. He further offered his vision of the impact that polygraph could make on the assessment, treatment and supervision of these offenders. The reception given by the Board to Dr. Abrams was cordial yet skeptical and his ideas were viewed as experimental and potentially revolutionary. Today, professionals everywhere associated with post-conviction sex offender treatment and supervision are indebted to Dr. Abrams. We say "thank you for your wisdom and foresight."

In the development of PCSOT it is also important to recognize the work of Kim English and her colleagues with the Colorado Department of Justice. Their definition of the Containment Model and the principles they adopted as vital to effective sex offender supervision identified polygraph examiners as equal partners with treatment providers and supervision officials in holding sex offenders accountable for their past and future behaviors. This gave further credibility to PCSOT.

Wilcox and his colleagues suggest that like any developing field, PCSOT testing will be continuously evolving and responsibly evaluated for its contributions. This process will be enhanced by the cooperation and mutual support of collateral professionals including treatment, corrections, probation/parole, risk assessment and jurists along with scientists whose research continuously provides guidance. I am not aware of any publication today that offers such a broad spectrum of views, information, and future-focused thinking as does this edition by Wilcox and the other invited authors.

Issues abound and are constantly debated about what role polygraph testing should have in post-conviction supervision. The reality is that polygraph testing is not perfect in its predictive capability but it is the best method available anywhere today for distinguishing truth from deception. This claim is virtually undisputed among practitioners involved in sex offender work. The reality is that involved and responsible professionals need to learn as much as possible from each other and continue to improve the collaboration process. These collaborating professionals have learned from each other during this evolution what it takes to maximize treatment potential and with this the benefit to society. The reality is what Gavin DeBecker wrote in his Foreword to Anna Salter's thought-provoking book *Predators: Pedophiles, Rapists, and Other Sex Offenders* (2004) - *"The solution to sexual violence is acceptance of reality."* First, the reality is confronting denial which is credited with being key to successful sexual abuse treatment. Then, the reality is that polygraph testing has demonstrated itself to be a vital element to assess denial by virtue of its ability to confront and simultaneously verify. Finally, the reality is that without polygraph, evaluators may only speculate about numbers of actual victims, acceptance of responsibility, guilt/innocence, and the myriad of other factors associated with successful treatment. More recidivism is the alternative.

Dan Wilcox and the other authors contributing to this text will help every professional interested in or associated with sex offenders. The material in this book will help us all to better understand how polygraph testing can assist in achieving our overall goal - the prevention of future assaults on children and vulnerable adults everywhere. Dan Wilcox has brought together a strong and diversified collection of authors covering a variety of topics that takes the reader on a journey from past to present and into the future. The reader will become familiar with polygraph testing in general and PCSOT in particular. The chapters cover current and future aspects of sex offender management and supervision as well as offering exciting new ideas for future collaboration between clinical specialties, government and polygraph professionals. While the authors emphasize throughout the book that PCSOT is both fluid and evolving, they also endeavor to anchor this process recognizing that we must understand our past to better predict our future. This text is a milestone to that end.

Eric J. Holden, M.A., L.P.C.
Past President, American Polygraph Association
Chair, APA PCSOT committee, 2007–2009

CHAPTER 1

Overview: Opportunities and Responsibilities

Daniel T. Wilcox

Over recent years there has been a steady accumulation of information about post-conviction uses of the polygraph, particularly in work with sex offenders. The polygraph has been employed to investigate the range of sexual interests and behaviors that offenders can demonstrate (Heil, Ahlmeyer & Simons, 2003; O'Connell, 1998; Simons, Wurtele & Durham, 2008; Wilcox, Sosnowski, Warberg & Beech, 2005). These studies have confirmed significant levels of crossover sexual offending. In the past it was popularly held that men who are known to sexually abuse in one area were unlikely to 'cross over' and show concomitant deviant sexual interests and involvements in other areas e.g. there was a belief that individuals who sexually abuse adults would not sexually abuse children, that those who abuse girls would not abuse boys, that those who offend within the family would not have deviant extra-familial interests and that those who commit non contact offences do not have any susceptibility to committing contact sexual crimes.

However, these more recent studies have consistently rejected the notion that crossover is rare and have regularly evidenced disclosures of more wide ranging sexual offending interests and involvements than

The Use of the Polygraph in Assessing, Treating and Supervising Sex Offenders: A Practitioner's Guide
Edited by Daniel T. Wilcox.

standard methods have identified. Further, this has frequently had direct treatment implications, giving therapists the opportunity to engage more fully with offenders to produce more robust relapse prevention strategies. This work allows treatment facilitators to better address crimes for which offenders have been convicted, as well as areas of sexual interest or activity for which they have not been criminally charged but pose a risk to the public by their own admission during polygraph examination. Importantly offenders with treated profiles have a much greater potential for remaining offence-free in the future (Allam, 2000), and as the polygraph serves to identify the magnitude of the offending risk in terms of incidence of past offending, numbers of victims and types of offending behaviors, effective treatment becomes more achievable. Relatedly, the polygraph has been shown to be an effective tool in breaking down denial among offenders, and as most sex offender treatment programs focus considerable attention on offenders taking accountability for their offending behavior, (Allam, 2000; Salter, 1988), the polygraph again offers a beneficial way forward enabling convicted offenders to engage in the treatment services that are most readily available to them.

Nonetheless there continues to be controversy about the use of the polygraph in working with post conviction sex offenders (Ben-Shakhar & Gershon, 2008; Gannon, Beech & Ward, 2008; Grubin, 2008; Meijer, Verschuere, Merckelbach, Harald & Crombez, 2008). However, this application of the polygraph has demonstrated considerable utility in particular to professional practitioners in the sex offender field and this has led to the expanding employment of this technology.

In the UK, the recently passed Offender Management Act (2007) makes provision for polygraph testing of sex offenders who are released on license or parole from a custodial sentence of twelve months or more. This law specifies that post-conviction polygraph testing for assessment, treatment and monitoring sex offenders can be employed, though it prohibits the use of any evidence obtained in this way being used in criminal proceedings where the offender is the defendant. Through employment of these powers, plans have also been developed for further research to proceed such that convicted offenders are legally compelled to engage in polygraph testing thus enabling additional systematic assessment of the polygraph to be undertaken on a larger scale. It is recognized that in some studies, including the British and Dutch work referenced in this book, the offenders who have been polygraphed have volunteered and have not been legally mandated to do so (Buschman, Wilcox, Foulger, Sosnowski, Bogaerts & Mulder, 2008; Grubin, 2006; Grubin, Madsen, Parsons, Sosnowski & Warburg, B. 2004; Wilcox & Sosnowski, 2005; Wilcox,

Sosnowski & Middleton, 2000; Wilcox, Sosnowski, Middleton & Grubin, 2003). The Offender Management legislation will enable polygraph to be used with riskier sexual offenders on parole/license following custodial sentences for the commission of serious sexual offences. They will be required to be regularly polygraphed and engage in compulsory treatment work, evaluation and supervision.

Based on current research drawn upon to produce this book it is asserted that the different post-conviction polygraph examinations have important utility in the management of offender behavior. Periodic polygraph testing appears to have a deterrent effect on criminal attitudes and behavior. With regard to monitoring and supervising the behavior of sexual offenders, research in this area by Grubin (2006) suggested that the polygraph has considerable utility. Disclosure testing facilitates the therapeutic process offering a potential to more accurately gauge the range of deviant sexual interests and risk behaviors in which offenders engage. Index offence or specific incident testing breaks down denial in a way that enables cognitive distortions to be addressed better in treatment. Salter (1997) described that sex offender workers in the North West of the United States would be unwilling to work with these individuals if they were not allowed to use polygraphy as an adjunct to their management and treatment work. The dialogue between supervising officer, therapist, polygraph examiner and other professionals including psychologists, provides a more comprehensive framework within which sexual offending behavior can be more effectively contained.

Grubin's UK polygraph pilot (2006) demonstrated the utility of polygraph in this regard. A further study by Wilcox and Donathy (2008) described the views of sex offender workers in England about the employment of the polygraph within the course of their work. Importantly, those professionals who had had the opportunity to use polygraphy in their work with sex offenders were more strongly supportive of its use in sex offender work than those individuals who did not have direct experience of polygraphy in their work. Indeed, where the use of polygraphy has been integrated into sex offender assessment, treatment and supervision, despite it possibly being looked upon skeptically at the outset, polygraph's continued employment has been strongly endorsed by professionals involved.

However, the application of polygraphy to post-conviction sex offender testing will continue to require careful integration in the UK with substantial attention directed at the development and maintenance of effective polygraph practice. It is important that sound guidelines for post-conviction testing should be agreed and adhered to where this technology is being introduced. The establishment of standards for professional practice is needed as well as a code of conduct for polygraph examiners working with sex offenders, in particular. Further the promotion of appropriate professional training in this field is essential as well as the introduction of a process of accrediting polygraph examiners at basic and specialist levels. Lastly, in my opinion, it would be of considerable assistance in the UK if a board or council were established to monitor the implementation of polygraph in this area, specifically as a safeguard against unprofessional practice and to ensure that the polygraphers' contribution is of a high standard.

The central focus of this book is to help professionals who work with sex offenders to have a clearer understanding of how post-conviction polygraph testing can assist them in assessing, treating and supervising sexual offenders. The book deals with accuracy, validity, and utility issues, together with ethical considerations and discussion about effective management integration of this tool within the field. The book also represents a 'work in progress' volume to be revisited and revised as further research is generated. The chapters endeavor to set out polygraph development and its use with sex offenders. From this central theme the book extends its brief to consider other applications of post-conviction polygraphy, and to explore related areas including interview and interrogation techniques, alternative technologies for detecting deception, and a systematic review of current methods for assessing sexual interest and deviance.

In the following chapter, Whittingham describes the polygraph's clinical application as distinct from the many other pre-conviction investigative uses of polygraph. His consideration of 'caveats and limitations' provides an important backdrop to Chapter 3 by Wilcox and Madsen, which explores polygraph development broadly over the last century or so and emphasizes the establishment of post-conviction uses of this instrument. Both chapters provide historical and contextual information regarding the use of the polygraph more generally, allowing the reader to gain a sense of the rationale and basis behind its current use with sex offenders.

Following on from this, Madsen and Wilcox in Chapter 4 set out the empirical evidence of the utility of the polygraph, describing its value particularly within the field of sex offender work. Chapter 5 by Sosnowski and Wilcox offers direction and clarification to professionals about the basic application of post-conviction polygraph to sex offenders from the perspective of a trained and experienced polygraph examiner in this field. While there is a great deal of evidence supporting the utility of the polygraph, it is important that the complexities and subtleties associated with this technology are acknowledged and understood.

In Chapter 6, Wilcox, O'Keeffe and Oliver present case studies where the polygraph has been employed in collaboration with supervision, assessment and treatment processes already in use within Probation Services. The chapter highlights a need for careful communication among professionals and describes ways that the various participants can contribute to improving the effectiveness in sex offender management. A re-occurring theme in this arena of work is the need for constant interdisciplinary teamwork and communication if sex offenders are to be most effectively assessed, treated and supervised.

Chapter 7 by Buschman explores the unique opportunities presented by polygraphy as a means of assessing the interests, behaviors and risks presented by internet child pornography downloaders. The polygraph has been employed with this population and has provided insights about these offenders not readily accessible through other means. This work has given indications of important links between downloading child pornography and the risk of contact sexual offending behavior. Chapter 8 by Gannon, Ward and Beech, provides a helpful consideration of the polygraph's potential role in assessing risk among sex offenders. The authors describe the ideological model of risk (Beech & Ward, 2004) and discuss how the disclosures obtained through polygraph may influence the risk assessment process.

Chapter 9 by Madsen, considers the accuracy of the polygraph and focuses most centrally on work conducted by Grubin, Madsen and colleagues. Their research has significantly impacted on the field of polygraphy and to date provides perhaps the best evidence of the accuracy of this instrument.

Chapter 10 by Heil and English, gives a detailed account of the polygraph's employment with Sex Offenders in the United States where its use has been established for a much longer period of time. Besides having considerable research acumen, the authors convey a unique and insightful perspective about post-conviction polygraphy, in describing their 'containment model' for working with sexual offenders. In Chapter 11 by Addison and Criscella, other post-conviction uses of the polygraph are explored. The authors discuss its application with individuals convicted of drug offences, domestic violence issues and consider other areas of probation and parole work, suggesting approaches that might enable workers to supervise, assess and treat offenders more successfully.

The book concludes with several chapters that address some other areas related to offender assessment and engagement. The potential for these methodologies to further improve effectiveness in working with sex offenders and inform assessment and supervision is a principal focus of these chapters. This begins with Blair's Chapter 12 on interviewing and interrogation techniques. He considers how these approaches may relate to polygraph testing, as well as how they can be employed independently.

In Chapter 13, Vendemia and her colleagues provide an up-to-date appraisal of alternative technologies for detecting deception, considering methods that are in some ways complimentary to polygraphy and other approaches which employ distinctively different paradigms to identify deceitful responding.

Chapter 14 by Kalmus, Beech and Warberg reviews forensic assessment tools that are currently employed to assess sexual interest with a particular emphasis on being able to identify deviant arousal patterns in offenders.

Polygraphy can provide helpful assistance in tailoring more effective treatment programmes as well as dealing with practical problems like denial. Polygraphy also presents an opportunity to improve offender management and risk assessment in the community. However, differences may arise about how best to integrate, implement, monitor and evaluate this tool. As a consequence the challenge to responsible practice will be one of continuously weighing the opportunities that this technology offers against the responsibilities associated with using it.

REFERENCES

Allam, J. (2000). *Sex Offender Groupwork Programme: Evaluation Manual Accredited Programme*. Submitted for Home Office Accreditation: West Midlands Probation Service, Birmingham, UK.

Beech, A.R. & Ward, T. (2004). The integration of etiology and risk in sex offenders: A theoretical model. *Aggression and Violent Behavior*, *10*, 31–63.

Ben-Shakhar, & Gershon. (2008). The case against the use of polygraph examinations to monitor post-conviction sex offenders. *Legal and Criminological Psychology, 2008. 13*, 191–207.

Buschman, J., Wilcox, D.T., Foulger, S., Sosnowski, D., Bogaerts, S., & Mulder, J. (2008). Sexual history disclosure polygraph examinations among a group of 25 Dutch men who downloaded child pornography. *Panopticon, 2008.2*, 36–47.

Gannon, T., Beech, A.R., & Ward, T. (2008). Does the polygraph lead to better risk prediction for sexual offenders? *Aggression and Violent Behaviour, 2008. 13*, 29–44.

Grubin, D. (2008). The case for polygraph testing of sex offenders. *Legal and Criminological Psychology, 2008. 13*, 177–189.

Grubin, D. (2006). *Polygraph Pilot Study: Final Report*. London: Home Office. Retrieved on May 18, 2007 from http://www.probation.homeoffice.gov.uk.

Grubin, D., Madsen, L., Parsons, S., Sosnowski, D., & Warburg, B. (2004) A Prospective Study of the Impact of Polygraphy on High Risk Behaviors in

Adult Sex Offenders. *Sexual Abuse: A Journal of Research and Treatment 16* (3): 209–22.

Heil, P., Ahlmeyer, S., & Simons, D. (2003). Crossover sexual offenses. *Sexual Abuse: A Journal of Research and Treatment, 15*, 221–236.

Meijer, E.H., Verschuere, B, Merckelbach, Harald, L.G., & Crombez, G. (2008). Sex offender management using the polygraph. A critical review. *International Journal of Law and Psychiatry, 2008. 31*, 423–429.

O'Connell, M.A. (1998). Using polygraph testing to assess deviant sexual history of sex offenders. *Dissertation Abstracts International, 58*, 3023.

Offender Management Act (2007). Her Majesty's Stationery Office, Office of Public Sector Information. Available electronically from http://www.opsi.gov.uk/Acts/acts2007/pdf/ukpga_20070021_en.pdf

Salter, A. (1988). *Treating Child Sex Offenders and Their Victims*. London: Sage.

Salter, A. (1997). *Sex Offender Assessment and Risk Management Issues*. National Organisation for the Treatment of Abusers (NOTA) Annual Conference. Southampton, England.

Simons, D.A., Wurtele, S.K., & Durham, R.L. (2008). Developmental experiences of child sexual abusers and rapists. *Child Abuse and Neglect. 2008. 32*, 549–560.

Wilcox, D.T. & Donathy, M.L. (2008). The utility of the polygraph with sex offenders in England. *Conférence Permanente Européenne de la Probation*, July. [http://www.cep-probation.org:80/news/polygraphE.shtml]

Wilcox, D.T. & Sosnowski, D. (2005). Polygraph examination of British sexual offenders: A pilot study on sexual history disclosure testing. *Journal of Sexual Aggression, 11* (1), 3–25.

Wilcox, D.T., Sosnowski, D., & Middleton, D. (2000). Polygraph and the community management of sex offenders. *Forensic Update, 61*, 20–25.

Wilcox, D.T., Sosnowski, D., Middleton, D., & Grubin, D. (2003). Use of the polygraph in sex offender work. *Probation Journal, 50* (1), 61–64.

Wilcox, D.T., Sosnowski, D., Warberg, B., & Beech, A.R. (2005). Sexual history disclosure using the polygraph in a sample of British sex offenders in treatment. *Polygraph, 34*, 171–181.

CHAPTER 2

The Clinical Use of the Polygraph with Sex Offenders: Caveats and Considerations

DAVID WHITTINGHAM

SCOPE AND NATURE OF THE PROBLEM

It is estimated that between 1 % and 2 % of the male population will accrue convictions of a sexual offence by the age of 40 (Marshall, 1997). Less than 2 % of reported cases result in successful conviction (Myhill & Allen, 2002), and increasingly female sex offenders are being recognized for their small, though under-reported, contribution (Fergusson & Mullen, 1999; Home Office, 2004). Approximately one-third of reported sexual offences are committed by offenders under 18 years of age (Fisher & Beech, 2004) and while overall sexual recidivism rates are considered low, even over the long term (i.e., 10–15 % over 5 years), some higher risk offenders may recidivate at rates up to 50 % (Hanson & Thornton, 2000).

Victimization surveys of the prevalence of child sexual abuse range from 6 % to 62 % for girls and 3 % to 31 % for boys, reflecting methodological, sample and definitional variations (Peters, Wyatt & Finkelhor, 1986). Recent trends in Australia have seen the rate of sexual assault

The Use of the Polygraph in Assessing, Treating and Supervising Sex Offenders: A Practitioner's Guide
Edited by Daniel T. Wilcox.

rising from 70 to 90 per 100,000 between 1993 and 2003 (Australian Institute of Criminology (AIC), 2006). Eighty-two percent of victims were female, with the highest rate of sexual assault reported by girls aged 10–14 years at 475 per 100,000 females, whereas for males, those under 10 years of age reported the highest rate of sexual assault at 90 per 100,000. Seventy-five percent of offenders were known to their victims and 65 % of all sexual assaults occurred in the home environment or private dwelling (AIC, 2006). Similar findings were reported in the British Crime Survey (Home Office, 2002) that sampled 6944 women aged 16–59 and found 4.9 % of women had been raped since the age of 16, and most were attacked by current partners (45 %) rather than strangers (8 %).

The increasing prevalence of sexual offenders in criminal justice settings in the United States (US) has been attributed to a rise in reporting, as well as the broadening of the definition of conduct liable for criminal prosecution (US Department of Justice, 2003). Increasingly public protection oriented legislation and policy initiatives, including preventive detention and selective incapacitation, have resulted in large numbers of sex offenders entering the criminal justice system, and staying under its auspices. According to the United Kingdom (UK) Home Office, as of 2001 approximately 8 % of the UK prison population, or 5039 inmates, were sexual offenders, and almost half of these were convicted for rape (Councell & Olagundoye, 2003). The National Probation Service was estimated to be supervising over 10,000 offenders in 2000 (Middleton, Taylor & Quayle, 2003), and the US has seen an estimated 265,000 adult sex offenders come under the control of the corrections in 1997, of which 60 % were under community supervision (US Department of Justice, 2003).

SEX OFFENDER MANAGEMENT STRATEGIES

The costs to the community of sexual offending are very substantial even in terms of the financial burden. Costs of medical, mental health and emergency services are significant while the adverse impact of sexual victimization on quality of life and future productivity is unquantifiable. The US Department of Justice (2003) estimated that rape/sexual assault and child abuse cost the community in 2003 US$109,778 and US$76,530, per case, respectively. A range of strategies have therefore been adopted to prevent, manage and address sexual offending in the community including: (a) increasing imprisonment and supervision; (b) the introduction of targeted public protection legislation; (c) the adoption of a public health approach to sexual violence

(Laws, 2000); and (d) delivering treatment. As a result the management of sex offenders has become increasingly complex, with many measures designed to enhance external control around the offender commensurate with their perceived risk to the community, while safeguarding the rights of victims.

Increasingly jurisdictions have adopted specific statutes to increase the detention and/or supervision of sexual offenders. Broadly speaking these strategies encompass measures for civil commitment of sexual offenders, selective incapacitation, preventative detention, lifetime supervision, and community notification and registration (Schlank, 2006; US Department of Justice, 2003). Originally certain statutes were designed to divert mentally disturbed sex offenders from prison into treatment, for example, Mentally Disordered Sex Offender Statutes (MDSO) (Schlank, 2006). Increasingly though jurisdictions have introduced preventative detention or selective incapacitation of high risk sex offenders, so-called Sexually Violent Predator Statutes (SVP) (Schlank, 2006). Prentky and Burgess (2000) reported 14 states in the US had adopted SVP measures, with this type of law preventing high risk sexual offenders being released into the community at the end of their term of imprisonment (their risk to the community considered to be too great and/or at such a time when treatment could be effective). Both the United States and Australia have seen constitutional challenges to the legal basis of such measures (see *Kansas v. Hendricks*, 1997; *Fardon v. The Attorney General of Queensland,* 2004).

Lifetime supervision, registration and community notification have also become increasingly common as part of the community-based supervision structure of sexual offenders (US Department of Justice, 2003). The former deals with certain sexual offenders being placed on lifetime supervision by probation/parole, while the community notification mandates law enforcement/officials to notify particular community members based on an offender's risk (LaFond, 1998). Perhaps the most well known example of community notification is Megan's Law in the US that authorized public disclosure of a sexual offender's personal information for protecting the community; akin to a public interest exception to confidentiality (LaFond & Winick, 1998). In the UK the Sex Offenders Act 1997 and Criminal Justice and Courts Service Act 2000 formalized multi-agency public protection arrangements (MAPPA) (Cobley, 2000). This legislation required convicted sex offenders to register their address with local police for five years, and established a statutory duty for the police in consultation with probation, to assess and manage their risk (Cobley, 2000). A recent review of MAPPA has highlighted problems with the process of risk assessment and management as well as with ongoing monitoring and follow-up, raising concerns about its utility and effectiveness (Maguire *et al.*, 2001).

There has been little empirical examination of the effectiveness of measures like Megan's Law in reducing sexual recidivism, with the Association for the Treatment of Sexual Abusers (2005) concluding such laws appear to reflect emotive responses to public events, rather than a considered approach demonstrating their effectiveness. There have been difficulties in identifying which offenders reach threshold for referral/enactment of the statute and defining what exactly is 'high risk' (Schlank, 2006). Often the basis of such incapacitation or detention is the diagnosis of a personality disorder (Falk, 1999), which historically has low diagnostic reliability and in some cases validity (Widiger & Samuel, 2005). There are significant concerns for the civil liberties of those detained under such legislation. The diagnosis of paraphilias can be unreliable and even the most state-of-the-art sexual violence risk assessment tools have notable false positive rates (Doren, 2006). Such legislation is particularly difficult to understand when effective treatment compares so favorably to these strategies in terms of cost, humanity and empirical effectiveness (US Department of Justice, 2003).

Further challenging the justification of these measures is the encouraging evidence of public health approaches to management of sexual offending, which offer credible alternatives to such measures (Chasan-Taber & Tabachnick, 1999). The public health approach effectively moves resources from criminal justice and child safety services to health, supporting a harm reduction model aimed at reducing the violence, intrusiveness and frequency of sexual offending (Laws, 2000). Such an approach integrates primary prevention or protection measures prior to the abuse occurring, secondary prevention by care for victims of sexual abuse and tertiary measures or treatment for the offenders themselves (Laws, 2000). This approach offers promise to treatment providers as a comparable alternative model to the criminal justice system responses outlined earlier, particularly so when some evaluations of the effectiveness of electronic monitoring and extended supervision on recidivism have been poor (Gendreau & Goggin, 1996).

ETIOLOGY, RISK AND TREATMENT

Given this context, efforts to understand the etiology of sexual offending have been immense. Contemporary explanations recognize that this behavior is a multifactorial, multidetermined phenomenon involving contributions from genetic predispositions, adverse developmental experiences, psychological dispositions and trait factors, social cultural structures and processes as well as contextual factors (Ward & Beech, 2005). Recent attention has turned to neuropsychological and biological levels of analysis, and the interaction between neurological systems and ecological factors to produce sexually abusive behavior (Ward & Beech, 2006).

Increasingly etiology has been linked with risk factors in attempts to bridge the gap between causative factors and clinical practice. Recent conceptualizations have been anchored in the general psychological literature, including distal developmental factors (i.e., attachment problems); psychological traits or disposition (i.e., stable dynamic risk factors); and the importance of contextual risks and triggering events (i.e., substance abuse, victim access) with acute dynamic risks factors (i.e., deviant fantasy) (Ward & Beech, 2005). Grounded theory analysis of the offence process has also helped guide the development of offence pathways (Polaschek *et al.*, 2001), where cognitive, affective, behavioral and physiological chains interact with triggering contextual factors to create the psychological and situational states of offending (Ward *et al.*, 1995).

This emphasis on various cognitive, emotional, behavioral and physiological deficits interacting to produce sexual offending has formed the basis for linking etiology to those dynamic risk factors and psychological variables traditionally targeted in treatment and relapse prevention (Ward & Marshall, 2004). Typical treatment program components target needs and/or deficits in respect to self-esteem, empathy, coping, intimacy, cognitive distortions, deviant sexual interests, negative emotional states (Marshall *et al.*, 2006), and more recently 'implicit theories' (Ward & Keenan, 1999) or offence-related schemas (Mann & Shingler, 2006).

The Relapse Prevention Model has formed the link between treatment of these risks and needs, providing a treatment framework and structure for the clinical management of the reoffence process (Ward & Marshall, 2004). This model's aim is to reduce the likelihood of recidivism through explicitly linking the identified internal and external risk factors for sexual offence relapse, to the acquisition and practice of coping skills to deal with the situations and psychological states that increase risk of reoffending (Pithers *et al.*, 1983). This model has been reformulated with psychological models of self-regulation guiding this process, consistent with the complexity of offending and the idea that not all such behavior is a consequence of deficit engineered failures to cope, but may in fact reflect positive affect approach goal-driven processes (Ward & Hudson, 1996).

Treatment Outcome and Management

The application of several principles of correctional rehabilitation and the results of meta-analytic studies (Hanson & Bussière, 1998; Hanson & Morton-Bourgon, 2005; Hollin, 1999) has led to a resurgence in optimism regarding the effectiveness of treatment for offenders generally, and specifically for sexual offenders. These principles of rehabilitation pioneered by Canadian researchers Andrews and Bonta (1994) include:

1. The risk principle: higher risk offenders should be targeted for intervention;
2. The need principle: programs should address individual offender criminogenic needs;
3. The responsivity principle: programs should be as responsive as possible to the characteristics of offenders (i.e., treatment motivation).

The risk principle involves actuarial and structured clinical risk assessment of the relevant static risk factors associated with sexual violence to assist a judgment about the individual's overall likelihood of reoffending; treatment targeting the higher risk offenders. This determines the intensity of the intervention in practice while the needs assessment targets dynamic risk factors or criminogenic needs which are empirically related to sex offending recidivism (see Table 2.1; Hanson & Morton-Bourgon, 2005).

Empirical support for the effectiveness of cognitive behavioral treatment programs in combination with relapse prevention is modest but reliable. Hanson and colleagues' (2002) meta-analysis of treatment

Table 2.1 Dynamic predictors of sexual recidivism with persistent sex offenders

Predictor variable*	Average effect size for sexual recidivism
Any deviant sexual interest	$d = .31$
Sexual preoccupations	$d = .39$
Antisocial personality	$d = .21$
Psychopathy Checklist Rating	$d = .29$
General self-regulation problems	$d = .37$
Employment instability	$d = .22$
Hostility	$d = .17$

*Hanson & Morton-Bourgon (2005) meta-analysis of 82 studies including 29 450 sexual offenders.

outcome with sexual offenders indicated a small but meaningful average treatment effect (Effect Size = 0.28), for this combination therapeutic program. A review by Dowden and colleagues (2003) attempted to dismantle the effect of relapse prevention components in sex offender treatment outcome. They found those programs that had more relapse prevention elements were more effective, and those components specifically associated with reduced recidivism were identifying offence antecedents, coping rehearsal for projected risks, and teaching the offender's support group to monitor and evaluate his risk factors (Dowden, Antonowicz & Andrews, 2003). It is those offenders who present with the most significant breadth and depth of sexual deviancy, and/or those with pronounced antisocial lifestyle orientation that appear to respond most poorly to treatment; the two strongest overall risk factors for persistent sexual offenders (US Department of Justice, 2003; Hanson & Morton-Bourgon, 2005).

Those who fail to complete treatment also appear to be at greater risk of recidivism (Hanson *et al.*, 2002), so substantial efforts have gone into methods to reduce sexual recidivism through increasing external controls for sexual offenders (i.e., clinical polygraphy), as well as attempts to maximize treatment effects through consideration of responsivity factors. In respect to the latter, treatment intensity may be titrated according to not only assessed level of risk and need, but also in response to clients' learning styles and needs and therapeutic process issues including therapist style considerations (Andrews & Bonta, 1994).

Recent reviews of treatment approaches to sex offenders have identified problems with therapeutic facilitation, including a limited emphasis on developing client optimism about, and self-efficacy in, behavioral change, as well as a lack of collaboration and humor with an undue focus on negative as opposed to approach-focused treatment goals (Marshall *et al.*, 2005). Confrontational approaches to treatment have been shown in fact to increase resistance and reduce treatment gain (Beech & Hamilton-Giachritsis, 2005; Drapeau, 2005), but perhaps this is not surprising in light of the emotive reactions treatment providers and supervising officers can have to offenders and their offending (Ennis & Horne, 2003). This is especially true in work with offenders exhibiting marked sexual deviancy and significant antisocial orientations, manifesting traditionally high levels of denial of their behavior (Salter, 1988).

Research has demonstrated that a 'positive therapist style' and a robust therapeutic alliance significantly predict the achievement of treatment targets including reduced cognitive distortion, improved empathy and pro-social attitudes, effective coping and greater intimacy, reduced deviance, and the identification of offence precursors (Beech &

Hamilton-Giachritsis, 2005; Drapeau, 2005; Marshall *et al.*, 2005). In 1996, Marshall described this style as:

> The optimal style is to display respect for our clients, help them distinguish their offensive behaviors from themselves, display compassion and empathy, model egalitarian attitudes and most of all, convey a belief in the redeemable nature of all people, including sexual offenders (Marshall, 1996, p. 332).

Such findings have clear implications for community-based treatment of sex offenders, which widely uses relapse prevention and where problems persist in the translation of the original collaborative philosophy of relapse prevention to practice (Shingler & Mann, 2006). Mann (2000) considered that the difficulties increasing collaborative aspects of treatment stem from longstanding strongly held views actively discouraging such perspectives (i.e., Salter, 1988). Traditional community supervision of sex offenders has been slow to embrace these findings with typical probation/parole involving individual case management incorporating regular office appointments, phone contact and community service requirements. These have increasingly been recognized as inadequate to effectively address the needs and risk of sex offenders (US Department of Justice, 2003). Consequently, some community-based supervision programs incorporate in addition to the factors already mentioned, specialist sex offender treatment, relapse prevention planning and support as well as specific conditions including monitoring and/or restrictions to areas that may pose a risk to the offender (US Department of Justice, 2003). Many of these restrictions and conditions aim to increase the external controls on the offender to reduce opportunities to reoffend, the risk to the public a primary concern of treatment; a 'containment' approach to sex offender management (English *et al.*, 2000). Clinical polygraphy is an integral component to this. In the Containment Model, the primary client is the community not the offender, with protecting the public and victim rights having primacy in the clinical management framework.

POST-CONVICTION POLYGRAPHY

It is within this risk management-focused community treatment and supervision framework for sex offenders that post-conviction polygraphy has flourished. Existing clinical polygraphy with sex offenders in post-conviction settings has traditionally included three types of evaluations: sexual history (SH), maintenance/monitoring (MM) and specific issue (SI) exams (Abrams, 1989). Sexual history exams involve the exploration of sexual experiences pre-index conviction, with an emphasis on establishing the degree of sexual deviance and tend to be applied between three and six months into treatment (Abrams, 1989). Maintenance exams establish the extent of compliance with treatment and supervision approximately every six months, including, but not limited to, adherence with legal conditions, relapse prevention and risk management plans. Specific issue exams explore a specific concern from treatment, history, or current behavior (US Department of Justice, 2003).

The primary aim with all of these exams is to obtain objective information about supervision compliance and treatment progress as well as encourage fuller disclosure and honest responding (Abrams, 1989; US Department of Justice, 2003). This typically results in disclosure of a higher number of victims, more facts regarding the offence and offences not previously reported (Ahlmeyer *et al.*, 2000). Supporters advocate that polygraph evaluations consequently provide more reliable sexual histories, more complete and accurate offence descriptions, and an increased likelihood of identifying high risk behaviors than existing methods of assessment and treatment (Ahlmeyer *et al.*, 2000; Blasingame, 1998; Wilcox & Sosnowski, 2005). Recent findings even suggest periodic polygraph exams may aid offenders to desist in reoffending or high risk behaviors (Grubin *et al.*, 2004; Grubin & Madsen, 2006).

In a recent study Wilcox and Sosnowski (2005) examined the effect of the polygraph on disclosures for victims, offences and sexual deviancy made by a sample of 14 community-based sex offenders in treatment. They found use of the polygraph produced increased disclosures when compared to existing probation records in the number of victims, offences, as well as revealing an earlier onset of offending and a broader range of paraphilic interests (Wilcox & Sosnowski, 2005). The probation records variable was a composite of psychometric data and supervision records, suggesting the polygraph outperformed a multimethod, multisource assessment method that is argued to typically produce more valid assessment findings (Grove & Meehl, 1996). The rate of deception was high with 72 % of the sample scoring 'deceptively', with only two offenders 'passing'; the remaining two produced inconclusive results (Wilcox & Sosnowski, 2005). Of interest was that the polygraph elicited information not previously disclosed to supervising probation officers, specifically concerning high risk behaviors and possible antecedents to relapse. Significantly 93 % of the sample endorsed alcohol use, 86 % reported use of pornographic material and 57 % admitted sexually associated cruising/stalking behaviors; a mixture of acute and stable dynamic risk factors for reoffending (Wilcox & Sosnowski, 2005).

A further study by Grubin and colleagues (Grubin *et al.*, 2004) reinforced the value of the polygraph over traditional assessment and monitoring methods, as well as suggesting it may play a role in reducing the occurrence of high risk behaviors, and have a deterrent effect on reoffending. They examined whether the expectation of polygraphy evaluation would reduce the probability of offenders engaging in high risk behaviors. Fifty of 116 community-based sex offenders agreed to participate in this prospective study knowing information disclosed would be reported to treatment providers or the supervising probation officer. Polygraph exams were administered at two intervals to two groups, a polygraph 'aware' and 'unaware' group although both groups were tested at Time One and Time Two. The maintenance exams employed the Control Question Test method and used specific risk behaviors relevant to the individual offender's offending history.

By Time One 32 of the 50 remained in the study and 31 (97 %) reported at a minimum of one high risk behavior, with only one offender known by treatment and supervising staff to previously be engaging in high risk behaviors (Grubin *et al.*, 2004). The majority of these disclosures were pre-examination either to the researcher or during pre-test interview with the polygrapher, indicating that the expectation of being polygraphed appears to play a role on its own in the disclosure process. At Time One 78 % failed (25) and of these 80 % (20) reported further high risk behaviors to those reported earlier. The nature of the high risk behaviors disclosed varied from reporting masturbation to deviant fantasies (27 or 84 %), unsupervised contact with children or vulnerable adults (9 or 28 %), to actually attempting to set up situations for contact with children (8 or 25 %), and going to areas to view children for sexual arousal (i.e., playgrounds; 8 or 25 %) (Grubin *et al.*, 2004).

By Time Two 15 (71 %) of the 21 passed the polygraph and the more significant high risk behaviors disclosed included masturbation to deviant fantasies (15 or 74 %), unsupervised contact with children or vulnerable adults (6 or 24 %) and attempting to set up a situation for contact with children (2 or 10 %). When surveyed 20 of the remaining 21 offenders considered the polygraph assisted them to avoid reoffending, and 57 %, or 12, said it helped them suppress their behavior.

Further confirmation of the utility of the polygraph in suppressing and avoiding high risk behaviors and situations can be found in a retrospective survey study of 176 community-based sex offenders in treatment attending treatment in the United States (Grubin & Madsen, 2006). Seventy-six or 56 % of the sample considered the polygraph to have assisted them to avoid reoffending, and 80 (63 %) thought it assisted them to avoid risk behaviors (Grubin & Madsen, 2006). Approximately a third of the sample considered they reduced their drug and alcohol consumption and were less likely to engage in several high risk behaviors including masturbation to offence-related fantasies, having contact with children or potential victims, and using or buying pornography (Grubin & Madsen, 2006).

IMPLICATIONS FOR PRACTICE

These findings need to be viewed cautiously given the high attrition rates, and the extent to which the results may generalize to all sex offenders, particularly rapists. Approximately half the offenders approached participated in both studies, and most high risk behaviors reflected the dominance of child sex offenders in the sample. The proportional percentage reduction in reported high risk behaviors is significant enough for clinical utility in practice. These three studies do nonetheless encourage early confidence in the role the polygraph had first, in assisting disclosure about unreported high risk behaviors, and secondly, based on the nature of such behaviors, in assisting treatment to target risks and needs more effectively; the disclosure effect considered helpful with treatment and desistance generally. Over two-thirds of those tested disclosed deviant sexual fantasies and almost one-third offence approach actions; both clinically significant given recent meta-analytic findings that suggested two of the stronger risk factors for sexual recidivism were any deviant sexual interest and sexual preoccupations (Hanson & Morton-Bourgon, 2005). Clinically monitoring such acute and stable dynamic risk factors for sexual offending has been and continues to rely heavily on client self-report or penile plethysmography findings, suggesting a clear role for the polygraph assisting disclosure of such sensitive phenomena; a method perhaps less sexually intrusive for the offender.

There are implications for these findings and the practice of risk assessment and clinical management. Historically there has been an emphasis on identifying static risk factors that are empirically associated with the risk of sexual recidivism, with findings from meta-analyses contributing strongly to these tools (Hanson & Bussière, 1998; Hanson & Morton-Bourgon, 2004). This has greatly assisted clinicians to establish, based on static unchangeable factors, the risk level for an individual in comparison to other offenders. Research on polygraphy assisted disclosures is more or less consistent with those studies carried out using confidentiality waivers or in health settings, reporting a higher incidence of sexual offences, multiple paraphilias, earlier onset of paraphilias and offending and greater crossover in respect to victim type (Abel & Osborn, 1992; Ahlmeyer *et al.*, 2000). This raises the question of how accurate current risk assessment devices are if they are not identifying the 'true' extent of the risk posed by the offender, although the more extensively research tools (i.e., Static-99) are heavily weighted to official criminal history and demographics, the victim items may be considerably affected by the crossover polygraph research.

Recently attention has focused on understanding an offender's risk state based on dynamic changeable variables; or their propensity to become violent or sexually violent in a given context (Douglas & Skeem, 2005; Hanson & Harris, 2000). Hanson and Harris (2000) examined dynamic predictors of reoffence that retrospectively separated sexual recidivists from non-recidivists, and grouped these in terms of stable or acute risk factors. Stable risk factors for recidivism were sexual preoccupations and entitlement, poor social influences and considering the self as posing no risk of reoffence, while the more immediate acute dynamic risks of reoffence were anger, access to victims and non-cooperation with supervision (Hanson & Harris, 2000). The studies reviewed indicate the polygraph allows the detection and monitoring of levels of sexual preoccupation (Grubin *et al.*, 2004). Polygraphy has also assisted offenders to be more honest in their interpersonal relationships, and conflict in intimate relationships has been significantly associated with sexual recidivism (Hanson & Harris, 2000; Kokish, Levenson & Blasingame, 2005). The polygraph has been found to be effective in the monitoring of supervision requirements generally, and such antisocial orientation factors have been found to significantly predict sexual recidivism (Hanson & Bussière, 1998; Hanson & Morton-Bourgon, 2004). It may also assist with honest reporting of acute deterioration of mood which has been linked to increases in deviant fantasies among sexual offenders (McKibben, Proulx & Lusignan, 1994).

It is the detection and monitoring of deviant sexual interests that is most emphasized in the post-conviction studies. As noted earlier this is not surprising as deviant sexual interest (i.e., self-report, offence history, specialized testing) has demonstrated strong empirical support as a predictor of sexual recidivism, although the results for phallometric assessments were mixed (Hanson & Morton-Bourgon, 2004). Sexual interest in children was a strong predictor, but sexual interest in rape/violence or boys demonstrated no significant relationship to sexual recidivism (Hanson & Morton-Bourgon, 2004). The polygraph by virtue of the disclosure effect offers the opportunity to confirm the existence of deviant sexual fantasies and monitor the effects of treatment generally and specifically for such a dynamic risk.

This is particularly important given that monitoring the topography of sexual fantasies may provide an indication of how close an offender is to relapse of reoffending. Gee, Devilly and Ward (2004) examined how the content and topographical process of sexual fantasies changed during the relapse phase of the offence process. This was a qualitative study of 24 male predominately child sexual offenders, and they found that the focus of the non-specific sexual offence fantasy (i.e., thoughts about sexual contact with a female) changed to become offence and victim specific, developed in detail and was experienced as more intense (Gee *et al.*, 2004). Tailoring polygraph questioning to such process models may increase the utility of such evaluations, from the identification of non-specific sexual fantasy to victim-specific fantasies or 'rehearsal'.

The challenging of denial is another advantage of the polygraph emphasized in several studies supporting post-conviction polygraphy (Ahlmeyer *et al.*, 2000; English *et al.*, 2000). Shame has been considered to play a significant role in maintaining levels of denial in sex offenders, through stigma about being a sex offender, and the phenomenology of shame itself (Marshall *et al.*, 2005; Proeve & Howells, 2002). The polygraph may provide a useful clinical tool to manage this therapeutically if it is employed in the context of a positive therapeutic relationship that is respectful, empathic, and enhancing of the self-confidence of the client (Marshall *et al.*, 2005). It may facilitate the therapeutic goal of reducing shame and increasing guilt by encouraging an emphasis on the specific behaviors and the offender's management of these (Proeve & Howells, 2002). The focus on an offender's own physiological responses to specific behaviors may challenge the global negative self-evaluations and externalizing of blame seen with shame. There is also a risk, however, that polygraph facilitated disclosures may negatively reinforce a client's negative beliefs about themselves, producing an intense affective response and increased resistance; one possible explanation for the high rates of deceptive polygraphy results in post-conviction studies.

The relative importance of surmounting denial in treatment, however, has been challenged by meta-analytic findings and small clinical studies (Hanson & Bussière, 1998; Hanson & Morton-Bourgon, 2004; Schlank & Shaw, 1996). The meta-analytic studies found no significant relationship between sexual recidivism and clinical presentation variables including levels of admission (i.e., denial and minimization), lack of victim empathy, and low motivation for treatment (Hanson & Bussière, 1998; Hanson & Morton-Bourgon, 2004). This relationship held for treated and untreated offenders. Schlank and Shaw (1996) also found combining elements of relapse prevention and victim empathy training modified denial in 50 % of their sample of sex offenders, raising concerns about the relevance of using the polygraph in lieu of other methods to reduce denial.

Effective cognitive behavioral treatments emphasize offenders taking responsibility for their offending and its impact on their victims, as well as form the basis for self-regulation maintenance and skill generalization in the community (Launay, 2001; Marshall & Laws, 2003). Logically, therefore, there is significant benefit from polygraph enhanced disclosure of information relevant to treatment targets and the formulation of a more specific relapse prevention plan, to monitoring of this plan and the effectiveness of treatment. The more effective monitoring of the relapse prevention plan is particularly useful given research supporting that lower recidivism rates were observed with high risk child sex offenders who met treatment goals, when compared to those who did not 'get' relapse prevention (Marques *et al.*, 2005).

Lastly, the polygraph may also assist disclosure of material relevant to identifying implicit theories or schemas argued to 'drive' offence-specific cognitive distortions (Beck, 1999; Ward & Keenan, 1999). Greater access to more sensitive material than 'surface level symptomology' could increase the focus on these hypothesized causal mechanisms in treatment and allow treatment to be more effectively tailored based on individual offence process formulations (Ward & Beech, 2006; Ward & Hudson, 1996).

CAVEATS TO USE

Useful guidelines already exist regarding the clinical use of post-conviction polygraphy with sexual offenders (Blasingame, 1998; US Department of Justice, 2003), and it is arguably the uncritical adoption and disproportionate weighting it may give to particular treatment issues that pose the most pressing practice concerns. Specifically these concerns include: (a) the focus on sexual deviancy at the potential expense of other contributing factors to sexual reoffence; (b) the dominant models contextualizing its current use; and (c) the limited empirical research base backing its application.

There is a risk that the emphasis on clinical polygraphy use with sexual offenders and its role in assisting assessment of sexual deviancy may focus treatment and management disproportionately on this risk. This particular use of the polygraph did not develop in isolation of clinical practice; in fact its application reflects long-standing concerns about sexual offenders, a focus on sexual deviance and concerns about high recidivism rates. When the first use of the polygraph was seen within post-conviction settings in the early 1970s, treatment of sexual offending was predominately guided by psychodynamic and behavioral therapy approaches based on the 'sexual preference hypothesis' (Consigli, 2002; Laws & Marshall, 2003). This approach emphasized the idea that deviant sexual interest developed and was maintained by a process of learning including the pairing of sexual fantasy, masturbation and enactment of deviant behavior. Central to this approach was the use of the penile plethysmograph and its use was promoted and adopted due to opinion that it offered a more objective and accurate assessment of sexual arousal preferences, degree of deviance and evaluation of the efficacy of behavioral treatments (Laws & Marshall, 2003); similar reasons to those used with post-conviction polygraphy.

These parallels between the use of the polygraph and penile plethysmograph with sexual offenders cannot be ignored and can reflect the unitary notion of deviant sexuality as the primary maintaining factor for offence onset, maintenance and recidivism. This view while clearly important to practice, does not critically reflect the contemporaneous understanding of the complex nature of this behavior, and may neglect the role of criminological variables (Marshall & Laws, 2003; Ward & Beech, 2006). Recent findings challenge this emphasis on specialism by sexual offenders in two ways: firstly, by demonstrating criminal versatility or a greater likelihood of conviction for non-sexual offences than sexual offences; both in pre- and post-sexual offence conviction in heterogeneous groups of sexual offenders (Hanson & Bussière, 1998) and among child sex offenders (Smallbone & Wortley, 2004a). Secondly, the findings challenge the relationship between paraphilias and sexual and non-sexual offending (Smallbone & Wortley, 2004b). In the Smallbone & Wortley (2004b) study, official criminal histories and confidential self-report data were used to examine empirical relationships between paraphilias, sexual offending and non-sexual offending among 221 child sex offenders. Results suggested an absence of relationship between paraphilias and sexual offending, but a significant association with non-sexual conviction.

Further support for criminological and situational contributions to sexual offending can be found in another study by Smallbone and Wortley (2000). This study of 182 child sex offenders utilized a confidential self-report method to examine the modus operandi of offending and rates of paraphilia. Their main findings indicated that child sex offenders were almost twice as likely to have previous convictions for non-sexual offences than for sexual offences (40.6 % versus 22.2 %), and that 37.1 % had no previous convictions. Of those with previous convictions, 82 % had first been convicted for a non-sexual offence, with theft being the most common. The rate of diagnosable paraphilias other than pedophilia was less than 5 %, in stark contrast to Abel and colleagues'

(Abel *et al.*, 1988) study where pedophilic acts accounted for 21.9 % of the total 291,737 paraphilic acts. The majority of offenders reported their offending did not begin in adolescence as opposed to 53.6 % of the Abel (1988) sample of adult offenders who reported onset of their deviant sex interest for two different paraphilias prior to the age of 18 (Smallbone & Wortley, 2000). Lastly and interestingly, 45 % of the sample had a history of counseling/treatment pre-offence for depression (23 %), alcohol or drug difficulties (18 %), family problems (14 %) and anger problems (13 %); suggesting opportunities for crime prevention and support for public health perspectives on sexual violence (Laws, 2000; Smallbone & Wortley, 2000).

Several of the studies of polygraphy with sex offenders in post-conviction settings have been conducted with offenders who were being treated and managed within a Containment Model (Ahlmeyer *et al.*, 2000; Heil, Ahlmeyer & Simons, 2003; Kokish *et al.*, 2005). The effects of this model of service on the use of the polygraph in post-conviction settings are unknown, as are empirical evaluations of effectiveness. Adopting this model may create a significant tension for the clinician who aspires to working positively with offenders (Marshall *et al.*, 2005). Marshall and colleagues (2005) investigated the relationship between therapeutic style and treatment targets in prison-based group sexual offender treatment and found evidence of strong correlations between these variables. Specifically, empathy, warmth, rewardingness and directiveness were all strongly associated with decreased denial of responsibility, victim blaming, and planning and minimizing features of the offence (Marshall *et al.*, 2005).

Marshall and colleagues (2005) argue that while the management of risk is a necessary feature of treatment, it should be in conjunction with a strengths focus and the attainment of good lives by enhancing hope, increasing self-esteem, developing approach goals, and working collaboratively with offenders (Marshall *et al.*, 2005). Some aspects of the Containment Model appear to be at odds with this approach and may encourage confrontational therapeutic encounters and rapport difficulties, coupled with the fact that there is some evidence that the therapeutic model the polygraph is employed within may affect the nature of the disclosures.

A study by Elliot and McConkie (2002) tested the difference between a collaborative team-based approach to polygraph assisted disclosure versus the traditional polygraph examiner-led disclosure. The team included the treating therapist, supervising probation officer and polygraph examiner; consistent with the Containment Model of management (Ahlmeyer *et al.*, 2000). All three types of polygraph exams were included in the study but not separately considered. Elliot and

McConkie (2002) found that the collaborative process produced significantly more unreported masturbatory fantasies and additional victims than the traditional polygraph process; the latter produced significantly greater disclosure of program compliance violations and masturbation to deviant sexual themes.

Finally, it is important to acknowledge the limited empirical research base underpinning the application of post-conviction polygraphy to sexual offenders, as well as the controversy about the polygraph generally. This matter is dealt more rigorously in Chapters 4 and 9, but the extant issues primarily concern construct and criterion validity of the polygraph – what it is in fact detecting and its ability to accurately detect such phenomena – as well as internal and external validity issues. While it has been accepted the polygraph reliably measures changes in autonomic arousal, it is the interpretation of this increased arousal as evidence of explicit deceptive cognitions that provokes controversy (British Psychological Society, 2004).

SUMMARY AND CONCLUSIONS

There is the potential for the post-conviction polygraph to usefully contribute as an adjunctive tool to contemporary sex offender assessment and treatment. The benefits appear useful to offender, practitioner and the community whether the effect is due to its role as a 'truth facilitator' (Grubin *et al.*, 2004), the 'bogus pipeline' (Gannon 2006; Roese & Jamison, 1993) or as a detector of deception. The potential benefits to its use may position it favorably over the costs and risks of its application, or of viable alternatives. This application, however, should reflect contemporary understanding of sexual offending and, that as a group, sex offenders are heterogeneous. The contributions of criminological and situational factors to this behavior and process should not be neglected. Exclusive reliance on sexual deviance and sexual preoccupation risks obfuscating the broadest application of this tool to intervening in the most optimal way. The monitoring of situational factors, a core psychological assumption to understanding human behavior, provides opportunities for contextual crime management or prevention. The challenge for post-conviction polygraphy is to position its use in the most collaborative treatment framework and to develop and broaden its research base to justify the extent of its application. Much of the research and opinion outlined in this volume does exactly that, providing a critically considered view of the utility of this tool to contemporary forensic clinical practice.

REFERENCES

Abel, G.G. & Osborn, C. (1992). The paraphilias: The extent and nature of sexually deviant and criminal behavior. *Clinical Forensic Psychiatry, 15*, 675–687.

Abel, G.G., Becker, J.V., Cunningham-Rathner, J.C. *et al.* (1988). Multiple paraphiliac diagnoses among sex offenders. *Bulletin of the American Academy of Psychiatry and the Law, 16*, 153–168.

Abrams, S. (1989). *The complete polygraph handbook*. Lexington, MA: Lexington Books/D.C. Heath and Co.

Ahlmeyer, S., Heil, P., McKee, B., & English, K. (2000). The impact of polygraphy on admissions of victims and offences in adult sex offenders. *Sexual Abuse: A Journal of Research and Treatment, 12*, 123–138.

Andrews, D. & Bonta, J. (1994). *The psychology of criminal conduct*. Cincinnati, OH: Anderson Publishing Co.

Association for the Treatment of Sexual Abusers (2005). *Facts about Sexual Offenders*. Available electronically at <http://www.atsa.com/ppOffenderFacts.html>.

Australian Institute of Criminology (AIC) (2006). *Australian Crime: Facts and Figures 2005*. Canberra: Australian Institute of Criminology.

Beck, A. (1999). *Prisoner of hate: The cognitive basis of anger, hostility and violence*. New York: HarperCollins.

Beech, A. & Hamilton-Giachritsis, C. (2005). Relationship between therapeutic climate and treatment outcome in group-based sexual offender treatment programs. *Sexual Abuse: A Journal of Research and Treatment, 17*, 127–140.

Blasingame, G.D. (1998). Suggested clinical uses of polygraphy in community-based sexual offender treatment programs. *Sexual Abuse: A Journal of Research and Treatment, 10*, 37–45.

British Psychological Society (2004). *A Review of the Current Scientific Status and Fields of Application of Polygraphic Deception Detection*. Leicester, UK: The British Psychological Society.

Chasan-Taber, L. & Tabachnick, J. (1999). Evaluation of a child sexual abuse prevention program. *Sexual Abuse: A Journal of Research and Treatment, 11*, 279–292.

Cobley, C. (2000). *Sex Offenders: Law, Policy & Practice*. Bristol: Jordans.

Consigli, J.E. (2002). Post-conviction sex offender testing and the American Polygraph Association. In M. Kleiner (Ed.), *Handbook of polygraph testing*. (pp. 237–250). San Diego, CA: Academic Press.

Councell, R. & Olagundoye, J. (2003). *The Prison Population in 2001:* A Statistical Review Home Office Research Findings No. 195. London: Home Office.

Doren, D.M. (2006). Recidivism risk assessments: making sense of controversies. In W. Marshall, Y. Fernandez, L. Marshall & G. Serran (Eds), *Sexual offender treatment: Controversial issues* (pp. 3–16). Chichester: John Wiley & Sons, Ltd.

Douglas, K. & Skeem, J. (2005). Violence Risk Assessment: Getting Specific about being Dynamic. *Psychology, Public Policy, and Law, 11*, 347–383.

Dowden, C., Antonowicz, D., & Andrews, D. (2003). The effectiveness of relapse prevention with offenders: A meta-analysis. *International Journal of Offender Therapy and Comparative Criminology, 47*, 516–528.

Drapeau, M. (2005). Research on the processes involved in treating sexual offenders. *Sexual Abuse: A Journal of Research and Treatment, 17*, 117–125.

Elliot, H. & McConkie, M.L. (2002). Collaborative multidisciplinary teams and polygraphs: One protocol for increasing rehabilitative integrity. *Public Administration and Management: An Interactive Journal*, *7*, 344–366.

English, K., Jones, L., Pasini-Hill, D., & Cooley-Towell, S. (2000). The value of polygraph testing in sex offender management. Research report submitted to the National Institute of Justice. Colorado: Colorado Department of Public Safety.

Ennis, L. & Horne, S. (2003). Predicting psychological distress in sex offender therapists. *Sexual Abuse: A Journal of Research and Treatment*, *15*, 149–157.

Falk, A.J. (1999). Sex offenders, mental illness and criminal responsibility: the constitutional boundaries of civil commitment after *Kanvas v. Hendricks*. *American Journal of Law and Medicine*, *25*, 117–47.

Fardon v. The Attorney General of Queensland (Qld) (2004) 210 ALR 50

Fergusson, D.M. & Mullen, P.E. (1999). *Childhood Sexual Abuse: An Evidence-based Perspective*. Developmental Clinical Psychology and Psychiatry Series, Volume 40. London: Sage.

Fisher, D. & Beech, A.R. (2004). Adult Male Sex Offenders. In H. Kemshall & G. McIvor (Eds), *Managing Sex Offender Risk*. London: Jessica Kingsley Publishers.

Gannon, T.A. (2006). Increasing honest responding on cognitive distortions in child molesters: The bogus pipeline procedure. *Journal of Interpersonal Violence*, *21*, 358–375.

Gee, G.G., Devilly, G.J., & Ward, T. (2004). The content of sexual fantasies for sexual offenders. *Sexual Abuse: A Journal of Research and Treatment*, *16*, 315–331.

Gendreau, P. & Goggin, C. (1996). Principles of effective correctional programming. *Forum on Corrections Research*, *8*, 38–41.

Grove, W. & Meehl, P. (1996). Comparative efficiency of informal (subjective, impressionistic) and formal (mechanical, algorithmic) prediction procedures: The clinical-statistical controversy. *Psychology, Public Policy, and Law*, *2*, 293–323.

Grubin, D. & Madsen, L. (2006). Accuracy and utility of post-conviction polygraph testing of sex offenders. *British Journal of Psychiatry*, *188*, 479–483.

Grubin, D., Madsen, L., Parson, S. *et al.* (2004). A prospective study of the impact of polygraphy on high risk behaviors in adult sex offenders. *Sexual Abuse: A Journal of Research and Treatment*, *16*, 209–222.

Hanson, R.K. & Bussière, M.T. (1998). Predicting relapse: A meta-analysis of sexual offender recidivism studies. *Journal of Consulting and Clinical Psychology*, *66*, 348–362.

Hanson, R.K. & Harris, A.J.R. (2000). Where should we intervene? Dynamic predictors of sex offence recidivism. *Criminal Justice and Behavior*, *20*, 187–202.

Hanson, R.K. & Morton-Bourgon, K. (2004). *Predictors of sexual recidivism: An updated meta-analysis*. Public Safety and Emergency Preparedness, Public Works and Government Services, Canada.

Hanson, R.K. & Morton-Bourgon, K. (2005). The characteristics of persistent sexual offenders: A meta-analysis of recidivism studies. *Journal of Consulting and Clinical Psychology*, *73*, 1154–1163.

Hanson, R.K. & Thornton, D. (2000). Improving risk assessments for sexual offenders: A comparison of three actuarial scales. *Law and Human Behavior*, *24*, 119–36.

Hanson, R.K., Arthur, G., Harris, A. *et al.* (2002). First report of the Collaborative Outcome Data Project on the Effectiveness of Psychological Treatment for Sex Offenders. *Sexual Abuse: A Journal of Research and Treatment, 14,* 169–194.

Heil, P., Ahlmeyer, S., & Simons, D. (2003). Crossover sexual offences. *Sexual Abuse: A Journal of Research and Treatment, 15,* 221–236.

Hollin, C.R. (1999). Treatment programs for offenders. *International Journal of Law & Psychiatry, 22,* 361–372.

Home Office (2002). *British Crime Survey.* <www.homeoffice.gov.uk>

Home Office (2004). *Recorded Crime Statistics 1898–2001.* Available online <www.homeoffice.gov.uk/rds/pdfs/100yearsxls>.

Kansas v. Hendricks (1997) 521 US 346

Kokish, R., Levenson, J., & Blasingame, G.D. (2005). Post-conviction sex offender polygraph examination: Client-reported perceptions of utility and accuracy. *Sexual Abuse: A Journal of Research and Treatment, 17,* 211–221.

LaFond, J. (1998). Sexually violent predator laws and registration and community notification laws: policy analysis and the costs of enacting a sexual predator law. *Psychology, Public Policy and the Law, 4,* 468–72.

LaFond, J. & Winick, B. (1998). Sexual offenders and the law. *Psychology, Public Policy and the Law, 4,* 11–16.

Launay, G. (2001). Relapse prevention with sex offenders: Practice, theory and research. *Criminal Behavior and Mental Health, 11,* 38–54.

Laws, D.R. (2000). Sexual offending as a public health problem: A North American perspective. *The Journal of Sexual Aggression, 5,* 30–44.

Laws, D.R. & Marshall, W.L. (2003). A brief history of behavioural and cognitive behavioural approaches to sexual offenders: Part 1. Early developments. *Sexual Abuse: A Journal of Research and Treatment, 15,* 75–92.

Maguire, M., Kemshall, H., Noaks, L. *et al.* (2001). *Risk Management of Sexual and Violent Offenders: The Work of Public Protection Panels.* Police Research Series Paper No. 139. London: Home Office.

Mann, R. (2000). Managing resistance and rebellion in relapse prevention intervention. In D.R. Laws, S.M. Hudson & T. Ward (Eds), *Remaking Relapse Prevention with Sex Offenders: A Sourcebook* (pp. 187–200). Thousand Oaks, CA: Sage Publications.

Mann, R. & Shingler, J. (2006). Schema-driven cognition in sexual offenders. In W. Marshall, Y. Fernandez, L. Marshall & G. Serran (Eds), *Sexual offender treatment: Controversial issues* (pp. 73–186). Chichester: John Wiley & Sons, Ltd.

Marques, J.K., Wiederanders, M., Day, D.M. *et al.* (2005). Effects of relapse prevention program on sexual recidivism: Final results from California's Sex Offender Treatment & Evaluation Project (SOTEP). *Sexual Abuse: A Journal of Research and Treatment, 17,* 79–108.

Marshall, P. (1997). *The prevalence of convictions for sexual offending.* Research Finding No. 55. Research and Statistics Directorate. London: Home Office.

Marshall, W.L. (1996). The sexual offender: Monster, victim or everyman? *Sexual Abuse: A Journal of Research and Treatment, 8,* 317–335.

Marshall, W.L. & Laws, D.R. (2003). A brief history of behavioural and cognitive behavioural approaches to offender treatment: Part 2. The modern era. *Sexual Abuse: A Journal of Research and Treatment, 15,* 93–120.

Marshall, W.L., Fernandez, Y.M., Marshall, L.E., & Serran, G.A. (2006). *Sexual offender treatment: Controversial issues.* Chichester: John Wiley & Sons, Ltd.

Marshall, W.L., Ward, T., Mann, R. *et al.* (2005). Working Positively With Sexual Offenders: Maximising the Effectiveness of Treatment. *Journal of Interpersonal Violence*, *20*, 1096–1114.

McKibben, A., Proulx, J., & Lusignan, R. (1994). Relationships between conflict, affect and deviant sexual behaviors in rapists and pedophiles. *Behavior Research and Therapy*, *13*, 571–575.

Middleton, D., Taylor, M., & Quayle, E. (2003). Child abuse and the Internet: Emerging treatment interventions. Paper presented at the National Organisation for the treatment of Abusers (NOTA) Annual Conference, Edinburgh, Scotland.

Myhill, A. & Allen, J. (2002). Home Office Research Study 237: Rape and sexual assault of women: The extent and nature of the problem. Research and Statistics Directorate. London: Home Office.

Peters, S.D., Wyatt, G.E., & Finkelhor, D. (1986). Prevalence. In D. Finkelhor (Ed.), *Sourcebook on Child Sexual Abuse* (pp. 15–59). Beverly Hills, CA: Sage Publications.

Pithers, W., Marques, J., Gibat, C., & Marlatt, G. (1983). Relapse prevention with sexual aggressors: A self-control model of treatment and maintenance of change. In J.G. Greer & I.R. Stuart (Eds), *The Sexual Aggressor: Current Perspectives on Treatment* (pp. 214–239). New York: Van Nostrand Reinhold.

Polaschek, D.L., Hudson, S., Ward, T., & Siegert, R.J. (2001). Rapists offence process: A preliminary model. *Journal of Interpersonal Violence*, *16*, 523–544.

Prentky, R. & Burgess, A. (2000). *Forensic management of sexual offenders*. Netherlands: Kluwer Academic Publishers.

Proeve, M. & Howells, K. (2002). Shame and Guilt in Child Sexual Offenders. *International Journal of Offender Therapy and Comparative Criminology*, *46*, 657–667.

Roese, N.J. & Jamison, D.W. (1993). Twenty years of bogus pipeline research: A critical review and meta-analysis. *Psychological Bulletin*, *114*, 363–375.

Salter, A.C. (1988). *Treating child sex offenders and victims: A practical guide*. Newbury Park, CA: Sage.

Schlank, A.M. (2006). *The Sexual Predator: Law and Public Policy, Clinical Practice*. Kingston, NJ: Civic Research Institute.

Schlank, A.M. & Shaw, T. (1996). Treating sex offenders who deny their guilt: A pilot study. *Sexual Abuse: A Journal of Research and Treatment*, *8*, 17–23.

Shingler, J. & Mann, R. (2006). Collaboration in clinical work with sexual offenders: treatment and risk assessment. In W. Marshall, Y. Fernandez, L. Marshall & G. Serran (Eds), *Sexual offender treatment: Controversial issues* (pp. 225–240). Chichester: John Wiley & Sons, Ltd.

Smallbone, S. & Wortley, R. (2000) *Child sexual abuse in Queensland: Offender characteristics and modus operandi*. Brisbane: Queensland Crime Commission.

Smallbone, S. & Wortley, R. (2004a). Onset, persistence, and versatility of offending among adult males convicted of sexual offences against children. *Sexual Abuse: A Journal of Research and Treatment*, *16*, 285–298.

Smallbone, S. & Wortley, R. (2004b). Criminal diversity and paraphiliac interests among adult males convicted of sexual offending against children. *International Journal of Offender Therapy and Comparative Criminology*, *48* (2), 175–188.

United States Department of Justice (2003). *Managing Sex Offenders in the Community: A National Overview*. Oregon: Lane Council of Governments.

Ward, T. & Beech, A. (2005). The Etiology of Risk: A Preliminary Model. *Sexual Abuse: A Journal of Research and Treatment*, *16*, 271–284.
Ward, T. & Beech, A. (2006). An integrated theory of sexual offending. *Aggression and Violent Behavior*, *11*, 44–63.
Ward, T. & Hudson, S. (1996). Relapse-prevention: A critical review. *Sexual Abuse: A Journal of Research and Treatment*, 8, 177–200.
Ward, T. & Keenan, T. (1999). Child molesters implicit theories. *Journal of Interpersonal Violence*, *14*, 821–838.
Ward, T. & Marshall, W. (2004). Good lives, etiology and the rehabilitation of sex offenders. *Journal of Sexual Aggression. Special Issue: Treatment & Treatability*, *10*, 153–169.
Ward, T., Louden, K., Hudson, S., & Marshall, W. (1995). A descriptive model of the offence chain for child molesters. *Journal of Interpersonal Violence*, *10*, 452–472.
Widiger, T.A. & Samuel, D. (2005). Evidence-based assessment of Personality Disorders. *Psychological Assessment*, *17*, 278–287.
Wilcox, D. & Sosnowski, D. (2005). Polygraph examination of British sexual offenders: A pilot study on sexual history disclosure testing. *Journal of Sexual Aggression*, *11*, 3–23.

CHAPTER 3

Pre-Conviction and Post-Conviction Polygraph Testing: A Brief History

DANIEL T. WILCOX AND LARS MADSEN

Post-conviction or clinical polygraph examination (lie detector testing) offers significant opportunities for assessing, treating and monitoring sex offenders (Holden, 2000; Wilcox, 2000). However, this application of the polygraph has been a relatively recent development in comparison with conventional (pre-conviction) polygraph testing (Abrams, 2000; Abrams & Abrams, 1993).

Importantly, there has also been a great deal of controversy surrounding the polygraph's application to criminal investigations as well as employee screening etc. This includes criticism of the theory base, accuracy, and the implications of various test outcomes (i.e., false positives and false negatives). While these criticisms may be justified in some contexts for pre-conviction testing, it is debatable whether they all equally apply to post-conviction polygraph.

It is, however, important to consider how these two approaches relate to each other. There are similarities and differences between pre- and post-conviction testing and the present chapter will concentrate on these issues. The authors will focus some attention on the

The Use of the Polygraph in Assessing, Treating and Supervising Sex Offenders: A Practitioner's Guide
Edited by Daniel T. Wilcox.

development of post-conviction sex offender testing (PCSOT), the most commonly used current application of post-conviction polygraph testing. The chapter will also explore current guidance (American Polygraph Association, 1997, 2007) for effective professional use of both types of tests.

BACKGROUND

Pre-conviction polygraph has an established history in the United States with legal precedents dating from the 1920s (*United States v. Frye*, 1924). Pre-conviction examinations refer to standard applications of polygraph testing, traditionally dealing with specific allegations (criminal or civil) currently under investigation. The use of the polygraph in these settings involves 'conflicting positions or statements, the outcome of which is pending and for which some type of punishment is likely if the guilt of or deception by the examinee is established' (Holden, 1997, p. 5).

Much of the early theory on polygraphy was based on the assumption that there existed a specific physiological profile for deception, in much the same way that Pinocchio's nose grew in size when he was dishonest. While the polygraph instrument does measure physiological correlates of arousal, contemporary polygraph theory does not claim to measure 'lying' per se. The Control Question Technique (CQT) was developed precisely because there is no specific or infallible response (Lykken, 1998). However, within some sections of the literature, a frequent criticism of the polygraph is that it endeavors to measure such a thing. For example, in a relatively recent article by Bashore and Rapp (1993), concerns were raised about 'the assumption that there is a physiological response that is specific to lying' (p. 5). Relatedly, Steinbrook (1992) also stated that 'lie detection assumes that telling a lie causes a specific and reproducible physiologic response' (p. 122).

Perhaps a reason for the continued myth of the lie response is the wider media's portrayal of the polygraph as a type of mind-reading machine. An example of this can be seen in the recent BBC1 television program 'Meet the Folks'. Here potential suitors to an individual are evaluated over a period of time by the parents. One of the methods used in this process is the polygraph. During this part of the show the suitor is seen attached to a polygraph instrument while the parents ask numerous questions (e.g., 'Do you like our daughter?' or 'Would you be faithful to her?' or 'Have you ever cheated on anyone?'). The individual responds 'Yes' or 'No', while the polygraph examiner (who is seated behind them) gives the thumbs up or down, ostensibly reporting the truthfulness of the individual's responses. These unstructured and sensationalized demonstrations mislead the public and imply that there is a specific lie response and appear to suggest that stress is exclusively associated with deception.

HISTORY OF THE POLYGRAPH

The American pioneer of modern lie detection was Hugo Munsterberg at Harvard University. Munsterberg published a book in 1908 (in which he pointedly avoided crediting any European scientists, some of whom certainly should have been referenced), proposing that research should be done to investigate the physiological correlates of deception. A student of his, William Marston, devised the 'systolic blood pressure deception test' in 1915. He reportedly got the idea after his wife said that her blood pressure rose when she got mad or excited (Lamb, 2001). In Marston's lie test, an individual's blood pressure was measured intermittently during questioning using a standard blood pressure cuff and stethoscope. In 1917, Marston reported high positive correlations between lying and changes in systolic blood pressure. He boldly claimed at that time to have discovered the specific lie response and predicted 'the end of man's long, futile striving for a means of distinguishing truth-telling from deception' (Marston, 1938, p. 45). Marston is credited with coining the term 'lie detector' (Lykken, 1998). He also gained fame, under the pseudonym Charles Moulton, for being the creator of the first female comic strip hero 'Wonder Woman', who was supposed to be a displaced Amazonian princess fighting the forces of evil and whose 'magic lasso' forced all who were encircled by it to tell the truth (<www.wonderwoman-online.com/fc-marston.html>).

In 1923, Marston was the first person to attempt to submit the results of his lie detector test as evidence in a court case (*United States v. Frye*, 1924). According to Marston's (1938) account, James Frye, a 19-year-old man, had been accused of robbery and murder, but after initially denying the offences he confessed and provided the police with accurate details of the crimes. Frye withdrew the confession a few days later, claiming that he admitted to the crimes because he had been promised a share of the reward for his own conviction. Marston administered his lie test and concluded that Frye was telling the truth. The trial judge, however, refused to permit Marston to either testify about the examination or to conduct a re-examination in court. Frye was convicted, but the case was appealed on the grounds that the trial judge had erroneously excluded Marston's testimony. The initial decision was upheld on appeal on the grounds that Marston's lie detector test had not gained sufficient acceptance within the scientific community to be considered valid evidence. Ironically, Frye, having been sentenced to life imprisonment, was later exonerated and set free – Marston had been right all along (United States Congress Office of Technology Assessment, 1983). This legal precedent became known as the 'Frye test' and remained a significant barrier to the inclusion of polygraph evidence in American courtrooms for the next 70 years. In 1979, the Kansas Supreme Court declared 'The Frye test has been accepted as the standard in practically all of the courts of this country which have considered the question of admissibility of new scientific evidence' (Segrave, 2004, p. 17).

The Frye test was eventually displaced in 1993 by the US Supreme Court's decision in *Daubert v. Merrill Dow Pharmaceuticals* (1993). The Daubert ruling did not specifically address the polygraph. It did, however, provide general guidelines for determining the admissibility of contentious scientific evidence. This included considering the known error rates, the reliability, and the general acceptance of the technique within the scientific community. These guidelines allowed courts to make decisions on admissibility of polygraph evidence on a case-by-case basis. As of 2003, polygraph evidence can be admissible in 19 states in the US.

John Larson, a forensic psychiatrist, was influenced by Marston's claims and commenced research into blood pressure and respiratory changes during police questioning. Larson is recognized as having created the first modern polygraph instrument in 1921. This was a device that made simultaneous recordings on paper of three physiological processes: blood pressure, pulse rate, and respiration. He reported a number of successes with this device, the most spectacular of which involved identifying a thief among 38 college girls living in the same house (Larson, 1932). Using a question technique that later became known as the Relevant-Irrelevant Test (RIT) he tested all the women in one day. The participants were presented with a series of yes or no questions of which only some were related to the topic of investigation. The underlying reasoning was that the guilty person would experience an increased physiological response to the questions related to the crime, while in innocent examinees there would be little difference in the strength of reactions to either type of question. For example, a series of questions might be 'Did you steal twenty dollars on Tuesday from the register?' (relevant) compared to 'Is your name Lucy?' (irrelevant). One woman displayed this deceptive profile, and when confronted with the results promptly confessed to the theft (Larson, 1932; Matte, 1996).

However, Larson became skeptical of the accuracy and value of the polygraph despite this and other successes. In one of the first published studies on polygraph chart evaluation, Larson (1938) had 9 psychologists independently evaluate 62 polygraph charts, of which 61 were truthful. The number of charts classified as deceptive, however, ranged from 5 to 33. Larson concluded that due to such a high disagreement in the interpretation of the charts 'the deception test alone should never be used as court evidence' (Larson, 1932, p. 896).

Leonarde Keeler, who was a protégé of Larson, developed the first portable polygraph instrument. This device could simultaneously record pulse rate, blood volume change and breathing. In 1939, he added the galvanic skin response channel to his lie detector and patented it. Keeler reasoned that a lying person would sweat more than a truthful person. This would then decrease skin resistance due to a higher concentration of negatively charged chloride ions on the surface of the skin. Keeler's device became the prototype for the modern polygraph, and it was the first instrument purchased by the Federal Bureau of Investigation (FBI). Keeler is recognized by many as being the 'father of modern polygraphy' (Harrelson, Gerow & Gerow, 1998). In contrast to Larson who tried to develop standardized approaches to the polygraph interview, Keeler stressed the role of the polygraph as an interrogative device and advocated enhanced examiner discretion.

Keeler is credited with developing the original polygraph testing formats: the previously mentioned Relevant-Irrelevant Test (RIT) (even though Larson and Marston had used similar testing procedures); and the Peak of Tension Test (POT) or Concealed Information Test (CIT) (Matte, 1996). The POT is based on a different premise to the RIT. Instead of detecting deception about having committed a crime, the POT's aim is to detect whether a suspect has information about the crime that only the guilty subject would have. During the test, participants are asked a series of multiple-choice questions, each question having only one correct alternative. In a car theft case, for example, a suspect might be asked: 'Regarding the car that was stolen do you know that it was: Yellow? Red? Blue? Black? White? Brown?' The theory is that the individual who committed the crime would know the correct alternative and display an augmented response to this critical item. An innocent suspect would, however, be unaware of the critical details and would show similar response patterns to all stimuli (Matte, 1996).

Keeler established the first polygraph unit within a police department in Chicago. This occurred primarily in response to the spiraling gang war between the gangs led by Al Capone and George 'Bugs' Moran. At that time, public outrage caused by the execution style murder of seven men in an incident that became known as the Saint Valentine's Day Massacre, forced officials to employ new methods of 'fighting crime'. This included the use of the polygraph (Segrave, 2004).

In 1938, Keeler and another polygraph enthusiast, lawyer John Reid, founded competing polygraph schools. Polygraph training proved a lucrative business for these initial schools. In 1942, the standard polygraph course available to police and military was two weeks long. Six years later the course had expanded to six weeks (Sullivan, 2001). Today the American Polygraph Association's (APA) accredited course is eight weeks in length.

Throughout the 1940s, polygraphy was increasingly becoming used by law enforcement agencies for criminal investigations and it was also taken up by various government agencies (Matte, 1996). In 1945, for instance, the US Government experimented with using the polygraph to screen German POWs for the purpose of identifying good candidates to train for a police force to be installed in the post-war Germany. That effort, with Keeler as the chief polygraph examiner, entailed testing 274 POWs, with the aim of identifying undesirable affiliations, sympathies or intentions. Many Nazi members and sympathizers were apparently uncovered. It was also reported that much criminal activity was discovered, including plans to commit sabotage. For unreported reasons, however, this polygraph program was abandoned (Sullivan, 2001).

During the 1940s and early 1950s the RIT technique was the standard polygraph questioning procedure. There was, however, an emerging awareness of the inadequacies of this question protocol. It was clear, for example, that some relevant questions such as 'Did you stab and kill Janice (suspect's mother) last night?' could be just as distressing for innocent as for guilty subjects. Indeed, as this example demonstrates, it is likely in some circumstances to be even more stressful for innocent participants. Reid (1947) therefore developed an alternative format that incorporated so-called 'comparison questions' that were not directly concerned with the crime under investigation but, unlike the irrelevant questions, were, nonetheless, calculated to induce an emotional reaction.

In Reid's new procedure the comparison question was presented in a way that led the examinee to believe that it was relevant to the case at hand. For example, he or she may be told: 'I need to ask you some other questions to determine whether you would be the 'type' of person that would lie about this (issue under investigation)'. This question was, however, general, non-specific, and difficult to answer confidently with an unequivocal 'no'. In regards to a specific theft, for instance, the examinee would be told that the comparison question 'Have you ever stolen from someone who trusted you?' was relevant, when in fact it was not. Reid argued that such an awkward question would cause the examinee to feel uncomfortable, and lead them to withhold information about past thefts, even extremely minor ones, because of their fear that disclosing these would make them appear like the 'type' of person that would steal. Reid's idea was to use the examinee's physiological responses to the comparison questions as a standard against which to measure their reactions to the relevant ones which were specifically about the issue under investigation. The theory was that an innocent person would be more concerned with the comparison questions and less concerned with the relevant questions, because they would know that they were innocent and thus be more confident in answering these latter questions. It was argued that an innocent 'non-deceptive' person would emit a larger physiological reaction to the comparison question when compared to the relevant, while it was expected that the reverse would be the case for the guilty examinee (Reid, 1947). This procedure was named the Control Question Test, although its name was later changed to the Comparison Question Test (CQT) because it was argued that the 'control' question was not a control in the true scientific sense (Honts & Perry, 1992; Lykken, 1998).

In response to these problems, Cleve Backster (1963), a student of both Keeler and Reid, developed the first numerical scoring system for evaluating polygraph charts. Backster's (1963) scoring system involved the systematic comparison of the reactions to each relevant question with the surrounding comparison questions. This process involved the assignment of numerical values on a 7-point scale ranging from –3 when the reaction to the relevant question was dramatically stronger, to 0 when there was no difference, and through to +3 when the reaction to the comparison question was very much stronger.

Summing these scores over all components and all charts gives a total score (Backster, 1963). If the global score exceeds +5 then the chart is typically considered to be 'No Deception Indicated' (NDI). If the score is less than −5 then the chart is classified as 'Deception Indicated' (DI). If the score is between −5 and +5 the chart is considered to be inconclusive. No other information is used when scoring the charts using Backster's system. Backster's innovation was important because it was the first time that a polygraph examination could lay claim to being a 'scientific' test, although the scientific basis of the scoring parameters themselves had still to be demonstrated.

By the beginning of the 1960s, polygraph use was widespread in the US while numerous other countries including Japan, China, Israel and Korea had started their own polygraph programs (Matte, 1996). At this time, US federal agencies were conducting approximately 19 000 polygraph examinations per year. The polygraph had also started to be used in the private sector (US Congress Office of Technology Assessment, 1983). Businesses, banks, fast-food chains and the like utilized the polygraph to vet job applicants not only to determine whether they were telling the truth on their applications, but also to determine whether they were the type of person worth employing. For example, the polygraph was used to examine whether applicants had ever stolen from previous employers, had used drugs, or engaged in other types of criminal or immoral behavior (Segrave, 2004).

During this time the polygraph was also introduced to periodically screen employees and determine whether they were stealing from the company or engaging in any other form of criminal behavior (Lykken, 1998). In 1965 a proposal to use polygraphy in a similar manner with federal employees prompted the Committee on Government Operation to conduct the first evaluation of polygraphy. Their report concluded that there was no scientific evidence to support this type of application, and that the research evidence for its accuracy was inadequate. The report also raised concerns about the ethics of using the polygraph for screening. It concluded 'there is no lie detector, neither man nor machine. People have been deceived by a myth that a metal box in the hands of an investigator can detect truth or falsehood' (Moss Committee, 1965, p. 1). In response to these conclusions and concerns President Kennedy indicated 'it was a mistake to suggest the polygraph' (Brooks, 1985, p. 348). In succeeding years a number of bills were proposed to restrict or ban polygraph use by federal agencies, although none were enacted (US Congress Office of Technology Assessment, 1983).

By the 1970s employee screening had become a multimillion dollar business, with approximately two million people each year in the US being required to take a polygraph to either apply for, or to keep a job in the private sector (Lykken, 1979). The pre-employment screening program used by the Coors brewery in Colorado provides an example of how the polygraph could be misused in such contexts. Company director William Coors is quoted as saying that the polygraph helped ensure 'that the applicant does not want the job for some subversive reason such as sabotaging our operation' (Segrave, 2004, p. 122). However, some of the actual questions used on the tests included: 'What are your sexual preferences?'; 'How often do you change your underwear?'; 'Have you ever done anything with your wife that could be considered immoral?' and 'Are you a homosexual?' (Segrave, 2004). A contrasting example of its successful use in an investigative capacity occurred in 1976, and has been described by Lykken (1998). A Californian bakery company was facing ruin because its products were being returned with glass and other materials in them. After an exhaustive investigation into the manufacturing process, it was concluded that an employee within the factory was deliberately contaminating its products. The police were unable to identify the culprit, and so the company decided to polygraph its employees. Apparently the eighth person tested confessed to the sabotage, having been angered after being overlooked for promotion (Lykken, 1998).

During the 1970s, the majority of law enforcement agencies established a staff of polygraph examiners, although federal government use of the polygraph had decreased dramatically to approximately 7000 tests per year (US Congress Office of Technology Assessment, 1983).

Yet despite its wide use, the polygraph was not universally accepted. The technique was vigorously criticized by some within the scientific community, notably Lykken (1974, 1979) who claimed that polygraph testing was no more than an elaborate gimmick, devoid of any theoretical or empirical foundation.

By the early 1980s testing had once again increased and it was estimated that in excess of 23 000 polygraph tests were being administered by various federal agencies, including the US Postal Service each year. Further, in the private sector approximately one million tests were being conducted yearly. Three hundred thousand of these tests were for employment purposes (Kleinmuntz & Szucko, 1984; US Congress Office of Technology Assessment, 1983). In 1983, in the wake of a damaging anonymous release of information regarding the funding of defense plans, President Reagan famously professed to being 'up to his kiester in leaks', and issued National Security Decision Directive 84 (Brooks, 1985). This authorized all federal agencies to polygraph their employees to identify any disclosures of classified information (US Congress Office of Technology Assessment, 1983). This directive affected more than 2.5 million government employees in addition to 1.5 million civilian employees at companies doing business with the US government (US Congress Office of Technology Assessment, 1983).

The Committee of Government Operations in the US House of Representatives responded, however, by formally requesting the US Congress Office of Technology Assessment (OTA) to conduct a thorough review and evaluation of the scientific evidence for polygraph tests. This report concluded, amongst other things, that the accuracy of the polygraph was still undetermined. It specifically highlighted the fact that there was no scientific evidence to support the polygraph's utility in a screening capacity. The report also raised concerns about the polygraph's vulnerability to countermeasures (i.e., strategies used to pass a polygraph test), and the rates of false positives (i.e., individuals erroneously identified as deceptive). The report additionally highlighted a number of methodological problems with much of the previous research into polygraphy, and recommended that additional research be undertaken in the area (Kleinmuntz & Szucko, 1984). President Reagan's directive was rescinded within three months of the publication of this report.

In the 1980s, there was also a growing concern within the wider community about the use of the polygraph. The case of Floyd Buzz Fay provides a compelling example of what can happen when the polygraph 'gets it wrong'. Fay was arrested after a botched armed robbery, in which a clerk was fatally wounded. The dying store clerk picked Fay as the man who had shot him. Fay was arrested but the prosecution, lacking any corroborative evidence, offered him a 'deal'. The charges would be dismissed if he could pass a polygraph exam. If he failed, however, another test would be administered and if he failed that one, Fay was to plead guilty to the lesser charge of murder. If he refused to do so, he would be charged with aggravated murder and the polygraph results would be submitted as evidence. Fay failed both and was eventually convicted of aggravated murder and given a life sentence. After serving two years in prison, Fay was released when another man confessed to the robbery and identified two other individuals involved (Sullivan, 2001). In a similar vein, the website <www.antipolygraph.org/statements.html> provides numerous testimonies of individuals claiming that the polygraph 'got it wrong' in pre-employment contexts.

The outcome of the OTA report, in conjunction with growing concern about the abuses associated with polygraph testing from both the general public and scientific community, led President Reagan to enact the 1988 Employee Polygraph Protection Act. This legislation restricted the polygraph's use within the private sector, although it specifically does not apply to federal agencies and public service employees such as the police (National Research Council, 2003).

Despite these apparent setbacks to the polygraph's credibility, its use by the US Federal Government has continued to increase dramatically. In 1986, a congressional mandate called for the expansion of the Department of Defense's polygraph program by allowing for the screening of federal employees in order to 'effect a significant deterrent for spying' (National Research Council, 2003, p. 12). The observable fruits of this legislation came in the case of Harold Nicholson, the most highly placed Russian spy in the CIA. In 1996, Nicholson was found to be deceptive in response to the question 'Are you working for a foreign intelligence service?' He subsequently failed two additional polygraph tests and was uncovered as a spy (Segrave, 2004). It is also worth noting that Aldrich Ames, another notorious although less illustrious CIA renegade, is said to have passed a number of polygraph tests (Lykken, 1998). However, this claim is disputed by the American Polygraph Association (D. Sosnowski, personal communication, January 20, 2004). In prison, Ames reportedly said that his Russian handlers had laughed at his worries about taking a polygraph test, telling him to relax because lie detectors did not work (Sullivan, 2001). It is of course possible that he was lying about this, or was not prepared to reveal the type of training he may have received to 'beat' the polygraph.

More recently in 1999, after the discovery of a significant security breach at the Los Alamos National Laboratory, allegedly by a spy from the Chinese government, Energy Secretary Bill Richardson ordered polygraph tests for all of the laboratory's nuclear weapons scientists. Richardson's swift resort to polygraph testing was meant to plug the holes in federal security and quell controversy (Segrave, 2004). Instead, it launched a debate about the accuracy of the tests and about whether federal agencies should use them on their employees, even though government officials claimed that the polygraph assisted with identifying Wen Ho Lee as the spy (Sullivan, 2001). Concerns about the polygraph's use in this screening and security vetting capacity led the Department of Energy to request that the National Academies of Science (NAS) conduct a scientific review of the research on the polygraph (National Research Council, 2003).

Alongside these developments there has been an increased interest in research in the area of post-conviction polygraph testing, for example, the specific application of the polygraph to individuals on parole/license or probation for new criminal activities. Distinct test protocols have been developed for this use of the polygraph to take account of the particular test requirements and different characteristics associated with pre- and post-conviction testing conditions. However, the use of post-conviction polygraph testing is not an entirely new occurrence.

POST-CONVICTION USE OF POLYGRAPH

During the 1970s, two judges, apparently unbeknownst to one another, informally initiated post-conviction polygraph testing in their jurisdictions. It was held by them that aside from the polygraph's ability to identify deception, it could also have considerable value in the supervision and management of men on probation (Abrams & Abrams, 1993). It was also argued that periodic polygraph testing would act as a deterrent for engaging in criminal activity, in addition to being an effective method of identifying when reoffences occurred.

Teuscher (1978), in an evaluation of these early initiatives, found that in a sample of 117 'career criminals' 60 had successfully completed probation over a four-year period. Despite the lack of comparison groups, the results led him to concur with initial impressions about its utility. He formed the view that the polygraph had been successful in reducing recidivism rates. He also reported that its use had led to the recovery of 'thousands of dollars' worth of stolen property and illegal substances' (Teuscher, 1978, p. 3). At this time, the polygraph was hailed as a valuable supervision tool, not only for ensuring community safety by preventing crime and identifying criminals, but also, potentially as a viable method of reducing prison populations (Consigli, 2002).

In 1973, Abrams, a psychologist and polygraph examiner in Jackson County Oregon, was the first to initiate the use of the polygraph specifically with sex offenders. He reasoned that the polygraph could improve supervision and treatment efficacy by counteracting the inherently secretive nature of sex offending (Abrams, Hoyt & Jewell, 1991). Throughout the late 1970s and 1980s, the polygraph was used by a small number of treatment and probation programs mainly on an ad hoc basis (Abrams, 1989).

In 1991 the first formal polygraph-testing program for sex offenders in the North-West of the US was established (Abrams & Abrams, 1993). Shortly after, similar programs developed in Hawaii, Texas and Tennessee. During this time English and colleagues in Colorado pioneered the 'Containment Approach' (English, 1998; Heil *et al.*, 2000). This model incorporates polygraphy as one of three components in an overall strategy that includes collaboration with treatment providers and probation officials, to 'contain' community-based sex offenders (English *et al.*, 2000).

A number of well-respected clinicians within the field of sex offender assessment and treatment have also come out in support of the polygraph's use. For example, Anna Salter (1997) claims that they do not have denier groups in the North-West of the US anymore because of polygraph. More recently the Center for Sex Offender Management (2000) in the US has described polygraph testing as 'an important asset in treatment and supervision of sex offenders' (p. 11). Gene Abel (1999) reported to colleagues, 'If you're not using the polygraph with sex offenders, you're missing the boat'. Indeed, even David Lykken, one of the most vehement critics of polygraphy, concedes that 'periodic testing might well serve both as a deterrent and also encourage more complete reporting', although he adds '... it should not be interpreted as a valid test for truth' (D. Lykken, personal communication, October 29, 2003).

In support of these developments, the Association for the Treatment of Sexual Abusers (ATSA) has established detailed standards for polygraph use. In ATSA's (1997) *Ethical Standards and Principles for the Management of Sexual Abusers* it states that the polygraph has 'significant clinical value' (p. 36), although it cautions professionals to avoid '... over reliance on the instrument' (p. 36). These guidelines further suggest that polygraph results 'should always be used in conjunction with other sources of information' (p. 36) and not be considered the sole 'determination of guilt or innocence' (p. 36).

In 1994 a telephone survey of 732 probation and parole supervisors in the US showed that 9.8 % reported that offenders in their programs were often or always required to take polygraph tests for treatment or supervision (English, Pullen & Jones, 1996). By 1996, this had increased to 16.3 % (English *et al.*, 2000). Simmons (1998) reported in a recent survey that 33 states used polygraphy with sex offenders. When considering this number, however, it should be noted that this is not an official figure but the perception of the interviewers (i.e., probation officers working in the various states). Bearing in mind the relatively small percentage of services reported in the English *et al.* (2000) study, Simmons (1998) data probably presents an exaggerated view of the use of polygraphy with sex offenders at that time.

Numerous states in the US have enacted legislation that requires sex offenders to take polygraph tests. The Supreme Court of the State of Washington, for instance, has ruled that Trial Courts have legal authority to subject sex offenders to polygraph tests (Spencer, 1998). In Texas, polygraph testing is mandatory in work with adolescents, and in an apparent rush of enthusiasm, the state also considered making monthly tests a requirement for all sex offenders. This proposal was abandoned, however, after the Texas Association of Polygraph Examiners advised against such a plan due to the concerns that such frequent testing might lead offenders to habituate to the examinations (McKay, 2000). In Tennessee, anyone convicted of two or more sexual offences is required to undergo periodic polygraph examinations. Colorado has also passed comprehensive legislation for the treatment of sex offenders that includes mandatory polygraph testing (Colorado Sex Offender Management Board, 2000).

The American Polygraph Association (APA) has also been quick to respond to this growing interest and demand for post-conviction polygraph examinations. In 1998, a Post-Conviction Sex Offender Testing (PCSOT) subcommittee was established and standards of practice were developed. At present, examiners wishing to conduct post-conviction testing are required to complete a 40-hour specialized training program (<www.polygraph.org>). By early 2004, 560 examiners had completed this course (D. Sosnowski, personal communication, January 20, 2004).

Much of the ongoing controversy surrounding the polygraph focuses on pre-conviction 'investigative-type' uses of the polygraph. It is argued that such uses are distinct from post-conviction polygraphy (Abrams & Simmons, 2000; Holden, 2000). In the former, issues of accuracy are particularly important, as someone may falsely be implicated in a crime or fail a pre-employment screen. In the latter, the focus is on its utility

(Cooley-Towell, Pasini-Hill & Patrick, 2000; Earls & Lalumière, 2002; Lundell, 2000; Wilcox, 2002). Within a post-conviction context, it is claimed that the polygraph is best not considered a 'test' but a treatment tool, used in conjunction with other tools, specifically to elicit as much information regarding past and current behaviors (Wilcox, 2000; Williams, 1995). Another important distinction is in the role of the polygraph examiner. In a post-conviction context, unlike in a pre-conviction context, the examiner is often considered part of a treatment team that includes the offender's therapist and probation officer. They develop supervision strategies and treatment interventions to ensure that the offender remains at lower risk of reoffending (Dutton, 2000; English *et al.*, 2000).

Research on both sides of the Atlantic in relation to post-conviction sex offender testing has been consistently encouraging (Grubin, 2006; Grubin & Madsen, 2005; Grubin *et al.*, 2004; Heil, Ahlmeyer & Simons, 2003; Wilcox, 2002; Wilcox & Sosnowski, 2005). These studies have employed sound research methodology and have consistently shown the benefits of polygraphy in this context, as a means of assessing risk, improving treatment and more effectively supervising convicted offenders.

There are three types of post-conviction polygraph examinations that are used at different times and stages of treatment and supervision (Lundell, 2000). Sexual history or disclosure examinations are usually utilized shortly after an offender has commenced treatment. Specific issue or denial tests are commonly used to verify the veracity of an offender's disclosures during treatment. Finally, monitoring and maintenance exams focus upon the offender's current behavior, and are used on a regular basis to monitor compliance with supervision or treatment conditions and to investigate concern about any current reoffending (Holden, 2000). All these exams work most effectively when the polygraph examiner, treatment provider and supervising officer work together to identify the most appropriate areas to target in polygraph testing (Consigli, 2002).

Post-conviction polygraphy has been developed for the assessment, treatment and monitoring of individuals who are subject to Court Orders. In fact, the term 'clinical polygraph' developed out of recognition that at post-conviction stage the polygraph could serve a therapeutic and evaluative purpose within treatment programs and also as an aid to supervising convicted offenders (Wilcox, 2002). Its use was therefore viewed as less focused on direct and specific investigative work than on facilitating clinical efforts and addressing risk and treatment issues following conviction. Most prominently, post-conviction testing has focused on convicted sexual abusers and to a lesser degree, drug offenders. However, other post-conviction applications have been employed (Abrams & Ogard, 1986). While polygraphy is used in a wide variety of ways at both pre- and post-conviction stages, there are important similarities in both examination formats.

Besides the similarities in terms of administration of pre- and post-conviction polygraphy, there are important similarities with regard to the kinds of errors that can be made. Holden (1997) asserted that most examination error is attributable to the polygraph examiner as opposed to the actual assessment process, though this position continues to be debated. This view was similarly cited by Matte (1996, p. 296) when he discussed research by Raskin, Barland and Podlesny (1978) where, for example, they specifically noted that their 'results were strongly contradictory to the common belief that psychopaths (sociopaths) can 'beat the lie detector". Importantly, however, Matte's further comments did not reject concern about testing psychopaths. Rather, he noted, 'perhaps the greatest danger is that a clever or convincing psychopath can talk a polygraph examiner into believing him, even though the polygraph charts indicate deception' (p. 296).

The authors would assert that effective, careful polygraph preparation, implementation, scoring and interpretation can reduce the likelihood of errors considerably. Nevertheless, polygraph examiners must adhere to established principles and rules governing the administration of either type of examination. For instance, data interpretation varies in important ways in pre- or post-conviction settings in each situation. Examples of common errors will assist the reader in gaining a better understanding of the parameters within which polygraphy can be utilized effectively. It is important to be aware of such parameters and they are detailed more fully in Chapter 4.

REFERENCES

Abel, G.G. (1999). Assessing and treating sex offenders. Paper presented at the Specialised Services Conference Presentation on Assessing & Treating Sex Offenders, Chicago, IL.

Abrams, S. (1989). *The Complete Polygraphy Handbook*. Lexington, MA: Lexington Books.

Abrams, S. (2000). Polygraph validity in the new millennium. *Polygraph*, *29*, 344–356.

Abrams, S. & Abrams, J.B. (1993). *Polygraph Testing of the Pedophile*. Portland, Oregon: Ryan Gwinner Press.

Abrams S. & Ogard E. (1986). Polygraph surveillance of probationers. *Polygraph*, *15*, 174–182.

Abrams, S. & Simmons, G. (2000). Post-conviction polygraph testing: Then and now. *Polygraph*, *29* (1), 63–67.

Abrams, S., Hoyt, D., & Jewell, C. (1991). The effectiveness of the disclosure test with sex abusers of children. *Polygraph*, *20* (3), 204–213.

American Polygraph Association (1997). *Manual for Polygraph School Accreditation*. Chattanooga, Tennessee: APA National Office.

American Polygraph Association (2007). Model policy for post-conviction sex offender testing. *Polygraph*, *36*, 177–181.

Association for the Treatment of Sexual Abusers (1997). *Ethical Standards and Principles for the Management of Sexual Abusers*. Beaverton, OR: Author.

Backster, C. (1963). New Standards in Polygraph Chart Interpretation – Do the charts speak for themselves? *Law and Order*, *11* (6), 67–68.

Bashore, T.R. & Rapp, P.E. (1993). Are there alternatives to traditional polygraph procedures? *Psychological Bulletin*, *113* (1), 3–22.

Brooks, J. (1985). Polygraph testing thoughts of a sceptical legislator. *American Psychologist*, *40* (3), 348–354.

Colorado Sex Offender Management Board. (2000). *Research Supporting Restricted Contact with Children*. Colorado: Author.

Consigli, J. (2002). Post-conviction sex offender testing and the American Polygraph Association. In M. Kleiner (Ed.), *Handbook of Polygraph Testing* (pp. 237–249). London: Academic Press.

Cooley-Towell, S., Pasini-Hill, D., & Patrick, D. (2000). The value of the post-conviction polygraph: The importance of sanctions. *Polygraph*, *29* (1), 6–19.

Daubert v. Merrill Dow Pharmaceuticals (1993) (509 U.S. 579, 113 S.CT.2786, 125 L.ED.2D 469.

Dutton, D.W. (2000). Guide for performing the objective scoring system. *Polygraph*, *29* (2), 177–184.

Earls, C.M. & Lalumière, M.L. (2002). A case study of preferential bestiality (zoophilia). *Sexual Abuse: A Journal of Research and Treatment*, *14* (1), 83–88.

English, K. (1998). The Containment Approach: An Aggressive Strategy for the Community Management of Adult Sex Offenders. *Psychology, Public Policy and Law*, *4* (1/2), 218–235.

English, K., Pullen, S., & Jones, L. (1996). *Managing Adult Sex Offenders: Containment Approach*. American Probation and Parole Association.

English, K., Jones, L., Patrick, D. *et al.* (2000). We need you to become experts in the post-conviction polygraph. *Polygraph*, *29* (1), 44–62.

Grubin, D. (2006). *Polygraph Pilot Study: Final Report*. London: Home Office. Available from <http://www.probation.homeoffice.gov.uk> [Accessed May 18, 2007].

Grubin, D. & Madsen, L. (2005). Lie detection and the polygraph: A historical review. *Journal of Forensic Psychiatry and Psychology*, *16*, 357–369.

Grubin, D., Madsen, L., Parsons, S. *et al.* (2004). A prospective study of the impact of polygraphy on high risk behaviors in adult sex offenders. *Sexual Abuse: A Journal of Research and Treatment*, *16* (3), 209–222.

Harrelson, L.H., Gerow, N., & Gerow, J. (1998). *Lie Test: Deception, Truth and the Polygraph*. Fort Wayne, USA: Jonas Publishing.

Heil, P., Ahlmeyer, S., & Simons, D. (2003). Crossover sexual offenses. *Sexual Abuse: A Journal of Research and Treatment*, *15* (4), 221–236.

Heil, P., Ahlmeyer, S., McCullar, B., & McKee, B. (2000). Integration of polygraph testing with sexual offenders in the Colorado department of corrections. *Polygraph*, *29* (1), 26–30.

Holden, E.J. (1997). Understanding pre- and post-conviction polygraph – the key to its successful use – a guide. *Voice for the Defence*, *26*, 4–12.

Holden, E.J. (2000). Pre- and post-conviction polygraph: Building blocks for the future – procedures, principles, and practices. *Polygraph*, *29* (1), 69–98.

Honts, C.R. & Perry, M.V. (1992). Polygraph admissibility. *Law and Human Behavior*, *16* (3), 357–379.

Kleinmuntz, B. & Szucko, J.J. (1984). Lie detection in ancient and modern times. *American Psychologist*, *39* (4), 766–776.

Lamb, M. (2001). *Who was Wonder Woman?* Bostonia [Online]. Available from <www.bu.edu/ alumni/bostonia/fall2001/ww/index.html>.

Larson, J.A. (1932). *Lying and Its Detection*. Chicago: University of Chicago Press.

Lundell, R.G. (2000). Sex offender testing: Still basic polygraph. *Polygraph*, *29* (1), 40–43.

Lykken, D.T. (1974). Psychology and the lie detector industry. *American Psychologist*, *29* (10), 725–739.

Lykken, D.T. (1979). The detection of deception. *Psychological Bulletin*, *86* (1), 47–53.

Lykken, D.T. (1998). *A Tremor in the Blood: Uses and Abuses of the Lie Detector*. New York: Plenum Press.

Marston, W.M. (1938). *The Lie Detector Test*. New York: Richard R. Smith.

Matte, J.A. (1996). *Forensic Psychophysiology Using the Polygraph: Scientific Truth Verification – Lie Detection*. New York: JAM Publications.

McKay, B. (2000). The state of polygraph testing on sex offenders under community supervision in Texas. *Polygraph*, *29* (1), 36–39.

Moss Committee (1965). Committee on Government Operations, Tenth Report; *Use of Polygraphs as lie detectors by the Federal Government*. Union Ca. No.88, House Report No. 198, March 22, 1965. Washington, DC: US Government Printing Office.

National Research Council (2003). *The Polygraph and Lie Detection*. Committee to Review the Scientific Evidence on the Polygraph, Division of Behavioral and Social Sciences and Education. Washington, DC: The National Academies Press.

Reid, J.E. (1947). A revised questioning technique in lie detector tests. *Journal of Criminal Law and Criminology*, *37* (6), 542–547.

Salter, A. (1997). *Sex Offender Assessment and Risk Management Issues*. National Organisation for the Treatment of Abusers (NOTA) Annual Conference. Southampton, England.

Segrave, K. (2004). *Lie Detectors: A Social History*. North Carolina: McFarland & Company.

Simmons, G.R. (1998). Survey of Polygraph Testing of Convicted Sexual Offenders for Monitoring Purposes in the United States. Unpublished study.

Spencer, H. (1998). *Lie Testing Upheld for Sex Offenders*. Retrieved from <www.seattletimes.com>.

Steinbrook, R. (1992). The polygraph test – A flawed diagnostic method. *The New England Journal of Medicine*, *327* (2), 122–123.

Sullivan, E. (2001). *The Concise Book of Lying*. Picador: New York.

Teuscher, T. (1978). The polygraph and probation. *Polygraph*, *7*, 1–4.

United States v. Frye 293 F. 1013 (D.C.Cir. 1924).

United States Congress Office of Technology Assessment (1983). *Scientific Validity of Polygraph Testing: A Research Review and Evaluation – A Technical Memorandum* OTA-TM-H-15. Washington, DC: US Government Printing Office. Available electronically from <http://www.fas.org/sgp/othergov/polygraph/ota/index.html>.

Wilcox, D.T. (2000). Application of the clinical polygraph examination to the assessment, treatment and monitoring of sex offenders. *Journal of Sexual Aggression*, *5* (2), 134–152.

Wilcox, D.T. (2002). Polygraph examination of British sexual offenders (pp. 148–248). Unpublished doctoral dissertation, University of Surrey.

Wilcox, D.T. & Sosnowski, D. (2005). Polygraph examination of British sexual offenders: A pilot study on sexual history disclosure testing. *Journal of Sexual Aggression*, *11*, 3–25.

Williams, V.L. (1995). Response to Cross and Saxe's 'A critique of the validity of polygraph testing in children sexual abuse cases'. *Journal of Child Sexual Abuse*, *4* (3), 55–71.

CHAPTER 4

The Empirical Evidence for the Value of Post-Conviction Polygraph in the Treatment and Supervision of Sex Offenders

LARS MADSEN AND DANIEL T. WILCOX

The polygraph, often referred to as a 'lie detector', has been widely used in the United States over the last 70 years, where it has typically been utilized in criminal investigations and for employment vetting (Grubin & Madsen, 2005; National Research Council, 2003). More recently the polygraph has also been increasingly used in a post-conviction capacity in the treatment and supervision of sex offenders (English *et al.*, 2000a). Proponents claim that, within this context, polygraph examinations assist with gaining additional information about an individual's background and current behavior. Numerous clinicians have endorsed the use of the instrument in this manner (Salter, 1997). The international Association for the Treatment of Sexual Abusers (ATSA, 1997) also recommends the use of the polygraph for validating an offender's self-report. While many of these claims appear to have face validity, little research has actually been undertaken in the area, and the polygraph

The Use of the Polygraph in Assessing, Treating and Supervising Sex Offenders: A Practitioner's Guide
Edited by Daniel T. Wilcox.

continues to be subject to considerable scientific and public controversy (Cross & Saxe, 2001; Fiedler, Schmidt & Stahl, 2002; Lykken, 1998).

Much of the ongoing controversy surrounding polygraphy has focused on applications, such as its use in criminal investigations, in employee screening and in security vetting. It is argued, however, that these uses are distinct from the post-conviction polygraph testing with sex offenders (Holden, 2000; Wilcox, 2000). In the former, the issue of accuracy is particularly important, whilst in the latter the focus is on its utility in eliciting disclosure of information (English *et al.*, 2000b). Thus, it is argued that within this context, the polygraph is not considered a 'test' per se but rather a *treatment tool* that is typically used in conjunction with other tools (Abrams, 1991; Chambers, 1994; Earls & Lalumière, 2002; Williams, 1995).

Currently the most common treatment approach for sexual offenders is the relapse prevention (RP) model (Launay, 2001; Marshall, Anderson & Fernandez, 1999). The central tenet of this approach is that a sexual reoffence is not an impulsive act, but rather a sequence of behavioral and cognitive steps that result in sexual offending if no interventions are made. These 'high-risk' features can be idiosyncratic for each offender and could include private behaviors such as, masturbating to deviant (offence-related) fantasies or more public activity such as visiting a park where there are children (Beech & Fisher, 2002). Whilst such behavior may be difficult to observe or appear relatively benign to others, each of these mini-decisions (in theory) moves the individual closer to an actual sexual offence.

In the initial stages of RP treatment substantial efforts are focused on identifying the individual's high risk factors that are linked to sexual offending (Mann, 2004). The therapy then shifts the focus to assisting the offender develop skills and strategies to manage these high-risk factors (Maletzky, 1998). At the completion of treatment a Relapse Prevention Plan will have been developed by the offender that details his high-risk behaviors and also outlines strategies to manage such factors (Marshall *et al.*, 1999). Community supervision dovetails with the plan by monitoring and restricting the offender's identified risk behaviors to ensure that his risk of a reoffence remains as low as possible (Mandeville-Norden & Beech, 2004). Traditionally, however, it has proven difficult to ensure that offenders honestly engage in therapy (i.e., fully disclose the nature of their sexual behavior problems) and also comply with their particular supervision conditions, such as avoiding contact with children. The development of risk assessment tools, such as the Static-99, and the identification of dynamic risk factors associated with sexual recidivism, help to address this problem to some degree by differentiating the offenders most likely to reoffend

(Hanson & Bussière, 1998; Hanson & Harris, 2000). Supervisors can therefore specifically target the more high-risk offenders with more intensive and appropriate strategies. Nonetheless, a large portion of supervision and treatment remains reliant on the offenders' self-report, and studies have generally found that deception occurs with the majority of sexual offenders (Gannon, Beech & Ward, 2008).

Maletzky (1991), for example, reported that 87 % of offenders in his research denied all or parts of their crimes. Barbaree (1991) similarly observed that 54 % of rapists and 66 % of child molesters completely denied having offended, and indeed 98 % of all the sexual offenders in his sample either completely denied or minimized their offences. In response to this apparent barrier, a number of methods have been suggested for monitoring an offender's behavior in the community, and these include 'tagging' and 'intensive' supervision. While such methods have merit they remain problematic in some respects. For example, 'tagging' provides information only about an offender's location and does not serve to gauge explicit behavior, whereas twenty-four hour supervision for all community-based sex offenders is infeasible. Thus, the inability to effectively determine the veracity of an offender's disclosure during therapy and supervision, in addition to the complications associated with monitoring an individual's behavior in the community, represents an obvious limitation of current practices. Polygraphy could provide an elegant solution to this difficult position.

POST-CONVICTION POLYGRAPHY

There are several types of post-conviction polygraph examinations that are used at different times and stages of treatment and supervision (Blasingame, 1998). Sexual history or disclosure examinations are usually utilized shortly after an offender has commenced treatment, and is specifically focused on the offender's previous sexual behaviors. Specific issue tests (sometimes also referred to as denial tests) are commonly used to determine the veracity of an offender's index of offence-related disclosures during treatment. Typically, such tests are used for offenders in denial or if their version of the crime varies substantially from the victim's version. Finally, monitoring or maintenance exams focus upon the offender's current behavior, and are used on a regular basis to monitor compliance with supervision and treatment conditions (English, Pullen & Jones, 1996; Holden, 2000).

Therapeutically, advocates argue that sexual history and specific issue polygraph examinations enable clinicians to obtain more reliable sexual histories and more accurate offence behavior descriptions, both of which assist in overcoming denial and improve the assessment of treatment need and risk of reoffending (Salter, 1995). In terms of supervision, it has been argued that maintenance polygraph exams have the potential to identify not only breaches in supervision and outright offences, but it also acts to deter offenders from engaging in problematic behavior in the first place. Remarkably little empirical research has evaluated these claims with much of the published literature on post-conviction polygraphy being either theoretical or anecdotal in nature (e.g., Blasingame, 1998; English, 1998; Kokish, 2003; Wilcox, 2000). What little research that has been done, however, has generally tended to be supportive.

USE OF POLYGRAPHY IN THE ASSESSMENT OF SEX OFFENDERS

In one of the earliest published studies on post-conviction polygraphy, Emerick and Dutton (1993) compared an offender's assault history (i.e., number of victims and offences) on three occasions:

- What was known from file information;
- What was known after an intake interview; and finally,
- What was known after a polygraph examination.

The results showed that there was a dramatic increase in the known information after the polygraph examination. For example, the mean number of victims increased from 1.5 to 1.9 and then 2.8, whilst for number of offences it increased from 20.6 to 27 and then 76.6 after a polygraph examination. They further reported gaining additional information regarding the nature of force used during their offences, the use of pornography, and the number of paraphilic interests. Emerick and Dutton concluded that the polygraph assisted with gaining significant amounts of additional information.

The approach taken by Emerick and Dutton's study represents the typical methodology utilized to investigate the impact of polygraphy on admissions in sex offenders. Generally, other studies have reported findings consistent with these early results. In unpublished research, for instance, O'Connell (1998) reviewed 127 archival clinical files of adult sex offenders. In this study an offender's admissions were compared on three different occasions:

- At the referral interview;
- After a clinical interview; and,
- After polygraph testing.

Again the results indicated significant increases in the incidence of sexually abusive behaviors and numbers of victims reported after a polygraph test. In another study, Chambers (1994) found that the mean number of known victims and offences increased by 5.8 and 13.9 respectively after a polygraph test. More recently, research has also been conducted in the United Kingdom (UK). In a small study (n = 14), Wilcox, Sosnowski, Warberg and Beech (2005) found that the polygraph, when compared to clinical interviews, assisted in gaining significant amounts of additional information. This included an increase in number of known contact (16 to 73) and non-contact (32 to 110) offences. The offenders also reported much earlier onset of offending behavior as well as a wider range of deviant paraphilic sexual interests than had previously been known (Wilcox *et al.*, 2005).

In a study that includes a type of comparison group, Ahlmeyer, Heil, McKee and English (2000) compared the admissions of inmates and parolees on four different occasions during the course of treatment. Again consistent with the earlier studies, the results suggested that the polygraph assisted with gaining significant amounts of additional information in both groups. For example, the 35 inmates in this study initially reported a mean of 83 victims and 394 offences after completing a Sexual History questionnaire, these numbers increased to 183 and 528 respectively after polygraph testing. This effect was less apparent for parolees (whose pre-polygraph reporting consisted of 2 victims and 3 offences versus their post-polygraph reporting of 7 and 23 respectively).

The difference in the degree of admissions between the groups is notable, especially considering that both groups had similar sexual offending histories according to their pre-sentence reports. It is of course conceivable that the incarcerated participants were more deviant in ways not assessed in these measures than the parolees, thus explaining why they were in prison, and also, why the larger amounts of additional information was disclosed. There are perhaps a variety of psychological and contextual factors that could also have affected the nature of the admissions by the two groups.

It was noteworthy that the parolees were mandated to engage in therapy, whilst the inmates volunteered. Furthermore, the parolees had spent less time in what was described as 'less intensive therapy' than had the inmate sample. It is possible, therefore, that the increased amount of information reported by the inmates may partly be due to a treatment effect. That is, offenders that have been in treatment longer are less likely to be in denial and perhaps more motivated to engage fully in the treatment. This may therefore have resulted in the inmates being more likely to disclose information following a polygraph. One must also bear in mind that making additional disclosures regarding offending behaviors is likely to be considered favorably at parole hearings, so inmates may have been further motivated to appear to be co-operating by disclosing information. Parolees have arguably less to gain from making additional disclosures, and perhaps, even more to lose. Consider, for instance, the likely change in their circumstances should they disclose an extensive previously unknown history of sexual offending or deviance. If parolees were withholding information it would be expected that they would be more likely to fail the polygraph than inmates. The study does not present data on failure rates for the two groups, although it is reported 21 % of parolees did not disclose additional information after a failed polygraph test compared to only 5 % of inmates, suggesting that this may indeed have been a factor. As such, this may suggest that in spite of more disclosures from both groups, the community-based parolees may have felt they had more to lose by being entirely open and honest than the inmates.

In a similar study, Heil, Ahlmeyer and Simons (2003) investigated the admissions of 'crossover' offending in a sample of inmate and parolee sex offenders participating in treatment and engaging in polygraph testing. They defined crossover offences as those in which victims are from multiple age, gender and relationship (familial versus non-familial) categories. Broadly speaking the results showed that overall the sample disclosed a greater amount of crossover offending after polygraph testing. For instance, pre-sentence investigation reports showed that 7 % of the inmate sample (n = 223) had committed sexual offences against both children and adults; however, after polygraph testing 70 % disclosed having done so. A similar pattern was observed for parolees.

Taken together the results from these studies are promising, however, the lack of true control groups makes it difficult to determine whether the polygraph is solely responsible for the additional disclosures. For instance, the possibility cannot be discounted that the offenders would have disclosed the same information if asked without the polygraph or during the course of treatment. However, in view of the extensive amounts of assessment, treatment and supervision before polygraph testing (O'Connell, 1998; Wilcox, 2002) this kind of spontaneous openness does not seem very probable, and is not often encountered.

In an interesting study that attempts to overcome this problem, English *et al.* (2000a) compared sex offender treatment programs that were conducted with and without polygraph testing as well. The results showed that polygraphed offenders were more likely to report having offended against both male and female victims, and also against both juveniles and adults. These offenders generally disclosed greater amounts of sexually deviant activity than the offenders not required to complete a polygraph examination. This study also compared information known before and after a polygraph test. Again consistent with the research mentioned earlier, the findings suggested that significantly more information was gained from the polygraph test. In the sample of 180 sex offenders, for example, almost twice as many admitted to having male victims (20 % to 36 %) and three times as many admitted to perpetrating offences against both sexes (10 % to 29 %) after a polygraph test.

In a similar study, Hindman and Peters (2001) retrospectively compared the histories of sex offenders whose self-reports were verified by polygraph with those who did not take a polygraph. Consistent with English *et al.* (2000a), polygraphed offenders reported on average more victims (13.6 compared to 2.5) and a higher incidence of having offended as juveniles (68 % compared to 22 %). Notably, they also reported less history of having been sexually victimized themselves (32 % compared to 65 % previously). Upon closer analysis of these data, however, these findings are perhaps not so unexpected, considering that some of the non-polygraphed offenders were seen only for an evaluation, whilst all the polygraphed offenders were seen for treatment and also offered immunity from prosecution for reporting prior unknown sex offences.

USE OF POLYGRAPH IN THE MONITORING OF SEX OFFENDERS

Even less research has been conducted with regards to the use of the polygraph in the supervision of sex offenders. Abrams and Ogard (1986) compared the recidivism rates of probationers required to take periodic polygraph tests for supervision with probationers for whom there was no polygraph requirement. Whilst the study did not specifically investigate sex offenders, it was reported that over a two-year period 69 % of men who received periodic polygraph examinations remained offence-free, whereas only 26 % who did not receive polygraphs successfully completed their supervision. However, because participants were not randomly allocated, and general criminality and previous treatment were not controlled for, it is unclear how much the polygraph actually contributed to a reduction of recidivism. The difference between the groups, for instance, may simply have been due to one being less criminal than the other.

In a retrospective study that specifically investigated sex offenders, Edson (1991) reported that 95 % of 173 sex offenders on parole or probation, and who were required to undertake periodic polygraph testing, did not reoffend over a nine-year period. Yet again the absence of a comparison group makes it difficult to conclude that the low recidivism rate was due to use of the polygraph for monitoring.

In a prospective study that does include comparison conditions, Grubin, Madsen, Parsons, Sosnowski and Warberg (2004) evaluated whether the expectation of a polygraph test would reduce the likelihood of offenders engaging in high-risk behavior. In this study, conducted in the UK, a small sample of sex offenders (n = 49) were seen on three occasions. On the first occasion offenders were placed into one of two conditions and four high-risk behaviors were identified. One group was told to expect a polygraph test focused on their specified high-risk behaviors ('Polygraph aware'), whilst the second group was not told to expect a polygraph test ('Polygraph unaware'). On the second occasion, three months later participants were again interviewed about their identified behaviors. However, all the offenders were then asked to submit to a polygraph test focused upon these behaviors. The offenders who had disclosed engaging in high-risk behaviors were then told to expect a polygraph test in three months' time, whilst the participants that did not disclose any high-risk behavior and passed their polygraph were not.

At the initial polygraph the majority of offenders (67 %) were deceptive regarding whether they had engaged in risk behavior over the preceding three months. Indeed nearly all the offenders (97 %) disclosed having engaged in at least one of their monitored risk behaviors. The majority of the behaviors reported involved masturbating to deviant fantasies. However, a significant portion also included more serious victim acquisition type behaviors, such as contact with previous victims. Comparison between the two conditions showed that there was no difference in the number of behaviors reported by men in the 'Polygraph aware' (M = 2.4, SD = 1.6) and the 'Polygraph unaware' conditions (M = 2.7, SD = 1.9). This suggests that knowledge of the polygraph test had not acted as deterrence for engaging in risk behavior.

Because all but one of the offenders admitted to having engaged in risk behaviors, all were told to expect a polygraph examination. At the final polygraph only 28 % of the sample failed the polygraph. Seventy-one percent reported engaging in risk behaviors; however, 29 % reported no risk behavior and passed their polygraph test. Of the participants who reported risk behaviors, 60 % had already disclosed these to their supervisors compared with just 1 (3 %) who had done so at the initial polygraph. The offenders that attended both polygraphs reported significantly less behavior at Time Two (58 versus 33 behaviors), these were also evaluated as being less serious in nature (Madsen, Parsons & Grubin, 2004). The researchers speculated that because polygraphy was not integrated into the treatment and supervision process, and none of the offenders had experienced a polygraph previously, this unfamiliarity may have contributed to there being no difference between the two conditions at the initial polygraph test. It appears that the polygraph acted as a deterrent for offenders only *after* they had experienced a test.

Grubin *et al.* (2004) also examined the times when offenders disclosed risk behaviors. All the offenders had three opportunities to disclose risk behaviors: to the researcher at the interview prior to the polygraph test, during the pre-test interview with the polygraph examiner, and after the polygraph test. At the time of the first polygraph, only 37 % disclosed all their risk behavior during the initial or pre-test interviews, compared with 80 % that did this at the second. This finding suggests that periodic polygraph testing may prompt offenders to volunteer information regarding risk behavior.

Overall, whilst the results from the Grubin *et al.* (2004) study appear encouraging, the high attrition rate limits its value. Only 21 offenders completed the study, this represented only 42 % of the original sample, and only 18 % of the offenders were approached to take part in the study. However, sex offenders in the UK at that time were under no obligation to engage in the polygraph study and their voluntary attendance was precluded from the outset to lead to higher rates of attrition.

EVIDENCE FROM QUESTIONNAIRE STUDIES

There are a number of questionnaire studies of note, which provide some complementary evidence of the polygraph's value in a post-conviction context. Harrison and Kirkpatrick (2000) asked a small sample of sex offenders (n = 28) whether the polygraph assisted them in their treatment and with the problem of adhering to their probation conditions. A slight majority (57 %) reported a general decrease in risk behaviors that they attributed to use of the polygraph. This included having contact with potential victims and masturbating to deviant fantasies. In a larger study Kokish, Levenson and Blasingame (2005), in a sample of 95 sex offenders mandated to take periodic polygraph tests in California, found that 72 % reported that periodic polygraph testing was helpful in avoiding high-risk behaviors and reoffences.

In a more recent study Grubin and Madsen (2006) asked 114 sex offenders who were required to take biannual polygraph tests, whether the polygraph affected their behavior. Overall, 44 % claimed that they were more truthful with their probation officers and treatment providers than they otherwise would have been because of the polygraph. Slightly over half (56 %) reported that the polygraph was 'moderately' to 'extremely' helpful in assisting them to remain offence-free, 64 % found that it was useful in assisting them to avoid engaging in risk behaviors, and 67% found that it was generally helpful with respect to their treatment. With regards to specific risk behaviors, 33% claimed that they were less likely to masturbate to deviant fantasies, 31% reported they were less likely to have contact with children, 27% found that the polygraph contributed to less drug and alcohol use, and 25% claimed that they were less likely to use or buy pornography. Taken together, the results from these studies provide some support for the view that the polygraph has therapeutic value in the treatment and management of sex offenders. Furthermore, the results from this study indicated that the majority of sex offenders reported polygraphy to be helpful in terms of both treatment and avoiding risk behaviors and reoffending. It should be noted, however, that these findings were based on the responses of 55% of the program participants who agreed to take part in the study, and it is possible that the other 45% might have had very different views on the value of polygraph testing.

THE BOGUS PIPELINE EFFECT

There is also indirect evidence within the realm of social psychology to provide some support for the potential value of post-conviction polygraphy. In a study by Jones and Sigall (1971), for example, students were asked various personal questions regarding racial attitudes while attached to a machine that they were told was a highly accurate 'lie detector' (it was not). Those questioned under this 'bogus pipeline' condition were more likely to disclose politically incorrect responses. It was concluded that because participants believed that the machine was an accurate lie detector they felt it was in their interest to tell the truth (even though it reflected poorly upon them) rather than be caught in a lie. In a similar study, students were given information in advance on how to cheat on a classroom test. Sixty-five percent later admitted to receiving this information when connected to a bogus pipeline, compared to only 5% who did so without being connected (Quigley-Fernandez & Tedeschi, 1978). A meta-analysis review has recently supported the conclusion that participants offer socially undesirable information because of their fear of being caught in a lie by the bogus pipeline, and not just because of the expectations of the experimenters (Roese & Jamieson, 1993). Whilst the bogus pipeline research is not necessarily analogous with post-conviction polygraphy, it does demonstrate a likely placebo effect that the polygraph may have within a post-conviction context.

CONFESSIONS AND FALSE CONFESSIONS

It is only in recent years that research has investigated the psychological aspects of confessions, examining this literature provides some insight into the reasons why sex offenders may disclose information during a polygraph test rather than in other contexts. Gudjonsson (2003) reviewed five theories of what makes suspects confess to crimes they have committed during police questioning. These, combined with empirical evidence (Moston, Stephenson & Williamson, 1992), indicated that there are three main reasons why suspects confess to crimes that they have committed (Sigurdsson & Gudjonsson, 1996a). These were: the perception of the strength of evidence against them, external pressure (i.e., fear of custody), and internal pressure (i.e., wanting to 'clear conscience'). Usually more than one of these factors is present when a suspect confesses, but the empirical evidence suggests that it is the perception of the evidence against them that is the most powerful reason for confessing to the offence. In this regard, the polygraph in a post-conviction context may enhance the perception in the offender mind that the evidence is 'stacked against them', and thus, prompt them to 'confess'. This of course also raises the issue of false confessions.

False admissions during a polygraph test have not been addressed by any published literature. In the previously mentioned survey study, Kokish *et al.* (2005) also examined 'defensive lying' (false admissions). In this study participants were asked whether they had ever made false admissions after they had failed a polygraph exam. Only five offenders (5 %) reported making false admissions at this time, suggesting that this issue is not a significant problem. Grubin and Madsen (2006) found that 9 % of their sample claimed to have done so, suggesting that whilst the incidence is not high it is of relevance. Notably, the false confessors were more emotionally disturbed and impulsive when compared to others.

Within the wider empirical literature little research has been published on the issue of false confessions in criminal justice contexts. Gudjonsson and Sigurdsson (1994) and Sigurdsson and Gudjonsson (1996a, 1996b) carried out research into alleged false confessions among prison inmates. In both studies, 12 % of inmates reported that they had made false confessions to the police at sometime in their lives. Three main reasons were given for having made a false admission: (1) to protect someone else; (2) to avoid police pressure, and (3) to escape police detention. Comparison of alleged false confessors with other prison inmates showed that the 'false confessors' were significantly more personality disordered (Sigurdsson & Gudjonsson, 2001).

Gudjonsson, Sigurdsson, Bragason, Einarsson and Valdimarsdottir (2004) reported similar findings in a more recent study with a large sample of students (n = 1050). Only a small minority (4 %), who had previously been interrogated by police, claimed to have made false admissions to the police. Again the false confessors were significantly more personality disordered than the other volunteers.

Overall, whilst these findings suggest that false confessions are likely to be reasonably low in criminal justice contexts, individuals with personality disorder may be predisposed to making erroneous admissions. This is concerning, because sex offenders as an overall sample have generally been described as having a high prevalence and a broad range of personality disorders (Fazel *et al.*, 2002; Fraedrich & Pfaefflin, 2000; Madsen, Parsons & Grubin, 2006). False admissions may be more of an issue, therefore, in sex offender populations, particularly when the polygraph is used in a therapeutic manner focused upon an offender's disclosure of risk behavior and offences.

ACCURACY

Finally, it is important to highlight the issue of accuracy (Vrij, 2008), as professionals need to be able to rely on the results of such tests. Within the literature proponents of post-conviction polygraphy have tended to ignore or dismiss the unease within the wider scientific community regarding the polygraph's accuracy, focusing instead on its potential utility. Whilst it may be correct to argue that these issues are theoretically distinct, they are very much related in practice. For example, the utility of the polygraph as a deterrent depends inherently on the offender's belief that the procedure will reveal any deceptions and that the costs of being judged deceptive are undesirable. If the polygraph is not particularly accurate, then offenders are not going to maintain a belief in its accuracy over time. The continued value of this technique would then greatly diminish. In such circumstances, overconfidence in the polygraph could create a false sense of security among supervisors, treatment providers and the general public, which may in turn lead to inappropriate relaxation of other methods of supervision and treatment. The long-term usefulness of post-conviction polygraphy depends intrinsically, therefore, upon the procedure being an accurate method of detecting deception.

A limited number of studies have attempted to evaluate the accuracy of the polygraph in a post-conviction context. In the previously mentioned survey by Kokish *et al.* (2005) subjects were asked about the accuracy of the polygraph tests they had completed whilst on probation.

The offenders reported that the polygraph accurately identified truth-telling 92% and deception 82% of the time. In the Grubin and Madsen (2006) study the offenders' self-report indicated that the polygraph had accurately identified deception 84% and truth-telling 85% of the time. In the only experimental study, Grubin and Madsen (2006) found that the polygraph, when scored by 'blind' examiners, was reasonably accurate in identifying truth-telling (80%) and deception (100%) in a sample of community-based sex offenders. The findings from these studies suggest that the polygraph is reasonably accurate in this context. The issue of accuracy, however, will be discussed in greater detail in Chapter 9.

CONCLUSIONS

Proponents of post-conviction polygraphy make a persuasive case for its introduction in the management of sex offenders. When used in this context, the polygraph has the potential to overcome limitations in current supervision practices, as well as generally improving the assessment and treatment of sex offenders. Its use in such a capacity has increased markedly over the last decade in the United States. This expansion is likely to continue as professional organizations and leading sex offender practitioners endorse its utility. Whilst enthusiasm to polygraph sex offenders is perhaps understandable, the empirical evidence demonstrating its value in these settings is still emerging. To date much of this research has been complicated by methodological problems, such as small sample sizes, retrospective methodologies, lack of comparison groups and the use of non sex-offender samples. Clearly additional research needs to be conducted that not only replicates the earlier research, but also examines the long-term impact of periodic polygraph use in a supervision and treatment context. Nonetheless, from studies that have been conducted we can be cautiously optimistic that polygraphy can make a valuable contribution to the treatment and supervision of sexual offenders.

REFERENCES

Abrams, S. (1991). The use of polygraphy with sex offenders. *Annals of Sex Research*, *4*, 239–263.

Abrams, S. & Ogard, E. (1986). Polygraph surveillance of probationers. *Polygraph*, *15*, 174–182.

Ahlmeyer, S., Heil, M., McKee, B., & English, K. (2000). The impact of polygraphy on admissions of victims and offenses in adult sexual offenders. *Sexual Abuse: A Journal of Research and Treatment*, *12*, 123–138.

Association for the Treatment of Sexual Abusers (ATSA). (1997). *Ethical Standards and Principles for the Management of Sexual Abusers*. Beaverton, OR: Author.

Barbaree, H.E. (1991). Denial and minimization among sex offenders: Assessment and treatment outcome. *Forum on Corrections Research*, *3*, 30–33.

Beech, A.R. & Fisher, D.D. (2002). The rehabilitation of child sex offenders. *Australian Psychologist*, *37*, 206–214.

Blasingame, G.D. (1998). Suggested clinical uses of polygraphy in community-based sexual offender treatment programs. *Sexual Abuse: A Journal of Research and Treatment*, *10*, 37–45.

Chambers, H. (1994). Snohomish county juvenile court sex offender treatment programme policy statement on the use of polygraph in treatment of juvenile sex offenders. *Interchange*, November, 1– 6.

Cross, T. & Saxe, L. (2001). Polygraph testing and sexual abuse: The lure of the magic lasso. *Child Maltreatment*, *6*, 195–206.

Earls, C.M. & Lalumière, M.L. (2002). A case study of preferential bestiality (zoophilia). *Sexual Abuse: A Journal of Research and Treatment*, *14*, 83–88.

Edson, C. (1991). *Sex Offender Treatment*. Medford, OR: Department of Corrections.

Emerick, R.L. & Dutton, W.A. (1993). The effect of polygraphy on the self-report of adolescent sex offenders: Implications for risk assessment. *Annals of Sex Research*, *6*, 84–103.

English, K. (1998). The Containment Approach: An Aggressive Strategy for the Community Management of Adult Sex Offenders. *Psychology, Public Policy and Law*, *4*, 218–235.

English, K., Pullen, S., & Jones, L. (1996). *Managing Adult Sex Offenders: Containment Approach*. American Probation and Parole Association.

English, K., Jones, L., Pasini-Hill, D., & Cooley-Towell, S. (2000a). *The Value of Polygraph Testing in Sex Offender Management*. Research report submitted to the National Institute of Justice. Colorado: Colorado Department of Public Safety.

English, K., Jones, L., Patrick, D., Pasini-Hill, D., & Gonzalez, S. (2000b). We need you to become experts in the post-conviction polygraph. *Polygraph*, *29*, 44–62.

Fazel, S., Hope, T., O'Donnell, I., & Jacoby, R. (2002). Psychiatric, demographic and personality characteristics of elderly sex offenders. *Psychological Medicine*, *32*, 219–226.

Fiedler, K., Schmidt, J., & Stahl, T. (2002). What is the current truth about polygraph lie detection? *Basic and Applied Social Psychology*, *24*, 313–324.

Fraedrich, S. & Pfaefflin, F. (2000). The prevalence of personality disorders in a prison population/Zur Praevalenz von Persoenlichkeitsstoerungen bei Strafgefangenen. *Recht und Psychiatrie*, *18*, 95–104.

Gannon, T.A., Beech, A.R., & Ward, T. (2008). Does the polygraph lead to better risk prediction for sexual offenders? *Aggression and Violent Behaviour*, *13*, 29–44.

Grubin, D. & Madsen, L. (2005). Lie detection and the polygraph: A historical review. *Journal of Forensic Psychiatry and Psychology*, *16*, 357–369.

Grubin, D. & Madsen, L. (2006). The utility and accuracy of post-conviction polygraph testing with sex offenders. *British Journal of Psychiatry*, *188*, 479–483.

Grubin, D., Madsen, L., Parsons, S., Sosnowski, D., & Warberg, B. (2004). A prospective study of the impact of polygraphy on high risk behaviors in

adult sex offenders. *Sexual Abuse: A Journal of Research and Treatment, 16*, 209–222.
Gudjonsson, G.H. (2003). *The Psychology of Interrogations and Confessions: A Handbook*. Hoboken, NJ: John Wiley & Sons, Inc.
Gudjonsson, G.H. & Sigurdsson, J.F. (1994). How frequently do false confessions occur? An empirical study among prison inmates. *Psychology, Crime and Law, 1*, 21–26.
Gudjonsson, G.H., Sigurdsson, J.F., Bragason, O.O., Einarsson, E., & Valdimarsdottir, E.B. (2004). Confessions and denials and the relationship with personality. *Legal and Criminological Psychology, 9*, 121–133.
Hanson, R.K. & Bussière, M.T. (1998). Predicting Relapse: A meta-analysis of sexual offender recidivism studies. *Journal of Consulting and Clinical Psychology, 66*, 348–362.
Hanson, R.K. & Harris, A.J.R. (2000). *The Sex Offender Need Assessment Rating (SONAR): A Method for Measuring Change in Risk Levels*. (User report 1998–01). Ontario: Department of the Solicitor General.
Harrison, J.S. & Kirkpatrick, B. (2000). Polygraph testing and behavioral change with sex offenders in an outpatient setting: An exploratory study. *Polygraph, 29*, 20–25.
Heil, P., Ahlmeyer, S., & Simons, D. (2003). Crossover sexual offenses. *Sexual Abuse: A Journal of Research and Treatment, 15*, 221–236.
Hindman, J. & Peters, J. (2001). Polygraph testing leads to better understanding adult and juvenile sex offenders. *Federal Probation, 65*, 8–15.
Holden, E.J. (2000). Pre- and post-conviction polygraph: Building blocks for the future – procedures, principles, and practices. *Polygraph, 29*, 69–98.
Jones, E. & Sigall, H. (1971). The Bogus Pipeline: A new paradigm for measuring affect and attitude. *Psychological Bulletin, 76*, 349–364.
Kokish, R. (2003). The current role of post-conviction sex offenders polygraph testing in sex offender treatment. *Journal of Child Sexual Abuse, 12*, 175–194.
Kokish, R., Levenson, J.S., & Blasingame, G.D. (2005). Post-conviction sex offender polygraph examination: Client-reported perceptions of utility and accuracy. *Sexual Abuse: A Journal of Research and Treatment, 17*, 211–221.
Launay, G. (2001). Relapse prevention with sex offenders: practice, theory and research. *Criminal Behaviour and Mental Health, 11*, 38–54.
Lykken, D.T. (1998). *A Tremor in the Blood: Uses and Abuses of the Lie Detector*. New York: Plenum Press.
Madsen, L., Parsons, S., & Grubin, D. (2004). A preliminary study of the contribution of periodic polygraph testing to the treatment and supervision of sex offenders. *British Journal of Forensic Psychiatry and Psychology, 15*, 682–695.
Madsen, L., Parsons, S., & Grubin, D. (2006). A comparison of DSM-IV Personality Disorders and the Five Factor Model in a sample of child molesters. *Journal of Personality and Individual Differences, 40*, 227–236.
Maletzky, B.M. (1991). *Treating the Sexual Offender*. Newbury Park, CA: Sage Publications.
Maletzky, B.M. (1998). The paraphilias: Research and treatment. In P.E. Nathan & J.M. Gorman (Eds), *A Guide to Treatments that Work* (pp. 472–500). New York: Oxford University Press.
Mandeville-Norden, R. & Beech, A. (2004). Community-based treatment of sex offenders. *Journal of Sexual Aggression, 10*, 193–214.

Mann, R.E. (2004). Innovations in sex offender treatment. *Journal of Sexual Aggression*, *10*, 141–152.
Marshall, W.L., Anderson, D., & Fernandez, Y.M. (1999). *Cognitive Behavioral Treatment of Sexual Offenders*. Chichester: John Wiley & Sons, Ltd.
Moston, S., Stephenson, G.M., & Williamson, T.M. (1992). The effects of case characteristics on suspect behaviour during questioning. *British Journal of Criminology*, *32*, 23–40.
National Research Council (2003). *The Polygraph and Lie Detection*. Committee to Review the Scientific Evidence on the Polygraph, Division of Behavioral and Social Sciences and Education. Washington, DC: The National Academies Press.
O'Connell, M.A. (1998). Using polygraph testing to assess deviant sexual history of sex offenders. *Dissertation Abstracts International*, *58*, 3023.
Quigley-Fernandez, B. & Tedeschi, J.T. (1978). The bogus pipeline as lie detector: Two validity studies. *Journal of Personality and Social Psychology*, *36*, 247–256.
Roese, N.J. & Jamieson, D.W. (1993). Twenty years of bogus pipeline research: A critical review and meta-analysis. *Psychological Bulletin*, *114*, 363–375.
Salter, A. (1995). *Transforming Trauma. A Guide to Understanding and Treating Adult Survivors of Child Abuse*. California: Sage Publications.
Salter, A. (1997). *Sex Offender Assessment and Risk Management Issues*. National Organisation for the Treatment of Abusers (NOTA) Annual Conference. Southampton, England.
Sigurdsson, J.F. & Gudjonsson, G.H. (1996a). The psychological characteristics of 'false confessors'. A study among Icelandic prison inmates and juvenile offenders. *Personality and Individual Differences*, *20*, 321–329.
Sigurdsson, J.F. & Gudjonsson, G.H. (1996b). The relationship between types of claimed false confession and the reasons why suspects confess to the police according to Gudjonsson Confession Questionnaire (GCQ). *Legal and Criminological Psychology*, *1*, 259–269.
Sigurdsson, J.F. & Gudjonsson, G.H. (2001). False confessions: the relative importance of psychological, criminological and substance abuse variables. *Psychology, Crime and Law*, *7*, 275–289.
Vrij, A. (2008). Credibility assessments in a legal context. In D. Carson, B. Milne, F. Pakes, K. Shalev, & A. Shawyer (Eds), *Applying Psychology to Criminal Justice*. Chichester: John Wiley & Sons, Ltd.
Wilcox, D.T. (2000). Application of the clinical polygraph examination to the assessment, treatment and monitoring of sex offenders. *Journal of Sexual Aggression*, *5*, 134–152.
Wilcox, D.T. (2002). Polygraph examination of British sexual offenders (pp. 148–248). Unpublished doctoral dissertation, University of Surrey.
Wilcox, D.T., Sosnowski, D., Warberg, B., & Beech, A.R. (2005). Sexual history disclosure using the polygraph in a sample of British sex offenders in treatment. *Polygraph*, *34*, 171–181.
Williams, V.L. (1995). Response to Cross and Saxe's 'A critique of the validity of polygraph testing in children sexual abuse cases'. *Journal of Child Sexual Abuse*, *4*, 55–71.

CHAPTER 5

Basics of Post-Conviction Sex Offender Polygraph Testing

DANIEL E. SOSNOWSKI AND DANIEL T. WILCOX

INTRODUCTION

This chapter was written for professionals working with sex offenders to give them a broad, basic understanding of how the polygraph can be employed in this area of work. Readers who wish to gain a more comprehensive understanding about polygraph procedures and techniques may find it helpful to refer to a polygraph text such as Abrams (1989), Matte (1996) or Kleiner (2002).

BACKGROUND

Throughout history judges, leaders, philosophers and scientists have tried to understand how to detect deception though largely with limited success. Investigators like Lombroso (1882) and Benussi (1914) first monitored physiological variations in the body to see if they coincided with psychological changes (Grubin & Madsen, 2005). They hoped that this information might provide a more accurate way of differentiating between truthfulness and deceit.

The Use of the Polygraph in Assessing, Treating and Supervising Sex Offenders: A Practitioner's Guide
Edited by Daniel T. Wilcox.

By the early twentieth century, the first instrument that might rightly be viewed as a 'polygraph' was developed. Since then the polygraph has come to be viewed by many as a 'lie detector' (Keeler, 1934; Larson, 1932; Marston, 1917, 1938). The modern polygraph typically combines a blood pressure cuff, skin sensors for thumb and forefinger that measure Galvanic Skin Response (GSR), and a respiratory gauge (Kleiner, 2002; Wilcox, Sosnowski & Middleton, 1999). The physiological responses an individual produces are recorded continuously during the data collection part of a polygraph examination. Historically, this was accomplished through the use of separate pens moving independently of one another, slowly unraveling a roll of paper on a moving cylinder where the different physiological responses are recorded. Questions are systematically asked during the polygraph administration process and physiological changes are simultaneously recorded. In recent years, the more cumbersome 'paper and ink' units have largely been replaced by smaller computerized laptop instruments.

The scientific principles underlying polygraphy relate to the recognized 'fight or flight' response. Physiological reactions are produced in response to activation of the sympathetic component of the autonomic nervous system following an individual perception of threat whether it is of a physical or psychological nature (Wilcox, 2000, 2002). These reactions generally take the form of increases in respiration, heart rate, skin conductivity (perspiring), blood pressure and blood flow to the arms and legs. The central scientific premise of polygraph examination is that the psychological threat or fear of detection produced by telling a lie will activate the nervous system, giving rise to these normally involuntary changes. When questions are presented to examinees, some of these automatic reactions are recorded and analyzed by an appropriately trained polygraph examiner in order to render opinions regarding the polygraphee's honesty.

Conventional (pre-conviction) polygraphy was developed for a different purpose and pre-dated post-conviction polygraph testing. Pre-conviction polygraphy normally explores specific issues like 'Did you do it?' or 'Were you there?' This use of the polygraph is routinely quite focal in its approach such that it often evokes strong feelings of distress, particularly in individuals who know that they are guilty of being involved in the actions under investigation (Abrams & Abrams, 1993).

Besides criminal or police inquiries, civil investigations are sometimes addressed through pre-conviction polygraphy. This conventional polygraph application is also employed to address other types of disputes. Examples include fidelity issues, for instance where a jealous spouse employs a polygraph examiner to investigate relationship apprehensions. Various competitions may also be subject to routine polygraph examination, for example, to assist in the judging of fishing and other contests to ensure that participants are behaving honestly. Polygraphy has even been considered to curb cheating in organized sports like cricket ('Cronjegate'; King, 2001).

Notably, conventional polygraph examinations were also the subject of considerable criticism when, in the 1980s they were increasingly used for 'employment vetting' by a number of poorly regulated polygraph examiners. These individuals have collectively been referred to as 'polygraph prostitutes' (Wilcox, 2000) and their practice of producing low cost, high volume, poor standard examinations cast a shadow over the polygraph field during this period. Unfortunately, this practice discredited polygraph use quite broadly in the United States (US) and tarred good examiners with the same brush that poorer ones no doubt deserved.

The introduction of agreed standards (APA, 1999; Dutton, 2000; Joint Polygraph Committee on Offender Testing, 1998) was aimed at curbing this activity and regulations were introduced by the American Polygraph Association (APA) to enable more professional polygraph practice. The APA was established in 1966 and is the largest professional polygraph organization in the world, comprising approximately 2500 members across 33 countries. The APA has a code of ethics, standards of practice and grievance procedures (see also www.polygraph.org) in addition to accrediting 15 US polygraph academies and a further 4 schools internationally. Further, a range of non-APA accredited schools also exist offering training to become a polygraph examiner. However, 20 states in the US require polygraph examiners to be registered with the APA in order to practice. Indeed, apart from this, there is little regulation of polygraphy in the US or abroad since individuals do not have to be licensed or have undergone any particular training in order to either purchase a polygraph instrument, practice privately or refer to themselves as a 'polygraph examiner'. Unfortunately, neither the APA nor any other formal body has power to exert much control over poor practice. However, the APA can end an individual's membership if unprofessional or unethical practice is determined.

HOW THE POLYGRAPH WORKS

The modern day polygraph instrument is not a 'lie detector' per se as thought by many people. Rather, it monitors and records changes to an individual's physiological reactions in response to stimuli presented by the polygraph examiner. Importantly, effective polygraph examinations necessitate the establishment of 'psychological set' from the outset of testing (Holden, 1997). Importantly, 'psychological set' is regarded as an adaptive psychophysiological response to the presence of fear and anxiety. Psychological set can be induced by focusing on a particular issue or situation which poses the greatest threat to the wellbeing of the polygraphee during testing.

A hypothetical situation may serve to illustrate this concept. Imagine an individual who is confronted by three assailants. One has a gun, another a club, and the third a large knife. The confronted individual is likely to quickly 'assess' the level of threat posed by each assailant in an effort to determine which one presents the greatest threat to their overall wellbeing.

Though all three of the assailants are a threat, even in these circumstances the confronted individual will likely focus more attention on the danger that they perceive to be the greatest. A not dissimilar psychological stratification of risk is created when an individual undergoes a polygraph examination. The issue becomes 'which of the questions asked during the pre-examination and data collection phases poses the most significant perceived threat or danger to the examinee's overall sense of safety or wellbeing'. Different questions will likely evoke responses of differing magnitude as the examinee engages in an internal weighting of the personal significance of each question.

Concerns have been raised about possible errors in the interpretation of physiological measures since some polygraphees may be troubled by high anxiety or other factors that are irrelevant to the determination of truth and deception. Critics (Ekman, 1985; Lykken, 1981) have expressed concerns that this might lead the polygrapher to provide a 'false positive' opinion (render the examinee as deceptive when they are actually telling the truth) or alternatively render the examinee as having shown no deception when they have actually been lying ('false negative').

Holden (1997, 1999) advised that false negative findings can be very substantially reduced when the examiner takes sufficient time with the examinee to establish appropriate 'psychological set'. In relation to this, Holden emphasized the necessity of impressing upon the examinee how important the polygraph examination results will be to the referring party or parties, i.e., probation, court, police, treatment services. Indeed, the authors note that guilty polygraph examinees have the greatest opportunity to successfully pass a polygraph examination if they have little reason to fear a 'Deception Indicated' result. It is therefore essential for the examiner to thoroughly clarify the consequences of being deceitful during the polygraph examination and in doing so establish the appropriate psychological set required for effective testing. Importantly, specialized polygraph training and the employment of standardized test administration and interpretation procedures markedly reduce the potential for such errors to arise (D. Sosnowski, personal communication, September 24, 1999; Holden, 1996, 1997; Wilcox, 1999).

With both pre- and post-conviction testing the risk of false positives is also further decreased once the examinee is shown how the polygraph is administered, what it measures and a 'trial run' (acquaintance test) is conducted. This 'acquaintance' test has considerable utility since it generally gives confidence to the examinee that deceitfulness can be distinguished from generalized anxiety. Consequently, 'innocent individuals' tend to relax after completing the acquaintance test whilst individuals who possess relevant and incriminating information in relation to the examination usually become more anxious at this stage (D. Sosnowski, personal communication, September 18, 2000).

All competent and conscientious polygraph examiners recognize that individuals being polygraphed likely experience considerable levels of general anxiety. For this reason, the polygraph subject is carefully interviewed to ensure the development of suitable relevant and comparison questions prior to embarking on the data collection phase. The comparison questions are individually developed with examinees and whilst they are independent of the factors underlying the reason for referral (i.e., offending behavior, adherence to license conditions) they are essential for determining a truthful examinee from a deceptive examinee.

The 'relevant' questions are formulated to define key events (i.e., those relating to the offence or adherence to license conditions) and importantly they are developed in a morally neutral and objective manner. Well-constructed relevant questions do not readily lend themselves to rationalizing or reinterpretation. For example, an acceptable relevant question might be, 'Did you put your hand on (child's) vagina for sexual gratification?' An example of a less helpful question would be 'Did you touch (child) in a sexual manner?' since a guilty examinee who intends to lie to this question may have more scope to rationalize their behavior. To clarify, a guilty examinee may argue their interaction with the child was for healthcare or educational reasons (i.e., I was applying cream to her vagina to alleviate soreness; I was showing him where he should not allow other people to touch him). Further, such an examinee may believe that because their actions did not involve penetration, for instance, or could be construed as normal parenting behavior (applying cream to their genital region as directed by a doctor) then they were not touching the child in a 'sexual manner'. Such an examinee could potentially reply 'No' to this question without producing physiological reactions reflective of deceit, since in their mind the original question does not apply to them. However, by including the term 'for sexual gratification' an examinee who has touched a child as a consequence of harboring deviant thoughts and feelings will experience significant difficulties attempting to rationalize their behavior. Responding 'No' (to the question 'Did you put your hand on (child's) vagina for sexual gratification?') will result in responding indicative of deceit because they did touch the child and found this sexually gratifying, irrespective of whether penetration was involved or indeed whether their actions could be construed as innocent behavior. Conversely, for those individuals who have been wrongly accused of sexual impropriety, for example, they are capable of confidently responding 'No' to questions such as 'Did you put your hand on (child's) vagina for sexual gratification?' because even if they had had contact with the child's genital region in the course of applying cream for instance, their actions would have been motivated by a need to alleviate the child's discomfort as opposed to being sexually gratifying.

Comparing physiological responses to comparison and relevant questions enable extraneous variables like transient anxiety, chronic generalized tension and unrelated guilt to be substantially factored out since they reflect a 'baseline' within the individual's typical or average level of responding. The individual is evaluated in relation to their own physiological reactivity as opposed to the norms of others. Therefore a normal response range is determined for the individual and deviations from this reflect whether the examinee is being truthful or deceptive to questions asked during the data collection phase.

Leading proponents of post-conviction polygraphy (D. Sosnowksi, personal communication, September 18, 2000; Abrams & Simmons, 2000; Dutton, 2000; Holden, 2000; Lundell, 2000) have emphasized that reliable and accurate polygraph test results can best be achieved by carefully adhering to established, recognized test protocols as taught during APA approved training programs.

BRIEF HISTORY OF POST-CONVICTION POLYGRAPH SEX OFFENDER TESTING

Employment of post-conviction polygraphy first occurred when US judges used it to make decisions about applications for probation (Partee, 1975) and further to identify violators of probation conditions (Tuttle, 1969). Both judges found it helpful in these contexts and also agreed that offenders who were polygraphed admitted to other criminal activities.

Based on his experience in this area, Judge Tuttle formed the opinion that periodic polygraph examinations could act as a deterrent to further criminal involvement and additionally make it less desirable for other active criminals to associate with these polygraphees for fear that their activities might also be detected through testing. For this reason, in commenting on Tuttle's work, Schmidt, Soloman and Johnson (1973) described the periodic polygraph examination as an 'artificial conscience'. Judge Tuttle further believed that the polygraph might even influence what offenders 'allowed' themselves to think about because these views might be revealed through polygraph examination.

In 1973 Judge Beatty began a polygraph surveillance program for offenders in the State of Oregon (Riegel, 1974). He used this approach with offenders who were regarded as so dangerous that they would not have been granted probation without agreeing to undertake periodic polygraph examinations. Teuscher (1978) published the four-year follow-up results of Judge Beatty's initiative which involved over 100 'high risk offenders'. He reported 54 failures and 60 successes among these 'career' criminals as regards facing new charges. He further reported extensive admissions by these men to additional crimes such that thousands of dollars' worth of stolen property and illegal drugs were recovered. He held the view that significant savings were also made in terms of public expenditure since the majority of these men had no further convictions and no longer warranted the expense of imprisonment.

Subsequently, Abrams and Ogard (1986) began a two-year study of convicted criminals including burglars, drug users and sex offenders. They reported that 69 % of the men who received periodic polygraph examination successfully completed their probation and did not reoffend whereas only 26 % of those offenders receiving probation supervision alone successfully completed their probation and refrained from reoffending. These highly significant results offered substantial evidence of the utility of the polygraph for surveillance and offence reduction purposes.

English, Pullen and Jones (1996) discussed the polygraph's role in monitoring convicted sexual offenders, advising that it should be viewed as one of several tools needed to effectively control and contain sexual offending behaviors. They advised that 'the goal of the polygraph examination is not to get the offender to fail the exam but, rather to pass, meaning that disclosing the offender's sexual assault pattern will increase the likelihood that an appropriate treatment and supervision plan will be developed' (p. 211).

In recent years, the polygraph has increasingly been used for sex offender treatment and monitoring. Members of the American

Polygraph Association's Post-Conviction Sex Offender Treatment Committee (Dutton, 2000) have worked, trained and published extensively in support of employing post-conviction polygraph testing for sex offender assessment, treatment and monitoring (Abrams, 2000; Abrams, Hoyt and Jewel, 1991; Holden, 1999, 2000; Lundell, 2000; Wilcox & Sosnowski, 2005; Wilcox *et al.*, 2005).

The experts in this field have expressed substantial agreement with regard to the different types of polygraph examinations needed to meet the range of requirements currently in existence. They have acknowledged the importance of various types of assessment, therapy and supervision in addressing the difficulties created by this particular client group. Accordingly, specific post-conviction procedures have been developed to obtain detailed information about past sexual behavior and potentially undisclosed victims (sexual history disclosure examination) as well as addressing denial (specific issue denial examination) which is commonly encountered by professionals working with individuals who have committed sexual offences. Further, the monitoring examination has been designed to monitor whether an offender has engaged in behavior contrary to the conditions mandated by their order since conviction or release from prison. Similarly the maintenance examination can be used to ascertain whether an offender has been complying with not only the requirements of their Order but also with the expectations agreed during groupwork sessions and/or supervision (i.e., refraining from masturbating to pro-offending fantasies). These different types of post-conviction polygraph examinations are discussed in greater detail below.

POST-CONVICTION POLYGRAPH EXAMINATION FORMATS

Specific Issue Denial Testing

This type of post-conviction polygraph examination is often described as a specific issue test since it addresses the elements of denial that are often found in convicted sex offenders. Treatment professionals frequently identify at least four different types of denial commonly employed by sex offenders (Salter, 1988; Trepper & Barrett, 1989; Wilcox & Coles, 2006; Winn, 1996):

1. Offenders very often deny the facts concerning the case and the behaviors for which they have been convicted. Indeed, they often vehemently assert that they 'were not there and did not or could not have done it'.

2. Offenders also deny being aware of their offending or exonerate themselves of culpability for their actions, reporting, for example, that they may have inadvertently touched someone sexually, were sleepwalking or were under the influence of alcohol.
3. Offenders may also deny responsibility by alleging that the victim's actions precipitated and triggered the events that formed the basis of their conviction but which were not acknowledged or taken into consideration by the investigating authorities.
4. Some offenders deny that there was a sexual component to their offending behavior and report that their actions were misconstrued as sexual, when in fact they were educative, hygiene-related or associated with health/treatment issues.

Further, offenders can also deny the impact of the offence or harm caused to the victim. Importantly, it is held by most experts on sex offending (Laws, Hudson & Ward, 2000; Marshall, Anderson & Fernandez, 1999; Marshall, Laws & Barbaree, 1990; Salter, 1988) that all of these stances or ploys will likely increase the chances of an offender committing further acts of sexual abuse. These 'excuses' implicitly give 'permission' for offending to reoccur since rationalization and justification admonishes the offender of holding themselves wholly accountable and responsible for their sexually abusive behavior.

The specific issue denial test can be used to break through these levels of denial, though in the experience of the authors, it is most helpful in breaking down the primary denial issues, for example, acknowledging the commission of the offence and responsibility for engaging in this activity. This is particularly useful since mainstream sex offender group involvement is very difficult with individuals who adamantly deny committing their offence. Thus polygraph examinations are used in collaboration with treatment work to aid in the addressing of denial issues as the offender moves through Court-ordered intervention (Markall, Wilcox & Goodwill, 2007). Although treatment work can be conducted with individuals who are in denial (Marshall, Anderson & Fernandez, 1999; Roberts & Baim, 1999), it is nonetheless generally accepted that work with sex offenders can be facilitated when these individuals accept that they committed the offences for which they were convicted. Salter (1997) reported that the effectiveness of the polygraph has been so substantial that denier groups are no longer run in the North-West of the United States where post-conviction sex offender polygraph testing has been widely employed.

Importantly, specific issue denial tests specifically focus on denial issues in relation to an offender's current sexual offence and its scope is restricted to these issues. This type of examination is often best used pre-treatment or at a very early point in the treatment process as confronting the denial of facts, awareness and responsibility can often be quite satisfactorily addressed through polygraph examination.

Importantly, denial-related polygraph questions frequently address very specific stumbling blocks to treatment (Abel, 1999). For example, specific denial questions might ask: 'Did you know the victim's actual age?' or 'Do you recall having touched your daughter for sexual reasons?' It is not uncommon for an offender to maintain that they were duped into a sexual encounter with a minor, had been mistakenly identified as the offender or were under the influence of a substance at the time and did not realize what they were doing. The creativity of offenders in denying and minimizing their behavior will be well known to treatment workers with implausible explanations often readily forthcoming, for example, 'I was only rubbing her back', 'She also said her father did it' or 'She was having sex with her boyfriend when she was fourteen and wanted to get me into trouble for interfering'.

However, some denial issues and in particular those associated with the impact of abuse may be best approached through sex offender treatment work (Marshall, Anderson & Fernandez, 1999). Such denial of impact usually involves minimization of damage (physical and/or psychological) to the victim. In these circumstances, a combination of the two (treatment and polygraphy) can often successfully address even these types of denial and minimization issues 'paving the way' towards the development of more effective treatment and relapse prevention work.

The Sexual History Disclosure Examination

The sexual history disclosure examination (SHDE) is employed to obtain a more thorough understanding of an offender's past sexual behavior and interests and allows for greater exploration of any involvement in previously undisclosed sexual activities. The sexual history information obtained from such examinations can assist in the tailoring of treatment for the offender in addition to providing an opportunity for a more comprehensive assessment of risk. A guarantee of some immunity from prosecution for previously undisclosed and unreported offences revealed during the sexual history disclosure has in some situations been given and thus produced fuller participation by the offender (English, 1998, 2002; Wilcox, 2000). Another method more commonly employed to increase the likelihood of openness/honesty is to have the examinee refer to unknown victims without giving details as to their names, addresses, etc. Rather, the examiner is provided with information about the age, gender and general circumstances concerning victims and previously undisclosed offences. In this way, disclosures may assist in understanding offence patterns and behaviors and subsequently the estimation of potential risk together with facilitating the development of more relevant and complete relapse prevention strategies while not necessarily leading to further criminal investigations/proceedings.

More recently, some practitioners employing sexual history disclosure examinations have advised limiting the scope of the SHDEs to investigate 'undisclosed victims' in particular rather than conducting an entire examination of the offender's sexual history (Lundell, 2000; Wygant, 1980). Abrams (2000) referred to potential problems associated with full disclosure examinations. This is based on the rationale that an offender will be likely to withhold some relevant information regarding undisclosed past sexual behaviors and interests and therefore the probability of a deceptive polygraph is high. As such, more focused sexual history examinations may be more beneficial. Even so, earlier studies employing full SHDEs have consistently revealed much more extensive histories of sexual offending, including significantly higher numbers of victims, offences and paraphilic involvements as well as earlier onset of offending behavior (Heil *et al.*, 2000; Wilcox & Sosnowski, 2005).

However, due to the breadth of the issues addressed in comprehensive SHDEs, the APA's approved Post-Conviction Sex Offender Testing materials now stipulate that the current preferred method for SHDEs would be to initially test on the issue of undisclosed victims and later, as deemed appropriate, test for undisclosed sexual behaviors if this is considered a relevant issue within the context of ongoing treatment.

Prior to the conducting of the sexual history disclosure examination the polygraphee should complete a sexual history form as recommended by the most recent APA guidelines (APA, 2007). This form affords the examinee an opportunity to provide the polygrapher with information about their past sexual thoughts and behaviors. During the pre-test interview the contents of this form are reviewed in addition to specific attention being paid to the extent to which they have engaged in deviant, obsessive and sexually disinhibited activities. Further, through dialogue with the treatment provider and supervising officer any more specific known or suspected issues can be discussed to enhance the successful treatment and monitoring of the offender. For example, areas of sexual concern to consider would include, but not be limited to, engaging in partner swapping, visiting adult book stores, massage parlors or prostitutes. Even more specifically, enquiries may address autoerotic behaviors, sexually sadistic activities, having or seeking sexual contact with hitchhikers, employing vegetables, fruit, etc. in sexual activities, touching someone (for sexual reasons) while they were sleeping or otherwise unaware/non-consenting in an effort to review a full range of potential paraphilic interests.

The employment of the sexual history questionnaire impresses upon the examinee a need to fully consider their sexual behavior over the course of their life. The breadth and depth of the sexual history questionnaire highlights recognition of the widest range of possible sexual activities in which an individual could engage (see Appendix A for a sample of sexual history disclosure examination questions). An informed, facilitative attitude should be maintained by the polygrapher throughout the interview and polygraph testing with individual items being considered in a neutral and objective manner to facilitate fuller disclosure. Notably, the number of disclosures made by offenders often increases (Abel, 1999) when the polygrapher discusses a range of sexual behaviors and interests whilst posing questions in a non-judgmental manner by asking 'When? How often? Where?' as opposed to 'Have you ever?' Importantly, as with other information gathered during polygraph testing, it is necessary for the polygrapher to review disclosures with the supervising officer and treatment provider post-examination. Through this process the individual issues identified can be addressed, clarified and corroborated in other settings with the net result of hopefully improving public safety and treatment response.

Maintenance Polygraph Examination

A third type of post-conviction polygraph test is the maintenance examination. Such examinations focus on an offender's adherence to conditions mandated by the Court (i.e., Community Rehabilitation Order) as well as addressing compliance with treatment/intervention. However, many, if not most trained polygraphers believe that examinations should either focus exclusively on matters relating to 'treatment' or on those concerning Court violations This relates to the generally accepted maxim within polygraphy that the narrower the focus of the examination, the greater the likely accuracy of the test. However, it is important to recognize that many areas concerning treatment also have direct bearing on probation or parole requirements. As such, while distinctly different polygraph examinations have been developed, information disclosed may overlap into other areas of significant interest. For example, an offender being given a maintenance examination may spontaneously report engaging in past risky behaviors where present circumstances mirror past offending conditions.

The maintenance examination is used to evaluate a sex offender's activities and truthfulness during their time on probation or license. It is generally administered every three to six months to ensure offender compliance with conditions mandated by their Order and also their treatment provider. A range of conditions may be listed for the offender to adhere to, for instance: (1) not having unsupervised contact with children, (2) refraining from viewing specific types of sexually explicit material, (3) abstaining from alcohol or illegal drug use, or (4) avoiding specified sexual behaviors. Ascertaining whether an offender has engaged in prohibited behaviors can be achieved through this type of polygraph test.

The maintenance test concentrates on whether the offender has been involved in various risky behaviors that might lead to further post-conviction acting out and reoffending. Many treatment providers believe that if they 'know' that the offender is engaging in activities that are similar to those associated with their previous offending, then they may have an opportunity to intervene early in the cycle before further offences occur. For instance, one area often investigated through 'maintenance testing' relates to masturbation to deviant or inappropriate fantasies. Enquiries here will relate directly to issues concerning the individual offender, for example, masturbating while thinking about children or forced sexual activity with adults.

Importantly, the polygraph cannot be employed to assess an offender's intentions nor will it predict future behavior, for example, will this individual reoffend. However, the maintenance examination can assist those professionals responsible for the treatment and supervision of offenders in understanding whether an offender is engaging in behaviors associated with being 'in cycle' (Wolf, 1984) and as such make more informed decisions about the level of input and monitoring they require. Specific disclosures made during testing can give helpful indications as to what kinds of risky behaviors the offender has been carrying out.

Quite understandably, treatment providers and related professionals will be concerned about whether or not an individual has actually reoffended. Many polygraph examiners believe that such a specific question can be most appropriately addressed through use of a 'monitoring examination' (see below) as opposed to a 'maintenance test'.

Monitoring Polygraph Examinations

Monitoring polygraph examinations specifically explore issues relating to new offences or breaches that have occurred since conviction/probation or parole. The issues covered by this type of exam will only focus on probation requirements and not specific treatment concerns. As such, the monitoring polygraph examination is similar to the specific issue test that is conducted when the offender has denied all or part of their initial index offence. If there is a specific allegation made against the offender, this type of 'monitoring test' should be administered and focus only on the particular issue presenting. For example, if a supervising officer is informed that an offender breached the conditions of their License/Order because they were witnessed alone and unsupervised with a minor, seen accessing inappropriate Internet images at a public library or observed in an area where they are prohibited from being, then a monitoring examination should be employed if the offender denied any wrongdoing when questioned about the allegation.

THE CONTAINMENT APPROACH

A collaborative multidisciplinary team strategy is required for the polygraph to be used effectively as a tool. The common goal for any team of professionals responsible for supervising a convicted sexual offender is to contain and modify the offender's behaviors in an effort to prevent further victimization. Importantly, to achieve this goal, close communication between probation/parole officers, law enforcement workers, therapists and the polygraph examiner is required.

This 'containment' team approach has proven very useful in sex offender work (English *et al.*, 1996). For example, in the state of Oregon its introduction gave rise to a lower rate of recidivism and reduced numbers of probation/parole revocations (R. Gindstaff, personal communication, July 1, 1993). Significantly, it was also determined that the 'pass or fail' rate on polygraph testing was largely dependent on the vigilance and combined efforts of the therapist, probation officer and polygraph examiner, for example, with the benefit of clear shared aims and open communication offenders were more likely to pass their polygraph examinations. As such their behavior was viewed as increasingly transparent and their attitudes as congruent with the aims of therapy and supervision.

COMMON ERRORS THAT REDUCE THE ACCURACY OF POLYGRAPH TESTING

Notably, the accuracy of polygraph testing is influenced by a range of variables such as corroboration amongst the key professionals involved and strict adherence to recognized testing procedures as stipulated by the APA's 'Standards of Practice' (APA, 2007) `http://www.polygraph.org/bylaws.cfm`. The closing section of this chapter therefore considers the types of problems that can arise and potentially impact on the accuracy of polygraph examinations administered.

Importantly, when framing questions for polygraph examination purposes the task must be approached in an objective and emotionally neutral manner since the mere inference or suggestion of guilt on the part of the examiner would be anticipated to unhelpfully bias test results and reduce accuracy.

Polygrapher Preparation Requirements and Style of Engagement with the Examinee

It is very important for adequate time to be taken by the polygraph examiner to review and familiarize themselves with all relevant documentation pertaining to the case (APA, 2007). This is particularly important when conducting post-conviction examinations where different accounts or levels of acceptance of guilt and responsibility exist. In the case of specific issue denial polygraph examinations, in-depth knowledge about the crime/offence is the key consideration since this test is used to obtain further details about the index offence for which an individual has been convicted but about which they continue to be in some significant degree of denial.

Appropriate Examinee Preparation

Prior to their appointment, examinees should be informed of how long the examination is likely to take. If this is not established then the offender's focus during the test may waver, particularly if the examinee thought the process would be completed quicker than they had anticipated. If, for example, an examinee has made an appointment to follow their polygraph test, then their attention could be unnecessarily disrupted and, as such, physiological reactivity might vary for reasons not associated with the polygraph test. The individual might simply be more concerned or even preoccupied with hurrying the test along so that they will have time to keep their further appointment.

It is also essential to establish at the outset that the examinee clearly understands the purpose of the polygraph examination. As referenced previously, once this is properly accepted and verbalized by the examinee, the examiner should take steps to reinforce this position. Further, it is important to be very clear about what the procedure will entail and the type of questions that will be asked. This is necessary to allay any possible fears or misguided notions associated with the test, for example, 'Is there pain involved? Will I receive an electric shock? Will the questions come as a surprise to me?' Such preparation can also address issues relating to how information may be used following the test, for example, 'If I fail will I go back to prison? If I 'prove' my innocence on the test will my Order/License be revoked? Will I be re-arrested for divulging previously unknown information or victims?' Addressing these matters before polygraph testing will serve to minimize the possible interfering effects of irrelevant and extraneous variables.

In post-conviction polygraph testing adherence to established, chart running procedures are critically important to ensure that the validity, accuracy and utility of the test is maximized. Polygraph examinations should take place in a quiet environment free from distractions such as wall decorations, the possibility of outsiders peering into the room, intercom announcements and telephone calls, for example. Pre-examination procedures should include verification of an examinee's identity, review of materials from referral parties, signing of a consent form, discussion of the examination's purpose, formulation/review of test questions, and establishing the examinee's fitness to undertake the polygraph test. Importantly, a clear and objective rationale for the polygraph examination should be agreed with the referring party or parties prior to performing the exam. This would require devoting time to discussing the key purpose for the polygraph referral (i.e., denial being a 'stumbling block' to treatment; suspicions regarding an offender's adherence to Order conditions; concerns arising from specific paraphilic interests).

Poorly Developed Questions (Comparison and Irrelevant)

Certainly, a key skill for appropriately trained polygraph examiners is to possess the ability to construct appropriate, unambiguous questions that serve to quite clearly reflect the examinee's thoughts and behavior in relation to the relevant issues being explored. Particular efforts must be taken to ensure that the examinee fully understands the meaning of each question and that through discussion with the examiner, the questions are not subject to different interpretations. In any polygraph test (pre- or post-conviction) when questions are not clearly formulated, the information obtained during the examination becomes much less helpful, reliable and accurate. As such, extreme care needs to be taken to ensure that the offender is not given any opportunity to attribute sexually abusive and sexually self-gratifying behaviors to more acceptable ulterior motives and thereby improve their chances of 'passing' the polygraph examination.

In post-conviction polygraph testing some sex offenders are able to engage in 'convenient' misinterpretation particularly when questions are poorly worded. Therefore, a thorough understanding of each case is critical to enable effective formulation of questions that will subsequently be reviewed and carefully clarified with the offender before polygraph testing is undertaken. This approach provides the best opportunity to obtain helpful and informative responses from the examinee.

It is the experience of the authors that many sex offenders have a remarkable capacity for justifying, minimizing and denying various aspects of their offending. For example, asking whether an individual has contravened the conditions of their Probation Order or License by having 'been alone and unsupervised with anyone below the age of 16' may seem quite a simple enquiry. However, paying more attention to the words 'contact' and 'unsupervised' can in some circumstances impact on the examinee's physiological responses. For instance, if an offender has had contact with a child whilst in a room full of people, they could respond 'No' to this question, without causing significant reactions because they have reasoned that technically they were not unsupervised at the time. The examiner is responsible for ensuring that such errors do not occur and this is largely achieved by devising simple unambiguous questions in addition to clarifying that 'unsupervised and alone' means just that. The polygrapher then thoroughly reviews and agrees what each question means so that the examinee does not have 'room for maneuver' in terms of interpreting questions in a way that meets their self-protective needs or supports their cognitive distortions.

Another type of error can occur when the examiner fails to appreciate and understand the impact that certain phrases or words can have on an examinee. This could, for example, give rise to poorly controlled but unrelated physiological responses which are not directly associated with truthfulness or deception with respect to the relevant polygraph issues. For this reason, the use of coarse or sexually explicit language during question preparation should be avoided if possible since such words may increase physiological reactivity during testing for reasons not pertinent to the test administration. Notably, examinees may be more comfortable using one term (often colloquial) over another and with this in mind, some words or phrases, provided they are deemed appropriate and not likely to independently generate an undue physiological response, might acceptably be used during the pre-test and question construction/chart-running phase of polygraph testing. However, the examiner must use professional judgment to compile questions in a way that minimizes the likelihood of an offender producing irrelevant physiological arousal. Relatedly, questions which have not been agreed during the pre-test interview stage of the polygraph examination are not appropriate to ask during the data collection polygraph testing phase. This would not only constitute an ethical breach of standard test procedures but also surprise or shock the examinee thereby increasing unhelpful and unrelated physiological reactions.

Importantly, useful information can be gathered whether an examinee passes or fails a polygraph examination. For example, an incestuous father undertaking treatment was administered a specific issue denial examination. After taking the polygraph, he returned to the treatment worker and with an air of apparent triumph reported that he had 'passed' his polygraph examination which 'proved' he had not 'forcibly' had sex with his adult daughter. However, whilst the examination gave indications that he had not (or believed he had not) 'raped' his daughter, significantly the results revealed that in his mind the sex with his daughter was consensual. Incredibly and clearly, he did not, however, appreciate that his 'passing' the polygraph reflected high levels of cognitive distortions and related deviance about his perceptions of roles, boundaries and accepted sexual practice within his family.

This 'passed' polygraph examination provided therapists with important treatment issues to process and gave supervising officers additional cause for concern about historical and current risk of harm to other family members. Further, the results offered both the polygrapher and probation workers scope for developing further subsidiary questions for subsequent testing in the future in relation to the examinee's sexual history and possible patterns of other intrafamilial offending.

As referenced previously the key feature of effective polygraph testing derives from heightening physiological arousal levels in a continuous manner over the course of the polygraph examination. Achieving this reflects establishment of 'psychological set' and, in doing so, significantly improves the accuracy of the test. 'Psychological set' is best achieved when the examiner takes deliberate steps to impress upon the examinee the importance of passing the polygraph examination and the damaging effects that failing would likely cause. It is of key importance that the examinee is aware that a failure to pass the polygraph examination will have marked and significant consequences for them since details regarding disclosures made and the outcome of testing will become known to the other relevant parties.

Although this may seem straightforward that is not always the case. For example, in a pre-conviction situation an individual may, through their legal representation, have the opportunity and resources to undertake a 'practice' polygraph conducted by an independent polygrapher as preparation for a 'formal' or 'official' polygraph examination. Even so, it is both possible and necessary to impress upon the examinee the significance of failing the practice examination as the trial examination would produce quite useless findings if these steps were not taken to establish appropriate psychological set. This may be done by asking questions such as 'Have you told anyone that you are going to be taking this practice polygraph examination?' or 'How will your solicitor react if you fail this preliminary polygraph examination?' These kinds of tactics serve to convey to the examinee that there are important consequences even for a 'practice' polygraph examination. Employing this approach is likely to produce more relevant preliminary results by realistically maintaining meaningful general physiological reactivity in the examinee so that he and his representative can properly consider their approach to the official polygraph examination.

Importantly, the above provides a helpful example of how polygraph results can be compromised. In circumstances where an examinee believes that the consequences of failing the polygraph are likely to be trivial and irrelevant, the likelihood of passing whilst being deceptive is increased. For example, if a probation officer informs an offender that they have been requested or required to undertake a polygraph examination but that the results will have no material consequence for them, then the effectiveness of the polygraph examination will be reduced. In contrast, if the probation officer expresses a view that the polygraph findings will be considered along with other information available and may impact on future supervision and therapy requirements then the polygraph results would be predicted to be more accurate and useful as this would accordingly serve to help in establishing appropriate 'psychological set'. Realistic and meaningful consequences attached to passing or failing are invariably associated with more accurate polygraph results.

Specific concerns may arise for those individuals taking tests where the scope of questioning is relatively broad, for example, in the administration of Maintenance and Sexual History Disclosure Examinations. Those who are overly worried about whether they have 'withheld' information across varied supervision or sexual history issues may obtain 'Deception Indicated' (DI) results though their failure to pass may be more indicative of generalized doubt and fear. Indeed, Blasingame (2001) advised that some individuals who experience chronic worry and self-questioning should probably be exempt from polygraph testing. Further, Gudjonssen (1992) referenced numerous variables that he thought could negatively affect polygraph test results. These included inordinately high levels of suggestibility or intense levels of anxiety that are reflected as prominent characterological features but are not readily distinguishable from the stresses of a particular situation. Further, individuals who may be viewed as very neurotic or diagnosed with a severe personality disorder would be predicted to be poorer polygraph candidates. As an example, an individual with very obsessive personality features may be more concerned than most people when trying to recall whether they have withheld any information. This can cause intense psychological reactions which are not rational or predictable from the point of view of the examiner. Again, this kind of uncontrolled interference may be more likely to occur with maintenance and sexual history disclosure examinations, where the scope of questioning may be relatively broad.

In the case of severe personality disordered offenders, it would be predicted that they may have difficulties regulating their affect in general. For example, they may demonstrate chronic levels of guilt, anxiety and paranoia. Thus, comparing their emotional reactions as manifested within their physiological responses to various questions may be invalid. For instance, an examinee may overreact to comparison questions because of personality characteristics that dispose them to be emotionally, cognitively and behaviorally dysregulated. Where this occurs there is an increased risk that the polygraph findings will be less accurate and reliable. As such, in these circumstances it is advisable not to use the polygraph.

Fortunately, in most circumstances an appropriate level of preparation can be achieved, so that the examinee's thoughts are centrally focused on the polygraph test and the matters of concern raised by supervision and treatment professionals. However, skilled sex offender workers and appropriately trained polygraph examiners are increasingly likely to identify the minority of individuals for whom (due to marked pressure features) polygraph testing is likely less useful.

Examiners are trained to work diligently and use their best judgment to determine whether extraneous emotions and thoughts can be dealt with effectively and in a way that enables the examinee to be fairly tested. For example, ascertaining why an examinee feels angry, nervous or agitated is very important at the pre-test stage. Further, the emotional affect of outside issues needs to be addressed before proceeding with the polygraph examination. The examinee's other concerns and emotions must be addressed and allayed sufficiently if the examinee is going to be able to place the polygraph examination to the forefront of their mind. This must be achieved before the test can proceed. If this crucial shift in the examinee's focus of mental attention cannot be satisfactorily achieved and maintained then the test must be stopped to prevent the remainder of the examination from likely being compromised. When the pre-test interview is inadequately conducted then an offender's attention may be distracted and turn toward current issues of importance to them such as arguments with loved ones, disagreements at work, financial pressures or even negative interactions with other professionals involved in their case.

Physical factors can also have an impact on an examinee's test performance and thereby reduce the accuracy of the polygraph test. For example, examinees presenting with cold or flu symptoms should not, as a rule, be tested in light of the effect that coughing, sniffing, sneezing, nasal blockage, labored breathing, chills and/or general body discomfort will have both indirectly on their motivation and concentration but also directly on chart tracings (physiological data gathered). Examinees suffering from pain, chronic or acute, may also be difficult to assess particularly if the discomfort should become more intense at irregular intervals. In these situations, testing should be employed when the examinee's physical discomfort is less apparent. For example, some individuals with these difficulties experience less problems at certain times of the day or when specific temperature or weather conditions prevail. In some instances, pain control medication can also assist, although the effect of the medication is an important consideration which may also influence the tracings and should thus be accounted for before a polygraph finding is rendered.

Inaccurate Interpretation of Test Results

The circumstances and 'demand characteristics' of post-conviction testing differ greatly from those of pre-conviction testing and this is reflected in the APA stipulation that examiners testing convicted sex offenders should undergo specific training beforehand (APA, 2007). When a sexual offender is tested post-conviction, they have already been sentenced in relation to a sexual offence and thus the examination is more likely to be focused on the offender's willingness to be open and honest with regard to treatment and supervision issues (Dutton, 2000). The exception to this rule is in relation to monitoring examinations where new offence allegations are being directly assessed. It is generally held at post-conviction stage that the likelihood of false negatives is greater, while at pre-conviction stage the stress associated with fears concerning police involvement and possible sentencing make the risk of false positive findings greater, particularly if examiners lack specific relevant post-conviction training (Holden, 1997).

Importantly, there are a number of differences between pre- and post-conviction polygraph testing that should be taken into account to assist the reader in understanding how to best utilize post-conviction testing. These differences include:

Time of reference and frame of reference. Prior to conviction, the time of reference (TOR) and frame of reference (FOR) for polygraph investigations are generally narrow and the issues linked together, for example,

'Did you take the money from that bank?' However, for post-conviction polygraph testing, these conditions do not necessarily hold since specific allegations are not always being investigated and therefore narrow timelines and frames of reference are less likely. Indeed during sexual history disclosure, maintenance and monitoring examinations, timelines can be relatively lengthy and might well incorporate questions like: 'Prior to your conviction did you . . .?', 'Since the time of your conviction have you . . .?', or 'Since your last polygraph examination have you . . .?'

At pre-conviction stage, victims, complainants or witnesses are identified within the context of investigations or proceedings. However, at post-conviction stage, this is not necessarily the case. Indeed, in many instances there are no known complainants or witnesses in relation to the polygraph examination.

At post-conviction, the scope can be broadened, such that, for example, an examiner can address issues relating to violation of an individual's Order as well as treatment concerns, for example, masturbation to deviant fantasies. Pre-conviction polygraph examinations have always employed protocols that ensure a narrow investigation focus and no mixing of issues.

Consequences of Deception Indicated (DI) and No Deception Indicated (NDI) opinions. Another very important distinction between pre- and post-conviction polygraph testing is the emotional impact of the examination on the polygraphee. Pre-conviction, there are very specific elements of fear of detection for those guilty of committing an offence or of having involvement or knowledge of such activities in addition to apprehension about the effects of being exposed and overriding worries about the possible consequences of their actions (e.g., criminal conviction and imprisonment). Post-conviction examinees in many circumstances will likely experience the fear of making admissions differently than pre-conviction examinees since they have already been convicted. However, it should be impressed upon post-conviction examinees that a 'Deception Indicated' result would reflect that they have been dishonest and conducted themselves in an untrustworthy manner during their supervision by the Probation Service. Such a finding might lead the professionals involved to consider intensifying supervision or involving the examinee in more extensive treatment. A failed post-conviction polygraph test would suggest that the offender's thoughts, feelings and behaviors in relation to their past sexual behavior or the actions they have taken since being convicted are not adequately understood. The failed polygraph would also give indications that the individual's willingness to be open and disclosing in this regard is inadequate. Heightened supervision and treatment requirements would be viewed as appropriate until such time as the offender can consistently pass the polygraph and give the examiner, probation officer and therapist greater confidence that they are being sufficiently open. Regularly passing the polygraph signifies that an offender is largely to be seen as a 'known quantity' in terms of being appropriately disclosing about risk to the public and in demonstrating motivation to change.

Denial issues. At pre-conviction stage an examinee is a 'suspect' and is being polygraphed because they deny involvement or knowledge of a particular event/crime. At post-conviction stage an offender is ordinarily not viewed as a suspect of a new crime. Post-conviction polygraph examinations frequently explore an offender's capacity for being open about their conviction and key issues relating to treatment, assessment and supervision. In some circumstances, an offender's capacity for being open about their offence, their sexual history or their adherence to treatment and supervision requirements may be viewed as inadequate or a cause for concern among workers who are attempting to develop effective treatment and an informed relapse prevention strategy. At post-conviction stage TOR and FOR are unlikely to be sufficiently narrow in most circumstances to identify specific victims or incriminating behaviors in a way that may expose the examinee to risk of criminal charges in the manner of most pre-conviction polygraph tests where complainants and specific circumstances are usually known to the examiner.

Indeed, in many circumstances further post-conviction admissions within the context of probation, supervision and treatment may appropriately be viewed as the offender being cooperative with the polygraph examiner and the treatment/supervision team. Where an examinee is sufficiently open, such that they pass (i.e., obtain a 'No Deception Indicated' result) a polygraph examination, their needs can be better understood for treatment and monitoring purposes than individuals who do not disclose and fail.

Post-conviction, an offender is likely to receive approval and encouragement for disclosing information via the polygraph examination in the same way that they would if new information was divulged during group or supervision sessions. Generally, such cooperation is equated with increased accountability and motivation to engage in treatment. The more honest an offender is about their deviant thoughts and behaviors, the more likely they will benefit from treatment which targets specific problem areas that could precipitate actual offending. Cooperation of this sort would be seen to reduce acute risk factors. Further, such polygraph findings could be employed either in group or during individual supervision sessions in order to tailor relapse prevention strategies to address the full range of dynamic risk factors that may exist (Abrams & Abrams, 1993; Ahlmeyer *et al.*, 2000; Heil *et al.*, 2000; O'Connell, 1998; Wilcox, Sosnowski & Middleton, 1999, 2000).

SUMMARY

In conclusion, pre-conviction polygraph examinations seek to establish guilt or exonerate the innocent and, as a result guilty examinees fear consequences that may occur as they rightly reason that disclosures will be criminally punished. Most often, post-conviction polygraph examinations are employed to establish responsibility for previous offending rather than guilt in relation to new offences (with the exception of monitoring polygraph examinations). The accountability associated with post-conviction polygraph testing can relate to acceptance of offending and openness about past sexual behavior.

To achieve this, the polygraph examiner must maintain the examinee's mental concentration on realistic and meaningful consequences of being deceitful. By concentrating the examinee's attention on apprehensions about being revealed as a liar and by clarifying that such information will be reported to the probation officer and therapist, then the appropriate 'psychological set' of the examinee should be established, thus maximizing the accuracy of testing. Notably, at post-conviction stage, disclosures are reinforced by therapists and supervising probation officers to a considerable degree since passing the polygraph is likely to reflect cooperative behavior with regard to the offender's ongoing engagement in treatment and supervision. It is therefore not difficult to understand that the demand characteristics for pre- and post-conviction polygraph examinations will be different since examinees in pre-conviction circumstances recognize that disclosures may lead to very quantifiable punishment including legal action and possible imprisonment, whilst examinees at post-conviction stage may see particular benefits in being honest and disclosing. Indeed, this is more likely to occur where men who have had the benefit of vicariously sharing polygraph experiences with other men engaging in their group treatment program are polygraphed. In particular, honest, open engagement in the polygraph may likely lead to a more positive working relationship with supervising officers as well as further gains in working with treatment facilitators.

Post-conviction polygraph testing is a field which developed much more recently than conventional pre-conviction polygraph. It has frequently been referred to as a clinical polygraph examination because of its relationship to treatment issues and is concerned with the testing of individuals (post-conviction) whilst under court supervision (probation, deferred adjudication, license/parole). The purposes of some tests are to establish and verify issues prior to the date of conviction (specific issue or sexual history disclosure examinations) whilst others monitor activities and behaviors of the offender after supervision began (maintenance and monitoring). These examinations have increasingly found support amongst court officials, supervising offices and specialized treatment workers in this field. Whilst there can be differences between interview and procedural rules for both pre- and post-conviction examinations, the established rules/protocols for each must be adhered to otherwise the reliability and validity of the test will be compromised.

REFERENCES

Abel, G.G. (1999). Assessing and Treating Sex Offenders. Symposium conducted at the conference of Specialized Training Services, Chicago, IL.

Abrams, S. (1989). *The Complete Polygraphy Handbook*. Lexington, MA: Lexington Books.

Abrams, S. (2000). Polygraph validity in the new millennium. *Polygraph, 29*, 344–356.

Abrams, S. & Abrams J.B. (1993). *Polygraph Testing of the Pedophile*. Portland, Oregon: Ryan Gwinner Press.

Abrams, S. & Ogard E. (1986). Polygraph surveillance of probationers. *Polygraph, 15*, 174–182.

Abrams, S. & Simmons, G. (2000). Post-conviction polygraph testing: Then and now. *Polygraph, 29*, 63–67.

Abrams, S., Hoyt, D., & Jewel, C. (1991). The effectiveness of the disclosure test with sex abusers of children. *Polygraph, 20*, 204–213.

Ahlmeyer, S., Heil, M., McKee, B., & English, K. (2000). The impact of polygraphy on admissions of victims and offenses in adult sexual offenders. *Sexual Abuse: A Journal of Research and Treatment, 12*, 123–138.

APA (1999). *The Validity and Reliability of Polygraph Testing*. Chattanooga, TN: American Polygraph Association.

APA (2007). Model policy for post-conviction sex offender testing. *American Polygraph Association, 36*, 112–116.

Benussi, V. (1914). Gesetze der inadäquaten Gestaltauffassun. (Die Ergebnisse meiner bisherigen experimenteelen Arbeiten zur Analyse der sogen. Geometrisch-optischen Täuschungen [Vorstellungen *ausserssinnlicher* Provenienz]). *Archiv für die gesamte Psychologie, 32*, 396–419.

Blasingame, G.D. (2001). *Developmentally Disabled Sexual Offender Rehabilitative Treatment*. Oklahoma City, USA: Wood 'N' Barnes Publishing.

Dutton, D.W. (2000). Guide for performing the objective scoring system. *Polygraph, 29*, 177–184.

Ekman, P. (1985). The polygraph as lie catcher. In *Telling Lies*. New York: Norton & Co.

English, K. (1998). The Containment Approach: An Aggressive Strategy for the Community Management of Adult Sex Offenders. *Psychology, Public Policy and Law, 4*, 218–235.

English, K. (2002). *The Containment Approach for Managing Sexual Offenders*. Keynote presentation, National Organisation for the Treatment of Abusers.

English, K., Pullen, S., & Jones, L. (Eds) (1996). *Managing Adult Sex Offenders: Containment Approach*. American Probation and Parole Association.

Grubin, D. & Madsen, L. (2005). Lie detection and the polygraph: A historical review. *The Journal of Forensic Psychiatry & Psychology, 16*, 357–369.

Gudjonsson, G.H. (1992). *The Psychology of Interrogations, Confessions and Testimony*. Chichester: John Wiley & Sons, Ltd.

Heil, P., Ahlmeyer, S., McCullar, B., & McKee, B. (2000). Integration of polygraph testing with sexual offenders in the Colorado department of corrections. *Polygraph, 29*, 26–30.

Holden, E.J. (1996). The clinical polygraph's role in sex offender treatment, supervision and monitoring: Guidelines for use. Paper presented at the national conference of the Association for Treatment of Sexual Abusers, Chicago, Illinois.

Holden, E.J. (1997). Understanding pre- and post-conviction polygraph – the key to its successful use: A guide. *Voice for the Defence, 26*, 4–12.

Holden, E.J. (1999). Clinical polygraph examinations. Paper presented at the annual conference of the American Association of Police Polygraphists, Orlando, Florida.

Holden, E.J. (2000). Pre- and post-conviction polygraph: Building blocks for the future – procedures, principles, and practices. *Polygraph, 29*, 69–98.

Joint Polygraph Committee on Offender Testing (1998). *Recommended Guidelines for Clinical Polygraph Examinations of Sex Offenders*. Dallas, Texas: JPCOT.

Keeler, L. (1934). Debunking the 'lie detector'. *American Journal of Police Science, 25*, 153–160.

King, E.L. (2001). Commission of inquiry into cricket match fixing and related matters: Final report presented to the Honourable Mr T.M. Mbeki, President of the Republic of South Africa. Retrieved April 1, 2008 from `http://www.polity.org.za/polity/govdocs/commissions/2001/kingfinal.pdf`.

Kleiner, M. (2002). *Handbook of Polygraph Testing*. San Diego: Academic Press.

Larson, J.A. (1932). *Lying and its Detection*. Chicago: University of Chicago Press. [Reprinted by Patterson Smith, 1969.]

Laws, D.R., Hudson, S.M., & Ward, T. (2000). *Remaking Relapse Prevention with Sex Offenders: A Sourcebook*. Thousand Oaks, CA: Sage.

Lombroso, C. (1882). *Genio a Follia: In Rapporto alla Medicina Legale, alla Critica ed alla Storia* (Fourth Edition). Rome: Bocca.

Lundell, R.G. (2000). Sex offender testing: Still basic polygraph. *Polygraph, 29*, 40–43.

Lykken, D.T. (1981). *A Tremor in the Blood: Uses and Abuses of the Lie Detector*. New York: McGraw-Hill.

Marshall, W.L., Anderson, D., & Fernandez, Y.M. (1999). *Cognitive behavioral treatment of sexual offenders*. Chichester: John Wiley & Sons, Ltd.

Marshall, W.L., Laws, D.R., & Barbaree, H.E.. (Eds) (1990). *Handbook of sexual assault: Issues, theories, and treatment of the offender*. New York, Plenum Press.

Markall, H.F., Wilcox, D.T., & Goodwill, A.M. (2007). Denial and sexual offending: An initial intervention for a first conviction sex offender. Manuscript in preparation. University of Birmingham, UK.

Marston, W.M. (1917). Systolic blood pressure changes in deception. *Journal of Experimental Psychology*, *2*, 117–163.

Marston, W.M. (1938). *The Lie Detector Test*. New York: Smith.

Matte, J.A. (1996). *Forensic Psychophysiology using the Polygraph: Scientific Truth Verification – Lie Detection*. New York: JAM Publications.

O'Connell, M.A. (1998). Using polygraph testing to assess deviant sexual history of sex offenders. *Dissertation Abstracts International*, *58*, 3023.

Partee, C.E. (1975). Probation and the polygraph. *Legal Admissibility of the Polygraph* Springfield, Illinois: C.C. Thomas.

Riegel, L. (1974). Court use of polygraph in probation programs. *Polygraph*, *3*, 256–268.

Roberts, R.B. & Baim, C. (1999). A community-based programme for sex offenders who deny their offending behavior. *Probation Journal*, *46*, 225–233.

Salter, A.C. (1988). *Treating child sex offenders and victims: A practical guide*. Thousand Oaks, CA: Sage.

Salter, A. (1997). *Sex Offender Assessment and Risk Management Issues*. National Organisation for the Treatment of Abusers (NOTA) Annual Conference. Southampton, England.

Schmidt, H.K., Soloman, G.F., & Johnson, H. (1973). The artificial conscience. *Corrective and Social Psychology*, *23*, 93–100.

Teuscher, T. (1978). The polygraph and probation. *Polygraph*, *7*, 1–4.

Trepper, T.S. & Barrett, M.J. (1989). *Systemic Treatment of Incest*. New York: Brunner/Mazel.

Tuttle, J.C. (1969). Personal Communication. In *Polygraph Testing of the Pedophile*, Abrams, S. & Abrams J.B. (1993), Portland, Oregon: Ryan Gwinner Press.

Wilcox, D.T. (1999). Polygraph testing. *NOTA News*, *30*, 29–31.

Wilcox, D.T. (2000). Application of the clinical polygraph examination to the assessment, treatment and monitoring of sex offenders. *The Journal of Sexual Aggression*, *5*, 134–152.

Wilcox, D.T. (2002). Polygraph examination of British sexual offenders (pp. 148–248). Unpublished doctoral dissertation, University of Surrey.

Wilcox, D.T. & Coles, R. (2006). Static, Dynamic and Acute Risk Assessment with Sex Offenders. Presentation for the National Probation Service.

Wilcox, D.T. & Sosnowski, D. (2005). Polygraph examination of British sexual offenders: A pilot study on sexual history disclosure testing. *Journal of Sexual Aggression*, *11*, 3–25.

Wilcox, D.T., Sosnowski, D., & Middleton, D. (1999). The use of the polygraph in the community supervision of sex offenders. *Probation Journal*, *46*, 234–240.

Wilcox, D.T., Sosnowski, D., & Middleton, D. (2000). Polygraph and the community management of sex offenders. British Psychological Society Bulletin, *Forensic Update*, *61*, 20–25.

Wilcox, D.T., Sosnowski, D., Warberg, B., & Beech, A.R. (2005) Sexual history disclosure using the polygraph in a sample of British sex offenders in treatment. *Polygraph Journal*, *34*, 171–181.

Winn, M.E. (1996). The strategic and systematic management of denial in the cognitive/behavioural treatment of sexual offenders. *Sexual Abuse: A Journal of Research and Treatment*, *8*, 25–36.

Wolf, S. (1984). *A Multi-Factor Model of Deviant Sexuality*. Paper presented at the International Conference on Victimology, Lisbon.

Wygant, J.R. (1980). Pre-test premise and procedures. *Polygraph*, *9*, 86–91.

APPENDIX: SEXUAL HISTORY QUESTIONNAIRE

TYPE OF BEHAVIOR:	1st:	LAST:	#TIMES:
1. Sexual play with children (playing doctor or show me games)			
2. Masturbation			
Frequency			
Inappropriate fantasies			
Type of fantasy			
3. Sex/Masturbation in public (outdoors, restrooms, in vehicle)			
4. Masturbation to pornographic material (XXX films, magazines)			
5. Masturbation with under clothing/garments (stealing of clothes for masturbation)			
Who/What type			
6. Voyeurism (peeking/watching for sexual purposes)			
7. Exhibitionism (exposing your sexual anatomy to others)			
8. Incest (any sexual activity within family)			
9. Homosexual behavior (any sexual activity with same sex, childhood or adult)			
10. Obscene phone calls, including prank or nuisance calls			

TYPE OF BEHAVIOR:	1st:	LAST:	#TIMES:
11. Frottage (rubbing up against or touching others for sexual purposes)			
12. Molestation (any sexual contact with minors as adult)			
13. Aggravated molestation (penetration of minor with penis, finger, or other objects)			
14. Setting fires (sexual purposes)			
15. Prostitution (either paying or being paid for sex) with females			
15a. Prostitution with males			
16. Stalking (following another person without their consent)			
17. Phone sex calls (900, random, or someone known)			
18. Sodomy (mouth to penis, vagina, or anus)			
19. Transsexualism (thoughts or interest in wanting to be opposite sex)			
20. Transvestitism (activities involving dressing in opposite sex clothes)			
21. Sadism (deriving sexual pleasure from another's pain or humiliation)			
22. Masochism (deriving sexual pleasure from receiving pain)			
23. Taking photographs/videos of minors for sexual purposes			
24. Fetishism (sexual arousal from objects – underwear, feet, shoes, vibrators			
What type?			
25. Placing objects into anus for sexual arousal			
Type used			

TYPE OF BEHAVIOR:	1st:	LAST:	#TIMES:
26. Urolagnia (use of urine for sexual excitement–golden showers)			
27. Coprophilia (use of feces for sexual excitement – brown showers)			
28. Cruising (driving, walking searching for a sexual target)			
29. Arousal to odors (any odor associated with sexual arousal)			
30. Necrophilia (sexual contact with dead animals or people)			
31. Animal sex or cruelty to animals			
Type			
32. Sexual victimization (if you have been sexually abused)			
33. Grooming a minor or minor's guardian/parent with sexual intentions			
34. Contributed to the delinquency of minors – use of alcohol, drugs, shelter, porno			
35. Visiting areas where children frequent in order to have sexual contacts/fantasies			
36. Threesomes			
37. Nude bars			
38. Swingers clubs/private sex clubs			
39. Sexual contact with fruit/vegetable			
40. STDs			
41. Adultery			
42. Hurt anyone during a sexual experience			
43. Force someone to have sex			

TYPE OF BEHAVIOR:	1st:	LAST:	#TIMES:
44. Hitchhikers			
45. Kidnapping			
46. Nudist resorts			
47. Touch anyone while sleeping			
48. Auto erotica			
49. Choking games			
47. Others not listed			

SEXUAL CONTACT WITH INDIVIDUALS:		**LISTED ALL RELATED THEN OTHERS**	
RELATION & THEIR AGE	HIS AGE	TYPE OF CONTACT	# OF TIMES

CHAPTER 6

Case Studies in the Utility of the Polygraph

DANIEL T. WILCOX, ZERINE O'KEEFFE AND CAROLINE OLIVER

The present chapter provides case examples of how the polygraph can be used to work more effectively with convicted sex offenders. The authors explore case examples to assist the reader in understanding the use of this instrument in combination with other available tools and resources.

When used effectively, the polygraph offers unique opportunities to understand the thoughts and behaviors of sex offenders in a way that informs a wide range of areas central to the offender's probation order or conditions of parole/license. Wilcox, Sosnowski and Middleton (1999) highlighted case examples of the use of post-conviction polygraphy with convicted sex offenders within the context of preliminary British polygraph trials that they undertook. They noted that the polygraph 'produced disclosures that verified treatment or supervision concerns and raised new issues to be addressed in future work'. Relatedly, English, Pullen and Jones (1996) reported that the polygraph is an essential component of the sex offender containment approach. They reported that this approach promotes public safety by seeking to hold sex offenders accountable for their behavior through the

The Use of the Polygraph in Assessing, Treating and Supervising Sex Offenders: A Practitioner's Guide
Edited by Daniel T. Wilcox.

combined use of the offenders' internal self-control and external Criminal Justice control measures. They further strongly endorsed the use of the polygraph to monitor internal controls and compliance with external controls.

Wilcox, Sosnowski and Middleton's (2000) initial polygraph examination trial with convicted sex offenders on probation gave rise to a range of valuable findings that were subsequently taken into account within the further treatment and supervision work undertaken with these men. For example:

1. An incest offender admitted a hitherto unacknowledged primary sexual attraction to a further victim in the family, although he had previously denied this attraction during months of treatment.
2. A second examinee who had repeatedly denied substantial alcohol misuse, (which was thought to be a significant disinhibiting feature in his offending), admitted to continued excessive use of alcohol.
3. A convicted offender acknowledged violation of his probation order involving sexual contact and sadistic fantasizing about a teenage girl he had met. This prompted investigation and immediate steps to safeguard this youngster from very probable danger.
4. One 'specific issue' examination was given at the offender's request since he wanted to exonerate himself in relation to a claim that he had attempted to abduct his victim when exposing himself in his car during the commission of his index offence. However, he failed this polygraph test. Further, although no subsequent admission was obtained, these results supported the ongoing concerns that had arisen during treatment concerning his level of denial and risk to the public.

Since then, much more extensive probation-based polygraph testing became possible in some parts of England, wherein multiple examinations were sometimes used to incrementally gain information about offenders (Grubin, 2006). Further, the opportunity to have polygraph examiners permanently based in the area where the assessments were administered enhanced communication between treatment facilitators, supervising officers and polygrapher. This enabled the examiners to be both more informed about key issues concerning the offender and more focused with regard to applying polygraph examinations in a way that addressed specified treatment and supervision needs. Selected samples that reflected the utility of the polygraph in dealing with particularly challenging issues have been identified by the authors, and are described below.

BREAKING DOWN DENIAL

The following cases illustrate how the use of the polygraph can assist offenders in reducing levels of denial about their offences, thus making them more amenable/receptive to treatment and serving as a deterrent to further offending.

Mr A

Mr A indecently assaulted his twenty-year-old daughter in the home which they shared. Although he had completed 50 hours of the Community Sex Offender Groupwork Programme, his level of cooperation and disclosure was extremely limited. Mr A used a range of strategies to avoid engaging in treatment and over the course of his attendance Mr A's involvement in the groupwork programme and cooperation did not improve. For these reasons it was decided not to include him in the further scheduled treatment work after he had finished the induction group. Instead, he was referred for individual intervention to address his denial behavior in order to improve his suitability for groupwork, with the aim of reintegrating him into this group treatment programme (Markall, Wilcox & Goodwill, 2007).

Mr A had agreed to be polygraphed within the context of his order to address the denial issues. Notably during the pre-examination interview before taking the polygraph, Mr A admitted that he did remember his offence and explained that his longstanding amnesic presentation in group had always been used as a means to avoid engaging. However, his denial then took a different course, as Mr A then reported that he had already decided to commit suicide before carrying out the offence, and he alleged that his purpose in abusing his daughter had been so that she would hate him after he took his own life. He asserted that committing the sexual assault would aid her in terms of forgetting him and not grieving. However, rather vaguely and paradoxically, he also acknowledged that sexual arousal 'might have been part of the offence'. Nonetheless, he denied any 'conscious awareness' of a sexual motivation to his offence. In the circumstances, the polygraph examination was terminated at the end of the pre-test interview and no charts were run, nor was a post-test interview conducted. However, Mr A agreed to attend a further examination six months later.

During the intervening period, individualized intervention work continued and the impending polygraph appointment seemed to serve as an impetus for Mr A to begin to be more disclosing. The polygraph appeared to offer Mr A a 'face-saving' opportunity where he could purport 'memory problems' and express a hope that the polygraph would give some clarification about these matters. This seemed to help Mr A account for shifting from having no recollection of the offence (during his original police interview) to admitting what happened with respect to his daughter, albeit without direct acknowledgement of a sexual motivation.

During the individual treatment session, prior to his second scheduled polygraph examination, Mr A expressed the opinion that sexual feelings associated with thoughts of his ex-girlfriend motivated some of his offence behavior. He also tentatively agreed that there was some degree of sexual arousal to his daughter. At that time, Mr A said that he viewed the polygraph as an instrument which would help him, as well as others, 'find the truth'.

When Mr A attended the scheduled follow-up polygraph examination, he made a number of disclosures during the pre-test interview and thus replied 'Yes' to the following questions:

> Did you ever touch your daughter (name) for sexual reasons?
>
> Did you ever think about your daughter for sexual reasons?
>
> Did you ever masturbate to thoughts about (name) prior to the offence?

During the pre-test interview, Mr A admitted becoming sexually aroused on several occasions when thinking about his daughter, although he described these as 'fleeting' thoughts only, particularly when in her company. He also reported his penis becoming erect on numerous occasions when in close proximity to her, i.e., when 'cuddling and watching television'. Notably, however, Mr A continued to display elements of denial and persisted in reporting that sexual thoughts were not in his mind when close to his daughter, despite his physiological reaction. During the interview, Mr A also reported that when his daughter was under 16, he had thought she would become an attractive adult. Further, he also recalled having a sexual reaction to her when he saw her in the bath at the age of 16.

On the basis of Mr A's disclosures during the pre-test interview, the following questions were asked during the physiological data collection phase:

> Do you recall masturbating to thoughts about (name) after the offence?
>
> Do you recall becoming sexually aroused to thoughts about (name) after the offence?
>
> Do you recall having sexual thoughts about (name) after the offence?

The polygraph examiner rendered a 'Deception Indicated' (DI) result for each of the above questions. During the post-examination interview, Mr A conceded having had sexual thoughts after his offence, some of which related to his daughter. Mr A reported that guilty feelings associated with his offence made it difficult for him to acknowledge deviant arousal to his daughter. He also acknowledged that he could still be deceiving himself with regard to the nature and extent of his sexual thoughts in relation to his daughter.

However, during a subsequent polygraph debriefing interview, Mr A was somewhat ambivalent about accepting the polygraph findings and again pursued a different type of denial. Mr A reported feeling some anger toward his daughter since she had not given him reason to believe she did not enjoy his abusive advances. He reported, 'If she had told me I would have stopped immediately'. Through the collaborative use of individual intervention and polygraphy, Mr A's admissions moved from overt denial to justifications more typically associated with offenders engaging in group treatment.

Importantly, Mr A's progress during the course of individualized treatment, augmented by polygraph, was encouraging. It provided an opportunity to realistically review his potential for engaging in group-work treatment given the progress he had made in acknowledging offending behavior and motivations. The polygraph provided a vehicle for challenging his thinking and behavior in a collaborative way which assisted in eliminating different 'layers' of denial. The case of Mr A provides a compelling example of the advantages of polygraphing individuals in denial, whether they are engaging in group or individualized therapy.

Mr S

Mr S was convicted for being in possession of indecent images featuring children between the ages of 7 and 12, and consequently he was given a probation order with a condition to attend a Community-based Sex Offender Treatment Programme. His offending was discovered after his neighbor's granddaughter, aged seven, informed her parents that she had seen these images on his computer screen. She was a regular visitor to Mr S's home, which he shared with his wife and his own daughter. However, Mr S denied having shown indecent/pornographic images to his neighbor's granddaughter.

Mr S experienced marked difficulties engaging in the Sex Offender Treatment Induction Group since he denied any arousal to images of children. Further, he denied sexual interest in the seven-year-old granddaughter of his neighbor and continued to insist that he had never shown her pornographic images. While undergoing treatment, a UK Home Office pilot regarding the efficacy of polygraph testing with sex offenders had begun in his local area (Grubin, 2006; Wilcox & Donathy, 2008). Mr S volunteered for the pilot and agreed to undertake a polygraph examination.

A maintenance examination was conducted which focused on Mr S's behavior 'since being on probation'. Some of the important issues discussed during the pre-test interview concerned potential breaches of his probation order and engaging in pro-offending thoughts and behaviors. During the interview, Mr S denied arousal to individuals below the age of 16. However, he did admit to visiting chat rooms online where he would correspond with people within this age range. Mr S also stated that he had been invited to look at other people via their webcams. When asked about the nature of such interactions, Mr S reported that he had usually observed men masturbating and on some occasions, women engaging in similar sexual activities. Continuing, Mr S said that he would engage with others via his webcam on a monthly basis, but had never encountered children in this manner.

On the basis of issues discussed during the pre-test interview, the following questions were asked during the physiological data collection phase:

Since being on probation:

Have you been alone and unsupervised with anyone below the age of 16 for sexual reasons?

Have you attempted to set up a situation with anyone below 16 for sexual reasons?

Have you masturbated to thoughts or fantasies involving anyone below 16?

Have you attempted to access Internet images of anyone below 16 for sexual reasons?

The above questions were constructed on the basis that participants who volunteered for inclusion within the Home Office pilot should not be questioned directly about undisclosed offences or incriminating behaviors that could potentially lead to criminal proceedings. This decision was taken to ensure adequate numbers of offenders volunteered and thus were polygraphed for the large-scale pilot.

Mr S's physiological responses to the third and fourth items resulted in the polygraph examiner rendering a 'Deception Indicated' (DI) result. During the post-test interview, Mr S offered no plausible reason for why he had failed the test. Rather, he maintained his innocence and insisted that he had done nothing wrong 'since being on probation'. Of interest, the polygraph examiner, also a psychologist, noted that Mr S's manner, gestures, tone and verbal comments were all, on an observable behavioral level, consistent with his protestations of innocence, for example, he was clinically convincing and quite plausible. However, Mr S agreed to be re-tested in a further three months.

Given his previously failed maintenance examination, Mr S's re-test, in line with common practice, covered the same time period as before, i.e., since being on probation. Such action is taken in an effort to ascertain what had previously been omitted or lied about during the initial examination. However, prior to discussing his thoughts and behaviors since being on probation, Mr S said that he wanted to make amendments to his original offence account. He then admitted that he had shown pornographic images of both children and adults to his neighbor's seven-year-old granddaughter, and that his actions were intentional. Mr S said that when previously asked whether he had shown indecent images to his neighbor's granddaughter he had lied to both police and probation personnel because he 'felt stressed'.

Further, during the pre-test interview, Mr S admitted arousal and masturbation to thoughts of his neighbor's granddaughter and expressed relief that he had been found out, since he was sure he would have progressed to acting out these sexual urges against her. Additionally, Mr S disclosed having masturbated to thoughts involving individuals below the age of 16 'since being on probation' and said that he had observed a girl (below the age of 16) expose her breasts to him via the webcam. Lastly, he acknowledged an extramarital affair during this period.

On the basis of the disclosures made during the pre-test interview, Mr S passed his second maintenance examination. During the post-test interview he made a commitment to avoid entering chat rooms and, to reinforce this resolve, requested that a question regarding chat-room use be included at his next examination. When informed that his 'passed' examination meant his next test would be in six months' time, Mr S expressed a preference for being tested sooner. Mr S indicated that being polygraphed had acted as a deterrent to risky thoughts and behaviors, and believed that regular testing would have an inhibiting effect on his desire to offend.

DISCLOSURE OF NEW INFORMATION

The use of polygraph testing can not only break down denial, but also facilitate disclosure of new information about unknown offences or high risk behaviors, such as paraphilic interests. Such information is critical in enabling professionals to make a proper assessment of future risk. The following case examples illustrate this.

Mr Z

Mr Z was convicted of two counts of attempted buggery of horses and was sentenced to a three-year probation order with a requirement to attend a Community Sex Offender Groupwork Programme. Mr Z had a long history of sexual offending, with convictions relating to rape and numerous acts of both indecent assault and exposure. Mr Z volunteered for polygraph testing at a time when a small pilot study was being undertaken in 1999 among probationers within the West Midlands (Wilcox *et al.*, 1999).

A sexual history disclosure examination was undertaken and during the pre-test interview, Mr Z reported a wide range of sexually abusive behaviors for which he had not been convicted. He estimated an additional 700 victims of indecent assault, 300 victims of frottage and 30 to 50 different people to whom he had indecently exposed as an adult. As a child he also reported 50 to 80 individuals to whom he had indecently exposed, a further 10 who he had masturbated in front of while at school, and two people to whom he made obscene telephone calls. Mr Z further admitted 400 separate incidents of stalking as an adult and 20 to 30 separate occasions of public masturbation.

Unfortunately, the further polygraph examination was terminated early, after the acquaintance test was given and towards the conclusion of the post-test interview, since Mr Z became quite agitated and angry while discussing offences he had committed as a child (as referenced above). Notably the disclosures were not previously known to the authorities. Despite cessation of the examination (before the physiological data collection phase), information obtained during the course of the pre-test interview served to emphasize the extent and seriousness of Mr Z's sexually deviant interests and past behaviors. Further, the polygraph examiner opined that since the examination was terminated prematurely full offence disclosure may still not have been achieved (Wilcox, Foss & Donathy, 2005).

The array of information disclosed by Mr Z was reported back to both his supervising officer and relevant treatment facilitators. Consequently efforts were undertaken to identify and confirm additional areas of risk in order to develop a more robust relapse prevention plan. Information divulged during the polygraph examination was also reported to the Public Protection Panel and appropriate parties were notified in order to enhance community safety. During groupwork the newly identified risk factors were explored, with the facilitators having obtained further offence-related details to better understand, predict and control his behavior.

Mr D

Mr D was convicted of making indecent images of children, predominantly females between the ages of 7 and 14. Mr D's offending came to light after he had contacted the police expressing concern for a teenage girl (Miss M) with whom he had corresponded via a chat room. Subsequently, his computer was confiscated and indecent images of children were found. Mr D was sentenced to complete a three-year Community Rehabilitation Order (CRO) with a condition to attend a Sex Offender Groupwork Programme. Mr D was married with two daughters below the age of 13, and following his conviction had just begun a new job working with computers. He left his previous job following the discovery of his offence.

While being supervised by probation he was polygraphed to learn more about his offence-related attitudes and behaviors. During the pre-test interview, Mr D admitted having discussed sexual matters with Miss M via her telephone. Further, he admitted that on occasions he had masturbated while corresponding with her. Mr D claimed that after three to six months of contact with Miss M, she told him that her brother was sexually abusing her in a sadistic manner. Mr D reported that at this point, due to concern for her welfare, the sexual element of his communication with Miss M subsided and he suggested that she should inform a responsible adult about the abuse.

Following liaison with Mr D's supervising officer, the polygraph examiner advised that a sexual history disclosure examination (SHDE) would be helpful to explore his previous sexual interests and behaviors. During the SHDE, Mr D admitted arousal and masturbation to a number of paraphilias and fetish interests, including to bestiality, urination and menstruation. He reported having engaged in sexual activity with his younger brother as a child and with other unrelated adult males during his adulthood. Further, Mr D admitted to masturbating while online and stated that he had also engaged in such activities while being observed by others via his webcam. Further, he admitted to watching others perform such acts at the same time. Contrary to the various accounts given prior to his polygraph examination, Mr D also confirmed arousal and masturbation to thoughts of girls below the age of 16.

Prior to construction of the questions concerning his past sexual behavior, Mr D disclosed that since his conviction he had returned to conversing online with under-age girls and had consequently received indecent images of children. Mr D explained that the images had been sent by girls with whom he had been corresponding, one of whom, like Miss M, reported that she had been abused. He reported that he recently received a picture depicting a girl of around 12 years posing indecently in a car.

Defensively, Mr D asserted that he had not visited 'child pornography sites' per se, or requested that such images be sent to him. Mr D regarded himself as a 'confidante' to the girls online and enjoyed advising abused females to seek help, but reiterated he would never sexually harm a female child. Mr D rationalized his behavior by reasoning that he 'did not go looking for girls' and continued to insist that he did not enter chat rooms with the intention of obtaining indecent material.

The shift in Mr D's focus from past sexual thoughts and behaviors, to what potentially constituted reoffending, necessitated abandoning the Sexual History Disclosure Examination. However, despite premature termination of the examination Mr D was concerned that his further disclosures might result in him being sent back to court.

In accordance with established protocols regarding disclosure of potential reoffending, Mr D's case manager was informed and an urgent meeting was held with Mr D, his case manager and the police. A formal warning ensued and increased supervision by both the probation services and the police was deemed necessary. Additionally, formalized restrictions regarding his Internet use were initiated. In terms of treatment, the various justifications and rationalizations used by Mr D helped identify the different types of pro-offending distortions held by him, and this proved useful in developing a more focused and proactive treatment/relapse prevention plan.

Mr B

Mr B is a single, unemployed male, living at home with his parents. He came to the attention of probation following a conviction for two counts of indecent exposure and one of harassment, for which he received a CRO with compulsory attendance to a treatment group. Mr B had a previous conviction for indecent assault on a school girl (age unknown). At the time of polygraph testing, he had a further impending court attendance in relation to a further incident of masturbating behind a woman's back in the street. He pleaded guilty to this and was awaiting sentencing.

The purpose of testing was to investigate whether he was adhering to the conditions of his CRO, specifically whether he had exposed himself or masturbated in public since being on probation (other than the incident mentioned above). Mr B understood the reasons for testing and accordingly made reference to the above incident which, up until the time of testing, was his only known breach.

However, during the polygraph examination, Mr B admitted to ongoing indecent exposure and public masturbation, estimating a frequency of about twice a week. The last time he had done this was two days beforehand when he had exposed himself while watching two women in their 20s, although he stated that they had not seen him. He stated that his preference was to not be seen, as it was often more exciting to be masturbating in the presence of a woman without her knowing he was doing this. He stated that he had followed these two women for a couple of minutes prior to exposing himself, waiting for the right opportunity.

What was particularly striking was not only the frequency of Mr B's offending, but also the lengths to which he would go to commit such offences, such as following women onto trains with no thought of the destination, for the sole purpose of masturbating in close proximity to them. Of note, Mr B stated that he had been tempted to expose himself on his way to the polygraph appointment, but had not done so because he was worried that he would be late!

As the interview progressed, Mr B gave information not only about his continued exposing, but also about recent viewing of child pornography, in magazines and over the Internet. He said that it had been supplied to him by an acquaintance, who, he stated was 'always trying to put [him] on to it'. He informed the examiner that this individual 'tends to like schoolgirls' and would use his sports car to try and attract them. He continued, stating that this man had 'tried to set [Mr B] up with 13 year olds'. He continued that this had happened once, but that he did not have any sexual contact with her, although he had been tempted. Mr B refused to give the name of this friend, stating that he did not wish to get him into trouble. Despite volunteering the above, Mr B denied that he himself was interested in under-age girls, although later in the interview, he openly admitted to fantasizing about schoolgirls while masturbating. He acknowledged getting more excited thinking about schoolgirls than he did thinking about adult women. However, he added that he would never masturbate in front of a schoolgirl 'because they're only young'. Mr B's previous conviction for indecent assault against a schoolgirl would suggest otherwise. In fact, Mr B's reflection that he thought he would have gone further, had the girl in question not screamed and run away, suggested a much riskier individual than originally thought in terms of an apparent absence of internal controls. Further, he admitted a continued interest in trying to touch schoolgirls and acknowledged having engaged in 'frottage' since being on probation by brushing up against adult women in crowded places for the purposes of sexual stimulation.

In view of all of the information that Mr B volunteered during the pre-test interview, the examiner deemed it unnecessary to continue with the chart-taking phase of the examination as it was precisely these issues that he would have been tested on. Instead, Mr B was told that the information he had given would be passed on to his probation officer, who, in turn, notified the police.

In this instance, careful questioning by the polygraph examiner during the pre-test interview elicited information about a significant number of previously unknown and current offences. It provided a much fuller picture of an individual who, in terms of both number and types of offences committed, showed himself to be a much more risky individual than originally thought by those involved in his management.

Mr G

Mr G was charged with 14 counts of possessing indecent images of children. The pictures in question were of children, male and female, aged between 18 months and 6 years old. The images were categorized as level 3, 4 and 5 of the COPINE (Combating Paedophile Information Networks in Europe, University of Cork) scale, for example, depicting sadistic and bestial offence scenes involving children. This scale goes from 1 to 5, with 5 reflecting the highest level of severity. Mr G was also initially charged, along with a co-defendant, with photographing indecent images of children, after a complaint was made by a 13-year-old girl, who said that she had posed naked for the defendants on a number of occasions. This latter charge was, however, dropped in Mr G's case.

Having spent three months incarcerated, Mr G was released on license for a further three-year period. Since his arrest, Mr G denied any sexual interest in children, maintaining that the images in question had been given to him by his co-defendant on a computer disk. He said that he had not been aware of the disk's contents at the time and that even when he discovered the images, there was no sexual interest. In relation to the 13-year-old girl, Mr G maintained that his involvement had only extended as far as taking 'clothed' images of the girl at the request of the girl's parents, and that he had not been present when she was photographed topless. Despite attending weekly probation-based Sex Offender Treatment Group sessions, Mr G's denial of any sexual interest in children remained intractable.

Mr G was subsequently polygraph tested on two separate occasions. Given his vehement denial of sexual interest in children, the focus of

Mr G's initial examination was on his motivation for acquiring the images. The result of this specific issue examination was 'Deception Indicated' reflecting that he was not being honest in some of his responses. Specifically, results suggested that Mr G's motivation for obtaining the images of children from his co-defendant was sexual. When confronted with the examination results Mr G continued to deny any sexual interest, but admitted to having been present when topless photographs of the girl were taken by his co-defendant.

Three months later, Mr G was re-tested using a 'maintenance exam' format, in which questions are asked about *recent* behavior, in terms of whether individuals are adhering to the conditions specified in their license/community rehabilitation order. In this case, those involved in Mr G's case management were keen to establish whether he was continuing to try to access indecent images of children, for example, off the Internet, or indeed create his own images using photographic equipment. On this latter point, a condition of Mr G's license was that he was not permitted to use any sort of photographic equipment, which included cameras, camcorders, etc.

During the pre-test interview, prior to the chart-taking (physiological data collection) phase, Mr G admitted to recent use of adult pornography and also to use of a camera phone to record images of a relative's new baby at a family gathering, although he maintained that these pictures had been completely innocent. However, just prior to having the attachments placed on him, Mr G informed the examiner that he had recently 'been shown' a short video clip (recorded on the same mobile phone, allegedly by his wife) of his four-year-old granddaughter doing a ballet dance dressed only in a towel. Of particular significance, Mr G stated that his granddaughter had inadvertently 'cocked her leg up' while doing this dance, thus exposing her genital area. Mr G maintained that he himself had not noticed this detail, in that it had been pointed out to him by other family members. He also denied taking the video footage himself. Mr G appeared to try and underplay the significance of this piece of information, although his body language suggested he felt somewhat uncomfortable while discussing it.

Importantly, Mr G also reported daily contact with this previously unmentioned granddaughter doing school runs, transporting her to ballet classes, etc., although he denied ever being alone with her. By his account, his involvement with his granddaughter's daily activities led him to regularly visit places where other young children would always be present, such as indoor soft play areas, swimming pools, etc.

Given all of the above information, clearly, if Mr G had a sexual interest in children, as his first test result had suggested, his continued exposure to young children, not least to his own granddaughter, was of grave concern. Questions during the chart-taking phase of his second polygraph examination therefore focused on his behavior since being on probation, specifically in terms of whether any of his behavior around children had been sexually motivated. The following questions were posed:

> Since you've been on probation, have you looked at any sexually arousing images of anyone under the age of 16?
>
> Since you've been on probation, apart from what you've told me, have you taken or tried to take any photos or video footage of anyone under the age of 16?
>
> Since you've been on probation, have you tried to set up a situation to have sexual contact with anyone under the age of 16?
>
> Since you've been on probation, have you masturbated to any thoughts or fantasies of anyone under the age of 16?

Mr G responded 'No' to all of the above questions. The result of this was that his body showed significant physiological arousal to the fourth question above, suggesting that he had, at some point since his release from prison, masturbated to thoughts or fantasies of someone under the age of 16. An opinion of 'Deception Indicated' was therefore given. Mr G's probation officer was informed of the failed test result along with all of the information that Mr G had volunteered during the pre-test interview.

In this instance, despite continued denial of any sexual interest in children, the polygraph provided good evidence (two failed test results) to suggest that Mr G was, in fact, sexually aroused (at least) by thoughts or images of children. This, coupled with the information that he supplied during the pre-test interview, in relation to both his continued use of photographic equipment (in breach of his license conditions) as well as his frequent contact with young children, was clearly a cause for concern that would subsequently be taken into account within the context of supervision.

CONCLUDING COMMENTS

Earle (1998) focused particular attention on the helping role that polygraph testing can play within the treatment process. He noted that the polygraph examination could provide verification about known sexual offences as well as giving an indication of the offender's willingness to comply with treatment. Earle found that using the polygraph improved openness with therapists in addition to identifying elements of both the offence cycle and underlying cognitive distortions. By eliciting further information, the polygraph aided in the targeting of new areas of concern to be addressed during therapy and was capable of verifying progress made. Earle's paper concluded that the polygraph examination reduced denial and minimization.

English (1998) stressed the importance of collaboration between the probation officer, therapist and polygraph examiner to promote public safety by seeking to hold sex offenders accountable for their actions. English *et al.* (1996) asserted that combining such efforts could enhance supervision of offenders and contain offending behavior far more effectively than when such professionals operate independently of one another.

The case examples in this chapter are intended to illustrate some ways in which the polygraph can be applied as a monitoring, treatment and assessment tool. As suggested in these summaries, the polygraph works best when it augments established supervision and intervention strategies. Further, its utility is significantly improved when a dialogue exists between therapists, supervising officers and other professionals involved. Collaboration helps to complement and strengthen the efforts of all those responsible for supervising and monitoring offenders.

As a tool, the polygraph has fundamental utility in addressing denial issues. As illustrated within the case examples, the more informed and involved the polygrapher, treatment workers and probation officers in understanding and agreeing the nature of these issues, the more capable they are at 'peeling away' the layers of denial so that more comprehensive treatment efforts can be employed. The polygraph can also serve to explore dynamic and acute risk factors, helping to provide greater clarity about these issues and identifying areas of concern which had not previously been recognized. The polygraph can also assist in producing more thorough and relevant relapse prevention plans.

The authors have found that the potential for containing offending behavior increases through incorporating the polygraph with other established probation and supervision practices. Indeed, there are indications that the polygraph may encourage offenders to consider their offending feelings, thoughts and behaviors in a different way than standard probation resources do. Importantly, while the polygraph can be used in a reactive 'let's polygraph him' way, the instrument comes into its own when used in a thoughtful and reflective way where professional collaboration is evident and an intelligent dialogue occurs prior to each examination.

REFERENCES

Earle, J.H. (1998). Polygraph as a Vital Component for Sex Offender Treatment. Presentation to ATSA Conference, Vancouver, October.

English, K. (1998). The Containment Approach: An Aggressive Strategy for the Community Management of Adult Sex Offenders. *Psychology, Public Policy and Law*, *4* (1/2), 218–235.

English, K., Pullen, S., & Jones, L. (Eds) (1996). *Managing Adult Sex Offenders: Containment Approach*. American Probation and Parole Association.

Grubin, D. (2006). *Polygraph Pilot Study: Final Report*. London: Home Office. Retrieved on May 18, 2007 from <http://www.probation.homeoffice.gov.uk>.

Markall, H.F., Wilcox, D.T., & Goodwill, A.M. (2007). Denial and sexual offending: An initial intervention for a first conviction sex offender. University of Birmingham, UK. Manuscript in preparation.

Wilcox, D.T. (2002). Polygraph examination of British sexual offenders (pp. 148–248). Unpublished doctoral dissertation, University of Surrey.

Wilcox, D.T. & Donathy, M.L. (2008). The Utility of the polygraph with sex offenders in England. *Conférence Permanente Européenne de la Probation,* July. [http://www.cepprobation.org:80/news/polygraphE.shtml]

Wilcox, D.T., Foss, C.M., & Donathy, M.L. (2005). A case study of a male sex offender with zoosexual interests and behaviours. *Journal of Sexual Aggression*, *11* (3), 305–317.

Wilcox, D.T., Sosnowski, D., & Middleton, D. (1999). The use of the polygraph in the community supervision of sex offenders. *Probation Journal*, *46* (4), 234–240.

Wilcox, D.T., Sosnowski, D., & Middleton, D. (2000). Polygraph and the community management of sex offenders. British Psychological Society Bulletin, *Forensic Update*, *61*, 20–25.

CHAPTER 7

Polygraph Testing Internet Offenders

Jos Buschman and Stefan Bogaerts

INTRODUCTION

Post-conviction or clinical polygraph examination is a relatively new approach to fact verification interviewing. It has been shown to be of considerable assistance not only in the management of probation issues (Abrams & Abrams, 1993; English 1998; English *et al.*, 2000; Heil *et al.*, 2000; Kokish, 2003), but also in terms of identifying more reliable behavioral risk profiles among individual sex offenders (Holden, 2000; Wilcox, 2000).

The combination of assessment and clinical polygraphy is especially useful with sex offenders because of the inherently secretive nature of this type of offence (Abrams, Hoyt & Jewel, 1991). Since clinical polygraphy is an effective tool for obtaining behavioral information that offenders are reluctant to disclose, it helps them to overcome specific areas of denial in treatment (Abel, 1999; Salter, 1997).

The utility of clinical polygraphy has been recognized by the Association for the Treatment of Sexual Abusers (ATSA). Relatedly, the American Polygraph Association (APA) has established specific Post-Conviction Sex Offender Testing (PCSOT) standards (`www.apa.com`).

The Use of the Polygraph in Assessing, Treating and Supervising Sex Offenders: A Practitioner's Guide
Edited by Daniel T. Wilcox.

In the present study, the use of clinical polygraphy (Sexual History Disclosure Polygraph Examinations) has proven its usefulness in profiling the risk of first conviction downloaders of child abuse images who were mandated to receive therapy at De Waag, a forensic treatment facility in the Netherlands.

DOWNLOADERS OF CHILD ABUSE IMAGES

The subject of child abuse images has never before been such a major focus of law enforcement involvement and social concern as it is today (Taylor & Quayle, 2003). Therefore it is not surprising that the production, distribution and downloading of child sexual abuse images, generally referred to as child pornography, is one of the major Internet offences of the time (Quayle, Vaughan & Taylor, 2006; Quayle *et al.*, 2006). Internationally, treatment facilities are increasingly addressing the emergence of this vehicle of expression of sexual interest in children, the broader sexual appetites of downloaders of child abuse images and the seduction of children through Internet applications (Quayle & Taylor, 2003).

In addition, practitioners who are dealing with offenders in this area have never suffered from such a lack of published literature relating to these activities as they do in relation to Internet offenders (Quayle *et al.*, 2006; Taylor & Quayle, 2003). Nonetheless experts in this field assume that indecent images of children must serve a number of important functions for those individuals with a sexual interest in children (Taylor & Quayle, 2003). Research has already shown that sexual interest in children is more likely to be observed among adult child molesters (Freund & Blanchard, 1989; Freund & Watson, 1991), and recent meta-analysis of sex offender follow-up studies concluded that relative sexual interest in children was the single best predictor of sexual recidivism (Hanson & Bussière, 1998).

However, a comprehensive understanding of the role of child sexual abuse images in the spectrum of child molestation is still not clear. Data to support the function of child abuse images are limited because of doubts and questions about the self-report of pedosexuals. This has led many therapists to assert that child abuse images are part of a grooming behavior (Calder, 2004; Quayle & Taylor, 2002). Even so, professionals cannot state for certain that child sexual abuse images are directly associated with the development of contact sexual offending against children (Marshall, 2000).

Based on research and clinical experience concerning adult pornography, some practitioners argue that individuals already predisposed to sexually offend may preferentially seek out pornography that depicts content that is highly arousing for them (Seto, Maric & Barbaree, 2001). Some suggest that child abuse images are instrumental in the initiation and perpetration of child sexual offending (Itzin, 1997, 2002). It is also well recognized that pornography can be used as part of an offender's grooming behavior to lower victims' inhibitions, to entrap children and to normalize adult/child sexual behavior (Calder, 2004; Quayle & Taylor, 2002). Additionally, the Internet affords opportunities to engage in sexual 'conversation' and flirt with children through chat rooms. Cooper *et al.*, (1999) suggested that 'cybersex' allows the offender to operationalize many sexual fantasies that would otherwise have self-extinguished but for the fact that they received the immediate feedback available via online communication to reinforce this deviant interest. This is further facilitated through the Internet's unique ability to allow the user to adopt multiple personae of whatever age, gender or other orientation they choose (O'Connell, 2004).

However, most self-reported data from downloaders would suggest that child abuse images serve to prevent or replace actual contact abuse (Taylor & Quayle, 2003); but should this self-report data simply reflect another aspect of denial being employed by certain sex offenders, then placing any reliance on these statements diminishes protection of the public and increases the risk of recidivism. In order to address this potential gap between clinical understanding and possible offender deception, the Sexual History Disclosure Polygraph Examination (SHDE) has been employed as a more objective clinical assessment tool to attempt to verify the facts.

THE SEXUAL HISTORY DISCLOSURE POLYGRAPH EXAMINATION (SHDE)

The SHDE is a post-conviction polygraph examination designed to obtain additional information regarding any sexual deviancy that predated the current offence. The aim of the SHDE is to focus beyond the index offence. This may include previously undisclosed sexual offences and/or identified paraphilias (deviant sexual interests) which can subsequently inform risk assessment and treatment planning for that individual. The results of studies employing the SHDE (Holden, 2000; Wilcox, 2000) indicate that polygraph techniques can be employed to gain additional information about the interests and deviant behaviors of offenders in ways that no other methods have achieved. If this is indeed the case, it might be appropriate for the polygraph to become a more generally accepted and used tool for overcoming the denial that offenders demonstrate in their self-reporting.

To illustrate the contribution that the SHDE can make to improve risk assessment and treatment targeting, the authors present two studies that have underlined the important role polygraphy played in identifying risky behaviors among (Internet) sexual offenders (Buschman *et al.*, under review; Buschman *et al.*, 2008).

Tables 1 through 4 show the results of these two studies together. The results shown in Tables 5 and 6 specifically relate to the study of Buschman *et al.* (under review).

DEFINITION OF LYING

For the purpose of these studies, an operational definition of lying was based on a consideration of the different definitions that are used in the Netherlands (DePaulo *et al.*, 1996; Ekman, 1985; Krauss, 1981; Mitchell, 1986; Vrij, 1998). As such, lying is defined as consciously expressing the word 'yes' or 'no' when the respondent knows that this answer does not represent the facts. This knowing carries with it the intention of the speaker to mislead the listener in order to avoid negative consequences and (so) gain positive consequences.

Study One

The sample of the first study (Buschman *et al.*, 2008) comprised 25 adult men, all of whom had been arrested and convicted after an Internet child pornography infiltration by Interpol and the FBI. All were previously unknown to the police and none had been previously registered for sexual offences. The Internet offenders had all undertaken treatment between 2004 and 2005 at the De Waag treatment facility in the Netherlands, and volunteered to participate in a SHDE. The Internet offenders were all of white/European ethnicity and their ages ranged from 24 to 65 years, with an average age of 41.

Study Two

The second study (Buschman *et al.*, under review) comprised 38 adult men all of whom had been arrested and convicted for the possession of child (sexual) abuse images. All offenders were unknown to the police prior to arrest and none had been previously registered for sexual offences. The offenders had all undertaken treatment at different treatment centers between 2005 and 2006, and volunteered to participate in a SHDE. The offenders were all of Caucasian ethnicity, and their ages ranged from 26 to 64 years, with an average age of 41.

Procedure. In both studies the following overall procedure was followed. The polygraph examiner thoroughly reviewed the treatment records prior to examination. This information concerned the range of deviant interests, masturbatory behaviors, confirmation of type and use of pornography, interests in child abuse, and the type of child abuse image content that the offenders had disclosed during the standard self-report clinical intake assessment procedure.

The polygraph examination consisted of a pre-exam interview, the actual polygraph exam, and a post-exam interview, which took an average of two hours to complete. During the pre-exam interview the offenders were given an explanation of the underlying principles of the polygraph and shown how the instrument works. Further, they were given instructions concerning the topics of the actual polygraph exams. Areas of enquiry raised on the structured sexual history interview were explored and specific questions were asked about the individual's past involvement with, and interest in, child abuse images (see Appendix).

Specific questions about contact offences were left out of the questionnaire, but were addressed separately in the second study (Buschman *et al.*, under review) during a second separate exam. This separate exam was done because of the possibility that, in a case where they were lying about contact offences, offenders may be distracted from polygraph test questions regarding other less serious sexual behaviors about which they might also be lying, thereby reducing the salience of questions about the lesser offences.

The SHDE was conducted with each offender, and he was asked whether he had been truthful in answering the questions relating to child abuse images involvement/interest. The test format utilized was a single issue probable lie comparison question test (CQT) consisting of six content questions (three relevant questions and three comparison probable lie questions) and four padding (symptomatic and irrelevant) questions. The CQT test that was used had a reported accuracy across studies for deception detection that ranged up to 97% (see Krapohl, 2006).

The following relevant questions were used in polygraph exam Number One:

1. Have you purposely withheld any information on the questionnaire? [No].
2. Did you lie about your past behavior on any of the questions on the questionnaire? [No].
3. Did you tell the truth about your past behavior on all questions on the questionnaire? [Yes].

In the second study (Buschman *et al.*, under review) the following relevant question (repeated three times) was also used in a second polygraph exam:

Have you ever, in any way, touched children for sexual reasons? [No].

This second exam in Study Two was also done using a single issue probable lie comparison question test (CQT) consisting of six content questions (three relevant questions and three comparison probable lie questions) and four padding (symptomatic and irrelevant) questions.

In both studies the psychophysiological reactions to all questions were recorded with a Lafayette LX4000 polygraph instrument (Lafayette Instrument Company, Lafayette, IN, USA). Furthermore, in both studies offenders were informed in a post-exam interview about whether they had passed the polygraph examination (No Deception Indicated [NDI] as the final call) or had not passed (Deception Indicated [DI] as the final call). If the polygraph results were not strong enough to indicate a DI or NDI, then a NO (no opinion) was reported.

Respondents who did *not* pass the polygraph exam with an NDI on one of the two issues (questionnaire and touching children) were asked for additional information on the relevant questions. Those respondents who disclosed further facts in the post-exam interview were offered a follow-up exam after their further disclosures in order to get an NDI result on the exam questions. If no additional information was given (the respondent persisted that there was no additional information to tell), the respondent was offered a second exam in order to reconfirm the first DI results. Those respondents with an NDI or NO result were also offered a second exam to verify this first result. However, no respondent in the studies was willing to undergo additional polygraph testing.

Results. Table 7.1 shows the disclosures of categories of child abuse images viewed. In their self-report 21 men denied masturbating to the images. The remaining 42 offenders reported masturbating whilst preferentially using one of the forms of erotic and nude child images (category three through to six). Most of them denied masturbating to explicit sexual contact images between adults and children (category eight through to nine) or to scenes of sexual activity between animals and children (category 10).

During SHDE, all 21 men who had first denied masturbation, admitted masturbation to child images. Furthermore, 47 men admitted masturbating on category nine, and 48 men admitted masturbating on category eight. Moreover, another 26 men admitted also masturbating

Table 7.1 Categories of child pornography

Masturbation categories (Taylor & Quayle, 2003)	Self-report data N = 63		Polygraph report data N = 63	
Offenders who denied masturbating to downloaded images	Ranking # 6	n = 21	Ranking # 11	n = 0
1. Indicative images	Ranking # 6	n = 21	Ranking # 9	n = 30
2. Nude images	Ranking # 6	n = 21	Ranking # 8	n = 36
3. Erotic non-intended suggestions	Ranking # 3.5	n = 25	Ranking # 7	n = 38
4. Erotic posing partly dressed	Ranking # 3.5	n = 25	Ranking # 6	n = 39
5. Erotic posing naked	Ranking # 2	n = 30	Ranking # 5	n = 43
6. Showing private parts	Ranking # 1	n = 33	Ranking # 3.5	n = 47
7. Explicit sex between children	Ranking # 8	n = 13	Ranking # 1	n = 52
8. Explicit sex child and adult	Ranking # 9.5	n = 6	Ranking # 2	n = 48
9. Penetration by adult	Ranking # 9.5	n = 6	Ranking # 3.5	n = 47
10. Sex between animal and child / inflicting pain	Ranking # 11	n = 2	Ranking # 10	n = 26

on category 10. The preference for images changed from categories five and six (erotic posing naked and showing private parts) based on self-report to categories seven and eight (explicit sex between children and between adults and children) based on SHDE findings.

Table 7.2 shows that according to self-report the sexual interest was least associated with the youngest age group (six and younger) and most associated with pubertal children (14 and older). Furthermore a large group even denied any masturbational interest in the images. However, during SHDE, the preference ranking changed to an overall preference for younger children as well as toddlers and infants. Indeed the polygraph data revealed that the number of offenders expressing an interest in pre-pubertal children more than tripled for the age six and younger and more than doubled for the age of seven through 13 (from 12 to 32) (from 9 to 31 men).

Table 7.3 represents the reported number of offenders interested in images depicting different combinations of sexual partners engaging in explicit sexual activity. Self-report demonstrated a continuing denial, and also a main interest in child pornography images of activity, particularly involving a girl on her own. However, the polygraph data

Table 7.2 Age of victims acting in the pornographic material

Age groups (lower limits)	Self-report data N = 63		Polygraph report data N = 63	
Offenders who denied masturbating to downloaded images	Ranking # 2	n = 21		
6 years and younger	Ranking # 4	n = 9	Ranking # 2	n = 31
Between 7 and 13 years	Ranking # 3	n = 12	Ranking # 1	n = 32
Between 14 and 18 years	Ranking # 1	n = 30	Ranking # 3	n = 20

demonstrated a very marked increase interest in images depicting boys with boys, girls with girls, boys with girls and adult men with children in comparison to self-reported interests prior to polygraph administered. Furthermore self-reports revealed a low preference for image combinations concerning adults and children. But the preference for this combination increased significantly after SHDE.

Table 7.4 shows the self-reported and polygraph elicited disclosure of data concerning high risk behaviors towards children. The majority of offenders denied any high risk behaviors towards children in their self-report. However, following polygraph examination an additional 47 offenders disclosed having masturbated whilst engaging in fantasies about having sex with children. Further, 29 offenders acknowledged making plans in order to make sex with a child possible. An additional 36 offenders disclosed that they had sought contact with a child. According to the SHDE information, there was a slight preference for

Table 7.3 Interest in sexual depictions

Combinations	Self-report data N = 63		Polygraph report data N = 63	
Offenders who denied masturbating to downloaded images	Ranking # 1	n = 21		
1. Single boy	Ranking # 5.5	n = 18	Ranking # 6	n = 32
2. Single girl	Ranking # 2	n = 35	Ranking # 1	n = 51
3. Boys with boys	Ranking # 5.5	n = 12	Ranking # 4.5	n = 33
4. Girls with girls	Ranking # 4	n = 15	Ranking # 2	n = 48
5. Boys with girls	Ranking # 3	n = 18	Ranking # 3	n = 38
6. Adult man with child	Ranking # 7	n = 3	Ranking # 4.5	n = 33

Table 7.4 High-risk behaviors towards children

High-risk behavior towards children	Self-report data N = 63		Polygraph report data N = 63	
Masturbating on fantasies about having sex with children	Ranking # 1	n = 4	Ranking # 1	n = 51
Making plans for having sex with children	Ranking # 2	n = 3	Ranking # 3	n = 29
Seeking contact	Ranking # 3	n = 1	Ranking # 2	n = 36

seeking contact with children than for making plans for having sex with children.

Table 7.5 shows the self-report and polygraph elicited disclosure of data concerning delinquent behavior towards children (Buschman *et al.*, under review). All men denied any form of delinquent behavior towards children in their self-report. During SHDE, 21 of 38 men

Table 7.5 Delinquent behaviors towards children

Delinquent behavior towards children	Self-report data N = 38	Polygraph report data N = 38	
Having touched children for sexual reasons	n = 0	Ranking # 2	n = 21
			n = 10
Touching child's vagina/penis			*n = 10*
Touching girl's breast area			*n = 6*
Touching anal area			*n = 10*
Child touching penis with hands			*n = 10*
Child touching penis with mouth			*n = 9*
Penetrating child's vagina			*n = 6*
Penetrating child's anus			
Grooming children towards sex through MSN / chatting	n = 0	Ranking # 8	n = 7
Photographing children for sexual reasons	n = 0	Ranking # 4	n = 13
Peeping at children while masturbating	n = 0	Ranking # 3	n = 16
Public masturbation	n = 0	Ranking # 5	n = 12
Exhibitionism	n = 0	Ranking # 7	n = 9
Steeling children's clothing for masturbation purposes	n = 0	Ranking # 6	n = 11
Renewed possession of child abuse images	n = 0	Ranking # 1	n = 36

Table 7.6 Age and sex of the hands-on child molestation victims and relation to perpetrator

Age and sex of hands-on child molestation victims	Self-report data N = 0	Polygraph report data N = 21	
Number of victims (Minimal number)	n = 0		n = 37
Number of official reported victims			n = 3
Victim is a girl		Ranking # 1	n = 20
Victim is a boy		Ranking # 2	n = 17
Victim is 6 years and younger		Ranking # 2	n = 10
age 0			*n = 2*
age 3			*n = 1*
age 4			*n = 6*
age 5			*n = 1*
Victim is between 7 and 13 years		Ranking # 3	n = 8
age 7			*n = 1*
age 8			*n = 6*
age 9			*n = 1*
age 12			*n = 1*
Victim is between 14 and 18		Ranking # 1	n = 19
years			*n = 2*
age 13			*n = 4*
age 14			*n = 6*
age 15			*n = 5*
age 16			*n = 1*
age 17			
Relation to perpetrator *Family*			
members		Ranking # 3	*n* = 4
Acquaintances		Ranking # 2	*n* = 14
Strangers		Ranking # 1	*n* = 21

disclosed hands-on behavior towards children, involving penetration, penile masturbation and fondling. In addition, other admissions included grooming towards children via web chatting (seven), exhibitionism (nine), public masturbation (12), making pictures of children (13), masturbating in vivo on children (16) and renewed possession of child images (36).

Table 7.6 shows the self-report and polygraph elicited disclosure of data concerning hands-on sexual behavior towards children (Buschman *et al.*, under review). The 21 of 38 men who admitted having touched children for sexual reasons were responsible for 37 victims. Only three of these cases were reported to the police, but no files were made against the perpetrators. All 21 men were officially reported as first offenders at the beginning of their conviction on possession of child abuse images.

SHDE results indicated that half of the victims were boys and half were girls. In addition, half of the victims were under 12 years of age (pre-pubertal age). The other half were of pubertal age. Furthermore, SHDE results also indicated that only four reported victims were direct family members. Most of the victims were strangers to the perpetrators (e.g., children in the surrounding area of their homes; children playing in parks or playgrounds; foreign children who had to escape their country and who were living in childrens' homes), or were acquaintances.

CONCLUSIONS BASED ON THE TWO SHDE STUDIES

The SHDE (Holden, 2000; Wilcox, 2000) is one of four types of post-conviction polygraph examinations being undertaken in conjunction with sexual offender assessment, treatment and monitoring

The presented polygraph studies revealed a range of relevant information, including offence-specific and risk-related data, and information concerning the range and type of sexually offensive behavior that was disclosed during SHDE. These data showed that the true level of involvement in high-risk activities was not previously apparent to anyone based on standard assessment tools alone. The SDHE was used to investigate the entire sexual history, despite the suggestion that more narrow, focused examinations could be of greater benefit due to the lower probability of deceptive (first) polygraphy results in these more focused exams (Abrams, 2000). Nevertheless, these studies consistently revealed more extensive histories of sexual offending and deviant sexual interests that were indicative of heightened risk concerns particularly when taking account of their 'first offence' status and their individual self-report disclosures.

It is also notable that although, as suggested by Abrams (2000), the number of deceptive results after the first polygraphy exams was very high, this did not have any particular relevance to the practical clinical usefulness of the results. For the purpose of 'screening individual risk profiles', this broad examination was both effective and the least time-consuming to administer to achieve broad profiling information. It must be said, however, that in these studies the APA stipulation was adhered to that specifies the employment of separate tests on the issues of undisclosed victims and on other undisclosed sexual behaviors.

FUTURE DIRECTIONS

The results of the SHDE studies confirmed other findings of increases in the number of paraphilic interests, offences and victims that have been reported when employing polygraph use with sex offenders (Abrams & Abrams, 1993; Abrams, Hoyt & Jewel, 1991; Ahlmeyer *et al.*, 2000; Edson, 1991; English, Pullen & Jones, 1996; O'Connell, 1998; Wilcox, 2002; Wilcox, Foss & Donathy, 2005). In addition, the present research gave strong supportive indications that downloading child sexual abuse images is more strongly associated with actual sexual abuse of children than previously suggested and that these offenders self-report markedly deceptive and 'sociably desirable' responses to systematically conceal this information.

The SHDE revealed a collective denial of high-risk behavior towards children, and a significant denial of sexual interest as a motive for downloading child abuse images. It revealed many hitherto unreported victims of hands-on sexual abuse, including a greater prevalence of high-risk sexual behaviors perpetrated towards young children. Further, almost collectively these convicted offenders have renewed possession of child pornography images even before beginning therapy, with a primary interest in explicit sex images and penetration images of young children. By employing the SHDE in the assessment phase before treatment, it was shown that a group of convicted men deemed to be low risk first offence child pornography downloaders were actually seriously misrepresenting important risk factors that had covered a broad, very disturbing spectrum of sex offending behaviors.

In the interest of predicting potential victims of child sexual abuse, we would therefore encourage the further scientific investigation of Sexual History Disclosure Polygraph Examination (Holden, 2000; Wilcox, 2000) as a means of assessing risk profiles of offenders that are at the beginning of their therapy, in order to address denial issues and to enhance the effective delivery of treatment and supervision.

REFERENCES

Abel, G.G. (1999). Assessing and Treating Sex Offenders. Symposium conducted at the conference of Specialized Training Services, Chicago, IL.

Abrams, S. (2000). Polygraph validity in the new millennium. *Polygraph*, *29*, 344–356.

Abrams, S. & Abrams, J.B. (1993). *Polygraph testing of the pedophile.* Portland, OR: Ryan Gwinner Press.

Abrams, S., Hoyt, D., & Jewel, C. (1991). The effectiveness of the disclosure test with sex abusers of children. *Polygraph*, *20*, 204–213.

Ahlmeyer, S., Heil, M., McKee, B., & English, K. (2000). The Impact of Polygraphy on Admissions of Victims and Offences in Adult Sexual Offenders. *Sexual Abuse: A Journal of Research and Treatment*, *12*, 123–138.

Buschman, J., Bogaerts, S., Krapohl, D., Hacket, S., & Spreen, M. (under review). Sexual History Disclosure Polygraph Examinations: Behind the Validity of Self-report. An explorative study.

Buschman, J., Wilcox, D., Foulger, S., Sosnowski, D., Bogaerts, S., & Mulder, J. (2008). Onderzoek met de polygraaf naar bekentenissen betreffende de seksuele voorgeschiedenis onder 25 Nederlandse mannen die kinderporno hadden gedownload. *Panopticon*, *2*, 36–48.

Calder, M.C. (2004). The Internet: potential, problems and pathways to hands-on offending. In M.C. Calder (Ed.), *Child Sexual Abuse and the Internet: Tackling the New Frontier* (pp. 1–24). Dorset, UK: Russell House Publishing Ltd.

Cooper, A., Scherer, C., Boies, S.C., & Girdon, B.L. (1999). Sexuality on the Internet: From sexual exploitation to pathological expression. *Professional Psychology*, *30*, 154–164.

DePaulo, B.M., Kashy, D.A., Kirkendol, S.E., Wyer, M.M., & Epstein, J.A. (1996). Lying in everyday life. *Journal of Personality and Social Psychology*, *70*, 979–995.

Edson, C.F. (1991). *Sex Offender Treatment*. Jackson County, OR: Department of Corrections.

Ekman, P. (1985). *Telling lies*. New York, NJ: W.W. Norton.

English, K. (1998). The Containment Approach: An Aggressive Strategy for the Community Management of Adult Sex Offenders. *Psychology, Public Policy and Law*, *4*, 218–235.

English, K., Pullen, S., & Jones, L. (1996). *Managing Adult Sex Offenders: Containment Approach*. American Probation and Parole Association.

English, K., Jones, L., Pasini-Hill, D., Patrick, D., & Cooley-Towell (2000). The Value of Polygraph Testing in Sex Offender Management. Research Report submitted to the National Institute of Justice, Denver: Grant number D97LBVX0034.

Freund, K. & Blanchard, R. (1989). Phallometric diagnosis of pedophilia. *Journal of Consulting and Clinical Psychology*, *57*, 100–105.

Freund, K. & Watson, R.J. (1991). Assessment of the sensitivity and specificity of a phallometric test: an update of phallometric diagnosis of pedophilia. *Psychological Assessment*, *3*, 254–260.

Hanson, R.K. & Bussière, M.T. (1998). Predicting relapse: A meta-analysis of sexual offender recidivism studies. *Journal of Consulting and Clinical Psychology*, *66*, 348–362.

Heil, P., Ahlmeyer, S., McCullar, B., & McKee, B. (2000). Integration of polygraph testing with sexual offenders in the Colorado department of corrections. *Polygraph*, *29*, 26–30.

Holden, E.J. (2000). Pre- and post-conviction polygraph: Building blocks for the future – Procedures, principles, and practices. *Polygraph*, *29*, 69–98.

Itzin, C. (1997). Pornography and the organization of intrafamilial and extrafamilial child sexual abuse: Developing a conceptual model. *Child Abuse Review*, *6*, 94–106.

Itzin, C. (2002). Pornography and the construction of misogyny. *The Journal of Sexual Aggression*, *8*, 4–42.

Kokish, R. (2003). The current role of post-conviction sex offender polygraph testing in sex offender treatment. *Journal of Child Sexual Abuse*, *12*, 175–194.

Krapohl, D.J. (2006). Validated Polygraph Techniques. *Polygraph*, *35*, 149–155.

Krauss, R.M. (1981). Impression formation, impression management, and nonverbal behaviours. In E.T. Higgins, C.P. Herman & M. Zanna (Eds), *Social Cognition: The Ontario Symposium, Vol. 1*. Hillsdale, NJ: Lawrence Erlbaum.

Marshall, W.L. (2000). Revisiting the use of pornography by sexual offenders: Implications for theory and practice. *The Journal of Sexual Aggression*, *6*, 67–77.

Mitchell, R.W. (1986). A framework for discussing deception. In R.W. Mitchell & N.S. Mogdil (Eds), *Deception: Perspectives on human and nonhuman deceit* (pp. 3–40). Albany: State University of New York Press.

O'Connell, M.A. (1998). Using Polygraph Testing to Assess Deviant Sexual History of Sex Offenders. *Dissertation Abstracts International*, *58*, 3023.

O'Connell, R. (2004). From fixed to mobile Internet: The morphing of criminal activity on-line. In M.C. Calder (Ed.), *Sexual abuse and the Internet: Tackling the new frontier* (pp. 37–57). Lyme Regis, UK: Russell House Publishing.

Quayle, E. & Taylor, M. (2002). Paedophiles, pornography and the Internet: Assessment issues. *British Journal of Social Work*, *32*, 863–875.

Quayle, E. & Taylor, M. (2003). Model of Problematic Internet Use in People with a Sexual Interest in Children. *CyberPsychology and Behavior*, *6*, 93–106.

Quayle, E., Vaughan, M., & Taylor, M. (2006). Sex offenders, Internet child abuse images and emotional avoidance: The importance of values. *Aggression and Violent Behavior*, *11*, 1–11.

Quayle, E., Erooga, M., Wright, L., Taylor, M., & Harbinson, D. (2006). *Only Pictures? Therapeutic work with Internet sex offenders*. Lyme Regis, UK: Russell House Publishing.

Salter, A. (1997). *Sex Offender Assessment and Risk Management Issues*. National Organisation for the Treatment of Abusers (NOTA) Annual Conference. Southampton, England.

Seto, M.C., Maric, A., & Barbaree, H.E. (2001). The role of pornography in the etiology of sexual aggression. *Aggression and Violent Behavior*, *6*, 35–53.

Taylor, M. & Quayle, E. (2003). *Child pornography: An Internet crime*. Hove, UK: Brunner-Routledge.

Vrij, A. (1998). Nonverbal communication and credibility. In A. Memon, A. Vrij, & R. Bull. *Psychology and Law: truthfulness, accuracy and credibility* (pp. 32–59). Maidenhead, UK: McGraw-Hill.

Wilcox, D.T. (2000). Application of the Clinical Polygraph Examination to the Assessment, Treatment and Monitoring of Sex Offenders. *The Journal of Sexual Aggression*, *5* (2), 134–152.

Wilcox, D.T. (2002). Polygraph examination of British sexual offenders. Unpublished doctoral dissertation, University of Surrey.

Wilcox, D.T., Foss, C.M., & Donathy, M.L. (2005). A case study of a male sexual offender with zoosexual interests and behaviours. *Journal of Sexual Aggression*, *11* (3), 305–317.

APPENDIX A: SEXUAL BEHAVIOR CHECKLIST TOWARDS CHILDREN

Have you ever participated in the following behavior:	
1. Internet surf for child pornography	yes / no
2. Collecting child pornography	yes / no
3. Distributing child pornography	yes / no
4. Making child pornography	yes / no
5. Masturbating to child pornography with children in the age range of:	
a. 16 – 12 years	yes / no
b. 12 – 06 years	yes / no
c. 06 – < years	yes / no
6. Masturbating to child pornography participating children from the following sexes:	
a. Only girls	yes / no
b. Only boys	yes / no
c. Girls on girls	yes / no
d. Boys on boys	yes / no
e. Boys on girls	yes / no
f. Adult on child	yes / no
g. Animal on child	yes / no
7. Masturbating to child pornography of the following content:	
a. Indicative images of children playing	yes / no
b. Nude images of children playing	yes / no
c. Images with non-intended erotic suggestions (children bathing)	yes / no
d. Images with children posing partly dressed	yes / no

e. Images with children posing naked	yes / no
f. Images with children showing their private parts	yes / no
g. Explicit images of children having sex	yes / no
h. Explicit images of adults having sex with children	yes / no
i. Images of children being penetrated by adults	yes / no
j. Images of children being penetrated by animals	yes / no
8. Voyeurism incl. masturbation (watching for sexual purposes)	yes / no
9. Compilation of sex images with (known) children	yes / no
10. Filming unknown children as masturbation material	yes / no
11. Masturbating to fantasies about own sex with children	yes / no
12. Looking at children for sexual purposes (including cruising)	yes / no
13. Internet chatting with children with sexual intentions	yes / no
14. SMS with children with sexual intentions	yes / no

CHAPTER 8

Risk Assessment and the Polygraph

THERESA A. GANNON, ANTHONY R. BEECH AND TONY WARD

RISK ASSESSMENT AND THE POLYGRAPH

Only two decades ago, professionals had no reliable means of assessing offenders' risk of future reoffending. Thankfully, science has progressed to such a degree that a variety of professionals can now make well-informed estimations of offenders' risk to the public on a daily and ongoing basis. Nevertheless, there is no foolproof method available, although some individual methods are universally agreed to be better than others (see Doren, 2002). Pure clinical judgment, for example, in the absence of guiding theory, has been shown to be a fairly poor indicator of risk (Hanson, Morton & Harris, 2003), while statistical (i.e., actuarial) methods, based on research follow-ups of offenders, have generally been deemed most effective (Bonta, 2002; Craissati, 2004; Grove & Meehl, 1996; Hanson *et al.*, 2003). Combining a range of methods, however, provides the most comprehensive analysis of offenders' risk for use in treatment and community supervision (Beech, Fisher & Thornton, 2003). This combination results in a broad assessment, spanning a rich array of factors ranging from personal traits to environmental

The Use of the Polygraph in Assessing, Treating and Supervising Sex Offenders: A Practitioner's Guide
Edited by Daniel T. Wilcox.

context (Ward *et al.*, 2006). These factors include: *dispositional factors* (e.g., psychopathic traits, antisocial personality), *historical factors* (e.g., a history of crime and violence, adverse developmental experience), *contextual antecedents* to violence (e.g., criminogenic needs, deviant peers), and *clinical factors* (e.g., poor functioning level, substance abuse, Andrews & Bonta, 1998; Blackburn, 2000; McGuire, 2000). Within this chapter, we use the term 'risk' to refer to the *likelihood of further offending* (either sexual or violent), and the term 'risk factor' to refer to those variables associated with an increase in the likelihood of further offending.

Assessing offenders' level of risk plays a pivotal role in securing community safety through providing appropriately matched custody, treatment and community supervision. For example, upon first entering the correctional setting, risk is assessed for security classification and allocation of treatment resources, whilst further on in the correctional system, risk assessment is used to assess treatment gain and for monitoring released offenders in the community. One problem with assessing risk, of course, is the reliance placed on both file information and offenders' self-reports, both of which are likely to underestimate risk. In this chapter, we discuss a proposed progression to the scientific status of offenders' risk assessment – the polygraph machine. We recognize that there is some debate about the usefulness of the polygraph for assessing risk. For example, proponents of the polygraph argue that this device promotes community safety, through forcing offenders to be honest about their level of risk to the community (Emerick & Dutton, 1993; English *et al.*, 2000; Grubin, 2002; Wilcox, 2000). On the other hand, some professionals are more doubtful of the polygraph's overall worth, arguing that its use could damage important collaborative relationships between offenders and treatment professionals (British Psychological Society, 1986, 2004; Jackie Craisatti, personal communication, July 4, 2005). We shall return to address some of these issues later in the chapter.

We have structured this chapter as follows. First, we describe current methods of risk assessment used to allocate supervision resources, identify treatment need, and monitor ongoing progress in the community. Second, we describe a new model that integrates etiology and risk into one comprehensive framework. Third, we acknowledge the problem of risk underestimation using current approaches, and examine polygraph studies that tap into three main groups of risk factors. Fourth, we address some common criticisms of the polygraph in relation to risk assessment. Finally, we look towards the future, outlining what we believe to be the most fruitful course of action concerning the relationship between risk assessment, risk monitoring, and the polygraph.[1]

CURRENT METHODS OF ASSESSING RISK

There are three main methods that, in combination, provide a comprehensive risk assessment for sexual offenders, covering personal traits, historical factors, contextual antecedents and clinical factors (Beech *et al.*, 2003). These are: (i) a *functional assessment* of the offender's underlying motives and functions for offending, (ii) a reliable *statistical* (i.e., actuarial) *approach* for estimating an offender's current risk level, and (iii) a *clinically informed psychometric approach*, in which stable-dynamic risk factors and acute-dynamic risk factors are identified for treatment and supervision purposes. We will now outline these concepts in more detail.

Functional Assessment

An important part of any comprehensive risk assessment is a functional analysis. Typically, such assessments involve interviewing the offender to examine the events leading up to and following a sexual offence, to highlight the thoughts, emotions, behaviors and decisions that played a role in elevating risk. For a useful decision-chain model for guiding professionals, see Ward, Louden, Hudson and Marshall (1995). In this chain, a series of offence-related choices are outlined, showing factors that predispose an individual to offend, situations indicating the likelihood of offending, and how offence-related reactions heighten risk. This model provides a multi-pathway description of offending, and outlines the many functions and motives underlying a whole host of sexual offences.

Functional assessments are used to educate offenders about factors related to increases in offending (i.e., *acute-dynamic* risk factors), and to monitor ongoing progress in the community. However, many offenders will be reluctant to lay bare thoughts, feelings and goals that they feel are shameful, will delay their release into the community, or have

[1]Because much of the risk instruments, theory, and polygraph-related literature have been developed using sexual offenders, we choose to focus on this well-established body of literature here. In addition, we focus our chapter on British participants where possible, since debate concerning the adoption of risk-related polygraph procedures has recently gained momentum in Britain.

them recalled to prison. Consequently, extracting truthful risk-related information from offenders becomes largely dependent upon the clinical skills of the assessor. Thus, a valuable addition to such assessments would be an instrument capable of eliciting truthful thoughts, feelings and goals from sexual offenders (i.e., the polygraph).

Actuarial Assessment

A wealth of actuarial instruments are readily available for professionals interested in examining the statistical relationship between an offender's history or static factors (e.g., prior offences and sentencing, general criminality, victim types) and reconviction probability (for examples, see Static-99, Hanson & Thornton, 2000; Sex Offence Risk Appraisal Guide, Quinsey *et al.*, 1998; or the Risk Matrix 2000, Thornton *et al.*, 2003). Based on data from recidivism studies, actuarial instruments invite professionals to code for the presence or absence of factors empirically associated with reoffending, and then provide a numerical estimation of risk (that equates to different risk groups such as high, medium or low) for various time periods in the community.

Static-99 (Hanson & Thornton, 2000) is a good example of an actuarial assessment, based on data from two previous instruments (i.e., the Structured Anchored Clinical Judgment Scale, Thornton, 1997 reported in Grubin, 1998; and the Rapid Risk Assessment for Sexual Offence Recidivism [RRASOR], Hanson, 1997). It is used to assess adult male convicted sexual offenders' risk and contains 10 items to be coded as present or absent by the assessor. These include: prior charges and convictions for sexual offences, the presence of unrelated victims, stranger victims, or male victims, and whether the offender has ever cohabited with a partner. Depending on the combination of scores from each of these factors, offenders are assigned a final risk score indicating their risk of sexual and violent[2] recidivism (i.e., low, medium-low, medium-high, or high). Here, offenders with a number of previous sexual offences and/or charges, who have unrelated, male stranger victims are likely to score higher on Static-99 than those without such a history.

Effectiveness of risk prediction tools is typically evaluated using the Receiver Operating Characteristic Area Under the Curve Analysis (AUC). AUC provides researchers with an estimate of predictive accuracy (where .5 = chance prediction and 1 = perfect prediction).

[2]Other tools are available that focus specifically on violence risk prediction (see, for example, the Violence Risk Appraisal Guide, Quinsey *et al.*, 1998).

As with many actuarial assessments, Static-99 is a fairly accurate predictor of risk (AUCs = .71 and .69 for sexual and violent recidivism respectively; see Hanson & Thornton, 1999 or 2000 for more details).

Actuarial risk instruments are easy to administer and fair well in predictive accuracy. However, there are some downfalls. For example, unusual offenders may not be adequately represented in the research sample underpinning instrument development (Beech *et al.*, 2003; Grubin, 1999). Additionally, Beech *et al.* (2003) point out that such instruments underestimate *true* offending because they have been developed using studies that rely on official recidivism statistics. Thus, offenders are likely to have a number of undisclosed offences in their histories that have never been officially recorded, but could dramatically change their risk profiles. Finally, actuarial assessments, made up of only static factors, tend to view risk as largely *unchanging*, and so are of limited usefulness for *managing or treating* risk (Beech *et al.*, 2003; Bonta, 2002).

Dynamic Risk Assessment

In recognition of actuarial limitations, a number of researchers have introduced changeable variables into risk assessment measures. Instruments that take account of such dynamic domains or needs include Beech's 'deviancy' concept (Beech, 1998) developed from the Beech, Fisher and Beckett (1999) psychometric test battery; Thornton's (2000, 2002) Initial Deviance Assessment now part of the SARN (Structured Assessment of Risk and Need system); and Hanson and Harris' (2001) Sex Offender Need Assessment Rating (SONAR). Hanson and Harris' instrument is particularly novel in that it incorporates both stable-dynamic and acute-dynamic risk factors. In the latest version of SONAR, stable-dynamic factors include: general and sexual self-regulation, pro-offending attitudes, intimacy deficits, social influences and cooperation with supervision. Acute-dynamic risk factors include: substance abuse, victim access, hostility, negative affect, social support collapse, sexual preoccupation and rejection of supervision. Interestingly, Hanson and Harris also incorporate an individual's unique acute risk factors into the equation. These are typically personal factors that are emotionally painful in some way and may heighten risk. For example, the anniversary of a family member's death could spark anger and hostility, making it more likely than usual that an offender will abuse alcohol, a common precursor to sexual offending.

Unfortunately, the overall picture of an offender's stable- and acute-dynamic risk factors can often be clouded by sexual offenders' propensity to minimize information that points to them being at risk to the community. For example, researchers have reported that sexual offenders minimize their answers on offence supportive belief questionnaires (i.e., Gannon, Keown & Polaschek, 2007; Kolton, Boer & Boer, 2003), and attempt to fake penile plethysmograph (PPG) assessments of deviant sexual arousal (Conte, 1985). In addition, it would take a very foolhardy sexual offender to tell his probation officer that he is experiencing risky thoughts, or engaging in high-risk behaviors in the community.

AN ETIOLOGICAL MODEL OF RISK

While the combination of functional, actuarial and dynamic assessments provides a broad picture of an individual's risk, until recently, professionals were assessing risk, quite comfortably, in the absence of any guiding theory. Beech and Ward (2004) have developed a guiding theory for risk assessors, which draws together empirical research, clinical ideas and theoretical risk work into a strong explanatory theory. Within this model, the relationship between historical and dynamic factors is clearly described, ensuring that assessment of risk paints a fully integrated picture of the individual as a whole. In brief, the model (see Figure 8.1) contains *developmental factors*, *vulnerability factors* (i.e., historical/static risk markers and stable-dynamic risk factors), *triggering risk factors* and *acute-dynamic state risk factors*. We shall now briefly explore each one of these factors in turn.

Developmental Factors

Most risk assessments tend to focus upon offenders' criminal history. Yet research and etiological theory indicates that a variety of developmental factors play a role in sexual offending (see Bogaerts, Vervaeke & Goethals, 2004; Hanson & Bussière, 1998; Marshall, 1989; Marshall & Barbaree, 1990; Smallbone & Dadds, 2000; Ward, Hudson & Marshall, 1996; Weeks & Wisdom, 1998). For example, having a generally negative relationship with a parent has been linked to sexual aggression (see Hanson & Bussière, 1998; Smallbone & Dadds, 2000) as has childhood rejection (see Craissati, 2004), and being sexually abused as a child (Briere & Smiljanich, 1993). Thus, all three factors are included in the model and are hypothesized to play an important etiological role in the development of risk-related vulnerabilities or psychological dispositions.

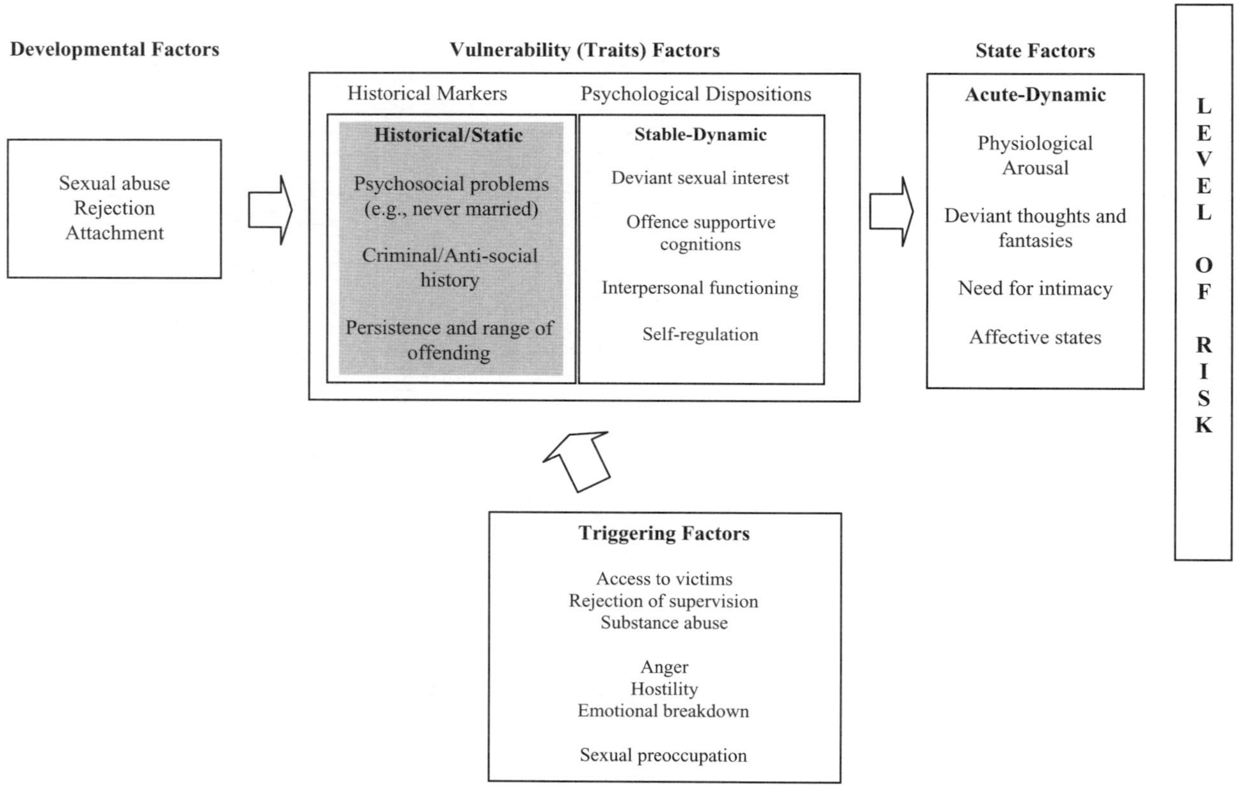

Figure 8.1 An Etiological Model of Risk. Reprinted from *Aggression and Violent Behavior*, *10*, Beech, A.R. & Ward, T., The integration of etiology and risk in sex offenders: A theoretical model, 31–63, Copyright (2004), with permission from Elsevier

Vulnerability Factors

An important distinction made by Beech and Ward (2004) is between psychological dispositions hypothesized to play a *causal* role in sexual offending (i.e., stable-dynamic deviant sexual interests, offence-related beliefs, socio-affective functioning and regulation management), and variables hypothesized to act as *risk identifiers* (i.e., historical/static marker variables).

Historical/static marker variables. Earlier in this chapter, we described how historical/static variables such as previous criminal convictions are typically used in actuarial risk assessments. To recap, historical risk factors are good estimators of an offender's risk to the community (Beech *et al.*, 2003; Bonta, 2002), although they are generally thought to be of little use for identifying offenders' treatment *need*s (Craissati, 2004; Grubin, 2003). Beech and Ward (2004), on the other hand, argue that static risk factors are actually important *markers* or identifiers of stable-dynamic risk factors (which Beech and Ward relabel as *psychological dispositions*: see below description). For example, static items that assess number and type of previous convictions may be useful indicators of offenders' sexual and more general self-regulation capabilities (with higher numbers of convictions indicating greater self-regulation deficiency). Similarly, items assessing previous cohabitation practices (e.g., Static-99, SORAG) may represent a useful indicator of offenders' interpersonal skills (with absence of serious long-term partners indicating greater intimacy deficits; Beech & Ward, 2004).

Stable-dynamic variables. Beech and Ward (2004) argue that commonly identified stable-dynamic variables are actually a type of *psychological disposition.* In other words, they reflect underlying causal features unique to the individual in question, likely to be predictive of an individual's future behaviors (Cattell & Kline, 1977; Matthews & Deary, 1998). Such traits are hypothesized to be the product of biological and cultural factors, as well as the various developmental adversities described earlier, and social learning history. Temporary manifestations of these traits (e.g., deviant sexual arousal, deviant thoughts and fantasies, need for intimacy, impulsivity) are hypothesized to be fluctuating *state* versions of these psychological traits (commonly termed *acute-dynamic* risk factors in the literature) and described in more detail below.

State-dynamic variables. Before stable-dynamic risk factors can be translated into their high-risk *state* versions, Beech and Ward (2004) argue that they have to be triggered in some way. Thus, it is hypothesized that a number of factors trigger psychological traits, producing their extremely risky state versions. *Behavioral triggers* include access to victims, rejection of supervision and abuse of substances; *affective triggers* include anger, hostility and emotional breakdowns; and *cognitive triggers* include sexual pre-occupation (see Hanson & Harris, 2001, described earlier). In summary then, state versions of core risk-related psychological traits act as central precursors to sexual offending and represent a proximal marker of an offender's causal psychological traits.

A strength of this model is the reframing of risk within an etiological framework. More specifically, Beech and Ward's (2004) model couches risk within general psychological theory, usefully describes how risk is related to a whole host of factors, and how risk should be explicitly tied to each offenders' own vulnerabilities or psychological traits. For example, an offender who experienced attachment problems during childhood (*developmental* risk factors) may have developed intimacy deficits, and find it extremely difficult to have fruitful interpersonal relationships with other adults (a *psychological disposition* signaled by the *marker variable* of never having been in a long-term relationship). Following a period of extreme isolation, and a request to babysit a neighbor's child (*triggering factors*), the offender may experience intense urges to create an intimate and adult-like relationship with that child, accompanied by extremely deep and satisfying loving emotions (i.e., this offender is experiencing an intense need for intimacy and possibly deviant sexual arousal accompanying this, both of which are *state factors* increasing the likelihood of a reoffence).

This model takes much of the guesswork out of risk assessment, allowing important etiological links to be made by assessors, so that a broad understanding of each individual's risk can be made, and relevant treatment and supervision provided. Most notably, in conjunction with the three methods of assessment outlined earlier, this model of risk can also act as a type of *map*, steering risk assessors towards points of risk that have particular relevance for the individual and allowing sensitive investigation of these areas. Put another way, we see this theory of risk as providing assessors and clinicians with a more substantial tool for gaining an honest and comprehensive picture of offenders' risk.

POLYGRAPH AND RISK

Although Beech and Ward's (2004) model of risk provides assessors with a strong etiological framework for obtaining more accurate clinical evaluations of risk, assessment of offenders' risk is still very much reliant on official file information, self-report measures, or the interviewing clinician's skill at uncovering sensitive information. Is there a more foolproof method which may be paired with these methods, and used alongside Beech and Ward's (2004) model for a supremely accurate view of offenders' risk?

One potentially useful indicator of deception that is receiving increased attention in the UK is the polygraph machine (Grubin, 2005; Wilcox, 1999). In brief, the polygraph assesses functions associated with the autonomic nervous system, such as respiration, cardiovascular and electrodermal responses (Grubin, 2005; Madsen, Parsons & Grubin, 2004), while the respondent is asked a series of specifically designed questions (see British Psychological Society, 2004). Physiological output is then recorded and used as a pointer for truthfulness (Madsen *et al.*, 2004). The polygraph has become a fairly popular method in the USA, being used within much sex offender treatment, and approximately one-quarter to a third of probationary management services (English *et al.*, 2000; Grubin, 2003). Proponents of the polygraph claim that the polygraph may inform the assessment, treatment and monitoring of risk through: (i) eliciting more realistic *historical/static profiles* of offenders' risk (e.g., previous number and type of victims, and possible offence *crossovers* [such as offending against girls *and* boys], Ahlmeyer *et al.*, 2000; Wilcox *et al.*, 2005); (ii) providing honest revelations of *stable-dynamic* psychological traits (Gannon, 2006; Gannon *et al.*, 2007); and (iii) encouraging honest disclosures of risky behaviors or *acute-dynamic* risk factors that may increase the likelihood of a sexual offender reoffending (i.e., masturbating to images or fantasies of children, Emerick & Dutton, 1993; Grubin *et al.*, 2004). In this section, we use empirical evidence to examine how the polygraph may inform each of these three major risk factor groups.

Historical/Static Risk Factors

Much of the risk-related research using the polygraph has focused on gaining more accurate information from offenders regarding historical offence-related information. Generally, studies have found that polygraph-assisted examinations provide the most comprehensive overview of previous offence history compared with clinical interviews, or information available from files (Emerick & Dutton, 1993; Heil, Ahlmeyer & English, 1998; Heil, Ahlmeyer & Simons, 2003; Wilcox & Sosnowski, 2005; Wilcox *et al.*, 2005). Heil *et al.* (2003), for example, found that substantially more offences and victims were revealed during polygraph examination administered during treatment, than the figures available from pre-sentence investigation reports for US sexual offender inmates (e.g., number of sex offence categories increased from 31% to 89% respectively). Similarly, in one of the first British pilot studies investigating treated sexual offenders' risk-related disclosures, Wilcox *et al.* (2005) found significantly more offence disclosures during polygraph examination compared to official file information (mean offence disclosures increased from 37.2 to 81.9 for 'hands-on' offences and from 26.2 to 80.8 for non-contact offences).

Hindman and Peters (2001) found five- to sixfold increases in the number of victims disclosed when they retrospectively compared US sexual offenders polygraphed *during* treatment with US sexual offenders who simply self-reported their histories prior to sentencing or dropped treatment before polygraph assessment.[3] They also found a fourfold increase when they compared a group of US sexual offenders who self-reported histories upon entering treatment, and then reported their history again post-polygraph once accepted for treatment. A particularly interesting aspect of these studies is what Hindman and Peters (2001) called the *Magical X*. This refers to the intriguing reversal of critical risk-related historical characteristics during polygraph examination. That is, while being polygraphed, sexual offenders significantly *increased* their disclosures of prior victims, but significantly *decreased* their own disclosures of childhood victimization. From these results, Hindman and Peters (2001) concluded that sexual offenders both minimize their own offending, and exaggerate their own childhood adversity when asked to self-report their history under standard conditions; most likely due to social stigma and/or legal consequences.

A reoccurring issue for professionals working with sexual offenders is whether offence and victim frequency are officially recorded or self-reported accurately. This issue becomes particularly meaningful for risk assessment when one examines the figures more carefully, for offence *crossovers*. Offence crossover refers to any offence disclosures indicating that victims vary in *sex*, *age* or *relationship* to the offender, and commonly increase the risk level assigned to offenders (see actuarial assessments described earlier). We focus on each of these crossover characteristics in the following sections, examining the quality of information elicited using the polygraph.

Sex of victim. The *sex* of child molesters' victims is an important risk-related variable, with molesters of boys being considered to be of

[3]Offenders do not appear to have been rigorously matched on confounding background variables.

particularly high-risk (Beech, 1998; Hanson & Bussière, 1998; Hanson & Harris, 2000; Hanson & Thornton, 1999; Quinsey *et al*., 1998), possibly because this victim preference marks significantly entrenched deviant sexual interests or stable psychological traits (see Beech & Ward, 2004). Thus, a realistic picture of the sex of offenders' chosen victims is vital for accurate risk assessment, appropriate treatment and subsequent risk supervision.

Heil *et al*. (2003) found that 35.9 % of her 223 inmate sexual offenders reported abusing both males and females during treatment-related polygraph assessment compared with a figure of only 8.5 % available from pre-sentence investigation reports. Similarly, in a review of 232 case files, English *et al*. (2000) reported that *one in three* sexual offenders disclosed having offended against male victims following treatment-related polygraph assessment, compared to only *one in five* recorded on file (made up of a combination of pre-sentence reports, police reports and supervising officer reports). Hindman and Peters (2001) suggested that non-polygraphed sexual offenders may routinely under-report their abuse of male victims. In their retrospective studies, for example, polygraphed offenders' victims were fairly evenly split across males and females, but non-polygraphed offenders self-reported a preponderance of female victims.

Age of victim. Offenders who cross the adult and child victim divide are deemed to be highly likely candidates for speedy reoffending, because their offence crossover indicates opportunism and impulsivity (Craissati, 2004). English *et al*. (2000) found that ready-to-hand file information showed only 10 % of sexual offenders had offended against both children and adults, whereas treatment-related polygraph disclosures increased this figure to 33 %. Heil *et al*. (2003) found that pre-sentence investigation reports indicated a mere 7.2 % of 223 inmate sexual offenders with both child and adult victims, whereas treatment-related polygraph assessment increased this rate to a massive 70 %. Wilcox *et al*. (2005) also reported an increase in adult-child victim crossover rates using the polygraph in their pilot research ($N = 14$), although the number was small (i.e., two offenders against adults admitted previously unknown offences against children).

Relationship to victim. More distant *relationships* between victim and perpetrator indicate increased risk (i.e., a stranger victim may indicate a higher level of risk to the community for both rapists and child molesters; Craissati, 2004; Hanson & Harris, 2000; Hanson & Thornton, 1999, 2000). Heil *et al*. (2003) found that sexual offender inmates showed an increased admittance to having committed offences against strangers as well as known victims (7–57 %) when comparing treatment-related polygraph self-report with pre-sentence investigation reports. Emerick and Dutton (1993) compared the sexual offence history of 76 US adolescent sex offenders across file information, clinical self-report and polygraph-assisted interview. They found that a polygraph examination led sexual offenders to acknowledge having victims of varying relationship types (46.7 %) compared to file data (22.2 %) and clinical interview (28.9 %).

In addition to the above mentioned offence crossovers, research has also shown that *offending onset age* appears to decrease when the polygraph procedure is introduced (Hindman & Peters, 2001; Wilcox *et al.*, 2005). For example, Wilcox *et al.* (2005) found that the polygraph decreased first offence mean age from 27.7 years (taken from file information and standard self-report) to 13.4 years. Similarly, Hindman and Peters (2001) found that adult sexual offenders typically underreported their sexual offence activity as juveniles. Of course, accurate information regarding age of sexual offending onset is crucial for risk assessment, given that earlier onset offenders are believed to be of a higher risk to the community, since they may hold more pervasive deficits in dynamic risk domains (Beech & Ward, 2004; Ward & Siegert, 2002).

From the variety of studies outlined above, it is clear to us that the polygraph does elicit a more realistic and comprehensive picture of offenders' offence history. Paired with Beech and Ward's (2004) etiological model of risk, the polygraph could provide the most realistic picture possible of sexual offenders' risk. For example, static risk factors are described by Beech and Ward (2004) as being *markers in time* of how an offender's psychological traits were once functioning in relation to the environment. Thus, accurate assessments of these *markers* or *historical* risk factors using the polygraph can provide assessors with a more reliable indicator of an offender's causal or psychological risk factors that need to be targeted during treatment. To illustrate, an offender who reports only offences against girls, yet who also regularly targets boys, is withholding vital historical information for accurate treatment and subsequent supervision. This offender is likely to have entrenched deviant sexual interests that need to be modified in treatment, explored for associated contextual triggers, and closely monitored upon community release.

What is not totally clear, however, is what the results of such historical risk-related polygraph research means for the development and use of actuarial risk instruments. The research suggests that historical risk factors are underestimated in both file information and standard self-report. Thus, the polygraph could be used alongside the research samples that are used to develop actuarial risk instruments; this may ensure our actuarial instruments are of the highest possible predictive quality.

Stable-Dynamic Risk

One only has to examine the techniques used to access psychological dispositions prior to, and post-treatment, (e.g., the PPG measures deviant sexual arousal) to realize that gaining untainted and objective information about an offenders' underlying psychological trait factors is critical for understanding their presenting risk and treatment needs. Our examination of the literature shows that most work with the polygraph has focused upon examining historical variables (Ahlmeyer *et al.*, 2000; English *et al.*, 2000; Hindman & Peters, 2001; Wilcox & Sosnowski, 2005; Wilcox *et al.*, 2005), or acute-dynamic factors in relation to risk (English *et al.*, 2000; Grubin *et al.*, 2004), with little controlled work having been conducted on traits of direct relevance to the *focus* of treatment.

It has been suggested that the polygraph leads to more honest risk-related disclosures because the participant believes 'the game is up', and the machine will catch him out (see Madsen *et al.*, 2004). Thus, presumably, one should find similar effects when using a bogus polygraph, as long as participants believe that the bogus polygraph really can detect lies. Studies of this type have been carried out by Gannon and her colleagues (see Gannon, 2006; Gannon *et al.*, 2007), focusing specifically on the detection of offence-related beliefs.

In the most recent, Gannon *et al.* (2007) asked 59 pre-treatment relatively high-risk child molesters (as measured on the Static-99) to complete Bumby's (1996) MOLEST offence-related beliefs questionnaire at two time points (Time One and Time Two), separated by a four to six week interval. At Time One, child molesters completed the questionnaire under standard, transparent, self-report conditions (in other words, they were free to impression manage). At Time Two, the same molesters were revisited, and asked to complete a randomized version of the questionnaire again. This time, however, half of the molesters were randomly allocated to the bogus polygraph condition, while the other half acted as controls (i.e., they completed the questionnaire again under standard, self-report conditions). The bogus polygraph was actually a skin conductance meter with electrodes and voice recorder, both attached to a laptop computer displaying real skin conductance output. Child molesters in the bogus polygraph condition were not only told that they should answer as truthfully as possible whilst connected to the apparatus, in case the machine 'caught them out', but they were also given a working demonstration of the machine's capabilities (in which 'test' questions were asked while the experimenter manipulated the screen output using a concealed foot pedal, see Gannon *et al.*, 2007 for details).

Results showed that molesters completing the questionnaire connected to the fake polygraph significantly *increased* their endorsements of offence-related beliefs compared to their own previous answers at Time One, and to control molesters' answers at Time Two. Put another way, this study showed that these high-risk child molesters had been hiding the true extent of their offence-related beliefs when assessed using standard conditions. A strength of this study compared to other polygraph-related research designs discussed earlier is rigorous *experimental control*. Risk-related polygraph research rarely employs adequate controls,[4] and the comparisons made *within* the same group are typically confounded by the provision of treatment (e.g., Emerick & Dutton, 1993; English *et al.*, 2000; Hindman & Peters, 2001).

To our knowledge, other risk-related *psychological traits* – deviant sexual interests, socio-affective functioning and regulation management – have not been assessed *directly* using either a bogus or authentic polygraph machine. However, as we have already seen, using Beech and Ward's (2004) model, one can make well-informed judgments about psychological trait deficiencies using polygraph-assisted research that taps relevant historical factors.

Acute-Dynamic Risk

One particularly appealing use of the polygraph concerns its usage for *risk monitoring* in the community. In other words, when sexual offenders are released under probation supervision, monitoring *acute-dynamic risk factors*, or those state factors indicating imminence of offending, is of the utmost urgency and importance. The dilemma here is obvious. At this stage in supervision, even the most compliant offenders are unlikely to volunteer highly risky thoughts and behaviors for fear of disappointing professionals, receiving more restrictive conditions, suspension of conditional release, recall to prison, or in severe cases, additional convictions. It is for this exact reason, that professionals have adopted the polygraph, to investigate whether it can: (1) bring supervising bodies' attention to imminent risk that previously would have gone undetected (English *et al.*, 2000), and (2) act as a major deterrent for offenders tempted to engage in high-risk

[4]With the exception of Grubin *et al.*'s (2004) study, which we describe in detail under *Acute-Dynamic Risk*.

behaviors or offending, and help them to stick to their relapse prevention plan (Abrams, 1991; Abrams & Simmons, 2000).

Research so far has reported positive results for both these areas (Abrams & Ogard, 1986; English *et al.*, 2000; Grubin *et al.*, 2004; Harrison & Kirkpatrick, 2000; Wilcox, Sosnowski & Middleton, 1999). In relation to the first, Wilcox *et al.*'s (2005) pilot research found that a number of important high-risk behaviors were disclosed by sexual offenders on probation using the polygraph. These included substance abuse, using pornography, sex chat lines and prostitutes, or visiting nude bars. Most worrying, however, was the fact that well over half of these men (57 %) reported stalking type behaviors, indicating that they may well have been on the brink of reoffending. This additional information would previously have gone undetected by supervising officials had the polygraph not been employed.

In a pioneering prospective study, Grubin *et al.* (2004) examined whether the polygraph would help British sexual offenders stick to their relapse prevention plan, and avoid high-risk behaviors associated with reoffending (e.g., masturbating to deviant sexual fantasies, or looking for victims). At stage one, 50 offenders (just under half of those approached to participate) were interviewed about their high-risk behaviors, and informed that they would be revisited three months later. Offenders allocated to the *Polygraph Aware* group were told to expect a polygraph examination, whereas the *Polygraph Unaware* group was simply told that they would have their behavior 'reviewed'. In fact, when sexual offenders were revisited at stage two, *all* sexual offenders received a polygraph examination; the prediction being that the Polygraph Aware group would report significantly lower frequencies of high-risk behaviors than the Polygraph Unaware group. By stage two, however, only 32 sexual offenders were able to be polygraphed as most ($n = 14$) failed to attend the session.[5] Surprisingly, men in the Polygraph Aware and Unaware groups did not significantly differ in their disclosures of high-risk behaviors. Overall, a massive 97 % of sexual offenders disclosed at least one risky behavior (range 0–7). Broken down, this amounted to a mean of 2.45 ($SD = 1.7$) high-risk behaviors per offender and included some serious threats to abstinence (e.g., looking for victims in public toilets). Following these disclosures, group allocations were discarded and all men were told to expect a further polygraph examination at stage three, six months later. A further 11 participants failed to turn up for polygraph examination at stage three leaving 21 sexual offenders for testing. During this third session, the

[5]Others could not attend for other reasons such as being recalled to prison, and one Polygraph Unaware participant refused to be tested.

most positive findings were attained. Almost three-quarters (71%) of offenders passed their polygraph examinations, and of the 15 men who disclosed risky behavior, the majority had reported these to their supervising probation officers already. All but one offender reported that the polygraph had helped them desist from offending, while 12 said that knowledge of the forthcoming polygraph strengthened their desistance from high-risk behaviors.

Using the same British sexual offenders described above, Madsen *et al.* (2004) inspected the data at stage three, to see whether, in addition to frequency, the polygraph also minimized the *severity* of reported high-risk behaviors. The results were affirmative, suggesting that knowledge of the polygraph had reduced not only high-risk behavior frequency, but in addition, severity.

Emerick and Dutton (1993) found similar increases in the types of high-risk behaviors disclosed by adolescent sexual offenders using the polygraph, although admittedly, their study was retrospective. To recap, they compared the sexual offence history of 76 adolescent sex offenders across file information, clinical self-report and polygraph-assisted interview. Comparisons showed that participants were significantly more likely to report having used exploitative or abusive pornography, and to have masturbated to such images under polygraph examination compared with clinical self-report. Interestingly, the polygraph data revealed a link between masturbating to abusive pornography and having a greater number of victims.

Similarly, English *et al.*'s (2000) analysis of case files showed extremely encouraging results concerning the monitoring of high-risk behaviors. First, disclosures concerning high-risk behaviors such as substance abuse, masturbating to deviant fantasies, indecent phone calls and pornographic Internet use increased overall following polygraph examination, compared to those admitted before. Second, polygraph examination identified 21 out of 147 individuals who continued to sexually abuse whilst under community supervision (14%). Finally, 44 of 122 offenders under community supervision disclosed engaging in high-risk behaviors whilst in the community.

Based on the small but growing risk-related polygraph studies we have presented here, we believe that a more comprehensive picture of each offender's risk factors is available using the polygraph. Research shows that historical information (i.e., frequency, diversity and onset of sexual offending), stable-dynamic information (i.e., offence-supportive beliefs), and acute-dynamic information, is almost always of a better quality when polygraph assessed. Clearly, having more realistic knowledge of each of these factors ensures that a more accurate picture is developed of each offender's level of risk. In combination with Beech and

Ward's (2004) theory of risk, the polygraph may represent a powerful force in the world of risk assessment. For example, a sex offender could admit, under polygraph examination, that he began having deviant sexual interests much earlier than his standard self-reports suggested. Given this more accurate information, Beech and Ward's (2004) theory of risk could be used to draw professionals' attention to factors of causal influence (i.e., stable-dynamic deviant sexual interest) early on, so that they can be appropriately dealt with in treatment.

FRIEND OR FOE: THE DILEMMAS OF POLYGRAPH-ASSISTED RISK ASSESSMENT

So far, our examination of polygraph-assisted risk assessments suggests that the polygraph does improve our understanding of a variety of risk factors. But what are the problems with using the polygraph for risk-related assessments? We believe that a number of issues need to considered; we have categorized them as falling under three main subheadings that we address in turn below: *violation of offenders' human rights*, *disclosure versus change*, and *false confessions*.

A Violation of Offenders' Human Rights?

The polygraph has received some criticisms concerning its ethical use and effectiveness (see the British Psychological Society (BPS), 1986, 2004; or Gale, 1988). The 1986 British Psychological Working Party report (BPS, 1986) appears to have acted as the major precipitator of concern about polygraph usage in Britain (Grubin, 2005) and many of these concerns were reiterated in the Working Party Report published in 2004. Wilcox (2000) has outlined three main ethical issues expressed by Gale, who led the 1986 Working Party. First, an objection was raised about the polygraph invoking *anxiety* in examinees. Wilcox (2000) acknowledged that fear of criminal offence detection will indeed be anxiety provoking. However, he pointed out that anxiety provoking assessments and procedures are commonly used during offender assessments, and cannot be avoided if one is to obtain information pertinent to the offending individual in question (e.g., Gudjonsson's suggestibility technique, 1983, 1984). Second, concerns have been raised surrounding the issue of the polygraph being a *violation of offenders' rights*. For example, the 2004 Working Party Report pointed out that many offenders may feel that they *have* to comply with polygraph testing to ensure optimal release conditions. Wilcox, however, argued that offenders are often made to comply with a number of assessment and treatment conditions once convicted. However, this argument does not necessarily mean that it is acceptable to add yet another test to the ones offenders already have to comply with, especially when the polygraph is still being discussed and researched. Third, concerns have been expressed concerning the *privacy invasions* associated with the polygraph. Wilcox highlighted that personal questions, outside the realms of offence-related questions discussed with the offender, are not allowed under APA guidelines. In addition, Wilcox pointed to other commonly accepted practices such as the PPG, which he argued entail much more personal invasions of privacy, but are necessary for both scientific and therapeutic progression.

Clearly, the above concerns are legitimate, and merit serious consideration in any risk-related (or indeed other uses) of the polygraph or believable fake polygraphs.[6] Yet if the risk-related information disclosed by offenders under polygraph examination is more valid than file information or standard self-report (e.g., Emerick & Dutton, 1993; Gannon *et al.*, 2007; Heil *et al.*, 2003), surely this opens up further ethical dilemmas of *not* using the polygraph for risk-related work (Sigall, 1997). Clearly, there are serious ethical considerations of not using the polygraph for community surveillance of high-risk behaviors given the positive evidence that we outlined earlier. Put another way, research suggests that supervised sexual offenders in the community may underreport behaviors of concern to their probation officer using standard self-report techniques, but dramatically increase reports of sensitive and potentially harmful behaviors when examined periodically using the polygraph (English *et al.*, 2000; Grubin *et al.*, 2004). Thus, risk assessment in the *absence* of the polygraph may well be lulling clinicians, treatment providers, probation officers and the public, into a false sense of security.

Disclosure versus Change

In a series of recent articles, we have argued that offenders' internal motivation to change is extremely important for promoting long-term sexual offending desistance (see Collie, Ward & Gannon, 2006; Ward & Gannon, 2006). Thus, one concern that could be directed at polygraph risk-related assessments is that consistent usage, throughout the correctional system, could severely compromise relations between offenders and treatment providers. Most notably, by primarily focusing

[6]See Sigall (1997) for an excellent general discussion of the ethical considerations of fake polygraph-related research.

assessments on polygraph-related disclosures, the danger is that sexual offenders receive a strong message from important professionals that they are unworthy, deceptive individuals rather than worthwhile individuals capable of change. An important focus of sex offender assessment, rehabilitation and monitoring should be to focus therapeutically upon the offenders' *strengths* to promote internally driven long-term change (Collie *et al.*, 2006). The promotion of such change may be maximized if offenders' self-esteem, and emotional wellbeing, are respected in the therapy process.

Notably, however, a large proportion of sexual offenders (72 %) have anonymously reported that the polygraph has been helpful to them during treatment (Kokish, Levenson & Blasingame, 2005),[7] although one participant wondered himself whether his new found honesty really had promoted any longer term change in lying behavior. Generally, however, the use of polygraph for community supervision has been well supported.

False Disclosures

So far, we have concentrated on the polygraph as a type of 'truth facilitator' (Grubin *et al.*, 2004) instead of focusing on the accuracy of *deceptive*, or *non-deceptive* results per se. In relation to *deceptive* results, of particular concern is the possibility of some unstable or particularly distressed individuals disclosing crimes they did not actually commit (i.e., *false confessions*; Cassell, 1999; Gudjonsson, 1992; Gudjonsson & Sigurdsson, 1994). So what are the chances of a sexual offender fabricating offences upon hearing an inaccurate deceptive result? At the time of writing this chapter, we could only find one published study directly addressing this important issue. Kokish *et al.* (2005, described above) surveyed 95 sexual offenders who had extensive personal experience of mandatory polygraph testing, on how often they had *falsely* disclosed crimes after having failed a polygraph examination; responses were anonymous. Five percent of participants ($n = 5$) reported making false disclosures, with the majority ($n = 4$) stating that these disclosures lead to a further *acceptable* polygraph examination. Madsen *et al.* (2004) have suggested that five false confessions represents a problem that is 'more theoretical than actual' (p. 692). We believe, however, (as do others, for example, Jackie Craisatti, personal communication, July 4, 2005) that this figure is high enough for concern,

[7] Also, Harrison and Kirkpatrick (2000) found that just over half of their 28 sex offenders believed their lack of risky behaviours could be attributed to the helpfulness of the polygraph.

although further investigation is warranted before drawing any firm conclusions.

FUTURE DIRECTIONS AND CONCLUSIONS

Reliable assessments of sexual offenders' risk are essential for adequate treatment and supervision of sexual offenders. In the first half of our chapter, we described the methods and theory required for a comprehensive assessment of sexual offenders' risk. Then, we examined how the polygraph may be able to further improve our current assessments of risk through considering current empirical research. Our examination of the evidence shows that polygraph-assisted risk interviews provide substantially more risk-related information for sexual offenders than file information or standard self-report. The implications of this growing body of research are obvious: if current risk assessments routinely underestimate risk, then our treatment and subsequent supervision of such individuals may be severely impaired. Despite this seemingly positive research base, we do not blindly advocate for polygraph use. At present, the research base in Britain is still in infancy, and a more systematically controlled research program is needed before adopting the polygraph routinely for risk assessment purposes. For example, many present studies confound treatment or prosecution immunity with polygraph implementation (e.g., English *et al.*, 2000; Grubin *et al.*, 2004; Madsen *et al.*, 2004), are small pilot studies (Wilcox *et al.*, 2005), or have a high percentage of offenders dropping out of the study proper (Grubin *et al.*, 2004; Madsen *et al.*, 2004). A well-designed research program could shed light on just how useful widespread implementation of the polygraph could be, and which parts of the corrections system it will most benefit.[8] We believe the polygraph may show most promise for the monitoring of risk when public safety is paramount, and offenders need extra incentive to disclose high-risk situations and behaviors to their probation officers. Whatever view one takes of the polygraph's overall usefulness for assessing risk, one thing is for sure: only a comprehensive program of tightly controlled research will be able to inform us just what the polygraph can offer long term both in Britain and worldwide.

[8]The Probation Services in the UK are about to implement a pilot polygraph program which is likely to provide information regarding the usefulness of risk-related polygraph testing.

REFERENCES

Abrams, S. (1991). The use of the polygraph with sex offenders. *Annals of Sex Research*, *4*, 239–263.

Abrams, S. & Ogard, E. (1986). Polygraph surveillance of probationers. *Polygraph*, *15*, 174–182.

Abrams, S. & Simmons, G. (2000). Post-conviction polygraph testing: Then and now. *Polygraph*, *29*, 63–67.

Ahlmeyer, S., Heil, P., McKee, B., & English, K. (2000). The impact of polygraphy on admissions of victims and offenses in adult sexual offenders. *Sexual Abuse: A Journal of Research and Treatment*, *12*, 123–138.

Andrews, D.A. & Bonta, J. (1998). *The psychology of criminal conduct* (2nd edn). Cincinnati, OH: Anderson Publishing Co.

Beech, A.R. (1998). A psychometric typology of child abusers. *International Journal of Offender Therapy and Comparative Criminology*, *42*, 319–339.

Beech, A.R. & Ward, T. (2004). The integration of etiology and risk in sex offenders: A theoretical model. *Aggression and Violent Behavior*, *10*, 31–63.

Beech, A.R., Fisher, D., & Beckett, R.C. (1999). *An evaluation of The Prison Sex Offender Treatment Programme*. UK Home Office occasional report. (Available from Home Office Information Publications Group, Research, Development and Statistics Directorate, Room 201, 50 St Anne's Gate, London SW1 9AT.) Available electronically from <www.homeoffice.gov.uk/rds/pdfs/occ-step3.pdf>.

Beech, A.R., Fisher, D., & Thornton, D. (2003). Risk assessment of sex offenders. *Professional Psychology: Research and Practice*, *34*, 339–352.

Blackburn, R. (2000). Risk assessment and prediction. In J. McGuire, T. Mason & A. O'Kane (Eds), *Behavior, crime and legal processes: A guide for legal practitioners* (pp. 178–204). Chichester, UK: John Wiley & Sons, Ltd.

Bogaerts, S., Vervaeke, G., & Goethals, J. (2004). A comparison of relational attitude and personality disorders in the explanation of child molestation. *Sexual Abuse: A Journal of Research and Treatment*, *16*, 37–47.

Bonta, J. (2002). Offender risk assessment: Guidelines for selection and use. *Criminal Justice and Behavior*, *29*, 355–379.

Briere, J. & Smiljanich, K. (1993, August). *Childhood sexual abuse and subsequent sexual aggression against adult women*. Paper presented at the 101st annual convention of the American Psychological Association, Toronto, Ontario.

British Psychological Society (BPS) (1986). Report of the working group on the use of the polygraph in criminal investigations and personnel screening. *Bulletin of the British Psychological Society*, *39*, 81–94.

British Psychological Society (BPS) (2004). *A review of the current scientific status and fields of application of polygraphic deception detection. Final report from the working party*. Leicester: BPS.

Bumby, K.M. (1996). Assessing the cognitive distortions of child molesters and rapists: Developments and validation of the MOLEST and RAPE scales. *Sexual Abuse: A Journal of Research and Treatment*, *8*, 37–54.

Cassell, P.G. (1999). The guilty and the 'innocent': An examination of alleged cases of wrongful conviction from false confessions. *Harvard Journal of Law and Public Policy*, *22*, 523.

Cattell, R.B. & Kline, P. (1977). *The scientific analysis of personality and motivation*. NY: Academic Books.

Collie, R.M., Ward, T., & Gannon, T.A. (2006). The management of sex offenders: Introducing a good lives approach. In R.D. McAnulty & M. Burnette (Eds), *Sex and Sexuality*. NY: Praeger Press.

Conte, J.R. (1985). Clinical dimensions of adult sexual abuse of children. *Behavioral Sciences and the Law, 3*, 341–353.

Craissati, J. (2004). *Managing high-risk offenders in the community. A psychological approach*. Hove, UK: Brunner-Routledge.

Doren, D.M. (2002). *Evaluating sex offenders: A manual for civil commitments and beyond*. London: Sage.

Emerick, R.L. & Dutton, W.A. (1993). The effect of the polygraph on the self-report of adolescent sex offenders: Implementation for risk assessment. *Annals of Sex Research, 6*, 83–103.

English, K., Jones, L., Pasini-Hill, D., Patrick, D., & Cooley-Towell, S. (2000). *The value of testing in sex offender management*. Research report submitted to the National Institute of Justice. Denver, Colorado: Division of Criminal Justice, Office of Research and Statistics.

Gale, A. (1988). *The Polygraph Test: Lies, truth, and science*. London: Sage.

Gannon, T.A. (2006). Increasing honest responding on cognitive distortions in child molesters: *The Bogus Pipeline Procedure*, *Journal of Interpersonal Violence, 21*, 358–375.

Gannon, T.A., Keown, K., & Polaschek, D.L.L. (2007). Increasing honest responding on cognitive distortions in child molesters: The bogus pipeline revisited. *Sexual Abuse: A Journal of Research and Treatment, 19*, 5–22.

Grove, W.M. & Meehl, P.E. (1996). Comparative efficiency of informal (subjective, impressionistic) and formal (mechanical, algorithmic) prediction procedures: The clinical statistical controversy. *Psychology, Public Policy and Law, 2*, 293–323.

Grubin, D. (1998). *Sex offending against children: Understanding the risk*. Police Research Series Paper 99. London: Home Office.

Grubin, D. (1999). Actuarial and clinical assessment of risk in sex offenders. *Journal of Interpersonal Violence, 14*, 331–343.

Grubin, D. (2002). The potential use of polygraph in forensic psychiatry. *Criminal behavior and mental health, 12*, 45–55.

Grubin, D. (2003). The role of the polygraph. In A. Matravers (Ed.), *Sex offenders in the community: Managing and reducing the risks*. Devon, UK: Willan Publishing.

Grubin, D. (2005). Lie detection and the polygraph: A historical review. *Journal of Forensic Psychiatry and Psychology, 16*, 357–369.

Grubin, D., Madsen, L., Parsons, S., Sosnowski, D., & Warberg, B. (2004). A prospective study of the impact of the polygraphy on high-risk behaviors in adult sex offenders. *Sexual Abuse: A Journal of Research and Treatment, 16*, 209–222.

Gudjonsson, G.H. (1983). Suggestibility, intelligence, memory recall, and personality: An experimental study. *British Journal of Psychiatry, 142*, 35–37.

Gudjonsson, G.H. (1984). A new scale of interrogative suggestibility. *Personality and Individual Differences, 5*, 303–314.

Gudjonsson, G.H. (1992). *The psychology of interrogations, confessions, and testimony*. Chichester, UK: John Wiley & Sons, Ltd.

Gudjonsson, G.H. & Sigurdsson, J.F. (1994). How frequently do false confessions occur? An empirical study among prison inmates. *Psychology, Crime and Law*, *1*, 21–26.

Hanson, R.K. (1997). *The development of a brief actuarial risk scale for sexual offence recidivism*. (User Report 1997-04.) Ottawa: Department of the Solicitor General of Canada.

Hanson, R.K. & Bussière, M.T. (1998). Predicting relapse: A meta-analysis of sexual offender recidivism studies. *Journal of Consulting and Clinical Psychology*, *66*, 348–362.

Hanson, R.K. & Harris, A.J.R. (2000). *The Sex Offender Need Assessment Rating (SONAR): a method for measuring change in risk levels*. (User report 1998-01). Ontario: Department of the Solicitor General.

Hanson, R.K. & Harris, A.J.R. (2001). *The Sex Offender Need Assessment Rating (SONAR): a method for measuring change in risk levels*. Available electronically from `<www.sgc.gc.ca/epub/corr/e200001a/e200001b/e200001b.htm>`. Please note this is an older version of SONAR and should not be used.

Hanson, R.K. & Thornton, D. (1999). *Static-99: Improving actuarial risk assessments for sex offenders*. Ontario: Department of the Solicitor General.

Hanson, R.K. & Thornton, D. (2000). Improving risk assessments for sex offenders: A comparison of three actuarial scales. *Law and Human Behavior*, *24*, 119–136.

Hanson, R.K., Morton, K.E., & Harris, A.J.R. (2003). Sexual Offender Recidivism Risk: What We Know and What We Need to Know. In R. Prentky, E. Janus & M. Seto (Eds), *Sexually Coercive Behavior: Understanding and Management* (pp. 154–166). Annals of the New York Academy of Sciences, Vol. 989. NY: New York Academy of Sciences.

Harrison, J.S. & Kirkpatrick, B. (2000). Polygraph testing and behavioural change with sex offenders in an outpatient setting: An exploratory study. *Polygraph*, *29*, 20–26.

Heil, P., Ahlmeyer, S., & English, P. (1998, October). *Maximising the use of the polygraph with sex offenders: Policy development and research findings*. ATSA conference, Vancouver.

Heil, P., Ahlmeyer, S., & Simons, D. (2003). Crossover sexual offences. *Sexual Abuse: A Journal of Research and Treatment*, *15*, 221–236.

Hindman, J. & Peters, J.M. (2001). Polygraph testing leads to better understanding adult and juvenile sex offenders. *Federal Probation*, *65*, 8–15.

Kokish, R., Levenson, J.S., & Blasingame, G.D. (2005). Post-conviction sex offender polygraph examination: Client-reported perceptions of utility and accuracy. *Sexual Abuse: A Journal of Research and Treatment*, *17*, 211–221.

Kolton, D.J.C., Boer, A., & Boer, D.P. (2001). A revision of the Abel and Becker Cognition Scale for intellectually disabled sexual offenders. *Sexual Abuse: A Journal of Research and Treatment*, *13*, 217–219.

Madsen, L., Parsons, S., & Grubin, D. (2004). A preliminary study of the contribution of periodic polygraph testing in the treatment and supervision of sex offenders. *British Journal of Forensic Psychiatry and Psychology*, *15*, 682–695.

Marshall, W.L. (1989). Intimacy, loneliness, and sexual offenders. *Behaviour Research and Therapy*, *27*, 491–503.

Marshall, W.L. & Barbaree, H.E. (1990). An integrated theory of sexual offending. In W.L. Marshall, D.R. Laws & H.E. Barbaree (Eds), *Handbook of sexual assault: Issues, theories and treatment of the offender* (pp. 363–385). NY: Plenum.

Matthews, G. & Deary, I.J. (1998). *Personality Traits*. Cambridge, UK: Cambridge University Press.

McGuire, J. (2000). Explanations of criminal behavior. In J. McGuire, T. Mason & A. O'Kane (Eds), *Behavior, crime and legal processes: A guide for legal practitioners* (pp. 135–159). Chichester, UK: John Wiley & Sons, Ltd.

Quinsey, V.L., Harris, G.T., Rice, M.E., & Cormier, C.A. (1998). *Violent Offenders: Appraising and managing risk*. Washington, DC: APA.

Sigall, H. (1997). Ethical considerations in social psychological research: Is the bogus pipeline a special case? *Journal of Applied Social Psychology*, *27*, 574–581.

Smallbone, S. & Dadds, M. (2000). Attachment and coercive sexual behavior. *Sexual Abuse: A Journal of Research and Treatment*, *12*, 3–15.

Thornton, D. (2000, March). *Structured risk assessment*. Paper presented at the Sinclair Seminars Conference on sex offender re-offense risk prediction, Madison, WI. (Videotape available from www.sinclairseminars.com.)

Thornton, D. (2002). Constructing and testing a framework for dynamic risk assessment. *Sexual Abuse: A Journal of Research and Treatment*, *14*, 139–154.

Thornton, D., Mann, R., Webster, S.I. *et al.* (2003). Distinguishing and combining risks for sexual and violent recidivism. In R.A. Prentky, E.S. Janus & M.C. Seto (Eds), *Sexually Coercive Behavior: Understanding and Management* (pp. 225–235). Annals of the New York Academy of Sciences, Vol. 989. NY: New York Academy of Sciences.

Ward, T. & Gannon, T.A. (2006). Rehabilitation, etiology, and self-regulation: The comprehensive good lives model of treatment for sexual offenders. *Aggression and Violent Behavior: A Review Journal*, *11*, 77–94.

Ward, T. & Siegert, R. (2002). Toward a comprehensive theory of child sexual abuse: A theory knitting perspective. *Psychology, Crime, and Law*, *8*, 319–351.

Ward, T., Hudson, S.M., & Marshall, W.L. (1996). Attachment style in sex offenders: A preliminary study. *Journal of Sex Research*, *33*, 17–26.

Ward, T., Louden, K., Hudson, S.M., & Marshall, W.L. (1995). A descriptive model of the offense chain for child molesters. *Journal of Interpersonal Violence*, *10*, 452–472.

Ward, T., Vess, J., Collie, R.M., & Gannon, T.A. (2006). Risk management or goods promotion: The relationship between approach and avoidance goals in treatment for sex offenders. *Aggression and Violent Behavior: A Review Journal*, *11*, 378–393.

Weeks, R. & Wisdom, C. (1998). Self-reports of early childhood victimization among incarcerated adult male felons. *Journal of Interpersonal Violence*, *13*, 346–361.

Wilcox, D.T. (1999). Polygraph testing. *NOTA News*, *30*, 29–31.

Wilcox, D.T. (2000). Application of the clinical polygraph examination to the assessment, treatment and monitoring of sex offenders. *The Journal of Sexual Aggression*, *5*, 134–152.

Wilcox, D.T. & Sosnowski, D. (2005). Polygraph examination of British sexual offenders: A pilot study on sexual history disclosure testing. *Journal of Sexual Aggression*, *11*, 3–25.

Wilcox, D.T., Sosnowski, D., & Middleton, D. (1999). The use of the polygraph in the community supervision of sex offenders. *Probation Journal*, *46*, 234–240.
Wilcox, D.T., Sosnowski, D., Warberg, B., & Beech, A.R. (2005). Sexual history disclosure using the polygraph in a sample of British sex offenders. *Polygraph Journal*, *34*, 171–183.

CHAPTER 9

The Accuracy of Polygraphy in the Treatment and Supervision of Sex Offenders

LARS MADSEN

INTRODUCTION

The polygraph is increasingly being utilized in the treatment and supervision of sex offenders (Grubin & Madsen, 2005). Proponents argue that the polygraph overcomes limitations in current supervision practices, as well as generally improving the assessment and treatment of sex offenders. Research has generally been supportive of these claims, with studies showing that the polygraph assists with gaining additional information regarding an offender's sexual offence history, paraphilic interests and general risk behavior (Ahlmeyer *et al.*, 2000; Emerick & Dutton, 1993; English *et al.*, 2000; Grubin *et al.*, 2004; Heil, Ahlmeyer & Simons, 2003; Hindman & Peters, 2001; Wilcox *et al.*, 2005). Periodic polygraph testing also appears to act as a deterrent for reoffending and engaging in risk behavior (Abrams & Ogard, 1986; Edson, 1991; Grubin *et al.*, 2004; Madsen, Parsons & Grubin, 2004). Indeed, even offenders have reported finding it useful in their treatment and supervision (Grubin & Madsen, 2006). Such research says nothing about the

The Use of the Polygraph in Assessing, Treating and Supervising Sex Offenders: A Practitioner's Guide
Edited by Daniel T. Wilcox.

accuracy of the instrument, which remains a contentious issue within the scientific literature. A good understanding of the accuracy of post-conviction polygraph tests is vital for professionals to know how best to respond to the different test outcomes. Indeed, if the polygraph is not reasonably accurate then its long-term value as a treatment and supervision tool is debatable.

SOME IMPORTANT CONCEPTS

It is important to define a number of key psychometric concepts prior to evaluating the scientific evidence for the polygraph. The term 'validity' refers to whether an instrument measures the phenomenon that it is supposed to measure. In regard to the polygraph it refers, therefore, to whether the instrument is actually accurate in discriminating between truthfulness and deception. There are several aspects to validity that are important to distinguish. *Construct validity* refers to the theory of how and why a particular test works. A test is considered to have high construct validity when the theory underlying it provides a plausible explanation for the empirical findings (Grimm & Yarnold, 2000). *Criterion validity*, on the other hand, refers to the accuracy of the instrument. It is important to further differentiate two concepts related to accuracy. These are *sensitivity* and *specificity* (Swets, 1996). With regards to polygraph testing, *sensitivity* refers to how well the test actually identifies 'liars', while *specificity* refers to how well it identifies 'truth-tellers'. Examinees who are misdiagnosed are referred to as either *false positives* (examinees erroneously identified as deceptive) or *false negatives* (examinees erroneously identified as non-deceptive) (Swets, 1996). Inconclusive results are typically excluded when presenting the data. Table 9.1 presents the four possible combinations of polygraph test results.

The 'percentage correct' for *sensitivity* and *specificity* is the typical format for presenting data on the accuracy of the polygraph. Some early studies have utilized an overall percentage correct to describe the accuracy of the polygraph, but such a figure is essentially meaningless. Consider the example where base rates of deception are quite low, for example, 10 out of 100. Simply by assuming that everyone is innocent and passing all the polygraphs would theoretically yield 90 % 'accuracy'. Even randomly failing 10 out of these 100 would still yield a respectable 82 % 'accuracy'.

Other related statistics that are of value when considering the accuracy of the polygraph are *positive* and *negative predictive power* (National Research Council, 2002). *Positive predictive power* refers to the

Table 9.1 Diagnostic classification statistics

	True Condition		
Polygraph Test Result	Positive (Truly Deceptive)	Negative (Truly Truthful)	Total
Deception Indicated (Lying)	True Positive (TP)	False Positive (FP)	TP + FP
No Deception Indicated (Truthful)	False Negative (FN)	True Negative (TN)	FN + TN
Total (n)	TP/(TP + FN) Sensitivity	TN/(FP + TN) Specificity	TP + FN + FP + TN

percentage of individuals testing positive (deceptive) on the polygraph who are actually deceptive. This measure is obtained by dividing the true-positive rate (total number of actual liars) by the total number of individuals who have tested deceptive. *Negative predictive power*, on the other hand, is the percentage of individuals scoring negative (non-deceptive) on the test who are truly negative. This statistic is calculated by dividing the true negative (total number of truth-tellers) by the total number of individuals who have scored negative on the test (McCann, 1998). The value of these statistics is that it provides an indication of how confident one can be that a 'failed' or 'passed' polygraph result is actually correct.

Some studies have recently applied scientific methods based on signal detection theory (National Research Council, 2002). A Receiver Operating Characteristic (ROC) curve is used to assess the quality of the discriminatory power of a test using *sensitivity* and *specificity* data (Swets, Dawes & Monahan, 2000). The actual curve is a graphical display with the *false-positive* rate on the horizontal axis and the *true-positive* rate on the vertical axis. Such a curve allows one to identify how well a test discriminates between positive (Deception Indicated) and negative (No Deception Indicated) results and to identify the best trade-off between *sensitivity* and *specificity* when evaluating a test. A convenient overall quantitative index of accuracy is the proportion of correct identifications that is made by a polygraph examiner when confronted repeatedly by pairs of random test outcomes, one of which is deceptive and the other truthful. For example, a polygraph examiner will make the correct choice 8 out of 10 times when using a test with ROC = 0.8. Its possible range is from 0.5 at the 'chance' diagonal to 1 and 'perfection' (Swets, 1996).

Other important concepts related to validity to bear in mind when considering studies on the accuracy of the polygraph are those of *internal* and *external validity*. *Internal validity* refers to whether studies have been sufficiently controlled for extraneous variables that may affect the accuracy of the test, typically a prospective design and the presence of control groups enhances a study's internal validity. The term *external validity* refers, on the other hand, to whether the findings from a study can actually be generalized to other contexts or circumstances (Grimm & Yarnold, 2000). *External validity* is enhanced when the testing conditions and the sample replicate the situations and participants that the polygraph would be used with.

POST-CONVICTION SEX OFFENDER TESTING

To date, only three studies have attempted to investigate the accuracy of the polygraph in a post-conviction context with sex offenders (see Table 9.2). In two of these studies, offenders were asked to complete a confidential survey asking them about their experiences with the polygraph. In the first, Kokish, Levenson and Blasingame (2005) approached 113 sex offenders engaged in treatment and also required to complete regular polygraph tests. In total, 95 offenders agreed to take part and reported having completed 404 tests, of which 337 were identified as truthful and 61 as deceptive. Only 6 tests were scored as inconclusive. According to the offender's self-report the polygraph accurately identified truth-telling (i.e., specificity) 92 % of the time and only wrongly accused offenders of lying (i.e., false-positive rate) on 8 % of such occasions. On the other hand, deception was accurately

Table 9.2 Polygraph accuracy rates in PCSOT studies

	Kokish, Levenson & Blasingame (2005) N = 95	Grubin & Madsen (2006) N = 121	Madsen & Grubin (2006) N = 51
Sensitivity (%)	82	84	100
False negative probability	18	16	0
Specificity (%)	92	85	79
False positive probability	8	15	21
Positive predictive value	69	47	29
Negative predictive value	97	97	100
Deception base rate	12	14	8

identified 82 % of the time (i.e., sensitivity), and the offenders claimed to have 'beaten' the polygraph on 18 % of occasions (i.e., false-negative rate). When considering only the accuracy of the individual test outcomes, the 'passed' outcomes were correct 97 % (i.e., negative predictive value) of the time, whereas the 'failed' outcomes were correct only 69 % (i.e., positive predictive value) of the time. These findings suggest that the offenders generally agreed with the outcomes of polygraph tests they had completed whilst in treatment.

It is, however, noteworthy that offenders in this study who had failed their most recent polygraph test were excluded. The researchers reasoned that this requirement would maximize the probability that participants were 'capable of passing a polygraph test'. This stipulation, however, creates an inherent sampling bias which is likely to inflate the 'agreement' rate, and hence, the reported accuracy of the procedure.

In a similar study, which did not discriminate between offenders who had failed or passed their most recent polygraph test, Grubin and Madsen (2006) asked a sample of 121 sex offenders about the instrument's accuracy. Broadly consistent with the results from the Kokish *et al.* (2005) study, in a total of 263 tests, the sensitivity of the polygraph was 84 % (false-positive rate = 16 %), and the specificity was 85 % (false-negative rate = 15 %). Ninety-seven percent of passed outcomes were correct, whilst only 47 % of failed outcomes were correct. The participants were also asked about their perception of the polygraph's accuracy. Seventy percent reported that they believed the polygraph to be 'moderately' to 'highly' accurate.

Taken together it would seem that offenders taking regular polygraph tests report the polygraph to be reasonably accurate. When considering such data it is important to recognize, however, that these questionnaire studies are likely to be complicated by a variety of biases that could affect the results in important ways. For instance, it would seem unlikely that offenders who are successfully 'beating' the polygraph (i.e., false negatives) would disclose doing so. Such offenders may be motivated to endorse the view that the polygraph is highly accurate and thus reduce the possibility that a 'passed' outcome would be viewed more skeptically. Similarly, some offenders may be anxious to please authority figures and under-report problems. Alternatively, offenders who are resentful at having to complete such tests may report false information in an attempt to undermine the acceptance of this procedure. Finally, it is possible that the actual methodology of the Comparison Question Test (see Chapter 4 for detailed description of this testing format) may predispose some individuals to believe they have in fact 'beaten' the polygraph. This is because most offenders would be unaware if they are being deceptive to the comparison or relevant issues. Because the distinction between these issues is not made for examinees it is possible that some may have believed that they had 'beaten' the polygraph when in reality they were 'lying' to the comparison questions. This effect, therefore, is likely to increase the self-reported false-negative rates. So whilst the data from these self-report studies present a somewhat optimistic view of the polygraph's accuracy, they are limited in important ways that curb the general value of the findings.

The most compelling type of accuracy study is an experimental field study. Only one study has attempted to experimentally investigate the polygraph's accuracy in a post-conviction context. In this investigation, Madsen and Grubin (2006) recruited community-based sex offenders in the US mandated to complete regular polygraph tests. The researchers arranged to include in the volunteers' regular polygraph test a question about drug use. (i.e., 'Over the last three months have you used any of the following illegal drugs?'). At the completion of this polygraph test the offenders were asked to supply a hair sample, which was subsequently analyzed for the drugs that they were questioned about during their test. By having blind examiners evaluate the charts it was possible to compare the objective drug test result with the polygraph result regarding drug use. Because illicit drug use could potentially incur significant sanctions for all the participants, this issue represented an authentic concern. Likewise for the examiners their performance could readily be evaluated, and it could be expected that they would be highly motivated. Utilizing this methodology, therefore, provided an opportunity to objectively examine the accuracy of the polygraph in a 'real-life' context for both the examinee and examiner.

Perhaps not surprisingly when considering the methodology used, only a small number of offenders (n = 5) were found to be taking drugs and lying about having done so. The examiners correctly identified four of these individuals, and scored the fifth as inconclusive. Overall the polygraph was reasonably accurate in identifying truth-telling (79 %), while 21 % were wrongly accused of drug-taking when their drug test indicated otherwise. The positive predictive value was only 29 %, whilst the negative predictive value was 100 %.

Follow-up analyses revealed that the offenders who were wrongly accused of lying were more likely to have previously experienced a sanction due to a polygraph test. This may suggest that for some individuals, having been punished due to a polygraph result might predispose them to react to the relevant issues at a later test.

Madsen and Grubin (2006) also compared the accuracy rates for the field and blind examiners. Notably, the field examiners were much less likely to evaluate examinees as inconclusive when compared to the blind examiners (6 % versus 27 %). They were, however, much less accurate with the sensitivity being only 40 % and the specificity 84 %. When considering the accuracy of the different test outcomes, similar to the blind examiners, failed (15 %) polygraph outcomes were much less likely to be accurate than passed (95 %) polygraph outcomes.

The poor reliability between the examiners suggested that the field examiners used additional information when analyzing the charts. The only feature that distinguished the false positives from the examinees accurately identified was the personality trait of extraversion. High scorers on this trait tend to be sociable and talkative, whilst low scorers are generally inclined to be introverted and reserved (Costa & McCrae, 1992). This finding perhaps indicates how the field examiners may have made their evaluations. The implication is that their determinations were based on their assessment of the examinees interpersonal behavior during the testing process. For example, examinees that were less talkative or forthcoming during the pre-test or post-test interviews might have been regarded with suspicion by examiner and subsequently failed.

Whilst these results are interesting, the low participant numbers limit the value of the findings. Only five individuals were identified to be lying about drug use. This low base rate of deception may have affected the results in important ways. For instance, in circumstances where base rates of deception are low, even a highly accurate test will produce more false than true positives (Murphy, 1987). For example, if only 10 % out of a sample of 1000 individuals are deceptive, a test that is 90 % accurate will correctly identify 90 of the 100 'liars', but it will also falsely label as 'liars' 90 of the 900 truth-tellers, resulting in 50 % of failed outcomes being incorrect. This phenomenon is illustrated with varying base rates and accuracy levels in Table 9.3. Thus, in the Madsen and Grubin (2006) study if the deception rate had been 50 % and everything else being equal, the positive predictive rates would have been 79 % (equal to the specificity).

It is important to bear in mind that because the polygraph was used to detect drug use, it might not generalize to actual sexual offending behaviors. In addition it is possible that the examiners' behavior (e.g., time spent discussing drug issue, presentation of questions) varied in important ways that may have affected the results. For example, an examiner that believes that the examinee is unlikely to be taking drugs because they have no drug abuse history or convictions may be motivated (either unconsciously or consciously) to produce a non-deceptive result. Such a bias, because of the very low base rate, would inflate the accuracy rate.

Table 9.3 The impact of base rates on the positive and negative predictive values at 90 % & 95 % accuracy

Sensitivity & Specificity 90 %

Deception Base Rates	Positive Predictive Value (Correct Deception Indicated)	Negative Predictive Value (Correct No Deception Indicated)
10 %	50 %	99 %
50 %	90 %	90 %
90 %	99 %	50 %

Sensitivity & Specificity 95 %

Deception Base Rates	Positive Predictive Value (Correct Deception Indicated)	Negative Predictive Value (Correct No Deception Indicated)
10 %	68 %	99 %
50 %	95 %	95 %
90 %	99 %	68 %

THE RESEARCH EVIDENCE FOR THE POLYGRAPH ACCURACY IN A PRE-CONVICTION CONTEXT

In the wider scientific literature the accuracy of the polygraph remains a contentious issue. At the core of much of this debate is the value of the different research methodologies used to investigate accuracy, these being field versus laboratory studies. *Field studies* are retrospective evaluations of the accuracy of 'real-life' polygraph tests conducted on criminal suspects. In these studies, the result of a polygraph test is compared with some other indicators of the 'truth', such as judicial outcomes. The two main problems with this approach are identifying who is actually lying, and then the bias introduced by the retrospective nature of the evaluation. *Laboratory studies* overcome these limitations by assigning volunteers to deceptive or non-deceptive categories. Because these studies involve simulations of crimes with volunteers who know they are participating in 'lie detection' research, it is debatable, however, whether the findings can be generalized to real-life contexts (Ben-Shakhar, 2002; Honts & Perry, 1992).

A number of substantive reviews have examined the evidence for the polygraph's accuracy. The most recent of these was conducted by the National Academy of Sciences (NAS) (2003), which was specifically charged with reviewing the polygraph's validity in relation to its use in personnel security screening. This review, amongst other things, concluded that the polygraph in certain circumstances (i.e., 'specific issue' testing and examinees being untrained in countermeasures) is likely to discriminate lying from truth-telling at rates well above chance, though well below perfection (National Research Council, 2003). However, the review highlighted that the general quality of studies examining the accuracy of the polygraph was poor, and suggested that the inherent limitations of the respective methodologies (i.e., field versus laboratory), has encumbered the development of a more robust body of evidence. Similarly, an earlier review conducted by the Office of Technology Assessment (OTA) (1983) concluded that the accuracy of the polygraph is difficult to assess and may vary widely between applications (i.e., criminal investigations versus security vetting). The NAS review further argued that in populations with extremely low base rates (e.g., spies in a national security organization) large numbers of innocent employees would fail, and thus, be implicated in such behavior. Partly because of these issues both of these reviews recommended against using the polygraph for security screening.

Without going into the pros and cons of the various arguments regarding polygraphy in security settings, it should be recognized that the issues are not identical in post-conviction contexts as there are a number of important differences between the two applications. Firstly, the base rate of deception in sex offender samples is likely to be much higher. Indeed, as highlighted in Chapter 4, research has suggested that up to 90 % of offenders are dishonest about their offending behavior and offence history during treatment (e.g., Barbaree, 1991; Maletzky, 1991). Of course this does give rise to a somewhat paradoxical situation that the more honest the examinees are the less confident one can be with a 'Deception Indicated' result. Secondly, in post-conviction contexts the emphasis is less on 'passing' or 'failing' the polygraph and more on gaining information relevant to the offender's supervision and treatment. Finally, the consequences associated with inaccurate outcomes in pre-conviction contexts are different to those in post-conviction settings. In a pre-conviction context, for example, innocent examinees could have their career terminated or interrupted, whilst in a post-conviction context consequences are comparatively minor (e.g., addressing additional issues in treatment, additional supervision sessions, etc.).

RESEARCH EVIDENCE FROM FIELD STUDIES

As briefly highlighted above, field studies are commonly 'real-life' situations, such as a criminal investigation. In these studies, 'accuracy' is usually based on gaining a confession, the outcome of an investigation or on the recording of a conviction. Critics of such research have asserted that the inability to assure criterion validity (i.e., knowing who is really lying) limit the value of the findings. For instance, using polygraph elicited confessions can be problematic. The polygraph examiner typically elicits confessions when they confront an individual in the post-test interview after a 'failed' test result. Participants that 'pass' are unlikely to be confronted in a similar manner. Thus deceptive examinees that pass the polygraph (i.e., false negative) are excluded from the research. Similarly, innocent individuals wrongly accused of lying (false positive) are also excluded from the research, because there is no confession. Examinees that confess in the pre-test interview also cannot be included in the research because they did not complete the test. Reliance on an examinees' post-test confession as a criterion for accuracy is, therefore, likely to artificially inflate overall accuracy rate.

Another concern with field studies is that due to their retrospective nature, the internal validity is likely to be low. Extraneous factors that may affect polygraph outcomes cannot be controlled. It is conceivable, for instance, that the examiner's decision can be 'contaminated' by other information. In real-life criminal investigations polygraph examiners are typically aware of, and have access to, other information related to the suspect. This could include victim statements, medical evidence, police intelligence, impressions of other investigators and records of previous convictions (Saxe, Dougherty & Cross, 1985). Thus it is unclear whether an examiner's decision is based solely upon the physiological data gained during the polygraph test.

The scientific merit of field studies can be appraised by considering four factors: sample; sampling strategy; polygraph evaluations; and criterion development. Firstly, the sample must represent the population for generalization. Secondly, cases should be selected randomly without reference to the accuracy of the original examiner's decision or to the quality of the physiological data. Thirdly, the outcome of the polygraph should be exclusively determined by the physiological data, with information about the case facts or other pertinent details withheld from the examiner. Finally, the truthfulness of the subjects must be confirmed by a criterion independent from the outcome of the polygraph examination. It is important to recognize that whilst these criteria may go some way to improve the quality of field studies, they do not overcome the inherent problems associated with these studies (Honts & Quick, 1995; National Research Council, 2003).

In the review conducted by the Office of Technology Assessment (1983), nine field studies evaluating the comparison question test (CQT) were considered. All polygraph tests had been conducted with suspects in criminal investigations for a range of crimes including sexual assault, theft and homicide. Two studies used panel decisions for determining criterion validity, while the remainder used confession. Unfortunately, none of the studies met all the previous mentioned criteria. Kleinmuntz and Szucko (1984), for instance, used 'trainee' examiners and only completed one polygraph chart, as opposed to the standard three. A number of other studies used global chart evaluations rather than blind numerical scoring procedures (Bersh, 1969; Hunter & Ash, 1973; Slowik & Buckley, 1975; Wicklander & Hunter, 1975).

The sensitivity of these studies ranged from 70 to 98 %, with a mean of 86 % and a mean false-negative rate of 11 %. Specificity displayed greater variability with a range from 12 to 94 %, the overall mean being 76 %, and a mean false-positive rate of 19 %. Inconclusive polygraph results for both liars and truth-tellers ranged between 0 and 25 %, with the means being 2 % and 5 % respectively. Further analysis showed that a 'failed' polygraph result was accurate 82 % of the time (i.e., the positive predictive value), whilst a 'passed' polygraph test was correct 87 % of the time (i.e., the negative predictive value).

Since this time, an additional four studies have been conducted that met the above-mentioned criteria (Honts, 1996; Honts & Raskin, 1988; Patrick & Iacono, 1991; Raskin *et al.*, 1988). When considered together, the sensitivity for these studies, similar to the OTA review, ranged from 73 % to 100 %, with the mean being 89 % and false-negative rate only 1 %. Specificity was only 59 % with the range being between 30 % and 83 %, and the false-positive rate 10 %. It was also notable that there was a significantly higher rate of inconclusive test results for 'truth-tellers' when compared to 'liars' (29 versus 10). Ninety percent of failed polygraph tests were correct, whilst 98 % of the passed polygraph results were correct.

The National Research Council (2003) evaluated 194 studies and identified only seven field studies that passed their minimal scientific criteria. This included six studies on the CQT. The inclusion criteria used by this review, in addition to the previously described conditions, also required studies to report the questions, physiological measures, instrumentation and scoring methods used. Again a large variation in the accuracy was observed between the different studies with the Receiver Operating Characteristic (ROC) being between .71 and .99, and the median value being .89.

RESEARCH EVIDENCE FROM LABORATORY STUDIES

Laboratory studies, on the other hand, are investigations in which field methods of polygraph examinations are used in simulated criminal situations. Such studies investigate either mock crimes set up by an experimenter with knowledge and collaboration of some participants or actual small crimes induced by the experimenter (Kircher, Horowitz & Raskin, 1988; Patrick & Iacono, 1989). Criterion validity is assured because the researcher sets up the crime. Such studies are not, however, actual criminal investigations and participants are usually aware that they are participating in research. They are often students who have little to lose by 'failing' a polygraph test.

Critics, such as Fiedler, Schmidt and Stahl (2002) have generally dismissed the value of such studies for estimating field accuracy because of the substantial differences that exist between laboratory settings and real-life situations. In the laboratory, the guilty participants usually do not have much at stake, and are aware that, whatever the result of the polygraph test, they will be released from further involvement with the 'crime'. By contrast the stakes are higher in real-life scenarios, and the examinee is likely to be greatly concerned about the outcome of the polygraph test, whether he or she is guilty or innocent. The emotional 'environment' between the two testing situations is, therefore, vastly different.

The OTA (1983) review considered 20 laboratory studies. The majority of these studies had been conducted with university students, four used paid volunteers, and single studies used inmates, psychiatric patients or police candidates. For the CQT, sensitivity was 64 % (range 37 to 100), and the false-negative rate 10 % (range 0 to 29). Specificity was 57 % (range 33 to 100), and the false-positive rate 14 % (range 0 to 50). Inconclusive polygraph results for both liars and truth-tellers ranged between 0 and 50 %, with average rates being 22 % and 27 % respectively. Two studies had notably less than 12 participants in the lying condition (Dawson, 1980; Ginton *et al.*, 1982). The positive predictive value for these studies was 82 %, whereas the negative predictive value was 85 %.

Since this review, a number of laboratory studies have been completed that are worthy of mention. Patrick and Iacono (1989) evaluated the accuracy of the CQT with incarcerated inmates as participants in a threatening context. In this study, the participants were led to believe that their personal performance could decide benefits or penalties for the sample as a whole. They were told specifically that if they failed the group would lose all rewards and they would be named to the other participants. Patrick and Iacono reasoned that because of the potential for physical violence, participants would be highly motivated to pass the polygraph test. Overall, the study reported a high sensitivity rate of 92 % and a low false-negative rate of 2 %. Innocent participants were, however, only correctly identified in 30 % of cases, and were wrongly accused of lying 24 % of the time. Inconclusive rates were also greater for innocent participants (46 % versus 6 %). This data suggest that the increased threat might be critical factor in false-positive and inconclusive rates.

Honts and Peterson (1997) filed an *amicus curiae* with the Supreme Court in the US. They reported on nine laboratory studies of the CQT, and consistent with the earlier OTA (1983) review, there was large variation in the rates reported by the different studies, with sensitivity ranging between 53 to 100 % (M = 80 %) and specificity between 75 to 90 % (M = 84 %). The mean for both false-negative and positive rates was 8 %, with the positive predictive value being 90 % and the negative predictive value 91 %.

The National Research Council review considered 52 studies. This review included many of the studies also used in the OTA (1983) and the Honts and Peterson (1997) reviews. In addition, various unpublished studies by the Department of Defense Polygraph Institute (DoDPI) were also included. The results indicated overall that the accuracy ranged between .81 and .91, with the median being .86 (National Research Council, 2002).

A GOOD ACCURACY STUDY

To date there is only one published study that appears to have overcome the inherent limitations of both field and laboratory studies. In this study, Ginton, Daie, Elaad and Ben-Shakhar (1982) gave an aptitude test to 21 policemen taking part in a course. The participants were led to believe that this test was potentially important for their careers. The researchers set up the situation so that each participant had an opportunity to 'cheat', not knowing that the researchers could identify the ones that did so. In total seven participants cheated. All 21 participants were subsequently recalled and told that it was believed some of them had cheated on the test and all would be required to complete a polygraph exam. They were further told that the results of the polygraph could affect their careers. Three of the seven cheaters confessed immediately, another two cheaters and one innocent participant refused to take the polygraph. In total, therefore, only 15 of the 21 original participants took the polygraph test – 2 cheaters and 13 non-cheaters.

The original examiner, utilizing both chart information and the behavior of the participant during the test, correctly identified both cheaters and also 11 of the 13 non-cheaters. Two truthful participants were wrongly accused of cheating. Blind re-scoring of these charts by 8 other examiners correctly identified the 2 cheaters 15 out of 16 times. For the innocent participants, there was greater variability. On average these participants were correctly identified 81% of the time, and wrongly accused of cheating 17% of the time. With consideration of the original examiner's decisions, even though his false-negative rate was 0 and his false-positive rate was 17%, when he said an individual was deceptive he was only correct two out of four, or 50%, of the time. Interestingly, one of the false positives, when interviewed after the study, reported that he had been focusing (unintentionally) upon a previous incident of cheating (A. Ginton, personal communication, August 4, 2004). This suggests that it is perhaps the saliency of an issue that contributes to an individual's reacting to the relevant issue.

The small participant numbers in Ginton's study make it impossible to say anything about the overall accuracy of the polygraph; however, the study does further illustrate the inherent difficulties associated with evaluating the polygraph.

SURVEYS OF EXPERT OPINION

It is worth noting that proponents and opponents have also presented findings from various surveys as evidence of the polygraph's value or lack thereof (Iacono & Lykken, 1997; Raskin *et al.*, 1997). A telephone survey by the Gallup Organization (1984), for example, found that 62% of the polled members ($n = 152$) from the Society of Psychophysiological Research believed that the polygraph was a 'useful diagnostic tool when considered with other available information'. Only three percent believed that the polygraph as a method of lie detection was of no use. Amato and Honts (1994) replicated these findings in an identical survey study. By contrast, two later surveys conducted by Iacono and Lykken (1997), also with members from the Society of Psychophysiological Research, found that only 36% in one, and 30% in the other, agreed that, 'the CQT is based on scientifically sound psychological principles or theory' (p. 430). This apparent discrepancy in professional opinion may, however, be due to their respective foci rather than reflect a shift in attitudes.

The earlier surveys conducted by the Gallup Organization and Amato and Honts (1994) addressed the utility of the polygraph as an aid to decision-making while the latter studies by Iacono and Lykken

(1997) focused upon the underlying theory of the CQT. When considering the issue of utility two broad conclusions can be drawn from the literature on 'lie detection': firstly, people are poor lie-catchers and are generally not able to detect deception at a rate better than random chance (Vrij, 2004); secondly, despite the confusing literature, there does seem to be a general trend that under normal circumstances, the polygraph produces better than chance success rates, and, in some circumstances actually appears to be quite accurate. It would seem reasonable, therefore, to conclude that if nothing else the polygraph could be a helpful aid in lie detection. With regards to the theory of the CQT, however, this is poorly developed and has not been subjected to sustained or rigorous scientific investigation. It would accordingly be difficult to endorse the view that this is based on 'scientifically sound psychological principles or theory'.

UNPUBLISHED EVIDENCE

Finally, it is valuable to consider unpublished and anecdotal evidence on the polygraph's accuracy. It is conceivable, for instance, that due to non-significant findings studies have not been published, and therefore are not easily able to contribute to the evidence base. In an early study which perhaps considers such evidence Abrams (1973) reviewed reports of the polygraph's accuracy dating to 1917, these included a large number of unpublished and anecdotal reports as well as experimental data. He calculated approximate estimates of overall accuracy from this data, noting however, 'it is almost meaningless to total and average these findings because of the great discrepancy in experimental paradigms and the instruments employed' (p. 316). Nonetheless, he reported that in studies where criterion validity was assured, the polygraph was 100 % correct. In field reports prior to 1963, Abrams calculated an accuracy rate of 98 %. In laboratory experiments prior to 1963, Abrams estimated the average accuracy rate of 81 %. Averaging the results of the reports between 1963 and 1973, Abrams' estimate of laboratory and field research accuracy was 83 % and 98 %, respectively.

In reality, these findings are of limited value because there is such variability in the technique and instruments used, the participants tested, and also the criteria for establishing criterion validity. In addition, many of the biases discussed earlier are likely to have inflated the accuracy observed in the reports that Abrams included in his review.

The more recent review by the National Academy of Science (NAS) (2003) utilized a particularly vigorous methodology to gain as much as possible of the published and unpublished polygraph accuracy literature. In addition to the more traditional literature searches using computerized databases, such as PsycLIT, Medline and so forth, they sent requests to a variety of individuals and organizations that they believed may have relevant research reports. These requests were sent to government organizations and agencies, polygraph websites and various researchers. The individuals contacted were also asked to forward their request to other professionals who may have potentially useful information. Indeed the NAS review deliberately attempted to limit the possibility of a 'publication bias' by being as inclusive as possible, and sought out studies regardless of whether or not they had undergone peer review.

In total 217 reports were collected of which 194 were identified as unique studies. Notably they highlighted that these studies varied greatly in the quality of research design, choice and standardization of measurement techniques, thoroughness of control of confounding variables, statistical analyses and various other factors. They evaluated these studies using the criteria described earlier (i.e., documentation to allow sufficient replication; independent verification of truth; blind scoring, and so on) and found that only 57 studies met their basic scientific criteria. Of these, 31 studies were gained from peer review journals, 7 were either unpublished studies or dissertations and 19 were reports submitted to government agencies or the like (i.e., Department of Defense Polygraph Institute). Taken together, these findings suggest that there is not a great deal of unpublished research on the polygraph's accuracy that is of sufficient scientific merit to contribute to the debate.

FACTORS LIKELY TO AFFECT THE ACCURACY OF THE POLYGRAPH

Countermeasures

Countermeasures are deliberate techniques used by examinees to produce a 'truthful' outcome on a polygraph test. The major types of countermeasures include drugs and alcohol, mental (such as meditation) and physical strategies (such as inducing pain). Numerous publications (e.g., Maschke & Scalabrini, 2000) and websites (e.g., `www.antipolygraph.org`) provide detailed information about how such strategies can be utilized to produce a non-deceptive polygraph result. As Maschke and Scalabrini (2000) suggest when referring to the CQT, '... the key to passing a polygraph test ... is to produce stronger physiological responses when answering control (comparison) questions than when answering the relevant questions' (p. 68). Most of the physical countermeasures described in the literature are consistently designed to augment responses to comparison questions. For instance, there are a number of subtle ways for examinees to induce pain when responding to these questions, such as by pressing on a tack placed in their shoe. Doing so during the data collection phase of the test would theoretically mimic the physiological profile of a truthful examinee.

Mental countermeasures have also been suggested as a method for enhancing responses to comparison questions. Maschke and Scalabrini (2000) suggest using arousing mental imagery during the comparison questions, such as thinking about falling off a cliff.

Numerous studies have also demonstrated that countermeasures can reduce the accuracy of the CQT. Honts, Raskin and Kircher (1994), for example, trained 80 participants to apply physical means (biting tongue) or mental countermeasures (counting backwards from 100 by sevens), while the comparison questions were being presented during their examinations. The mental and physical countermeasures were equally effective. Each enabled 50 % of the participants to erroneously pass the polygraph test (i.e., 42 % of countermeasure participants correctly classified compared with 75 % guilty non-countermeasure participants). The researchers reported, moreover, that the countermeasures were difficult to detect through observation. These findings are consistent with other studies in the area suggesting that training examinees in a combination of physical and mental countermeasures can substantially decrease the likelihood that deceptive participants will be detected by the polygraph (Honts, 1986; Honts, Hodes & Raskin, 1985; Honts, Raskin & Kircher, 1987, 1994; Honts *et al.*, 1996). All these studies have involved only short periods of training for examinees.

Like the research investigating accuracy, there are a number of important limitations worth noting. All the studies have involved mock crime scenarios where the examiners are researchers, and the examinees are volunteers. Again it is questionable whether the results can be applied to real-life circumstances, where the examiner is likely to be a skilled and experienced interviewer, and the consequences of failing the test for the examinee are high. It is possible, therefore, that the results from these studies overestimate the effectiveness of countermeasures.

A curious omission in the research on countermeasures is that no study has attempted to investigate the physiological correlates or features of the actual countermeasures. It is possible that utilizing countermeasures such as inducing pain would produce specific physiological profiles that are distinct from other physiological responses. Barland (2003) has presented anecdotal evidence suggesting that specific countermeasures display unique physiological features.

In response to the issue of countermeasures, polygraph practitioners have generally claimed that a skilled examiner is capable of identifying when an examinee is attempting to influence the polygraph recordings through movement or other methods (D. Sosnowski, personal communication, January 24th, 2004). This claim would appear more credible if there was actual research demonstrating the known physiological features for specific countermeasures. The polygraph manufacturer, Lafayette, has recently developed 'movement sensors', which it claims, can detect the use of physical countermeasures (`www.lafayetteinstrument.com`). Again, however, these claims have not been substantiated by any published research.

Expectations

Research within social psychology has shown that the expectations an individual holds can unconsciously affect their behavior and also the behavior of others. Perhaps the most well-known example of this phenomenon is the so-called 'Pygmalion effect'. This describes how a teacher's initial expectations about specific students can affect the student's future performance and behavior in the classroom and on standardized tests. It could be similarly expected that an examiner's expectation could influence the outcome of a polygraph test. Darley and Gross (1983) identified two forms of 'biases' that could affect a polygraph examiner's judgments and behavior – the '*cognitive confirmation effect*' and the '*behavioral confirmation effect*'.

The '*cognitive confirmation effect*' describes how an examiner's beliefs and expectations may influence the interpretation of ambiguous information. For example, if an examiner believes that an examinee is 'innocent', he may interpret information in a manner that confirms this assumption. For examinees considered deceptive or guilty, the converse could be expected to happen. Indirect evidence for the 'cognitive' confirmation bias can be derived from a number of sources. In a small study for example, Barland (1975) reported that in 17 out of 19 cases polygraph examiners who gave evaluations on an examinee's truthfulness based on information available to them prior to the administration of a polygraph test, maintained these conclusions after administering a polygraph test.

A second, and perhaps more dramatic example of this phenomenon, was provided by a CBS production of '60 minutes' broadcast in 1986. In this television program, three different polygraph examiners were independently approached to test for an alleged theft of a camera and lens from an office employing four employees. The polygraph examiners were told that only four employees had access to the equipment, which, therefore, must have been stolen by one of them. They were also told which one was most likely to have stolen the equipment, but that there was no evidence to prove this. In reality, no equipment was stolen, and each examiner was given a different name for the thief. All of the polygraph examiners examined each of the four employees using the CQT procedure and all reached the confident conclusion that the employee that had been named to them as the suspected thief had lied during the polygraph investigation, while the three others had spoken the truth. This anecdotal example provides a vivid demonstration of the possible impact of examiner biases on the outcome of CQT examinations, but again only a limited number of studies have empirically evaluated this phenomenon (Ben-Shakhar, 2002).

Elaad, Ginton and Ben-Shakhar (1994), in a study investigating the scoring of charts, manipulated the prior expectations of polygraph examiners by telling half the examiners that the suspect had confessed. The results indicated that prior expectations did have an impact on the examiner's judgments, although only when the charts were initially scored to be inconclusive. There was no effect for charts that were originally evaluated as either being deceptive or being truthful. In a follow-up study, Elaad, Ginton and Ben-Shakhar (1998) again manipulated the expectations of the polygraph examiner, although this time over the entire CQT examination. In this study, seven experienced polygraph examiners tested four innocent participants suspected of cheating on an aptitude test. The examiners were led to believe that two of the participants were probably guilty, and the other two were probably innocent. This manipulation had no discernable effect. It is of course possible that the examiners in the study were skeptical about the true purpose of the research. The evidence is too limited overall to enable one to draw any clear conclusions about whether examiner's expectations affect polygraph outcomes.

The '*behavioral confirmation effect*' refers to the effect of expectations on the behavior of the individual towards others. In the context of a polygraph examination, the effect occurs when an examiner develops a 'gut feeling' about the suspect's guilt or innocence, and then subconsciously influences the measurements to match this belief. For example, an examiner may present the questions in a different manner when he believes that the examinee is deceptive from when he believes he is testing a truthful suspect. This theoretical limitation has been recognized by several proponents, including Honts and Perry (1992) who point out:

> An examiner motivated to produce a deceptive result might ask over general or provocative relevant questions, and spend a great deal of

> time on their review and presentation. Subsequently, this unethical examiner could ask very narrow, specific, or inappropriate control questions and spend very little time on their review and presentation. An examiner predisposed to produce a truthful result could take the opposite approach. (p. 372)

The American Polygraph Association (APA) attempts to address problems of 'examiner bias' by emphasizing the importance of an impartial standardized approach (`www.polygraph.org/standards.htm`). It is perhaps also noteworthy, that while this concern is plausible because of the lack of research that has been conducted, it remains only speculation.

Personality

A limited number of studies have evaluated the impact of personality characteristics on the accuracy of the polygraph. Investigating 'normal' personality traits, Giesen and Rollison (1980) found that participants who described themselves as anxious responded stronger than participants identifying themselves as non-anxious on the CIT. Bradley and Klohn (1987) similarly showed that participants high in Machiavellianism (i.e., 'able to focus more directly on the relevant aspects of a situation', p. 747) displayed greater physiological responsivity when guilty than when innocent. Early studies, however, by Janisse and Bradley (1980) and Oksenberg (1970) had failed to find an effect for Machiavellianism. Other studies have generally failed to find effects for normal personality characteristics. Gudjonsson (1982), for example, found no relationship between personality traits as evaluated by numerous inventories, and the accuracy of the CIT. Bradley and Rettinger (1992) also found no difference between subjects high and low in their propensity to monitor their own social demeanor, a characteristic of social anxiety.

Waid, Orne and Wilson (1979) investigated the impact of socialization on the accuracy of the CQT in a mock crime scenario. They found that the three guilty participants who were misclassified (i.e., false negative) scored significantly lower on a socialization scale than the 12 guilty participants who were correctly classified. By contrast, innocent participants who were false positives had significantly higher socialization scores than the participants who were correctly classified, and also, the false negatives. The study tentatively concluded that poorly socialized individuals might be prone to false-negative errors, whilst highly socialized individuals may be prone to false-positive errors. This finding has not been replicated by other studies. Raskin, Barland and Podlesny

(1976), for example, failed to find any relationship between outcomes on the CQT and psychopathy (a construct related to socialization) as defined by the Pd scale of the Minnesota Multiphasic Personality Inventory (MMPI). In another study, Raskin and Hare (1978) reported on a laboratory experiment that utilized a mock crime scenario with psychopathic and non-psychopathic criminals as participants. Consistent with the Raskin *et al.* (1976) study, there was no difference between the groups, and indeed, all the deceptive psychopaths were correctly identified. Hammond (1980) also found no difference between a student sample, psychopaths and alcoholics in a mock crime scenario. Similarly, neither Honts, Raskin and Kircher (1985) or Patrick and Iacono (1986, 1989) found that socialization or psychopathy affected the accuracy of the polygraph.

The limited number of studies that have investigated the impact of personality have tended to show that this is probably not an important factor influencing polygraph results, although again, it would be premature to conclude that personality has no effect as two studies did find an effect.

CONCLUSIONS

The review of laboratory and field studies shows that there is considerable variability in the reported accuracy of the polygraph. This variation makes it impossible to make any precise quantitative estimate regarding the polygraph's accuracy. Broadly speaking, though, it would seem that at least in some circumstances the polygraph is highly accurate. However, in other circumstances innocent individuals may be prone to be branded deceptive. Overall, the quality of the studies varies considerably, and falls far short of what would be ideal. *Field studies*, for instance, cannot guarantee criterion validity and have problems with internal validity, whilst *laboratory studies* have problems with external validity. Survey studies evaluating the opinions of scientists in relevant fields, have further illuminated the lack of agreement, and perhaps, confusion within the scientific community regarding the value of the polygraph.

It is important to recognize that all of the literature discussed above has examined polygraph tests conducted in a pre-conviction capacity; generalization from them to uses for post-conviction treatment and supervision is not justified. In reality little can be said about the polygraph accuracy in a post-conviction context. It appears that when asked, sex offenders have tended to agree with the outcomes of the tests they have completed whilst in treatment. In the only experimental study, Madsen and Grubin (2006) found that the polygraph was reasonably accurate in detecting drug use, however, only when the charts were scored blindly. Nonetheless, examinees were more likely to be a false positive, and failed outcomes were also less reliable. Notably, imposing penalties for a specific test outcome may create a de facto involuntary condition that increases the chances of invalid or inconclusive test results on a later test. Thus applying sanctions for different test outcomes would mean that some offenders would be unjustly sanctioned for wrong outcomes. To reduce the probability of such a situation the polygraph could be viewed as a type of 'red flag' or warning mechanism. In such a situation a failed outcome should prompt further investigation by some other means, such as follow-up interviews or surveillance.

REFERENCES

Abrams, S. (1973). Polygraph validity and reliability: A review. *Journal of Forensic Sciences*, *17*, 313–327.

Abrams S. & Ogard E. (1986). Polygraph surveillance of probationers. *Polygraph*, *15*, 174–182.

Ahlmeyer, S., Heil, M., McKee, B., & English, K. (2000). The impact of polygraphy on admissions of victims and offenses in adult sexual offenders. *Sexual Abuse: A Journal of Research and Treatment*, *12*, 123–138.

Amato, S.L. & Honts, C.R. (1994). What do psychophysiologists think about polygraph tests? A survey of the membership of SPR. *Psychophysiology*, *31*, S 22.

Barbaree, H.E. (1991). Denial and minimization among sex offenders: Assessment and treatment outcome. *Forum on Corrections research*, *3*, 30–33.

Barland, G.H. (1975). Detection of deception in criminal suspects: A field validation study. Unpublished doctoral dissertation, University of Utah.

Barland, G.H. (2003). *Identifying countermeasures: More important today than ever*. Presentation to the Annual Seminar of the American Polygraph Association, Reno, NV, August.

Ben-Shakhar, G. (2002). A critical review of the control question test (CQT). In M. Kleiner (Ed.), *Handbook of Polygraph Testing* (pp. 103–126). London: Academic Press.

Bersh, P.L. (1969). A validation study of polygraph examiner judgements. *Journal of Applied Psychology*, *53*, 399–403.

Bradley, M.T. & Klohn, K. (1987). Machiavellianism, the control question test and the detection of deception. *Perceptual and Motor Skills*, *64*, 747–757.

Bradley, M.T. & Rettinger, J. (1992). Awareness of crime relevant information and the guilty knowledge test. *Journal of Applied Psychology*, *77* (1), 55–59.

Costa, P.T. & McCrae, R.R. (1992). *Revised NEO Personality Inventory (NEO-PI-R) and NEO Five-Factor Inventory (NEO-FFI) Professional Manual*. Odessa, FL: Psychological Assessment Resources.

Darley, J.M. & Gross, P.H. (1983). A hypothesis-confirming bias in labeling effects. *Journal of Personality and Social Psychology*, *44*, 20–33.

Dawson, M.E. (1980). Physiological detection of deception: Measurement of responses to questions and answers during countermeasure maneuvers. *Psychophysiology*, *17*, 8–17.

Edson, C. (1991). *Sex Offender Treatment*. Medford, OR: Department of Corrections.
Elaad, E., Ginton, A., & Ben-Shakhar, G. (1994). The effects of prior expectations and outcome knowledge on polygraph examiners' decisions. *Journal of Behavioral Decision Making*, *7*, 279–292.
Elaad, E., Ginton, A., & Ben-Shakhar, G. (1998). The role of prior expectations in polygraph examiners' decisions. *Psychology, Crime and Law*, *4*, 1–16.
Emerick, R.L. & Dutton, W.A. (1993). The effect of polygraphy on the self-report of adolescent sex offenders: Implications for risk assessment. *Annals of Sex Research*, *6*, 84–103.
English, K., Jones, L., Pasini-Hill, D., & Cooley-Towell, S. (2000). The Value of Polygraph Testing in Sex Offender Management. Research report submitted to the National Institute of Justice. Colorado: Colorado Department of Public Safety.
Fiedler, K., Schmidt, J., & Stahl, T. (2002). What is the current truth about polygraph lie detection? *Basic and Applied Social Psychology*, *24*, 313–324.
The Gallup Organization (1984). Survey of members of the Society for Psychophysiological Research concerning their opinions of polygraph test interpretation. *Polygraph*, *13*, 153–165.
Giesen, M. & Rollison, M.A. (1980). Guilty knowledge versus innocent associations: Effects of trait anxiety and stimulus context on skin conductance. *Journal of Research in Personality*, *14*, 1–11.
Ginton, A., Netzer, D., Elaad, E., & Ben-Shakhar, G. (1982). A method for evaluating the use of the polygraph in a real-life situation. *Journal of Applied Psychology*, *67*, 131–137.
Grimm, L.G. & Yarnold, P.R. (Eds) (2000). *Reading and Understanding More Multivariate Statistics*. Washington, DC: American Psychological Association.
Grubin, D. & Madsen, L. (2005). Lie detection and the polygraph: A historical review. *Journal of Forensic Psychiatry and Psychology*, *16*, 357–369.
Grubin, D. & Madsen, L. (2006). The utility and accuracy of Post-Conviction Polygraph Testing with sex offenders. *British Journal of Psychiatry*, *188*, 479–483.
Grubin, D., Madsen, L., Parsons, S., Sosnowski, D., & Warberg, B. (2004). A prospective study of the impact of polygraphy on high risk behaviors in adult sex offenders. *Sexual Abuse: A Journal of Research and Treatment*, *16*, 209–222.
Gudjonsson, G.H. (1982). Some psychological determinants of electrodermal responses to deception. *Personality and Individual Differences*, *3*, 381–391.
Hammond, D. (1980). The Responding of Normals, Alcoholics, and Psychopaths in a Laboratory Lie-Detection Experiment, a PhD dissertation submitted to the California School of Professional Psychology, San Diego.
Heil, P., Ahlmeyer, S., & Simons, D. (2003). Crossover sexual offenses. *Sexual Abuse: A Journal of Research and Treatment*, *15*, 221–236.
Hindman, J., & Peters, J. (2001). Polygraph testing leads to better understanding adult and juvenile sex offenders. *Federal Probation*, *65*, 8–15.
Honts, C.R. (1986). Countermeasures and the physiological detection of deception: A psychophysiological analysis. *Dissertation Abstracts International*, *47*, 1761B.
Honts, C.R. (1996). Criterion development and validity of the control question test in field application. *The Journal of General Psychology*, *123*, 309–324.

Honts, C.R., Devitt, M.K., Winbush, M., & Kircher, J.C. (1996). Mental and physical countermeasures reduce the accuracy of the concealed knowledge test. *Psychophysiology*, *33*, 84–92.

Honts, C.R., Hodes, R.L., & Raskin, D.C. (1985). Effects of physical countermeasures on the physiological detection of deception. *Journal of Applied Social Psychology*, *70*, 177–187.

Honts, C.R. & Perry, M.V. (1992). Polygraph admissibility. *Law and Human Behavior*, *16*, 357–379.

Honts, C.R. & Peterson, C.F. (1997). Brief of the Committee of Concerned Social Scientists as Amicus Curiae. *United States v. Scheffer*, in the Supreme Court of the United States. Retrieved from www.truth.boisestate.edu/polygraph/polylaw.

Honts, C.R. & Quick, B.D. (1995). The polygraph in 1995: Progress in science and the law. *North Dakota Law Review*, *71*, 987–1020.

Honts, C.R. & Raskin, D.C. (1988). A field study of the validity of the directed lie control question. *Journal of Police Science and Administration*, *16*, 56–61.

Honts, C.R., Raskin, D.C., & Kircher, J.C. (1985). Effects of socialisation on the physiological detection of deception. *Journal of Research in Personality*, *19*, 373–385.

Honts, C.R., Raskin, D.C., & Kircher, J.C. (1987). Effects of physical countermeasures and their electromyographic detection during polygraph tests for deception. *Journal of Psychophysiology*, *1*, 241–247.

Honts, C.R., Raskin, D., & Kircher, J.C. (1994). Mental and physical countermeasures reduce the accuracy of polygraph tests. *Journal of Applied Psychology*, *79*, 252–259.

Hunter, F.L. & Ash, P. (1973). The accuracy and consistency of polygraph examiners' diagnoses. *Journal of Police Science and Administration*, *1*, 370–375.

Iacono, W.G. & Lykken, D.T. (1997). The validity of the lie detector: Two surveys of scientific opinion. *Journal of Applied Psychology*, *82*, 426–433.

Janisse, M.P. & Bradley, M.T. (1980). Deception, information and the pupillary response. *Perceptual and Motor Skills*, *50*, 748–750.

Kircher, J.C., Horowitz, S.W., & Raskin, D.C. (1988). Meta-analysis of mock crime studies of the control question polygraph technique. *Law and Human Behaviour*, *12*, 79–90.

Kleinmuntz, B. & Szucko, J.J. (1984). Lie detection in ancient and modern times. *American Psychologist*, *39*, 766–776.

Kokish, R., Levenson, J.S., & Blasingame, G.D. (2005). Post-conviction sex offender polygraph examination: Client-reported perceptions of utility and accuracy. *Sexual Abuse: A Journal of Research and Treatment*, *17*, 211–221.

Madsen, L. & Grubin, D. (2006). Accuracy and utility of post-conviction polygraph testing with community-based sex offenders. *The British Journal of Psychiatry*, *188*, 479–483.

Madsen, L., Parsons, S., & Grubin, D. (2004). A preliminary study of the contribution of periodic polygraph testing to the treatment and supervision of sex offenders. *British Journal of Forensic Psychiatry and Psychology*, *15*, 682–695.

Maletzky, B.M. (1991). *Treating the Sexual Offender*. Newbury Park, CA: Sage Publications.

Maschke, G.W. & Scalabrini, G.J. (2000). *The Lie Behind the Lie Detector*. Available electronically from http://antipolygraph.org/lie-behind-the-lie-detector.pdf.

McCann, J.T. (1998). *Malingering and Deception in Adolescents: Assessing Credibility in Clinical and Forensic Settings*. Washington: American Psychological Association.

Murphy, K.R. (1987). Detecting infrequent deception. *Journal of Applied Psychology*, *72*, 611–614.

National Academy of Sciences (NAS) (2003). *The polygraph and lie detection*. Washington, DC: National Academies Press.

National Research Council (2002). *The polygraph and lie detection*. Washington, DC: National Academies Press.

Oksenberg, L. (1970). Machiavellianism and emotionality. In R. Christie & F.L. Geis (Eds.), *Studies in Machiavellianism* (p. 396). New York: Academic Press.

Office of Technology Assessment (1983). *Scientific Validity of Polygraph Testing: A Research Review and Evaluation – A Technical Memorandum*. OTA-TM-H-15. Washington, DC: US Government Printing Office.

Patrick, C. & Iacono, W. (1989). Psychopathy, threat, and polygraph test accuracy. *Journal of Applied Psychology*, *74*, 347–355.

Patrick, C.J. & Iacono, W.G. (1991). A comparison of field and laboratory polygraphs in the detection of deception. *Psychophysiology*, *28*, 632–638.

Raskin, D.C. & Hare, R.D. (1978). Psychopathy and detection of deception in a prison population. *Psychophysiology*, *15*, 126–136.

Raskin, D.C., Barland, G.H., & Podlesny, J.A. (1976). *Validity and Reliability of Detection of Deception*. Washington, DC: National Institute of Law Enforcement and Criminal Justice.

Raskin, D.C., Kircher, J.C., Honts, C.R., & Horowitz, S.W. (1988). *A Study of the Validity of Polygraph Examinations in Criminal Investigations*. Grant No. 85-IJ-CX-0040. Salt Lake City: Department of Psychology, University of Utah.

Raskin, D.C., Honts, C.R., & Kircher, J.C. (1997). The scientific status of research on polygraph techniques: The case for polygraph tests. In D.L. Faigman, D. Kaye, M.J. Saks, & J. Sanders (Eds), *Modern Scientific Evidence: The Law and Science of Expert Testimony*. St. Paul, MN: West Law.

Saxe, L., Dougherty, D., & Cross, T. (1985). The validity of polygraph testing. *American Psychologist*, March, 355–366.

Slowik, S.M. & Buckley, J.P. (1975). Relative accuracy of polygraph examiner diagnosis of respiration, blood pressure, and GSR recordings. *Journal of Police Science and Administration*, *3*, 305–309.

Swets, J.A. (1996). *Signal Detection Theory and the ROC Analysis in Psychology and Diagnostics*. Mahwah, NJ: Erlbaum.

Swets, J.A., Dawes, R.M., & Monahan, J. (2000). Better decisions through science. *Scientific American*, October, 70–75.

Vrij, A. (2004). Why professionals fail to catch liars and how they can improve. *Legal and Criminological Psychology*, *9*, 159–181.

Waid, W.M., Orne, M.T., & Wilson, S.K. (1979). Effects of level of socialization on electrodermal detection of deception. *Psychophysiology*, *16*, 15–22.

Wicklander, D.E. & Hunter, F.L. (1975). The Influence of Auxiliary Sources of Information in Polygraph Diagnoses. *Journal of Police Science and Administration*, *208*, 405–409.

Wilcox, D.T., Sosnowski, D., Warberg, B., & Beech, A.R. (2005). Sexual history disclosure using the polygraph in a sample of British sex offenders in treatment. *Polygraph*, *34*, 171–181.

CHAPTER 10

Sex Offender Polygraph Testing in the United States: Trends and Controversies

PEGGY HEIL AND KIM ENGLISH

AN IMPORTANT PREFACE

Sex offenses are carried out in secrecy and are seldom reported (Tjaden & Thoennes, 2006). Offenders may also conceal high risk behaviors that are frequently associated with sex offending. The polygraph examination is a useful tool for sex offender management professionals seeking to provide appropriate treatment for clients who are likely to have secretive lifestyles.

The polygraph is a lightning rod for controversy. This is unfortunate, but not because the use of the polygraph, like all intervention tools, requires ongoing scrutiny. It is unfortunate because the controversy distracts from the core dilemma. Sex offenders, like everyone else, must become honest to live a healthy, non-secretive lifestyle. The polygraph is to sex offender management what urinalysis testing is for drug treatment: a tool to assist the offender to stay the course of treatment. Its use underscores the need for honesty and serves as an

The Use of the Polygraph in Assessing, Treating and Supervising Sex Offenders: A Practitioner's Guide
Edited by Daniel T. Wilcox.

acknowledgment of the extreme difficulty in making significant and lasting lifestyle changes.

This chapter will review a myriad of issues that often overshadow polygraph testing generally and post-conviction polygraph testing specifically. First the history of the post-conviction polygraph examination is reviewed and this is followed by discussions of the value and controversies that surround its use.

HISTORICAL CONTEXT

The use of the polygraph in the United States is common. Polygraph testing is typically used in the military, employment screening and law enforcement interrogation. Prosecuting attorney's offices often employ polygraph examiners, and defense attorneys frequently request clients undergo examinations. The military conducts approximately 30,000 polygraph tests per year with crime suspects and monitoring of espionage activities. In 1986, Congress established the US Department of Defense Polygraph Institute (DODPI) to provide research, training and quality control of military tests. DODPI also funded the development of computerized polygraph systems. Although decisions are made based on polygraph examination findings, these findings are rarely used in criminal courts.

A History of Polygraph Testing of Sex Offenders in the United States

According to Abrams and Simmons (2000), polygraph testing with property offenders dates back to the mid 1960s in Chicago with a judge who considered its use a '24-hour tail'. A judge in Portland, Oregon used the polygraph in 1973 to allow offenders with extensive criminal histories to be supervised in the community (Abrams & Simmons, 2000). Probation and parole officers along with treatment providers in Oregon and Washington began to use polygraph testing with convicted sex offenders in the mid- to late 1970s.

Use of the polygraph with sex offenders grew in the western United States and eventually expanded to jurisdictions across the nation. In 2000, English and colleagues (English *et al.*, 2000) conducted a telephone survey with a nationally representative sample. Researchers surveyed 732 probation and parole agencies and found that jurisdictions in 30 states were using the polygraph in sex offender management in the late 1990s.

In 2000, Burton and Smith-Darden surveyed several hundred treatment programs in North America for Safer Society

(Burton & Smith-Darden, 2001). The researchers found that 60% of adult community-based treatment programs, and 37% of adult residential programs used the polygraph. About one-third of adolescent community-based treatment programs and 19% of adolescent residential programs used this tool. This was the first survey to differentiate polygraph use across program types. The findings indicated that polygraph was used more frequently with community clients than residential clients, suggesting recognition of the risk this population posed to public safety. The next survey, conducted by McGrath, Cumming and Burchard in 2003, found over 70% of adult and 45% of juvenile community-based programs were using the polygraph (as cited in Kokish, 2005). The results indicated an increase in polygraph use across adult and juvenile community-based programs from the Burton and Smith-Darden 2001 survey.

While the polygraph was primarily used with adults in early years, it was also used with juveniles in some jurisdictions. For example, treatment programs in Oregon have used it with juveniles since the early 1980s, and Colorado began in the early 1990s. The American Polygraph Association recommends that it not be used with youth younger than 14, but some programs occasionally use it with offenders as young as 10.

Although many jurisdictions have set age limits for the use of the polygraph with young offenders, functional age is probably more important than biological age in determining whether polygraph testing is appropriate. A polygraph client regardless of age must be able to sit still, concentrate and follow what is being said. The individual must fit well into the cuff (specialized components have been designed for smaller persons), maintain reality contact, use abstract thinking, understand right from wrong, know the difference between truth and lies, and understand potential rewards and consequences. When testing youth, generally informed consent is obtained from parents or guardians as well as the examinee. Although there have been concerns regarding the emotional impact of using the polygraph examination on juveniles, one study of youth aged 13–18 found no adverse emotional reactions on the part of the youth (English *et al.*, 2002).

Finally, the use of the polygraph in the context of sex offender management continues to grow. Perhaps more importantly, its use continues to evolve as important questions are raised and addressed. A serious issue concerning 'compelling' individuals to incriminate themselves was resolved when the court stated that individuals under probation supervision were not in custody (*Minnesota v. Murphy*, 465 U.S. 420, 1984) and were free to invoke their constitutional protections against self-incrimination under the 5th Amendment. However, there is considerable variation across jurisdictions in terms of implementation and consistency of practice remains an issue. Research and case law, along with practitioner experiences, will continue to define and refine practices in the US. Some of the current pressing issues in the use of the polygraph are discussed later in the chapter.

WHY IS POLYGRAPH TESTING NEEDED?

Under-Reporting of Sex Offences

The polygraph is vital to obtain information about offenders who are in treatment and under supervision; very little is known about their actual criminal past. This is because few sex crimes are reported to law enforcement, which assists offenders in keeping the secrets of their abusive pasts.

General population surveys in the US on sexual assault victimization suggest that few sex offences are reported to law enforcement agencies (National Victim Center and Crime Victims Research and Treatment Center, 1992; Tjaden & Thoennes, 2006). The most recent Violence Against Women survey in the US found that only 19 % of rapes of adult women and 13 % of rapes of adult males are reported to law enforcement (Tjaden & Thoennes, 2006).

Certain types of sexual assault victims, including younger victims and victims who know the perpetrator, are especially unlikely to report offences to law enforcement (Smith *et al.*, 2000). Not surprisingly, Hansen *et al.* (1999) found that stranger perpetration, physical injury, or life threat increased victims' disclosure.

Underestimation of Offenders' Past Histories

Moreover, criminal justice records frequently underestimate the extent of an offender's past history. This assumption is supported by Abel's groundbreaking research. In 1988, Abel, Becker, Cunningham-Rathner, Mittelman and Rouleau interviewed paraphiliacs under conditions of guaranteed confidentiality and found that only 3.3 % of the paraphiliacs' self-admitted hands-on sex offences, such as rape and child molestation, resulted in an arrest. Less than 1 % of hands-off sex offences, such as exhibitionism and voyeurism, resulted in the offender's arrest.

It is clear that additional information, beyond criminal justice records, is needed to accurately assess an offender's risk of offending and to develop individually tailored treatment/supervision plans. However, the offender's risk can be understood only by knowing the age of onset, frequency, variety and duration of the behavior. Research on sex offenders specifically, and criminology in general, has established these dimensions of criminal behavior as the strongest predictors of future crime. According to Monahan (1981), 'If there is one finding that overshadows all others in the area of prediction, it is that the probability of future crime increases with each prior criminal act' (p. 4).

Difficulty of Monitoring Offenders' Progress in Treatment

Another reason to use polygraph testing with sex offenders is that it is often difficult to monitor an offender's progress in treatment. For example, an offender may understand the material presented in treatment, but choose not to apply what has been learned, which makes it difficult to determine whether he is incorporating treatment skills into his lifestyle. Maintenance polygraph testing provides a useful tool to monitor these changes. Questions can focus on whether the offender is having unauthorized contact with children, masturbating to thoughts of a child, or engaging in other high-risk behaviors. Such information allows professionals to intervene before a new sex offence is committed. This is the objective of using monitoring polygraph tests. However, when new crimes are not prevented, monitoring polygraph exams can also be used as a tool to detect additional offences, allowing supervising officers to quickly initiate an investigation that might stop further offences.

A Deterrent to High-Risk Behaviors

There is an accumulating body of evidence to indicate that polygraphy also functions as a deterrent to high-risk behaviors. Slightly more than half of the offenders in Harrison and Kirkpatrick's (2000) anonymous survey reported that polygraph testing decreased their grooming and masturbation behaviors. Twenty-seven percent reported decreased sexual touching of children as a result of polygraph testing.

Grubin *et al.* (2004) also found polygraph testing to have a deterrent effect on high-risk behaviors in a sample of sex offenders voluntarily participating in polygraph exams. The average number of disclosed high-risk behaviors significantly decreased between the first polygraph test and the second, indicating that polygraphy was effective in decreasing these behaviors. At the same time, disclosures of high-risk behaviors to treatment providers and supervising officers increased.

Abrams and Ogard, 1986 also studied the deterrent effect of polygraph testing on a general population of probationers and determined that 69% of offenders who received polygraph testing along with supervision successfully completed probation as opposed to only 26% of offenders who received supervision alone. While this body of research is small and involves small sample sizes, it does indicate that the polygraph holds promise as a motivating factor to help offenders apply treatment skills, comply with supervision conditions, and avoid high-risk behaviors.

Identifying Risk Factors

Using the polygraph with sex offenders provides important information to supplement criminal justice records, as it can verify the accuracy of offenders' self- reported sexual histories and their compliance with supervision rules. This information can be used to assess individual risk factors. Several of the sexual recidivism risk factors identified in Hanson and Morton-Bourgon's meta-analysis (2004) can be further clarified through polygraph testing, including whether an offender has a sexual preoccupation (through knowledge of the frequency of sexual behaviors), has violated supervision rules, or has a history involving use of force in sex offences. Risk is ongoing, and research information is limited in terms of assessing factors that change over time, and in a moment. The polygraph examination can focus on relevant historical and recent factors that indicate risk behaviors and situations that might otherwise be overlooked.

INFORMATION REVEALED BY POLYGRAPH TESTS

Research has established that, in combination with treatment, polygraph testing provides significant information about sex offenders that can be used to effectively treat and supervise them (Ahlmeyer *et al.*, 2000; Emerick & Dutton, 1993; English *et al.*, 2000; Heil, Ahlmeyer & Simons, 2003a; Hindman & Peters, 2001; O'Connell, 1998). Offenders reveal more extensive sexually deviant histories than are typically disclosed in treatment settings without polygraph. Moreover, this information is quite similar to that obtained under conditions of guaranteed confidentiality or anonymous survey (Abel *et al.*, 1988; Freeman-Longo & Blanchard, 1998; Weinrott & Saylor, 1991).

The following offender characteristics are typical of sex offenders based on the research revealed in these studies: an under-identification of prior sex offences in official records; diverse sex offence behaviors; an earlier age of onset of sexually deviant behaviors; a detection lag-time between the initiation of sex offending and identification as a sex offender in the criminal justice system; and persistent risk, meaning that offending appears to be well established in the individual's lifestyle.

Information on Offences and Diverse Victims

In a sample of 222 incarcerated sex offenders with non-deceptive sexual history polygraphs, for example, pre-sentence investigation reports had indicated a median of only one victim and two offences per offender prior to polygraph tests. By the time the offenders had become non-deceptive on sexual history questions during a polygraph, however, they were admitting a median of 11 victims and 36 sex offences per offender (Simons, Heil & English, 2004). These admissions were hands-on offences involving sexual assault of an adult or child. Studies including information on non-contact offences have revealed even higher numbers (Ahlmeyer *et al.*, 2000; English *et al.*, 2000; O'Connell, 1998; Wilcox & Sosnowski, 2005).

In addition, 73 % of the non-deceptive sample acknowledged having both adult and child victims, 37 % acknowledged both male and female victims, 87 % acknowledged victims from two or more relationship categories (stranger, acquaintance, position of trust, or relative) including 83 % that acknowledged victimizing relatives, and 56 % that acknowledged bestiality. Although these numbers are shocking, they are consistent with the admissions made by Abel *et al.*'s (1988) community sample under conditions of guaranteed confidentiality.

In another study, researchers reviewed disclosures in 116 polygraph examination reports of youth in treatment for sex offences. The subjects ranged in age from 13 to 18. Important information about additional victims, abuse of prescription medication, bestiality and fire setting was obtained in the course of the examinations (English *et al.*, 2002). As a result of the testing, 42 % of the sample disclosed 141 additional victims, 8 of whom were siblings. Over 85 % of the victimizations involved hands-on crimes. Of the 64 youths who were taking their first examination, 8 reported previously undetected gender crossover offending.

Revelations of Earlier Onset of Sexually Deviant Behaviors

Along with revealing higher numbers of prior offences than otherwise known, studies indicate that most sex offenders began engaging in sexual offending behavior during childhood but were not apprehended until they were adults (Ahlmeyer *et al.*, 2000; English *et al.*, 2000; Freeman-Longo & Blanchard, 1998; Hindman & Peters, 1988). In 2001,

Hindman and Peters reported that after the program started using polygraph, 71 % of adult sex offenders disclosed sexually abusing others when they were children whereas only 21 % of offenders had disclosed childhood sex offences prior to use of polygraphy. Similarly, the average age of sex offending onset was 12 in the Ahlmeyer *et al.* (2000) study and 11 in the English *et al.* (2000) study.

With a younger age of onset, it is not surprising that polygraph studies have also uncovered a significant interval prior to detection as a sex offender. The average time between initiations of sex offending and detection were calculated in two small studies. The results ranged from 14 years in the Wilcox *et al.* (2005) study, to 16 years in the Ahlmeyer *et al.* (2000) study. This time period is slightly higher than the Freeman-Longo (1985) anonymous survey study, which found an average detection gap of 6 years for rapists and 13 years for child molesters. Therefore, it appears that polygraph testing in conjunction with treatment significantly increases information on the extent of prior sex offending behaviors and the length of time the offender has been able to hide these behaviors.

Such information is valuable to those providing treatment and supervision of sex offenders. Contrary to traditional treatment wisdom, it is clear that removing access to a known victim type may not stop sex offending behavior, as offenders may seek an available vulnerable substitute for their preferred victim type. In this way, sex offending may be similar to substance abuse. Someone who is an alcoholic may like a specific type of drink, for example, but if the preferred drink is not available, another type of alcoholic beverage might be substituted.

Identification of Persistent Risk: Maintenance Polygraphs

The goal of maintenance testing is to discourage offenders from engaging in high-risk behaviors and catch problematic behaviors early in the relapse cycle. The objective is to intervene before the offender reoffends. Maintenance testing can help determine whether offenders are applying what they learn in treatment and complying with supervision conditions. The small amount of research that has reviewed maintenance testing suggests that a high percentage of offenders continue to engage in high-risk behaviors and that a significant percentage commit new sex offences while they are in treatment and under supervision.

As Colorado began to use the polygraph systematically with sex offenders, Tanner and Veeder (1997) reviewed the results of maintenance polygraph tests in a sample of 128 probationers participating in treatment. As a result of polygraph testing, it was confirmed through offenders' self-reports that 82 % of offenders were engaging in high-risk behaviors during the time period covered by the maintenance exam. A more disturbing finding was that 48 % had committed new crimes, with 41 % committing new sex crimes involving a variety of hands-off and hands-on offences.

As these polygraph tests were administered during a time period when few consequences were associated with polygraph results, the tests may not have served as a deterrent. However, some studies have found a decrease in high-risk behaviors as a deterrent effect takes place (Grubin *et al.*, 2004; Harrison & Kirkpatrick, 2000). Interestingly, some proportion of the detected high-risk behaviors in the Tanner study correspond to decreases in high-risk behavior reported in the Harrison & Kirkpatrick survey (Table 10.1).

In addition to affecting current behavior, maintenance testing may also provide relevant information for conducting risk assessment protocols, and for evaluating ongoing risk. Further research is needed, but one preliminary study has shown a connection between a high rate of high-risk behaviors while in treatment and supervision, as determined through polygraph maintenance testing, with high numbers of prior victims and offences, as determined through non-deceptive sexual history tests (Simons, Heil & English, 2004). Outcome data are clearly needed to determine if this connection is indeed predictive of recidivism risk.

STANDARDS FOR POLYGRAPH TESTING OF SEX OFFENDERS IN THE US

As growing numbers of polygraph examiners became involved in sex offender testing, widespread debates emerged in the US about the best practices and procedures for using the polygraph. In recognition of this growing field of polygraph testing and the debate regarding best practices, the American Polygraph Association (APA) formed a Subcommittee for Post-Conviction Sex Offender Testing to increase field standards. This subcommittee developed minimum guidelines for sex offender testing along with a 40-hour examiner training program. Many jurisdictions have made the APA training a requirement for polygraph examiners conducting post-conviction sex offender testing. In addition, some states such as Illinois, Colorado and Texas, have adopted standards with specific requirements for polygraph examiners who test sex offenders supervised by the criminal justice system.

Table 10.1 Comparison of high-risk behaviors during treatment between Tanner and Veeder (1997) and Harrison and Kirkpatrick (2000) studies

	Tanner & Veeder (1997) Maintenance polygraph results on 128 probationers participating in treatment		Harrison & Kirkpatrick (2000) Anonymous survey of 28 offenders in community treatment	
Behaviors	Admitted behavior or scored deceptive (%)	Admitted behavior (%)	Decrease in behavior reported with polygraph testing (%)	Behaviors
Substance use	54 %	39 %	36 %	Substance use
Viewing sexually explicit materials	45 %	41 %	36 %	Frequenting adult book stores
Masturbation to deviant fantasies	32 %	29 %	57 %	Masturbation
Unauthorized contact with a minor	25 %	20 %	57 %	Grooming behaviors
Sexual contact with a minor	31 %	13 %	27 %	Sexual touching of children

THE POLYGRAPH IN THE CONTEXT OF A CONTAINMENT TEAM

In the US, polygraph testing is generally seen as only one component of a comprehensive sex offender management program. Sex offenders are best contained by a team approach that includes comprehensive programming. Generally, the polygraph is implemented within the context of a collaborative team approach to managing sex offenders, known as the Containment Model (English, Pullen & Jones, 1996). The five-part containment approach operates in the context of multi-agency collaboration, explicit policies and consistent practices that combine case evaluation and risk assessment, sex offender treatment and intense community surveillance – all designed specifically to maximize public safety. The five components were identified from comprehensive field research in dozens of jurisdictions across the country. The containment approach consists of the following aspects:

1. A philosophy that values victim protection, public safety and reparation for victims as the paramount objectives of sex offender management.
2. Implementation strategies that depend on agency coordination and multidisciplinary partnerships.
3. A containment-focused case management and risk control approach that is individualized based on each offender's characteristics.
4. Consistent multi-agency policies and protocols, and
5. Quality control mechanisms, including program monitoring and evaluation.

The victim orientation is paramount. When the societal or criminal justice system responses to a sexual attack place the victim at fault, the trauma is magnified and recovery may be delayed (Hindman, 1988). Explaining that sexual abuse is a complex process rather than an act or series of acts, Finkelhor (1988) notes, 'Clinicians have often observed that the harm of some sexual abuse experiences lies less in the actual sexual contact than in the process of disclosure or even in the process of intervention' (p. 77–78). Understanding this point is vital for professionals interested in implementing the containment approach. The power and authority of police officers, lawyers, judges and social workers can weigh as heavily on the victim as on the perpetrator.

The Containment Model for managing sex offenders in the community calls for the creation of intra-agency, interagency and interdisciplinary teams. These teams can overcome the fragmentation that usually results from the multilayered nature of the criminal justice system. These teams are valuable for several reasons:

- They vastly improve communication among the agencies involved;
- They allow for quicker and less intrusive responses to victims (Epstein & Langenbahn, 1994);
- They promote the exchange of expertise and ideas;
- They facilitate the sharing of information about specific cases;
- They increase team members' understanding of what everyone on the team needs to do his/her job well; and
- Perhaps most importantly, they foster a unified and comprehensive approach to the management of sex offenders.

Collaborating agencies should include sex offender treatment programs, law enforcement, probation, parole, schools, social services, rape crisis centers, hospitals, prisons, polygraph examiners, researchers and victim advocate organizations. In a call to collaborate across disciplines and within communities for the purpose of addressing the epidemic of sexual assault, the American Medical Association added the following to the list above: attorneys, emergency room staff, universities and victims' assistance centers (American Medical Association, 1995).

Interagency and multidisciplinary collaboration can occur in many ways. In Colorado, for example, a state-level Sex Offender Management Board with multidisciplinary membership is defined in legislation and meets monthly. The Board has issued guidelines for the evaluation, treatment and behavioral monitoring of adult sex offenders, including sex offenders with developmental disabilities. In Oregon, probation and parole officers who work with sex offenders meet quarterly for two-day meetings in various locations across the state. The group has strict ground rules for participants and makes decisions by consensus. The agenda focuses on ensuring consistent practices across counties, and has subcommittees that focus on training and public policy. The state department of corrections sponsors the meetings that are attended by local law enforcement, the state police, treatment providers and polygraph examiners who work in the region.

Officials in Maricopa County (Phoenix), Arizona have worked to ensure a strong interagency and multidisciplinary approach to managing adult and juvenile sex offenders. The district attorney's office and the local police department partnered to train prosecutors and law enforcement officers statewide on effective interviewing and sex crime investigation techniques. The prosecutor's office is in the same building as probation, enhancing communication and cross-agency activities.

These jurisdictions, Colorado, Oregon and Maricopa County, are examples of the team approach that is central to containing sex offenders in the community. In these settings, treatment providers, supervising officers and polygraph examiners form tight teams that monitor each sex offender. In Phoenix and some counties in Colorado, surveillance officers supplement the work of the supervising officer by working out of their cars to monitor each offender's location and activity in the community.

The containment approach can operate in a variety of environments, from probation and parole to prison settings. In Colorado, the prison sex offender treatment program partners with parole, community-based halfway houses, treatment providers in the community, victim advocate organizations, law enforcement officers and polygraph examiners. The containment team in prison is adapted from the community version. Therapists work closely with polygraph examiners who travel to the prison regularly. To fulfill some of the functions of supervising officers, therapists network with prison housing and work supervisors to monitor the offender's behavior outside of treatment. An important part of treatment delivery is the expectation that offenders will engage in community service activities by providing information on how they have selected victims and set up their crimes. This information is shared with law enforcement, prosecutors, school officials and victim advocates. When offenders prepare for release, therapists work with parole officers in the community. Treatment staff actively participate in the work of the state Sex Offender Management Board.

The core containment team should consist, at a minimum, of a therapist, supervising officer and polygraph examiner. All members of the team should have specialized training to work with sex offenders, and additional members should be added as appropriate. For example, a child protective worker or victim advocate who is involved in the case is often included in a containment team. In addition to information provided by the core team members and polygraph testing, therapists will need additional sources of information in order to treat an offender effectively. These additional information sources might include testing of sexual arousal or interest, psychological assessments or testing, and information from collateral contacts such as family members, victim advocates, employers and ministers. Supervising officers also depend on a variety of information tools, which can include collateral contacts, home visits, surveillance officers, GPS or pager monitoring, and urinalysis. In short, polygraph testing is just one in a varied set of tools that improve the treatment and supervision of sex offenders.

Polygraph testing should not be used in isolation. If teams believe that polygraph testing will eliminate the need for collateral sources of information or can be used in place of treatment, they have unrealistic expectations for the polygraph. Good supervision and treatment require an inquiry into more than three behavioral questions every three to six months, which is all that a polygraph usually covers. When a polygraph test does raise concerns, of course, containment team members must turn to their collateral sources of information and increase supervision of the offender to try and determine the meaning of the concerns raised by the polygraph.

It is also essential to use the polygraph in combination with treatment. Some supervising agencies have tried to implement polygraph testing in lieu of treatment, because they believed that treatment of this population was unlikely to succeed. However, research indicates that polygraph testing alone does not produce the number of admissions produced by treatment combined with polygraph testing (Ahlmeyer *et al.*, 2000). The reverse is also true: treatment alone does not produce the number of admissions as treatment with polygraph testing produces. Such admissions, of course, provide crucial information for the containment team.

Criminal Justice Incentives for Compliance

Criminal justice supervision is also important, as it provides the incentive for compliance with treatment and polygraph testing. Supervising officers are responsible for overall management of offenders in the community. They monitor and encourage the offender's compliance with court- or parole board- imposed conditions of community placement. Supervision conditions establish the structure and expectations that support lifestyle change. When offenders do not comply with conditions and pose a risk to community safety, it is the supervising officer's responsibility to report violations to courts and parole boards, resulting in potential revocation to prison.

Supervising officers accomplish their mandate through a variety of methods including in-office meetings with the offender, home visits, contacts with significant individuals in the offender's life, electronic or GPS monitoring, urinalysis, polygraph testing and offender treatment. Since confidentiality is waived with the supervising agency as a condition of treatment, information from offence-specific evaluations and therapists help officers recommend conditions that limit the offender's access to potential victim pools or high-risk situations. By enforcing treatment compliance, offenders are given opportunities to address problems that contribute to their offending behavior. Information provided through the process of polygraph testing should be combined with information from collateral sources such as community members, criminal justice records, treatment and psychological exams, and monitoring polygraph tests to form a more complete picture of the offender's risk and adjustment in the community.

Home visits provide clues to the offender's behavior in the community and, consequently, level of risk. The officer's knowledge of the offender's lifestyle and risk factors can be vital in developing critical polygraph questions. Officers also depend on such visits plus collateral sources of information obtained from neighbors and family members to investigate potential problems identified during the process of polygraph testing. Both polygraph testing and collateral sources of information are valuable complementary methods in the effective assessment and supervision of sex offenders.

Responding to Previously Undisclosed Offences

Because treatment combined with polygraph testing provides better information on prior offences and new criminal behavior, containment teams must resolve how they will handle the offences disclosed through polygraph tests. With respect to new offences, of course, teams generally inform offenders that there will be no confidentiality or immunity from prosecution.

Admissions of prior offences are handled in one of three ways in the United States. The first method involves no immunity. All admissions of previously unknown offences are disclosed to law enforcement or child protective services. This approach allows victims to be identified and treated, but as it subjects the offender to further prosecution, it may discourage admissions. A common variation of this method involves reporting only offences that fall under mandatory reporting laws, generally offences involving minors.

The second method commonly used in the US is to grant limited immunity on prior offences. In order to use this method, teams must seek cooperation from prosecuting attorneys. Under this approach, offenders sign a limited immunity agreement with the prosecutor's office that specifies that all crimes will be reported to the prosecuting attorney's office, allowing victims to be identified and treated. As long as the offender successfully completes treatment and supervision, however, he/she will not be prosecuted for prior sex offences. If the offender drops out of or fails treatment and supervision, the crimes can be prosecuted. Thus, this approach creates an extra incentive for complying with treatment and supervision.

Arranging immunity agreements with prosecutors can be difficult, however. As an elected official, a prosecutor may be concerned that the public will view such agreements as excusing sex offences. Moreover, offenders may disclose crimes that occurred in jurisdictions outside the purview of the prosecutor.

The third method entails no immunity for prior offences, but offenders are asked to disclose prior sex offences without providing details such as the name of the victim or location of the offence. As a result, sufficient facts are not provided to evoke requirements for mandatory reporting. Typically, the age, gender and general relationship category (relative, position of trust, acquaintance, or stranger) are recorded, which provides teams with knowledge of the variety and frequency of past offending behaviors. Unfortunately, this method does not allow victims to be identified and treated. Nevertheless, as case law evolves in this field, it appears that there will be increased pressures to use the second or third method to handle past offence admissions as those methods sidestep self-incrimination concerns.

EFFECTIVENESS OF THE CONTAINMENT MODEL

The Containment Model is a relatively new approach to dealing with sex offenders, and there are few studies evaluating its effectiveness. However, the studies that have been conducted show promising results. For example, Maricopa County Adult Probation Department in Arizona has been using the containment approach since 1986. A program evaluation indicated only a 2.2 % sexual recidivism rate and a 13.1 % criminal recidivism rate among 419 male offenders who had been on lifetime supervision for an average of 36 months (Hepburn & Griffin, 2002). In this study, recidivism was measured by arrest for a new sex offence or any new criminal offence. This compares favorably to the Hanson *et al.* (2002) meta-analysis that reported an average sexual recidivism rate, as measured by re-arrest or reconviction, of 12.3 % and criminal recidivism rate of 27.9 % over a median 46 month follow-up period.

Lowden *et al.* (2003) studied the implementation of the Containment Model at the Colorado Department of Corrections. This program employed intense treatment with polygraph testing in the institution. When paroled, the offenders participated in treatment, supervision and polygraph testing in the community. Researchers found that 84 % of the offenders who participated in the advanced phase of institutional treatment successfully completed parole versus only 52 % of the offenders who had not participated in treatment. By the third year following parole discharge, 21 % of the offenders who participated in the advanced treatment phase had been arrested for any crime versus 42 % of the offenders who had not participated in treatment.

A study of Jackson, County Oregon's probation and parole program also found support for the containment approach. Comparing outcome data on offenders in the Jackson County program with a comparison group from a nearby county, researchers found that offenders who stayed in treatment for at least one year were 40 % less likely to have a new felony conviction than those in the comparison group (England *et al.*, 2001).

Stalans (2004) studied probation sex offender programs in several counties in Illinois and concluded 'all specialized probation programs should be based on the containment approach and should include (a) at least three unannounced random field visits per offender every month, (b) a full-disclosure polygraph and a maintenance polygraph exam every six months, and (c) a tight partnership between probation officers and treatment providers that includes probation officers appearing at random times at the treatment site to check on offenders' attendance' (p. 599).

In sum, evidence is mounting that use of the post-conviction polygraph testing, when combined with intense specialized treatment and supervision, is an effective method for managing sex offenders.

CONTINUING ISSUES RELATED TO THE USE OF THE POLYGRAPH IN THE US

Polygraph testing for sex offenders has evolved in the US, however a number of issues are unresolved. Use of the polygraph continues to grow, nevertheless polygraph, treatment and supervision professionals continue to debate a number of aspects of the polygraph. Questions remain, for example, about the accuracy of the polygraph, about how specific polygraph questions should be worded, whether the polygraph increases false admissions, how effective the polygraph is with psychopaths, and what to do about sex offenders' use of countermeasures. Following is a discussion of these issues.

Accuracy

According to the National Research Council (NRC) 2003, the most researched and accurate type of polygraph test has a single-incident focus, that is, the test is limited to one specific event. NCR (2003) identified the median accuracy rate of this test at 89 %. A post-conviction sex offender test is rarely limited to one specific incident, however. Instead, it usually involves three or four questions addressing behavior within a specified time frame. This is a multiple issue test.

Such a multiple issue test is considered less accurate than a single issue exam and is somewhat comparable to an employment 'screening test', although these tests typically involve more than three to four relevant questions. The average accuracy rate for a well-executed screening test is 80 % (Krapohl, Senter & Stern, 2005). However, the overall accuracy of polygraph testing can be increased by applying a 'successive hurdles' approach (Meehl & Rosen, 1955). That is, if an offender scores deceptive on a multiple issue test, there should be a follow-up test. The focus of the follow-up test should be narrowed to the single issue of most concern. This second, single issue test will have a higher accuracy rate, and having greater specificity, the single issue test can better distinguish the true positives from the false positives.

The polygraph does compare favorably in terms of accuracy to many other instruments that are currently used with sex offenders. It has been well established that actuarial instruments are more accurate than clinical judgments in identifying risk for a new conviction for a reoffence. However, LaFond and Winick (2004) state, '... actuarial risk assessment can identify a group of sex offenders who will sexually reoffend at a rate that can 'conservatively be estimated at 50 % and could reasonably be estimated at 70 % to 80 %'. Even if this high accuracy is achieved, predictions will have a false-positive rate of from 20 % to 50 %' (p. 1177). Because actuarial assessments are not repeated, as polygraphs can, it appears that these tests may have a lower accuracy rate than polygraph testing.

Vigil and Jenks (2004) point out that many commonly relied on medical procedures have comparable accuracy to polygraph testing, from pap smears, mammography, and endoscopy for gastric cancer. Based on this information, it appears the accuracy rates on polygraph are similar to many commonly relied upon tests.

Utility versus Accuracy

One debate in the field is between the uses of broad questions versus very specific questions on the examination. Broad questions allow treatment providers and supervising officers to cover a wide range of concerns. For example, in some jurisdictions, containment team members attempt to validate the offender's self-reported sexual history during a single polygraph exam. Frequently these tests will ask whether the offender intentionally withheld information on their documented sexual history. Deceptive responses do not provide specific clues on the areas that the offender might be withholding information.

Over time this practice is becoming less common and has shifted to more focused tests covering three or four specific types of behavior. This is the utility versus accuracy debate: do we ask broad questions to obtain disclosures on a variety of issues, or do we narrow the question and increase accuracy of the examination result. When case management decisions are based on polygraph examination results, accuracy becomes a critical issue, not a casual one. Currently, the field appears to be moving in the direction of prioritizing accuracy.

Examiner Skill Impacts Accuracy

As with clinical practice, an important factor that affects the accuracy of polygraph results is the skill of the examiner. Examiners' skills vary based on their training and expertise in various components of the test: question construction (requires knowledge of sex offender minimizations), pre-test interviewing, post-test interviewing, chart scoring, machine calibration, testing environment and identification of countermeasures.

Because most treatment providers and supervising officers do not have sufficient knowledge to assess an examiner's skill, a quality assurance audit by a neutral polygraph examiner can help programs select the most appropriate examiners. Some programs require examiners to maintain videotape recordings, charts and reports to be used in random audits. In addition, programs that use multiple examiners may have a greater sense of the skill of individual examiners in comparison to others in the group.

One potential threat to accuracy may occur when offenders begin to anticipate too well the experience they will have at the examiner's office. Although past research on 'habituation' to an examiner or the testing process has found no effect, post-conviction testing is long term and requires safeguards against this possibility. Post-conviction sex offender testing is unusual in that the offender participates in multiple tests over the course of supervision, and the extent to which offenders might habituate to routine testing is unknown. Using multiple examiners may guard against habituation.

Question Construction Affects Accuracy

Other important elements of polygraph testing with sex offenders include asking behavioral questions and eliminating intent questions. Sex offenders have many rationalizations for their sexual offending behaviors. Intent questions can provide an out for the offender. Consider this question: 'Did you intend to drink at the party?' The offender might be able to legitimately pass the question, even if he drank alcohol at the party, if he had previously told himself that he would just drink pop at the party.

Question construction requires great skill and experience. Accuracy hinges on well-constructed questions (among other things). For this reason, examiners require special training and supervision before working with this population.

Offender Preparation Improves Accuracy

An essential part of the polygraph examination process involves offender preparation for the exam. Besides offering offenders the tools necessary for change, therapists help offenders to understand definitions of sex offences and help offenders to decrease rationalizations and denial. This is the beginning of helping offenders successfully engage in the polygraph examination process. Therapists also instruct offenders to carefully and thoroughly document their history of deviant sexual behavior. As a result, examiners are able to conduct more effective tests with the offender because the offender recognizes the behaviors of concern. It is also helpful if the polygraph examiner, treatment provider and supervising officers all use the same definitions for sexual contact and for different types of sexual offences.

The National Research Council's (2003) review of polygraph testing states: 'Both examinee and examiner may have difficulty knowing whether an answer to such a question is truthful unless there are clear and consistent criteria that specify what activities justify a 'yes' answer. Examinees may believe they are lying when providing factually truthful responses, or vice versa' (p. 1).

Consequences Improve Accuracy

It is an underlying theory of polygraph testing that the subject must have something at stake for the test to register a physiological response. In post-conviction testing, the offender must fear detection (Kircher *et al.*, 1988). Heil, Simons and Ahlmeyer (2003b) found the use of a decisions grid that provided a range of negative and positive consequences for polygraph results increased the percentage of offenders scoring non-deceptive on polygraph exams. These grids were designed to promote consistent decisions and to encourage offenders to disclose pertinent information to their therapists before the polygraph test. The study found that when offenders knew that the polygraph results would be related to consequences, they were more likely to provide accurate information in response to polygraph questions. During the time period when the decisions grid was implemented, only 9 % of the tests were scored non-deceptive. After full implementation of the grid, however, 55 % of the tests were scored non-deceptive, and the non-deceptive rate climbed to 67 % when all therapists in the program supported the use of the decisions grid.

Another factor that appears to affect the rate of non-deceptive results is the therapist's attitude toward polygraphy. Heil, Simons and Ahlmeyer (2003b) found that therapists who were rated by supervisors and polygraph examiners as supportive of polygraph testing were more likely than unsupportive therapists to have clients that scored non-deceptive on exams. Even when therapists were supportive of polygraph testing, however, a failure to complete paperwork and assign timely consequences decreased the percentage of non-deceptive results. Therapists with the highest proportion of clients with non-deceptive findings were both supportive of polygraph testing and consistent in assigning positive or negative consequences for test results.

Although consequences can be used to increase the accuracy of polygraph tests, most programs in the US do not base major case decisions on a deceptive polygraph exam alone. Even if an offender scores deceptive to sexually abusing a child, the information is ordinarily not considered sufficient to revoke an offender's parole, for example. The results of such a test should certainly signal further investigation, however, and may warrant moving the offender out of a home where a child resides until the deceptive response can be clarified. At the same time, programs and containment teams are more inclined to use non-deceptive polygraph results as support for positive case decisions. Thus, an incarcerated offender who appears to be progressing in treatment might be more likely to be recommended for parole if his polygraph tests are non-deceptive and tend to validate the offender's progress in treatment.

Is the Polygraph Effective with Psychopaths?

Several studies have addressed polygraph testing with psychopaths (Hammond, 1980; Patrick & Iacono, 1989; Raskin & Hare, 1978). No statistical differences were found in the accuracy rates of the polygraph with psychopaths compared to other offenders. Many clinicians assume that psychopaths have no conscience and therefore will have no detectable physiological responses when lying. However, like other criminals, psychopaths are invested in keeping secrets, and they generally do not want others to know what they have done. In this way, they do fear detection. Therefore, the test can be an especially useful tool given the risk this population presents to the public.

Does Polygraph Testing Increase False Admissions by Sex Offenders?

While it is certainly possible for offenders to fabricate admissions, there is no indication that this happens more often when the polygraph is used than when it is not used in treatment. Nevertheless, a prevalent concern in the field is that the polygraph process results in false admissions from sex offenders in response to sanctions for false-positive outcomes. As a result, some programs are leery of imposing consequences based on polygraph results.

Certainly, it is much easier to fabricate information successfully during therapy without the polygraph, since this intervention provides no checks on the information disclosed. However, it has been the experience of the first author that offenders report failing polygraphs when they report inaccurate numbers of crimes – by disclosing either too few or too many sex offences to the examiner. To ensure accuracy of the examination results, therapists should instruct offenders to prepare accurate sexual histories before they take a polygraph exam. When an offender provides inaccurate information, it is more likely that he or she will withhold information on prior offences than fabricate additional offences since additional offences are associated with increased restrictions. Therapists that are concerned about false admissions as a result of polygraph testing can simply seek collateral information to clarify the results and then retest the area of deception.

Accuracy: Let's do the math. Math equations can be used to illustrate the improved accuracy of repeat testing. At the mean accuracy rate of 80 % for a multiple issue polygraph, an offender has 20 chances out of 100 of being found deceptive when he is actually telling the truth (false positive). If the test were repeated, focusing exclusively on the area in which the offender was found to be deceptive, the accuracy rate would be closer to the single incident accuracy rate of 89 %. Using this rate, an offender has 11 out of 100 chances of making a false admission and being found truthful on the test (false negative). Therefore, the probability of the offender being found deceptive on a test in which he was telling the truth and then truthful on the next test when he was lying is only 2.2 %. Even if the second single focus test has the lower accuracy rate of 80 %, the chance of a false positive on the first test followed by a false negative on the follow-up test is only 4 %. If the single focus test were repeated a second time, the offender would have only a .24 % chance of being found initially deceptive when he was telling the truth and being found truthful on both follow-up tests when he was fabricating an admission.

$$20/100 \times 11/100 = 220/10,000 \text{ or } 2.2\%$$
$$20/100 \times 20/100 = 400/10,000 \text{ or } 4\%$$
$$20/100 \times 11/100 \times 11/100 = 2420/1{,}000{,}000 \text{ or } .24\%$$

One Final Point on False Admissions. If the polygraph process is producing fictitious admissions, these admissions are remarkably similar across studies employing guaranteed confidentiality (Abel *et al.*, 1988; Elliot, 1994; Weinrott & Saylor, 1991), anonymous survey (Freeman-Long, 1985) or polygraphy (Ahlmeyer *et al.*, 2000; Emerick & Dutton, 1993; English *et al.*, 2000; Heil *et al.*, 2003a; O'Connell, 1998).

High rates of adult and child crossover have been determined in multiple studies (Table 10.2). For instance, Abel *et al.* (1988) studied 244 paraphiliacs, who had committed acts against adults, under conditions of guaranteed confidentiality. The sample primarily consisted of individuals living in New York and Tennessee. Forty-nine percent admitted molesting children. O'Connell (1998) studied 127 probationers participating in community treatment with polygraph in Washington. Sixty-four percent of rapists admitted having child victims. Ahlmeyer *et al.* (2000) studied 143 inmates participating in treatment with polygraph in Colorado. Fifty percent of rapists acknowledged victimizing children. Freeman-Longo (1985) conducted an anonymous survey of 23 rapists participating in an institutional forensic sex offender treatment program in Oregon. The rapists reported 5090 sex offences including 319 child molestations and 178 rapes. Weinrott and Saylor (1991) using a confidential computer-administered interview found 32 % of incarcerated rapists in Washington admitted child molestation.

Comparable consistency was found in studies evaluating relationship crossover (Table 10.3). In a sample of 561 paraphiliacs, Abel *et al.* (1988) determined through guaranteed confidentiality that 66 % of interfamilial offenders had sexually assaulted outside the family. Weinrott and Saylor (1991) studied 99 institutionalized sex offenders in Washington using a confidential self-report survey. Fifty percent of incest offenders admitted extra-familial child sexual abuse. English *et al.* (2000) studied a sample of 180 probationers and parolees participating in polygraph testing in four different states. Sixty-four percent of sex offenders who had committed incest admitted sexually abusing victims outside the family. Heil *et al.* (2003a) studied 223 inmates with polygraph testing and found 64 % of offenders victimizing relative children admitted victimizing non-relative victims.

Table 10.2 Multiple studies using different methods find consistent information about rapists committing child molesting offences

	Abel *et al.* (1988)	O'Connell (1998)	Weinrott & Saylor (1991)	Freeman-Longo (1985)	Heil *et al.* (2003a)
Sample description	Community sample of paraphiliacs	Probationers in treatment & supervision	Civilly committed sex offenders in a hospital treatment program	Inmates in a forensic treatment program	Inmates in prison treatment program
Sample location	New York & Tennessee	Washington State	Washington State	Oregon	Colorado
Data collection technique	Self-report with Guaranteed Confidentiality	Self-report with Polygraph Testing	Self-report with Guaranteed Confidentiality	Self-report with Anonymous Survey	Self-report with Polygraph Testing
Rapist admitting child molestation	49 %	64 %	32 %	23 rapists admitted 319 child molestations	-

Table 10.3 Multiple studies using different methods find consistent information about incest offenders victimizing non-relatives

	Abel *et al*. (1988)	English *et al*. (2000)	Weinrott & Saylor (1991)	Heil *et al*. (2003a)
Sample description	Community sample of paraphiliacs	Probationers & parolees in treatment & supervision	Civilly committed sex offenders in a hospital treatment program	Inmates in prison treatment program
Sample location	New York & Tennessee	Oregon, Texas & Wisconsin	Washington State	Colorado
Data collection technique	Self-report with Guaranteed Confidentiality	Self-report with Polygraph Testing	Self-report with Guaranteed Confidentiality	Self-report with Polygraph Testing
Incest offenders victimizing non-relatives (%)	66 %	64 %	50 %	64 %

While the rates of these behaviors are relatively consistent across populations, a lower frequency of gender crossover has been established in these studies (Table 10.4). Emerick and Dutton (1993) studied 76 'high-risk' juvenile offenders in a hospital treatment facility in Arizona. Forty-three percent of the polygraphed juveniles acknowledged assaulting both male and female children. English *et al.* (2000) found 29 % of the parolees and probationers participating in polygraphy reported having both male and female victims. Similarly, Simons *et al.* (2004) found 37 % of the 222 inmates participating in polygraphy disclosed both male and female victims. If offenders are fabricating admissions, they are doing so consistently across 20 years of research in multiple locations across the US.

Offenders' Use of Countermeasures

As polygraph testing of sex offenders increases, offenders' use of countermeasures needs to be addressed. Because offenders usually participate in multiple tests, they have opportunities to experiment with countermeasure techniques and attempt to perfect them. Any information they may need on countermeasures is easily accessed over the Internet.

Fortunately, well-trained and experienced examiners easily detect most of the countermeasure techniques, and the result is typically an inconclusive, rather than a non-deceptive, test result. Increased use of countermeasures has the potential to invalidate results; so most containment teams develop significant consequences for an offender's established use of countermeasures. Offenders are generally warned ahead of time that major consequences can result from efforts to sabotage the test. Consequently, containment teams may be more inclined to make case decisions when it has been clearly established that the offender used countermeasures. Experienced examiners are more likely to detect the use of countermeasures, and they usually warn an offender during the test to discontinue the tactic.

If a major decision (i.e., revoking the offender to a more secure environment, terminating the offender from a treatment program, etc.) is contemplated because of an offender's attempt to sabotage a polygraph, the containment team frequently obtains a second opinion on whether the offender was actually using countermeasures. By conducting a quality assurance review of the polygraph charts and videotape, a second polygraph examiner can render an opinion on whether there is sufficient evidence to indicate sabotage before the team implements any major decisions. This places teams on stronger ground when implementing a consequence. If this manipulation effort is ignored, offenders

Table 10.4 Multiple studies using different methods find consistent information about gender crossover

	Emerick & Dutton (1993)	Abel *et al*. (1988)	English *et al*. (2000)	Simon *et al*. (2004)
Sample description	High-risk juvenile sex offenders in hospital treatment program	Community sample of paraphiliacs	Probationers & parolees in treatment & supervision	Inmates in prison treatment program
Sample location	Arizona	New York & Tennessee	Oregon, Texas, & Wisconsin	Colorado
Data collection technique	Self-report with Polygraph Testing	Self-report with Guaranteed Confidentiality	Self-report with Polygraph Testing	Self-report with Polygraph Testing
Offenders with gender crossover (%)	43 %	20 %	29 %	37 %

may attempt to use countermeasures to avoid disclosing information that is pertinent to effective treatment and supervision.

Influence of Base Rates

When the polygraph test is inaccurate, the base rate of behaviors queried can impact the direction of the error. Some clinicians express concern that the base rate of behaviors questioned in polygraph exams is low. As a result, they fear the direction of error will be toward finding offenders deceptive when they are telling the truth.

However, as first evidenced by Abel's research with guaranteed confidentiality, undetected offences are not rare events. Therefore, it appears that the base rate of undetected offences is relatively high. Tanner and Veeder's (2001) research also indicates that base rates of offenders engaging in high-risk behaviors while in treatment and supervision are relatively high. With a high base rate, errors are more likely to be in the direction of false negatives (i.e., scoring non-deceptive when the offender was lying) than false positive (i.e., scoring deceptive when the offender is telling the truth). This again points to the importance of using additional tools and sources of information to monitor the offender's risk.

If polygraph testing becomes an effective deterrent, offenders can discontinue high-risk behaviors and the error rate can shift in the direction of false positives. This again provides support for the practice of repeating tests when deception is indicated. It also lends support for the importance of using multiple sources of information to monitor offenders since an offender can score truthful on a polygraph when lying about a behavior or score deceptive when telling the truth.

ADVANTAGES FOR OFFENDERS: WHAT'S IN IT FOR THEM?

Why would anyone voluntarily give up information about him/herself that is likely to bring disapproval from others? Most offenders have successfully hidden the extent of their sex offending behavior for years, and they generally expect that prior behaviors will not be detected. They also have every reason to hide information about their sex offending histories, because full disclosure usually results in shame and, often, in rejection by significant others. When such behaviors are revealed, others may reassess whether they want to continue in a relationship with the offender.

Offenders also suspect that full disclosure will result in more severe sanctions, decreased access to previously undetected victims, as well as increased scrutiny and other limitations. Once their relationships with therapists and supervising officers have been established, offenders are likely to see potential disruption of the status quo as risky. It is much easier simply to acknowledge only the information that is available to the therapists in criminal justice records than to undergo a polygraph. However, without disclosing the extent, duration and variety of prior offending behavior, the offender is likely to stay in a perpetual 'pretend normal' state, and relapse prevention plans may not even address the offender's highest risk offence behaviors. In fact, offenders may be returned to living arrangements where undetected victims are present, as child relatives are less likely to report offences (Russell, 1986; Smith *et al.*, 2000).

Although offenders often resist taking the step of disclosing prior offences, once they actually do, they find that there are a variety of benefits. For instance, the offender no longer has to maintain secrets in his relationships with others. For the first time, he/she is free to form genuine relationships with others without fear of rejection should these other people discover 'who he/she really is'. Offenders often worry how others will react to their prior offences, and they may need emotional support after an initial disclosure. However, eventually they typically feel a sense of relief after disclosing the information.

In addition to allowing offenders to form more genuine relationships, disclosing complete information on past deviant sexual behavior allows treatment to address the offender's specific needs, thereby increasing opportunities for him/her to benefit from treatment, have a more satisfactory lifestyle and develop a sense of self-respect. This finding is supported by two studies that used anonymous surveys to query sex offenders' views about the relevance of polygraphs to their progress in treatment.

In both surveys, the majority of offenders believed that the polygraph was beneficial in their treatment progress (Harrison & Kirkpatrick, 2000; Kokish, Levenson & Blasingame, 2005). In particular, the offenders in Harrison and Kirkpatrick's (2000) survey reported that the polygraph helped them share information with treatment providers and comply with treatment and supervision rules. In addition, the majority of offenders, 25 out of 28, believed that they could not manipulate the polygraph. In the Kokish *et al.* study, 72% of the 95 offenders surveyed believed that the polygraph increased their honesty with self, therapists and group members. Many reported a positive impact on their social relationships as a result of their increased honesty.

On two separate occasions, sex offenders at the Colorado Department of Corrections were interviewed by newspaper reporters and child mentoring program staff to obtain information on detecting and preventing child molesters from abusing children in sports and mentoring programs. In both instances, sex offenders reported that the possibility of polygraph testing was one of the best deterrents to predators. Although most offenders would probably choose not to participate in polygraph if it were voluntary, it appears that testing helps offenders to become more honest, establish more genuine relationships, comply with treatment/supervision requirements and refrain from problematic behavior.

THE EFFECT OF THE POLYGRAPH INFORMATION ON PROFESSIONALS

The Value of Additional Information

Clearly, integrating polygraph testing with treatment creates additional work for both therapists and supervising officers. Therapists must review criminal justice records to determine documented offences, read the offender's written sexual history and determine areas that require polygraph testing. After the polygraph report comes back, professionals may have to question offenders about deceptive results and track follow-up testing. In addition, professionals need to be familiar with the offender's high-risk behaviors and provide input into aspects to be covered in maintenance polygraph tests.

Nevertheless, there are advantages to professionals in using the polygraph. The information obtained through the polygraph process improves both treatment and supervision, as it is not necessary to depend exclusively on an offender's admissions or criminal justice record for indications of risk and treatment need. In addition, the polygraph serves as a prompt for the offender to disclose more complete information. Treatment can therefore focus on real issues, as professionals waste less time on attempts to get the offender to divulge risk information. As a result, offenders tend to progress more rapidly in treatment.

As a consequence of having more accurate risk information, professionals are less likely to endorse relapse prevention plans or supervision plans that place the offender in situations where he is likely to fail. For example, an offender who is convicted of a crime involving the rape of an adult female may reveal during polygraph testing that he also sexually abused female children. Without this information, a therapist might support the offender's return to his home where his minor age daughter lives, thereby setting up a high-risk situation for the offender and daughter and increasing the offender's likelihood of reoffence.

Moreover, an occasional polygraph result supports an offender's claim that he has only committed one sexual offence. This information serves as a reminder that some offenders are telling the truth and that offenders have individual histories and levels of risk. As a result, more accurate treatment and supervision plans can be formulated.

Additional Information Can Be Hard to Bear

Of course, using the polygraph can also have some serious negative effects on professionals, as it deepens the exposure of therapists and supervising officers to the devastating impact of sexual assaults and the serious nature of sex offending. This increased exposure may prove overwhelming and can push containment team professionals to the point of burnout, especially when their self-esteem is tied to their clients' progress. Professionals may be disappointed when maintenance testing identifies ongoing problems, as this can cause them to question their skill and/or the effectiveness of treatment and supervision. As a result, they can develop a skeptical attitude that is apparent in their interactions with offenders.

Worse yet, professionals can take out their frustration on their clients, co-workers, or family. This 'parallel process' was first described in reference to victim treatment providers. Parallel process involves professionals taking on some of the characteristics of the population with which they are working, such as abuse, powerlessness, rage, secrecy and denial (McAllister, 1997). Professionals may be especially vulnerable to negative job impacts when they are experiencing high stress in other areas of their lives.

Sex offenders frequently try to manipulate professionals, so the professionals who are effective with them tend to scrutinize the offender's statements and behavior. However, this skill becomes problematic when the scrutiny carries over into interactions with co-workers. This process often affects team communication and functioning, and if offenders become aware of the breakdown, they tend to exacerbate splits between team members in order to take the focus off their own behavior. If team members are aware of the symptoms of parallel process and the resulting team dysfunction, they can try to intervene before the process becomes incurable. Symptoms of team dysfunction include team communication breaking down, team members avoiding each other, team members being intolerant of different opinions, team members making assumptions about other members and holding on to assumptions that maintain their anger, and team members recruiting others who will value their opinions and join their side.

Preventive measures include training new staff about the symptoms of trauma and parallel process, establishing a team culture that allows members to debrief the materials they are exposed to, and setting team rules for resolving conflicts. In a survey of therapists working at the Colorado Department of Corrections, most reported that they relied on their co-workers for support to deal with job impacts. If teams acknowledge negative job impacts, members can ask others on the team if they are feeling stress, thus creating opportunities for members to debrief. More formal opportunities can also be developed by scheduling periodic meetings where professionals can talk about job impacts in a safe environment.

Helpful team rules can include the following: agreeing to resolve conflicts at the lowest level by first trying to resolve them directly with the other member of the team, listening to and respecting each other's point of view, reviewing the file or interviewing the offender together, and always paying attention to others' concerns about the offender. On specialized units, it is always helpful if agencies allow professionals to rotate off a caseload either temporarily or permanently when a break is needed.

Prior to initiating polygraphy, administrators should prepare staff for potential negative job impacts. It is understandable that sex offenders attempt to maintain secrets about their offending history and ongoing problems, so the inability of a team member to obtain the same level of information without the polygraph does not reflect on his/her skill or the skill of the team. The polygraph simply provides an additional tool. Information obtained during testing emphasizes how difficult it is for offenders to change and highlights the importance of the containment team's work. Complete knowledge of the scope of the problem helps teams develop sound plans to help offenders change and promote public safety.

CONCLUSION

Polygraph testing with convicted sex offenders remains controversial. While the NRC (2003, p. 4) determined that polygraph testing could detect deception at odds well above chance, they also noted that it was far less than perfect. Cross and Saxe (2001) point out the risks of polygraph testing sex offenders: 'Errors with deceptive individuals can lead to new offences against children, whereas errors with truthful individuals can devastate people's lives' (p. 203). While this caution is important to remember, the same errors can be made without polygraph and result in similar consequences.

Will offenders be more honest about new offences without polygraph testing? Is clinical judgment of therapists and supervising officers more accurate than polygraph testing? These are pressing questions. Similar concerns arise with risk prediction. Actuarial assessment instruments, although far from perfect, have been found to be more effective than clinical judgment alone. Perhaps more appropriately, the questions should focus on whether use of the polygraph increases the team's ability to discern prior and current offences, promote honesty in offenders and deter high-risk behaviors. Errors in judgment regarding an offender's self-reported offence behavior most likely will happen at increased rates without the polygraph and have the same potential consequence as errors with polygraph.

In sum, many sex offenders have finely honed manipulation skills. Polygraph provides another tool that can be used as a more objective and independent source of information. Its use in any given jurisdiction requires a careful and thoughtful undertaking, with significant collaboration and communication among well-trained and knowledgeable professionals. Like the field of sex offender management itself, the use of the polygraph will evolve and improve with study and careful implementation.

ACKNOWLEDGMENTS

The authors wish to acknowledge the helpful comments and assistance from Don Krapohl, Ray Nelson, Karen Vigil and Barbara Krauth.

REFERENCES

Abel, G.G., Becker, J.V., Cunningham-Rathner, J., Mittelmann, M.S., & Rouleau, J.L. (1988). Multiple paraphilic diagnoses among sex offenders. *Bulletin of the American Academy of Psychiatry and the Law*, *16*, 153–168.

Abrams, S. & Ogard, E. (1986). Polygraph surveillance of probationers. *Polygraph*, *15*, 174–182.

Abrams, S. & Simmons, G. (2000). Post-conviction polygraph testing: Then and now. *Polygraph*, *29*, 63–67.

Ahlmeyer, S., Heil, P., McKee, B., & English, K. (2000). The impact of polygraphy on admissions of victims and offenses in adult sexual offenders. *Sexual Abuse: A Journal of Research and Treatment*, *12*, 123–138.

American Medical Association (November, 1995). *Sexual assault in America* (position paper). Baltimore, MD: Author.

Burton, D. & Smith-Darden, J. (2001). *North American survey of sexual abuser treatment and models summary data*. Brandon, VT: Safer Society Foundation, Inc. Responses to Safer Society 1999–2000 Survey – Polygraph Question Results, personal communication.

Cross, T. & Saxe, L. (2001). Polygraph testing and sexual abuse: The lure of the magic lasso. *Child Maltreatment*, *6*, 195–206.

Elliott, D.S. (1994). *The developmental course of sexual and non-sexual violence: Results from a national longitudinal study*. Paper presented at the meeting of the Association for the Treatment of Sexual Abusers 13th Annual Research and Treatment Conference, San Francisco, CA.

Emerick, R.L. & Dutton, W.A. (1993). The effect of polygraphy on the self-report of adolescent sex offenders: Implications for risk assessment. *Annals of Sex Research*, *6*, 84–103.

England, K., Olsen, S., Zakrajsek, T., Murray, P., & Ireson, R. (2001). Cognitive/behavioral treatment for sexual offenders: An examination of recidivism. *Sexual Abuse: A Journal of Research and Treatment*, *13*, 223–231.

English, K., Pullen, S., & Jones, L. (1996). *Managing adult sex offenders: A containment approach*. Lexington, KY: American Probation and Parole Association.

English, K., Jones, L., Pasini-Hill, D. *et al.* (2000). *The value of polygraph testing in sex offender management*. Final research report submitted to the National Institute of Justice for grant number D97LBVX0034. Denver, CO: Colorado Division of Criminal Justice, Office of Research and Statistics.

English, K., Lowden, K., DiTrolio, E. *et al.* (2002, February). *Using the polygraph examination with juveniles with sexual behavior problems*. Presentation to the Colorado Sex Offender Management Board, Lakewood, CO.

Epstein, J. & Langenbahn, S. (1994). *The criminal justice and community response to rape*. Issues and Practices in Criminal Justice series, National Institute of Justice. Washington: US Department of Justice.

Finkelhor, D. (1988). The trauma of sexual abuse: Two models. In G. Wyatt & G. Powell (Eds), *Lasting effects of child sexual abuse* (pp. 61–82). Newbury Park, CA: Sage.

Freeman-Longo, R.E. (1985). *Incidence of self-reported sex crimes among incarcerated rapists and child molesters*. Unpublished manuscript, Correctional Treatment Program, Oregon State Hospital.

Freeman-Longo, R. & Blanchard, G. (1998). *Sexual Abuse in America: Epidemic of the 21st Century*. Brandon, VT: Safer Society Press.

Grubin, D., Madsen, L., Parsons, S. *et al.* (2004). A prospective study of the impact of polygraphy on high-risk behaviors in adult sex offenders. *Sexual Abuse: A Journal of Research and Treatment*, *16*, 209–222.

Hammond, D. (1980). *The responding of normals, alcoholics, and psychopaths in a laboratory lie-detection experiment*. A PhD dissertation submitted to the California School of Professional Psychology, San Diego.

Hansen, R., Resnick, H., Saunders, B. *et al.* (1999). Factors related to the reporting of childhood rape. *Child Abuse and Neglect*, *23*, 559–569.

Hanson, K. & Morton-Bourgon, K. (2004). *Predictors of sexual recidivism: An updated meta-analysis*. Ottawa, Ontario, Canada: Public Safety and Emergency Preparedness Canada. Public Works and Government Services Canada. (Cat. No: PS3-1/2004-2E-PDF, ISBN: 0-662-36397-3)

Hanson, R.K., Gordon, A., Harris, A.J.R. *et al.* (2002). First report of the collaborative outcome data project on the effectiveness of psychological treatment for sex offenders. *Sexual Abuse: A Journal of Research and Treatment*, *14*, 169–194.

Harrison, J.S. & Kirkpatrick, B. (2000). Polygraph testing and behavioral change with sex offenders in an outpatient setting: an exploratory study. *Polygraph*, *29*, 20–25.

Heil, P., Ahlmeyer, S., & Simons, D. (2003a). Crossover sexual offenses. *Sexual Abuse: A Journal of Research and Treatment, 15*, 221–236.

Heil, P., Simons, D., & Ahlmeyer, S. (2003b). *Impact of incentives and therapist attitudes on polygraph results*. Presentation at the Association for the Treatment of Sexual Abusers 22nd Annual Research and Treatment Conference, St. Louis, Missouri.

Hepburn, J. & Griffin, M. (2002). *An analysis of risk factors contributing to the recidivism of sex offenders on probation*. Report submitted to the Maricopa County Adult Probation Department and the National Institute of Justice. Tempe, AZ: Arizona State University.

Hindman, J. (1988). *Just before dawn*. Boise, ID: Northwest Printing.

Hindman, J. & Peters, J. (1988, July/August). Research disputes assumptions about child molesters. *National District Attorneys Association Bulletin 1*, 3.

Hindman, J. & Peters, J. (2001). Polygraph testing leads to better understanding adult and juvenile sex offenders. *Federal Probation, 65*, 8–15.

Kircher, J.C., Horowitz, S.W., & Raskin, D.C. (1988). Meta-analysis of mock crime studies of the control question polygraph technique. *Law and Human Behavior, 12*, 79–90.

Kokish, R., Levenson, J., & Blasingame, G. (2005). Post-conviction sex offender polygraph examination: Client-reported perceptions of utility and accuracy. *Sexual Abuse: A Journal of Research and Treatment, 17*, 211–221.

Krapohl, D.J., Senter, S.M., & Stern, B.A. (2005). An exploration of methods for the analysis of multiple-issue relevant/irrelevant screening data. *Polygraph, 34*(1), 47–61.

LaFond, J.Q. & Winick, B.J. (2004). Sex offender re-entry courts: A proposal for managing the risk of returning sex offenders to the community. *Seton Hall Law Review, 34*(4), 1173–1212.

Lowden, K., Hetz, N., Patrick, D. *et al.* (2003). *Evaluation of Colorado's prison therapeutic community for sex offenders: A report of findings*. Denver: Colorado Department of Public Safety, Division of Criminal Justice, Office of Research and Statistics.

McAllister, G.J. (1997). When helping hurts: How trauma impacts our work. *The CCASA Connection, 6*(1–2), 5–9.

Meehl, P.E. & Rosen, A. (1955). Antecedent probability and the efficiency of psychometric signs, patterns, and cutting scores. *Psychological Bulletin, 52*, 194–216.

Monahan, J. (1981). *Predicting violent behavior: An assessment of clinical techniques*. Thousand Oaks: Sage Publication.

National Research Council (2003). *The polygraph and lie detection*. Committee to Review the Scientific Evidence on the Polygraph. Washington, DC: The National Academies Press.

National Victim Center & Crime Victims Research and Treatment Center (1992). *Rape in America: A report to the nation*. Arlington, VA: Author.

O'Connell, M.A. (1998). Using polygraph testing to assess deviant sexual history of sex offenders. *Dissertation Abstracts International, 58*, 3023.

Patrick, C. & Iacono, W. (1989). Psychopathy, threat, and polygraph test accuracy. *Journal of Applied Psychology, 74*, 347–355.

Raskin, D. & Hare, R. (1978). Psychopathy and detection of deception in a prison population. *Psychophysiology, 15*, 126–136.

Russell, D. (1986). *The Secret Trauma: Incest in the lives of girls and women*. New York, NY: Basic Books.

Simons, D., Heil, P., & English, K. (2004). *Utilizing polygraph as a risk prediction/treatment progress assessment tool*. Presentation at the Association for the Treatment of Sexual Abusers 23rd Annual Research and Treatment Conference, Albuquerque, NM.

Smith, D., Letourneau, E., Saunders, B. *et al.* (2000). Delay in disclosure of childhood rape: Results from a national survey. *Child Abuse and Neglect*, *24*, 273–287.

Stalans, L.J. (2004). Adult sex offenders on community supervision: A review of recent assessment strategies and treatment. *Criminal Justice and Behavior*, *31*, 564–608.

Tanner, J. & Veeder, G. (1997). *Incidence of sex offender risk behavior during treatment*. Research Project Final Report. Teaching Humane Existence, Inc., Wheat Ridge, Colorado, USA. Paper available from the authors.

Tanner, J. & Veeder, G. (2001). Incidence of sex offender risk behavior during treatment. Available from www.kbsolutions.com/polysumm.pdf.

Tjaden, P. & Thoennes, N. (2006). *Extent, nature, and consequences of rape victimization: Findings from the national violence against women survey*. Washington DC: National Institute of Justice (NCJ 210346).

Vigil, K. & Jenks, J. (2004). *Using the polygraph to ensure optimal treatment and supervision strategies*. Presentation at the Association for the Treatment of Sexual Abusers 23rd Annual Research and Treatment Conference, Albuquerque, NM.

Weinrott, M.R. & Saylor, M. (1991). Self-report of crimes committed by sex offenders. *Journal of Interpersonal Violence*, *6*, 286–300.

Wilcox, D.T. & Sosnowski, D. (2005). Polygraph examination of British sexual offenders: A pilot study on sexual history disclosure testing. *Journal of Sexual Aggression*, *11*, 3–25.

Wilcox, D.T., Sosnowski, D., Warberg, B., & Beech, A.R. (2005). Sexual history disclosure using the polygraph in a sample of British sex offenders in treatment. *Polygraph*, *34*, 171–181.

CHAPTER 11

Other Post-Conviction Applications of Polygraphy

Shay Addison and Lou Crisilla

INTRODUCTION

The treatment and supervision of offender populations has developed considerably in the past 15 years, primarily as a consequence of the application of the growing body of research focusing upon identifying and targeting the criminogenic needs of offenders (Hanson & Bussière, 1998; Towl & Crighton, 1997). Increased knowledge about what factors are predictive of recidivistic behavior enables the development of a range of strategies to counter such factors and therefore reduce the likelihood of recidivism among offenders identified predominantly within the criminal justice system.

'Risk-focused research' has had a profound impact upon what has shaped the approach to how we treat and supervise offenders (Andrews & Bonta, 2003). The terms 'risk assessment' and 'risk management' are now common to people who work in any capacity with offender populations, and are the cornerstone of the National Probation Service for England and Wales' primary goal of public protection.

While variations in approach to offender management exist across the globe, (i.e., legal frameworks, statutory bodies, treatment provision,

The Use of the Polygraph in Assessing, Treating and Supervising Sex Offenders: A Practitioner's Guide
Edited by Daniel T. Wilcox.

theoretical orientation), there is general agreement that a combination of targeted treatment and effective statutory supervision to monitor an offender's behavior whilst living in the community, are crucial components for achieving success in terms of preventing reoffending.

As our understanding of 'what works' with offenders becomes greater over time, so does our understanding of the shortcomings in the system and the gaps which need to be plugged. In recent years in England and Wales, a number of important initiatives have been developed in response to identified shortcomings across the criminal justice system. These have included changes in legislation, developing national registers of offenders, introduction of multi-agency public protection panels for high-risk offenders, provision of supervised residency via approved premises, imposing curfews and tagging, enabling specific prevention orders such as sex offence prevention orders and antisocial behavior orders to be administered, and mandating treatment of offending behavior as a condition of a statutory order.

In spite of these initiatives, one issue consistently highlighted as a major shortcoming is the over-reliance upon an offender's self-report, in respect to assessment, treatment and also supervision. For instance, Hudson and Ward (1997) identified this reliance as the "single greatest challenge facing the area (of sexual offender assessment and treatment)" and argued that professionals needed "credible alternatives to self-report" (p. 490). This view was reiterated by the Association for the Treatment of Sexual Abusers (ATSA), which proposed that polygraphy be used as a method of overcoming the problem of over-reliance on an offender's self-report (ATSA, 2001). Of course, the concern of being over-reliant upon an offender's self-report is not confined just to sex offenders, however, and is arguably relevant to most offenders within a criminal justice context.

In this regard, polygraphy as a method of verifying an offender's self-report appears capable of making a significant contribution to the management and treatment of offenders more generally.

WHERE DO THE GAPS EXIST IN THE TREATMENT AND SUPERVISION OF OFFENDERS?

Broadly speaking, treatment for various types of offences attempts to assist the individual to develop the necessary insight and skills to manage specific dysfunctional behaviors.

It is, of course, difficult to evaluate whether an offender is actively applying the newly acquired skills in his real life when necessary. In reality, evaluation can often be based upon what the offender says and does during statutory sessions with program facilitators or case managers.

The same is true with respect to gauging supervision compliance. In relation to the vast majority of offenders, probation officers are left to rely primarily upon whether an offender chooses to report any problematic or risky behavior. This is particularly so where an offender has been classified as being at low or medium static risk of reoffence. In a system where there are substantial consequences to be avoided by failing to report risk behaviors (i.e., possible loss of liberty, increased supervision, extra restrictions, further prosecutions) and rewards to be gained (i.e., easing of restrictions, engaging in desired antisocial behaviors, gaining access to potential victims), it is unsurprising that many offenders 'keep mum'.

When reflecting upon how the polygraph contributes to plugging these gaps within the framework of treating and supervising sex offenders, it is logical to expect that there could be benefits from using post-conviction polygraphy with other populations of offenders. This is particularly so given that the general supervision and treatment of many offenders in England and Wales is achieved in a similar way, and will thus also be vulnerable to the same 'gaps' in information (i.e., incomplete or misinformation) which occurs when staff lack access to alternatives to offender self-report.

A NOTE ON VALIDATION VERSUS DETECTION

Whilst most of the emphasis of post-conviction polygraphy literature is about detecting unknown behaviors (English *et al.*, 2003; Wilcox, 2005), the issue of verification of self-report (rather than invalidation) is an important, but often overlooked one. Knowledge that a significant number of offenders are likely not to recidivate (Hanson & Bussière, 1998; Hanson & Morton-Bourgon, 2005), in addition to the knowledge that treatment can work, means recognizing that offenders can and do change; a point which is relevant even for those deemed 'high risk' and 'very high risk', (as not all 'high- or very high-risk' offenders are thought to reoffend). In reality, however, how do we determine which of the offenders have genuinely implemented change? How does a probation officer supervising a violent offender with a history of offending and general antisocial tendencies decide that the offender's risk has changed? How much weight is put on the mere absence of any new arrest or complaint about his behavior? How much on the offender's assurances that he has been honest and is not failing to report? And how much on the progress reports from his group treatment and on the reports from hostel staff, and so on?

For those offenders where ongoing suspicion about their compliance is inevitable (and warranted), and where there is a lack of substantiating behavioral evidence of non-compliance, periodic polygraph testing can serve a functional purpose in terms of helping to provide direction about an offender. It can be used as a means for the offender to 'prove' or vindicate him or herself, while also reassuring the case manager or relevant authority that his/her suspicions remain unfounded, or otherwise. Without any process for verification, a sustained overestimation of offender risk can also occur, which has other implications for the criminal justice system, ranging from unnecessary deployment of resources right through to the indeterminate detention of an offender via a public protection sentence, legislated in England in 2003.

THE CASE FOR BROADENING APPLICATION OF POST-CONVICTION POLYGRAPHY TO ALTERNATE OFFENDER POPULATIONS

In terms of populations of non-sex offenders who have been identified as: (a) in need of treatment for their offending behavior; (b) likely to under-report relevant behavior or deliberately deceive; (c) where detection of compliance or lack of it is difficult to ascertain; and (d) where reoffending is likely to cause serious physical, psychological or other injury (i.e., financial) to the victim, the following three categories readily come to mind:

1. Domestic abuse
2. Stalking
3. General violence.

Looking at post-conviction polygraphy in a broader context is also pertinent when consideration is given to the prevalence rates for non-sexual offences within society. Home Office figures published in 2001 (Home Office, 2001) indicate that the majority of recorded victims within the criminal justice system are directly or indirectly victimized by someone who is considered to be a violent offender, not a sex offender. More effective monitoring of violent offender populations is therefore vital to achieve greater protection for the wider public.

Domestic Abuse

Domestic abuse represents the single greatest category of violence against British women, and accounts for one-quarter of all violent crime in the UK (Home Office, 2006). The *British Crime Survey* (BCS) of 2001 estimated that 26 % of females and 17 % of males aged between 16 and 59 had experienced at least one incident of domestic abuse in their lives. They also estimated that in one calendar year in England and Wales there are approximately 12.9 million (non-sexual) incidents of domestic abuse perpetrated against women, and 2.5 million (non-sexual) domestic incidents perpetrated against males. Around one-third of women are thought to be repeatedly victimized, with a small proportion of them (3.3 %) being subjected to a variety of abuses within the domestic context (i.e., combination of emotional, psychological and physical abuse, as well as rape and stalking). Ultimately, two women per week in the UK are murdered by a partner or ex-partner.

The extent of domestic abuse within the UK is clearly something which affects very many people. This estimation mushrooms further when 'unrecorded' victims of domestic abuse are considered, such as children, extended family members, friends, neighbors and others who either witness such incidents or who are indirectly exposed to the behavior.

Stalking

In relation to stalking, the BCS (2001) estimated that 19 % of females and 12 % of males aged between 16 and 59 have been stalked in their life, with 900,000 males and around one and a quarter million females having experienced stalking in one calendar year. Although stalking is often a form of domestic abuse (Mullen, Pathe & Purcell, 2000; National Probation Service for England and Wales, 2003; Sheridan & Davies, 2004), the BCS (2001) found that two-thirds of people reported being stalked by someone who was non-intimate.

Statistics from other countries suggest that it is an equally common problem. The Australian Bureau of Statistics (1996) national survey found that 15 % of adult women had been the victim of stalking in their lifetime, equating to around one million females. Ex-intimate victims reported being stalked for the longest duration (between six months to over two years), a trend consistent with data from North America (Tjaden, 1997). Prevalence rates in the US were reported to be between 8 and 12 % of the female population and between 2 and 4 % of the male population.

Intimate partner stalking appears to represent the most dangerous form, with some literature reporting that up to 75 % of victims of attempted or successful femicide had been stalked prior to being attacked or murdered (McFarlane *et al.*, 1999).

General Violence

Recent government crime statistics (Home Office, 2006) show that (with the exception of property crime) incidents of a violent nature represent the largest category of crime in England and Wales for the year 2004/05 with a total of 2,412,000 recorded by police. Two million of the overall figures represented the offences of assault, wounding, robbery and snatch theft. They excluded homicide and sexual crimes. Domestic abuse crimes were also included in the total, and were officially recorded at 401,000 for that calendar year. This figure stands in stark contrast to the BCS (2001) estimate of UK community prevalence being in the region of 15.9 million incidents per year, thus highlighting the problem of under-reporting.

Consequences of Violent Behavior and the Problem of Under-Reporting

It is generally agreed that violent crime is significantly under-reported to authorities, and particularly so when we consider cases such as sexual abuse, domestic abuse and stalking. The BCS (2001) found that in domestic abuse cases, 34 % of females and 62 % of males did not tell a single other person about the incident(s), and that when people did tell someone it was likely to be through informal networks, such as friends or family. In relation to stalking only around a third of both male and female victims in the UK informed police. Reporting rates for stalking appear to be consistent across some western countries, with only 38 % of Australian stalking victims reporting the behavior to the police, and a slightly better 50 % in relation to US victims (Australian Bureau of Statistics, 1996; Tjaden, 1997).

The impact of violent crime upon victims can be prolonged and debilitating. Violent crime also has significant 'knock-on effects' as it creates what has been described as "secondary victims" (Ruback & Thompson, 2001); those in the victim's immediate environment, such as children, extended family members, friends, colleagues, neighbors and the wider community. The impact and costs are difficult to calculate as consequences span across the spectrum of individual, community and system (i.e., criminal justice, mental health, social welfare, employment sector).

Mullen *et al.* (2000) highlighted that stalking may produce chronic stress reactions and other prolonged negative psychological consequences for the victim, as it is by definition a form of persistent, repetitive trauma. They also point out that because victims of stalking live in a state of vigilance and fear of the potential of future threat, the impact upon them can far outlive the duration of the actual harassing behaviors. In addition to the psychological and emotional effects that stalking has upon victims, many have also reported significant lifestyle consequences, ranging from minor alterations (i.e., changing phone numbers, installation of motion sensor lighting) through to major (i.e., relocating residence, loss of employment) and sometimes radical life changes (i.e., emigration).

Surveys indicate that significant proportions of victims of stalking report symptoms consistent with Post Traumatic Stress Disorder (PTSD) and that all victims experience a level of disruption and distress as a direct result of their stalker's behavior. In some cases the effects upon victims are completely devastating and represent a profound deterioration across all levels of functioning (Mullen *et al.*, 2000). Other research has found that a significant number of the 13,000 male and female victims of stalking who were surveyed reported being more prone to becoming injured or suffering from a chronic disease since they began to be stalked (Davis, Coker & Sanderson, 2002). Ninety-two percent of female victims of domestic abuse in England and Wales reported suffering some type of physical injury, while nearly one-third (31 %) also reported suffering from mental or emotional problems as a consequence of the abuse (Home Office, 2001).

Research has found that the reasons for lack of reporting are varied and complex. Those cited in a selection of adult victim surveys include: victim's fear of retribution from the offender towards them, their family or significant others (most common in domestic abuse cases); family pressures; lack of confidence in authorities and the legal system; age; vulnerability; lack of awareness of support and resources available for victims; and even a lack of appreciation of the significance (i.e., possible risk) that certain behaviors represent (Australian Bureau of Statistics, 1996; Mullen *et al.*, 2000; Tjaden, 1997).

As the BCS is a victim survey and police crime statistics are based on crime categorization, neither provide ready information about the proportion of perpetrators who may have been subject to probation/parole at the time. However, it is reasonable to expect that some will have been known to authorities responsible for their monitoring, management and for the prevention of further harm to known victims or possible future victims.

Given the many reasons why victims of various crimes do not report clear instances of abusive behavior which would result in action being taken by the probation service and/or police, it is imperative that with known offenders the vigilance for detection and onus of responsibility for monitoring their behavior, is placed, as much as possible, within the criminal justice system or other relevant authority, rather than disproportionately upon the victims of such crimes. Domestic abuse legislation in the UK, which enables police to pursue a prosecution without a formal victim complaint, is a good example of a recent initiative designed to achieve this aim. However, more work needs to be done to address this issue.

CURRENT THEORIES USED TO INFORM WORK WITH CONVICTED OFFENDERS

Cognitive Behavioral Therapy (CBT) Model

There is no one conceptual theory which fits in terms of understanding who commits offences, and why certain types of offending behaviors are committed by certain individuals. Indeed, in regard to research about different behaviors (domestic abuse, stalkers, sexual abuse), much debate continues in relation to the etiology, typology, legislative requirements, identification of criminogenic needs and treatment targets for the offences.

Arguably, there is general agreement that cognitive behavioral therapy (CBT) is the most effective method for working with a variety of clinical issues, including offending behaviors (Fernandez *et al.*, 2006). CBT has been adopted as the primary therapeutic method of practice for training clinicians in the UK, Canada, Australia, New Zealand and the USA. It is also the approved method of practice within accredited offending behavior programs throughout the England and Wales probation service.

The central tenet of CBT is that a person's thought processes drive their behavior. In terms of offending behavior, the theory posits that faulty thinking processes, (e.g., distorted thoughts, assumptive thinking, poor decision-making, lack of consequential thinking and so on) allow a person to give themselves permission to act in a way which violates the rights of other people.

Relapse Prevention (RP) Model

The Relapse Prevention Model was adopted from the addictions literature, and despite ongoing debate about its utility as a model of offending

(Briggs & Kennington, 2006; Laws & Ward, 2006), it continues to be the basis of the treatment model used with a variety of offender populations, including sexual offenders and domestic abusers.

Briefly, the RP model posits that prior to the commission of reoffence, an offender will generally encounter some type of destabilizing event, which leads to a cycle of unhealthy behaviors occurring, which in turn (if left unchecked) leads him/her closer to the act of committing a reoffence. The general goal of RP is to educate the offender about the cycle, to recognize the small cognitive, behavioral and situational steps along the way, and to assist them in anticipating and developing coping skills to manage these issues in the future (Laws & Ward, 2006).

The Relapse Prevention Model of treatment has been found to be effective in facilitating risk management in the community (Briggs & Kennington, 2006; Wilson *et al.*, 2000) primarily because the model provides a means of planning treatment with the offender and also enables structured follow-up work after treatment has been completed.

For the majority of offence types, current practices of offender management within the criminal justice system in England and Wales reflect the central tenets of a CBT Relapse Prevention Model. During treatment, each offender is required to develop an understanding of their specific offending behavior in terms of thoughts, feelings and behaviors, which in turn is used to design matched strategies to prevent a reoccurrence of the offending behavior in the future. The specific behaviors identified in offender's individual CBT and RP plans are used as core testing material for polygraph examinations.

HOW CAN POLYGRAPH CONTRIBUTE TO THIS MODEL?

Post-conviction polygraphy can contribute to three primary goals in managing offender behavior by:

1. Facilitating assessment *of the offending behavior*;
2. Facilitating *honest engagement in the treatment process / evaluation of treatment intervention*;
3. Facilitating the *monitoring of offender behavior in the community*.

Facilitating Assessment of the Offending Behavior

It is well recognized that an accurate assessment is necessary for the effective treatment and management of any behavior. This is best achieved by accessing information from a variety of sources, such as interviewing offender and other relevant individuals, psychometric tools, observation and historical documents (i.e., medical files, psychological and psychiatric reports). Not only is assessment essential for effective treatment, it is also crucial for being able to implement the most appropriate range of strategies to decrease the likelihood that the offender will recidivate or cause further harm to people.

The best possible assessment of an offender is also ethically imperative, given that serious decisions about offenders are made upon the basis of people's assessment of their needs and progress throughout the criminal justice system. Offenders are provided or denied access to services on the basis of the information contained in professional assessment and are routinely released or detained on the basis of the same process.

Polygraph history examination. The application of the polygraph history examination grew out of the knowledge that significant proportions of offenders will have a history (some a very substantial one) of offending which has remained undetected (Abrams, 1991). The first published research which brought this issue into clear focus was conducted by Gene Abel in relation to sexual offenders (Abel *et al.*, 1988). It has subsequently been reported in other populations of offenders, including domestic abuse offenders and stalkers (Mullen *et al.*, 2000).

History exams consider the index behavior (i.e., rape) and related behaviors (i.e., stalking, voyeurism, deviant fantasy) in terms of onset, duration and frequency over the course of an offender's lifespan.

As with other forms of assessment, history exams should be conducted at a time which enables the information gained from it to inform and direct treatment. In some cases this may mean conducting a polygraph history exam prior to treatment beginning (to uncover unknown information), while in other cases a history exam may be used in some way through the group treatment process (i.e., to test the veracity and completeness of reported information relating to the index offence).

Where the offending behavior involves the commission of an act against another person, a history exam always attempts to ascertain whether the offender has victimized any other person in a similar way. That is, it seeks to answer: are there any unknown victims?

History exams are broad, however, and can also assess for whether the offender has engaged in a variety of behaviors associated with the index offence. For example, in relation to the perpetration of intimate partner abuse, the pre-test interview phase can cover the whole range of abusive behaviors (i.e., from dictating home tasks based upon rigid sex roles, to controlling what the partner wore, to controlling finances, through to sexual coercion, serious physical assault and femicide).

Applying a history exam to a domestic abuse offender would in the first instance normally involve focusing upon the extent to which the offender has (or has not) abused/assaulted any intimate partner(s) prior to the current victim. A secondary version of the history exam could also then focus upon obtaining an accurate history of domestic abuse perpetrated against the current/index victim.

Likewise, for stalking behavior, a history exam would focus upon assessing the extent to which the offender has (if ever) stalked any other person prior to the victim of his index offence(s). It can also facilitate gaining a more accurate history of stalking behavior against the victim of the index offence. Again, the pre-test interview would also cover extensive stalking-related behaviors.

For general violent behavior, a history exam would focus upon assessing the extent to which the offender (if ever) has been violent with anyone prior to the victim of his index offence(s), with the pre-test interview focusing upon a broad range of behaviors associated with the type of violence perpetrated (i.e., hooliganism, pub brawls, gang violence, street muggings).

Facilitating Honest Engagement in Treatment and Evaluation of Treatment Intervention

Base rates of deception in offender populations have been consistently judged to be high, as much as 90% (Salter, 1997). It has also been shown that even when conditions for the offender to cooperate with the treatment process are 'ideal' (i.e., supportive environment, experienced facilitator, not asked to incriminate selves), some offenders will continue to deceive authorities about their true behavior (Salter, 1997). It is recognized that the more honest an offender can be with people about his risk behaviors (both staff and other support people), the greater the treatment gain will be. There is no doubt that some offenders require more than is currently available in order to be honest during treatment.

Denial polygraph examination. This exam is conducted when an offender either does not admit to committing the index offence, disputes certain parts of the offending, or seriously minimizes aspects of the offence when measured against victim/witness statements. The denial exam has obvious application in being able to facilitate an offender's more honest engagement in the treatment process.

It can also help to clarify aspects of an offender's index offence which may be unclear due to conflicting or incomplete file information (i.e., opposing witness statements), or where any offender states that he has no memory of the events.

Denial exams are normally done at the beginning of an offender's sentence (for those in complete denial or stating amnesia) or in the early stages of treatment (where there are serious discrepancies or minimization).

Maintenance and monitoring polygraph examinations. Maintenance and monitoring polygraph exams are conducted as part of evaluating how well the offender has been managing his dynamic risk behaviors and offending behavior whilst undertaking treatment and subject to supervision. Maintenance exams are general 'check-up' exams designed to be administered regularly (normally six-monthly); while monitoring exams are reactive and done when staff strongly suspect the offender of having engaged in specific inappropriate behavior (or actual reoffending), but have no overt proof of such. Monitoring exams are conducted only when a specific request is made, but this can be done at any time throughout the offender's supervision. Both of these exams provide relevant staff with an indication of how open an offender is being in treatment about their behavior, and how well they understand or are applying the concepts of treatment to their situation.

Hanson and Wallace-Capretta (2000) make the point in relation to sexual offenders that it is essential that a rigorous process of participant performance and outcome evaluation, using a range of methods, be used to evaluate intervention effectiveness. Relying upon offenders filling out post-treatment questionnaires to determine whether someone is 'treated' does not necessarily provide professionals with evidence that genuine attitude or behavior change has occurred, as it may be that the offender has simply become skilled in being able to answer questions in the way that they know professionals desire them to. The maintenance/monitoring exam is particularly important when the range of methods for evaluating behavior is limited.

Grubin *et al.* (2004) found 'faking good' to be a well-established trend within English sex offender probationees, and one which continued to be highlighted throughout a later three-year polygraph trial (Grubin, 2006). A common occurrence among men who were either current participants or program completers was that they reported a spontaneous extinction or complete absence of deviant and inappropriate sexual fantasy/masturbation involving children or adult rape. During polygraph examination, many offenders failed this issue and some went on to make disclosures in the post-test interview confirming the ongoing existence of deviant fantasy and arousal. For those where sexual deviancy was an active issue, the denial of its occurrence was seen as a possible function of offenders learning what others consider to be progress in treatment and what is seen as low or high risk in terms of staff expectations.

Given that both Hanson's meta-analyses (1998, 2005) have found deviancy to be the single greatest predictor of sexual recidivism, this is an area where it is crucial to assist offenders maintain honesty about their patterns of sexual arousal, and that without alternate means of verification, a significant number of men will not be truthful about this issue. This leaves treatment providers in the position of making decisions and evaluations about treatment outcome and risk on the basis of misinformation (if the offender is believed) or on the basis of suspicion alone rather than evidence (where the offender is not believed but continues to maintain his stance).

During treatment programs offenders spend considerable time working through the details of their index offending behavior so as to understand it within a CBT RP framework. It is this information which is used directly to inform the pre-test interview phase of both monitoring and maintenance polygraph exams. Whatever the offender's index offence is should determine what issues will be covered during the maintenance pre-test interview.

For example in RP, the 'pre-offence build-up phase' of an offending cycle requires the offender to describe all the relevant cognitive, emotional, situational and behavioral precursors to their index offence. The maintenance polygraph exam then utilizes this part of the offender's own work to discuss issues during the pre-test interview and then test whether or not over time they have been engaging in behaviors indicative of their particular 'build-up' to offending. The results of the maintenance polygraph examination and any new information are then used to assist the offender in providing a more honest account of their *current* behavior within the group context, which is then incorporated into their future group work. It also assists staff in informing their treatment plan which can include recommending that an offender moves on to the next part of the program, repeats part of the program, is referred to external agencies for specialist intervention(s) and so on.

Facilitating Monitoring of Offender Behavior in the Community

Follow-up is crucial. While there is an expectation that offenders will apply and maintain change strategies, as mentioned previously, behavioral evaluation of offender progress can be conspicuously absent from program manuals.

For the average offender who completes a treatment program, evaluation is done primarily by reviewing an offender's statements made throughout the course of the program and through administrating a variety of psychometric instruments. Psychometrics, however, predominantly measure attitudinal change. One of the primary reasons for a lack of overt measurement of behavioral progress is due to a lack of current viable means by which to do so. In reality it is very difficult to gain a meaningful behavioral evaluation of an offender in his/her own environment.

Some methods used in England and Wales designed to gauge overt offender behavior include:

- Curfew/tag (tells you where the offender is, not what he is doing);
- Surveillance (only viable for the 'critical few' due to cost);
- Home visits by criminal justice system staff (generally infrequent, most offenders will not leave 'evidence' lying around for their probation officer or police to find).

While each method has something different to contribute, all still leave considerable scope for an offender to be able to engage in undetected risk or offending behavior (as we know that an absence of concrete evidence of behavior at one point in time does not mean it is absent at other points in time).

Maintenance and monitoring exams. Once the offender has completed treatment, the focus of polygraph examination is purely to gauge risk behavior and/or reoffending. The offender's completed personal relapse prevention plan is utilized directly by the polygraph examiner to guide the pre-test interview and to formulate test questions. In a post-treatment context, the exam results and any new information are used primarily to inform the case manager's risk assessment and risk management strategies.

Maintenance and monitoring exams should continue after the offender has completed treatment up until their license or order expires and they are no longer subject to statutory supervision.

ALTERNATE OFFENDING POPULATIONS

Within each of the offending paradigms mentioned, there are core behaviors which all offenders who commit these types of offences will engage in to a greater or lesser degree. It is recognized that there is also considerable overlap of some of the offending behaviors within what can be considered to be 'domestic abuse', such as stalking. Notwithstanding this overlap, the following summaries of the different offence types will attempt to categorize the behaviors as they would apply to a polygraph examination.

Denial and monitoring polygraph exams are very similar; the main difference being that a denial exam focuses upon past behavior and monitoring focuses upon current behavior. Essentially the examiner is evaluating an offender's statement against that of a specific, known behavior or allegation.

While history and maintenance exams are also based upon past and present behavior respectively, they differ substantially from denial and monitoring exams, in that they are utilized as a form of assessment, by searching for behaviors which are unknown, or verifying the absence of the same. As such they are more complicated to administer. Consequently, this section will involve outlining the issues that need to be considered when administrating a history and maintenance exam as they apply to different offender populations.

Domestic Abuse

What does this behavior involve? The adoption of a broad definition of domestic abuse appears pertinent when considering the issue in a post-conviction context. This is designed to be in keeping with a therapeutic framework, as the treatment and rehabilitation of offenders often involves looking at behaviors which fall outside of the legal definition of an offence (i.e., anger expression). Dynamic risk behaviors predominantly fall into this category.

Consequently, a 'post-conviction' definition of domestic abuse is deliberately intended to be as inclusive as possible and for the purposes of this chapter it includes the following: the perpetration of threats or use of force against an intimate partner; the use of psychological manipulation or other means of deliberate intimidation to control a partner's behavior. It also includes isolating or deliberately preventing an intimate partner from accessing resources, including financial, social, professional or otherwise.

Current treatment/supervision methods of domestic abusers within the CJS. Males perpetrate domestic abuse upon their adult female intimate partners at an overwhelmingly higher rate than females perpetrate abuse upon males (Home Office, 2006). Consequently, treatment programs within the England and Wales criminal justice system focus exclusively on male offenders. Within this context a range of methods to treat and manage men convicted of domestic abuse is advocated (Kebbell & Gilchrist, 2005).

Treatment programs such as the Home Office accredited Integrated Domestic Abuse Program (IDAP) is group-based and delivered through a combination of psycho-education and cognitive behavioral techniques, within a RP framework. It is designed to target five domains: emotional mismanagement, problems of self-regulation, motivation for change, distorted thinking and social skills deficits (National Probation Service for England and Wales, 2003). From these domains, specific treatment targets for consideration are drawn from a range of 'precursors to battering' identified by Harway and Hanson (1994) which cover a range of cognitive, affective and behavioral indicators.

Specifically, intervention takes the form of: education about the power and control wheel/equality wheel model of domestic abuse, exploration of abusive attitudes and consequences for victims. Anger control training is facilitated through strategies such as assisting the offender to recognize his anger cues, use time out, use positive self-talk, coping with jealousy, perspective taking, being assertive, being aware of non-verbal behaviors, communication skills and conflict resolution.

In terms of monitoring domestic abuse offenders, they are generally subject to standard license or probation conditions, which can proscribe extra restrictions depending upon the case, such as residence. Offenders are also subject to any other court-sanctioned order such as a restraining order or child access order. Offenders are seen regularly by case managers and have treatment mandated as a statutory requirement.

Gaps in the system. There remains vigorous debate in the literature as to the effectiveness of treatment programs and rate of recidivism for domestic abusers. Despite the lack of clarity surrounding this issue, there is agreement in the literature that there exists a subgroup of domestic abuse offenders who continue to assault their female partners despite treatment, and that repeat assaults are among the most severe in terms of injury to the victim. For example, Gondolf (1997) found that within 15 months of completing treatment, 20 % of domestic abuse offenders had repeatedly reassaulted their partners. The men who persist in reoffending appear to be unresponsive to existing intervention strategies, and as such represent a significant danger to their partner/ex-partner.

Where current treatment strategies are not effective with men who remain in the community (i.e., an offender is considered 'intractable'), the only option to prevent reoffending and avoid further harm to victim(s) is strict, legally-sanctioned monitoring.

Polygraph information and results are maximized when used in both treatment and supervision contexts. However, when an offender's motivation to engage in treatment is diminished, periodic maintenance and monitoring polygraph testing could be a useful tool to gauge whether an offender who engages poorly with treatment is actually engaging in any inappropriate behavior. Mandated polygraphy could also provide a means by which to plug the gap in relation to offenders who drop out of treatment.

How polygraph could be applied. Conducting a domestic abuse history exam would involve interviewing the offender about a broad range of abusive behaviors, with test questions focusing on use of overt violence upon an intimate partner(s), in a historical context (prior to index conviction). All aspects of domestically abusive behavior should be covered.

A domestic abuse maintenance exam would focus upon testing the same range of abusive behaviors covered in the history exam, but would also interview the offender about whether he has engaged in any dynamic risk behaviors (i.e., not necessarily abusive behaviors). The context would be current; during the offender's community sentence (since index conviction/last six months).

Harway and Hanson (1994) identified 17 specific precursors to battering. These being:

- unreasonable jealousy
- controlling behavior, such as denying partner access to money, transport, restricting her socializing
- quick involvement with a partner and pressure to make quick commitment
- unrealistic expectations that partner will meet all needs
- isolation/cutting woman off from all resources
- blaming others for all his problems
- blaming others for his feelings
- hypersensitivity: easily hurt or insulted
- cruelty to animals, children
- use of force in sex 'playfully'
- verbal abuse
- rigid sex roles
- abrupt changes of mood
- past battering
- threats of violence
- breaking objects, especially prize possessions
- use of any type of force during an argument.

While most of the 17 factors could be included in a domestic abuse history or maintenance pre-test interview, it is important to remember that polygraphy is designed to test out overt behavior. Consequently, only 7 of the 17 specific precursors listed would be suitable to formulate as polygraph test questions: isolating and cutting woman off from all resources; cruelty to animals and children; 'playful' use of force in sex; verbal abuse; threats of violence; breaking/striking objects, especially prize possessions; and use of force during an argument.

The scope of a maintenance pre-test interview and test questions is likely to be most beneficial when tailored to the offender's personal relapse prevention plan. This should also consider contextual factors which may provide an estranged offender access to potential victims or other things which would be considered risky. In addition to some of the 17 precursors these may include, for example:

- Breaches of exclusion zones/restraining orders;
- Abusive phone calls or other types of direct abusive communication with victim;
- Indirect or third party communication with victim;
- Drive-bys;
- Following victim;
- Unauthorized contact with children;
- Contact with victim's family;
- Breaking and entering victim's property;
- Access/possession of weapons;
- Diary-keeping;
- Drinking/drug-taking;
- Intimidation;
- Preventing from leaving house/accessing others;
- Insults.

General Violence

Violent behavior is most commonly categorized into that of instrumental and expressive. For the purposes of the category of general violence (i.e., non-intimate partner violence), the possible application of polygraphy will be broken into these two groups. It is, however, important to note that the two subcategories of behavior are not mutually exclusive and that an offender's behavior can be driven by both types of motivation at different times, or indeed during the same incident. There are also some instances where it may be difficult to determine the motivation for the violent behavior, which makes categorization difficult, such as cases of child cruelty, and torture.

Instrumental violence can be described as 'means-to-an-end' violence. Armed robbery is a good example of this, where the offender generally uses the amount of violence necessary to complete their desired goal (i.e., steal the bank's cash) and that the act itself represents a person who is in control rather than out of control. It often involves premeditation and planning to achieve a specific purpose. Other examples of instrumental violence include: organized crime, football hooliganism, other gang-related activity, home invasion, kidnapping for ransom and street robbery. Due to the nature of premeditation this type of violent behavior is more likely to involve more than one offender.

Expressive violence is the result of someone who has lost control of their emotions. This is most commonly thought of as a response to conflict or build-up of stress, whereby a person becomes increasingly emotionally aroused and lashes out in an aggressive and physical manner as a means of managing and moderating the negative feelings. Expressive violence is often not premeditated and is less likely to involve a co-offender.

Drug and alcohol abuse has often been identified as a link to violent behavior. Murdoch, Pihl and Ross (1990) reported that 62 % of offenders had been drinking immediately prior to committing violent crime, while Chaiken and Chaiken (1990) found that those who were drug/alcohol dependent were more likely than non-dependent users to commit repeat acts of violence.

Contextual or situational factors have also been identified as important determinants for violent behavior, such as access to a potential victim and/or weapons. Hall (1987) also identified stressors such as the ending of a relationship and financial concerns as predictors of violent offending.

Current treatment / supervision methods of violent crime within the CJS. Treatment for violent offending is again offered throughout probation in the form of a range of CBT programs designed to meet the assessed need of the offender (i.e., instrumental/expressive violence, drug- and alcohol-mediated, etc). This often involves programs such as anger management, substance abuse and thinking skills programs.

The programs aim to facilitate change through the processes of cognitive preparation, critical thinking, self-monitoring and self-regulation, cognitive restructuring, social skills acquisition and rehearsal/practice. Treatment programs attempt to help offenders to stop behaving violently by teaching alternative means by which to deal with problems and issues in their lives. Typically programs also have a section dedicated to skills training and rehearsal.

How polygraph can be applied. The distinction between instrumental and expressive violence is a useful one for the polygraph examiner to understand in as much as it serves to guide the pre-test interview questions and also informs the types of questions which should be formulated for the test. Situational factors are also important precursors to violent crime occurrence, specifically the availability of a weapon and proximity to potential victim(s).

Examples of issues, some identified in the HCR-20 (2nd edition), which could be included in both violence history and maintenance exams include:

- Frequenting establishments known for trouble;
- Associating with peers who engage in violent behavior/previous co-offenders;
- Acquisition of tools/equipment to commit crime (stolen car, weaponry);
- Targeting particular premises or person/people/places looking for likely or possible victims;
- Direct communication with associates about planning criminal/violent behavior;
- Trial runs of crimes;
- Fantasy about engaging in certain behaviors (i.e., twisting child's arm, cutting child);
- Specific grievance thinking – directed towards a particular person or person from an identifiable group;
- Threatened victim/harmed victim/assaulted victim;
- Drinking/drug-taking;
- Breaking/smashing objects – property;
- Conflicts in life;
- General grievance thinking (poor me, victim stance);
- Verbal threats/abuse (received/metered out).

Stalking

What is stalking? Stalking is a term designed to cover a broad range of behaviors commonly termed as 'harassment' in the legal system. Stalking by legal definition must be a repeated, unwanted behavioral intrusion into somebody's life, although the details of what is and is not considered to be stalking can often be a point of conjecture within the CJS. Clinically, however, stalking is understood by the function or perceived nature of the stalking behavior.

A typology of stalkers has been put forward by Mullen *et al.* (2000), demonstrating the heterogeneity of the population, as it attempts to explain the motivation or goal of the stalking for the stalker. His typology included five specific categories: the rejected stalker, resentful stalker, predatory stalker, intimacy-seeking stalker and the incompetent suitor stalker.

Although research has found that anyone can become a victim of stalking, the most likely group of person to become a stalker is the ex-intimate partner of an adult female. Research has consistently found a strong link between domestic abuse and stalking, in that 80 % of the women who reported being stalked by a current or previous partner also reported having been assaulted by that person, and that in 60 % of cases the stalking behavior had begun prior to end of the relationship (Mullen *et al.*, 2000). Stalked ex-intimates are also subject to the widest range of harassing behaviors. Other groups of victims can be strangers, professionals (doctors, helping professionals), work colleagues, famous people and more unusual types such as well-known criminals.

Mullen *et al.* (2000) detailed the importance of identifying and treating mental health issues in this population, and also identified substance abuse as a crucial risk factor for continued stalking.

Current treatment/supervision within the CJS. Stalking experts advocate that for many perpetrators a range of treatment is likely to be necessary. This is particularly so given that stalkers have a high incidence of being co-morbid for a range of psychiatric illness, including delusional disorders, schizophrenia, depression, substance abuse disorders and personality disorders.

Consequently, it is generally advocated that a multidisciplinary approach based upon the principles of risk assessment is required to effectively manage the stalker. This means effective case management to include and coordinate provision from mental health professionals, offending behavior treatment providers, police, victim liaison staff and other relevant resources.

There are no stalking-specific treatment programs within the probation service of England and Wales. Typically those assessed as sexually-motivated 'harassers', are referred to sex offender treatment programs. Similarly, if the stalking takes place in the context of ex-intimate partner harassment, then offenders are referred to relevant programs for domestic abuse.

Gaps in the system. Stalking, more notably than the other offending groups, is a behavior which has only recently been recognized in a legal capacity. Most legislation in countries has only been implemented within the past decade. Academic understanding of stalking is also in its infancy which makes decision-making difficult for all involved. Rosenfeld's (2003) study is the only publication to examine recidivism in stalkers, finding that within 12 months almost half the sample recidivated, with personality issues and substance abuse being considered significant contributors.

Rosenfeld (2004) found threats to be the most consistent correlate of violence in almost every published study of stalking-related violence. They also found that a history of substance abuse typically correlates with an increased rate of violence among stalkers, and that personality disorder was also found to be statistically significant in terms of predicting stalking violence, although the effect was small.

Other research which looked at the prosecution of anti-stalking laws found that many offenders had failed to comply with them, with one 1997 US survey (Tjaden & Thoennes, 1998) finding that up to 70 % of female victims and 80 % of male victims reported that their stalker had violated a restraining order.

Some authors have highlighted a subset of stalkers that go to extreme lengths to perpetrate stalking behaviors and methods of harassment likely to cause significant distress to the victim, while also ensuring that the likelihood of their detection remains low. The given explanation of this includes when a stalker stays within the limits of the law, but exploits the weakness of the law to continue to deliberately harass their victim. For example, a stalker stands exactly 100 meters away from the victim's home because that is the distance proscribed on the restraining order (Sheridan & Davies, 2004).

How polygraph could be applied. While polygraph interviews should be comprehensive and should never make assumptions about what behavior someone has or has not engaged in, knowledge of typologies and application to specific offenders/offences can assist the polygraph examiner to ask questions during the pre-test interview and formulate test questions which best suit that offender's most likely risk(s). This type of approach takes into account the notion of offender heterogeneity and is similar to the anchoring questions for different types of violent or sexual offender.

Assessment – validation of offender's self-report. Depending upon the system that the stalker is being dealt with, he/she will be subjected to a range of interviews/psychometrics etc. designed to assess his/her stalking behavior in relation to the following offence-specific behaviors:

- Stalking behavior throughout lifetime;
- Extent of stalking behaviors that offender has engaged in;
- Number of people he/she has stalked;

- Types of victims;
- Duration of stalking;
- Type of stalking behaviors engaged in.

Polygraph examination can assist in verifying the stalker's account of his/her stalking history.

Other uses can be to assist the stalker engage more actively in treatment and to monitor their compliance with requirements of their order, or if not on an order, to ascertain any pursuance of the victim.

The following things would be targeted on a maintenance exam:

Nine distinct stalker behaviors (Sheridan & Davies, 2004):

- Telephone calls
- Harassing letters
- Surveillance of victim's home
- Following
- Unlawful entry to victim's home
- Destruction/theft of victim's property
- Direct unwanted approaches
- Threats to harm or kill victim
- Physical assault.

Mullen *et al.* (2000):

- Getting into a relationship suddenly/seeking partner;
- Targeting potential victim;
- Retaining memorabilia of victim/past relationship;
- Following person without their knowledge;
- Following person with their knowledge;
- Constantly surveilling victim/home/work – accessing surveillance equipment such as binoculars, video-recording equipment and cameras;
- Loitering outside places victim is known to visit;
- Visiting their home;
- Visiting their work;
- Any form of unwanted communication – direct/indirect (phone calls, letters, cards);
- Sending flowers;
- Attaching notes to victim's property;
- Killing or threats to kill victim's pet;
- Fantasy/masturbation;
- Physical contact with victim;
- Access/possession of weapons;
- Waiting/lingering;

- Diary-keeping;
- Letters published in print media;
- Malicious complaints to police/government departments;
- Making a complaint of stalking against the victim – trying to get victim prosecuted for stalking;
- House break-ins;
- Leaving unsolicited offensive material such as dead animal;
- Making bomb threats against company;
- Hacking into computer systems;
- Tampering with mail;
- Masturbated to sexual fantasies of victim;
- Tried to steal underwear of victim/other sexual paraphilias associated with victim.

CONCLUSIONS

The polygraph is not a panacea or magic lasso and is never intended to be used as a stand-alone technique. When used on its merits, while knowing the limitations, it can help plug gaps and reduce clinicians and other staff's over-reliance upon offender self-report. Best practice dictates that it be used cautiously in a clinical sense within a structured treatment and risk management framework. This means not using it in an evidentiary sense, but rather as an additional clinical tool to assist direct decision-making. Useful comparison can be drawn with tools commonly used in the forensic area, such as standard assessments (i.e., psychometric testing, phallometric assessment, clinical judgment, urinalysis and hair sample drug testing, and satellite tracking). No one tool has perfect accuracy or is without the capacity to be abused if not administered and interpreted appropriately by competent individuals.

While the case for periodic post-conviction polygraph testing as a means of facilitating the assessment, treatment and supervision of various offender populations appears to make logical sense, it also needs to be stressed that it is yet to be conducted, let alone empirically investigated. Until such time as the discerning polygraph researcher can provide the profession with evidence of its impact, as with any innovation, examiners who begin to utilize this type of post-conviction testing need to do so in a responsible and cautious manner.

REFERENCES

Abel, G.G., Becker, J.V., Cunningham-Rathner, J. *et al.* (1988). Multiple paraphilic diagnoses among sex offenders. *Bulletin of the American Academy of Psychiatry and the Law*, *16*, 153–168.

Abrams, S. (1991). The use of polygraphy with sex offenders. *Sexual Abuse: A Journal of Research and Treatment (4)*, 239–263.

Andrews, D.A. & Bonta, J. (2003). *The Psychology of Criminal Conduct*. Cincinnati, OH: Anderson Publishing.

Association for the Treatment of Sexual Abusers (2001). *Practice Standards and Guidelines for the Members of the Association for the Treatment of Sexual Abusers*. Beaverton, OR: Author.

Australian Bureau of Statistics (1996). *Women's Safety Australia*, Australian Bureau of Statistics, Canberra.

Briggs, D. & Kennington, R. (2006). *Managing Men Who Sexually Abuse*. London: Jessica Kingsley Publishers.

Chaiken, J. & Chaiken, M. (1990). Drug use and predatory crime. In J.Q. Wilson & M. Tonry (Eds), *Drugs and crime*. Chicago: University of Chicago Press.

Davis, K.E., Coker, A.L., & Sanderson, M. (2002). Physical and Mental Health Effects of Being Stalked for Men and Women. *Violence and Victims, 17*, (4), 429–443.

English, K., Jones, L., Patrick, D., & Pasini-Hill, D. (2003). Sexual offender containment. Use of the post-conviction polygraph. *Annals of the New York Academy of Sciences*, *989*, 411–427.

Fernandez, M.A., Storch, E.A., Lewin, A.B. *et al.* (2006). The principles of extinction and differential reinforcement of other behaviours in the intensive cognitive-behavioral treatment of primarily obsessional pediatric OCD. *Clinical Case Studies*, *5*, 511–521.

Gondolf, E. (1997). Patterns of reassault in batterer programmes. *Violence and Victims*, *12*, 373–387.

Grubin, D., Madsen, L., Parsons, S., Sosnowski, D., & Warberg, B. (2004). A Prospective Study of the Impact of Polygraphy on High-Risk Behaviours in Adult Sex Offenders. *Sexual Abuse: A Journal of Research and Treatment, 16*, 3, 209–222.

Grubin, D. (2006). *Polygraph Pilot Study: Final Report*. London: Home Office. Available electronically from <http://www.probation.homeoffice.gov.uk>.

Hanson, R.K. & Bussière, M.T. (1998). Predicting Relapse: A meta-analysis of sexual offender recidivism studies. *Journal of Consulting and Clinical Psychology*, *66* (2), 348–362.

Hanson, R.K. & Morton-Bourgon, K. (2005). The characteristics of persistent sexual offenders: A meta-analysis of recidivism studies. *Journal of Consulting and Clinical Psychology*, *73* (6), 1154–1163.

Hanson, R.K. & Wallace-Capretta, S. (2000). Predicting Recidivism Among Male Batterers. (Report No. 2000-06.) Ottawa: Solicitor General of Canada.

Harway, M. & Hanson, M. (1994). *Spouse Abuse: Assessing and Treating Battered Women, Batterers, and Their Children*. Sarasota, Florida: Professional Resource Press.

Home Office (2001). *British Crime Survey*. Available electronically from <www.homeoffice.gov.uk>.

Home Office (2006). *Crime in England and Wales 2005/2006*. Available electronically from <www.homeoffice.gov.uk>.

Hudson, S.M. & Ward, T. (1997). Future Directions. In D.R. Laws & W. O'Donohue (Eds), *Sexual Deviance: Theory, Assessment, and Treatment* (pp. 481–500). New York: Guilford Press.

Kebbell, M.R. & Gilchrist, E.L. (2004). The psychology of cross-examination. In J. Adler (Ed.), *Forensic Psychology*. Cullompton, Devon: Willan.

Laws, R. & Ward, T. (2006). When one size doesn't fit all: Reformulation of relapse prevention. In W.L. Marshall, Y.M. Fernandez, L.E. Marshall & G.A. Serran (Eds), *Sexual Offender Treatment. Controversial Issues*. Chichester, UK: John Wiley & Sons, Ltd.

McFarlane, J., Campbell, J.C., Wilt, S. *et al.* (1999). Stalking and Intimate Partner Femicide. *Homicide Studies*, *3* (4), 300–316.

Mullen, P.E., Pathe, M., & Purcell, R. (2000). *Stalkers and Their Victims*. Cambridge: Cambridge University Press.

Murdoch, D., Pihl, R., & Ross, D. (1990). Alcohol and crimes of violence: Present issues. *International Journal of the Addictions*, *25*, 1065–1081.

National Probation Service for England and Wales. (2003). *Integrated Domestic Abuse Programme*. Theory Manual.

Rosenfeld, B. (2003). Recidivism in stalking and obsessional harassment. *Law and Human Behavior*, *27*, 251–265.

Rosenfeld, B. (2004). Violence risk factors in stalking and obsessional harassment: A review and preliminary meta-analysis. *Criminal Justice and Behaviour*, *31*(1), 9–36.

Ruback, R.B. & Thompson, M.P. (2001). *Social and Psychological Consequences of Violent Victimization*. Thousand Oaks, CA: Sage Publications.

Salter, A. (1997). *Sex Offender Assessment and Risk Management Issues*. National Organisation for the Treatment of Abusers (NOTA) Annual Conference. Southampton, England.

Sheridan, L. & Davies, G. (2004). Stalking. In J. Adler (Ed.), *Forensic Psychology. Concepts, Debates, and Practice*, pp. 197–215. Devon: Willan Publishing.

Tjaden, P. (1997). *Crime of Stalking: How big is the problem?* Washington DC: National Institute of Justice: Rockville: United States. (FS000186)

Tjaden, P. & Thoennes, N. (1998). *Stalking in America: Findings from the National Violence Against Women Survey*. Washington, DC: National Institute of Justice and Centers for Disease Control and Prevention (NCJ 169592).

Towl, G.J. & Crighton, D.A. (1997). Risk Assessment with Offenders. *International Review of Psychiatry*, *9* (2/3), 187–193.

Wilcox, D.T. (2005). *Clinical Applications of the Polygraph in Sex Offender Work – Pre- Versus Post-Conviction Polygraphy*. Presentation for the International Academy of Law and Mental Health 29th Congress, July, Paris.

Wilson, R.J., Stewart, L., Stripe, T. *et al.* (2000). Community-based sex offender management: Combining parole supervision and treatment to reduce recidivism. *Canadian Journal of Criminology*, *42*, 177–188.

CHAPTER 12

Interviewing and Interrogation

J.P. Blair

INTRODUCTION

Contrary to what is portrayed in popular culture and the media, detectives obtain most investigative information by talking to people (Horvath & Meesig, 1996). Regardless of whether the investigation is conducted in the United States, Canada, Japan or England, physical evidence appears to play a very limited role in the solving of crimes (Horvath & Meesig, 1996). As such interviewing and interrogation play critical roles in the investigative process. Interviewing and interrogation also play critical roles in the polygraph process. For example, a thorough pre-test interview is critical in producing accurate test results, and while an accurate diagnosis of deception is of some value, a confession following this diagnosis is far more valuable to the investigation than the diagnosis of deception alone. This chapter is devoted to discussing the state of our knowledge regarding interviewing and interrogation techniques. Where possible, links to the polygraph context will be made. This chapter will proceed by: identifying the differences between interviews and interrogations; discussing the functions of interviews; discussing the interrogation process; and finally discussing how interrogations can produce incorrect results.

The Use of the Polygraph in Assessing, Treating and Supervising Sex Offenders: A Practitioner's Guide
Edited by Daniel T. Wilcox.

THE DIFFERENCES BETWEEN INTERVIEWS AND INTERROGATIONS

While the terms interview and interrogation are often used interchangeably by the public, the two terms refer to two distinct processes; therefore, before either can be discussed, the two processes must be differentiated. In distinguishing the two processes, it is useful to first discuss the different goals that each process attempts to attain.

The interviewing process has three goals. The first, and probably foremost, is to gather information (Inbau *et al.*, 2001). In regards to polygraph testing, the objective of developing test questions can be considered part of the goal of gathering information. The second is to assess the credibility of a person's statement, and the third is to prepare the suspect for interrogation in the event that it becomes necessary to confront the suspect at a later time. The interrogation process has a single goal. This goal is to obtain the truth from a person who is believed to be withholding information (Inbau *et al.*, 2001).

Because the goals of the two processes are different from each other, the two procedures have very distinct characteristics. The first distinction is that an interview is non-accusatory and an interrogation is accusatory (Inbau *et al.*, 2001). This distinction occurs because approaching an interview in an accusatory manner will obstruct the free flow of information from the victim, witness, or suspect to the interviewer and may make assessing the credibility of the information that is given more difficult. A person who is accused of involvement in a criminal act will hardly feel comfortable freely sharing information with the interviewer. Additionally, the innocent suspect who is accused may become frightened and this fear may make the innocent suspect display characteristics that are often associated with guilt. The interrogation is conducted in an accusatory manner because it is often necessary to tell the suspect that you are certain that they did the crime in order to overcome their resistance to telling the truth.

The second distinction between the process of an interview and an interrogation is that an interview is a dialogue and (at least the first part) of an interrogation is a persuasive monologue (Inbau *et al.*, 2001). Again this difference arises from the different goal structures of the two procedures. The dialogue format of the interview is necessary to facilitate the gathering of accurate information. It allows the interviewer to ask questions and the participant to answer these questions. This process also allows the participant to ask their own questions, which may further enhance the information exchange process. The persuasive monologue format of the interrogation is used to overcome the suspect's resistance to telling the truth. If the interrogator does not dominate the initial steps of the interrogation, the interrogation may devolve into an unproductive argument in which the interrogator repeatedly accuses the suspect of committing the crime and the suspect repeatedly denies involvement. The monologue is persuasive in that the interrogator attempts to change the suspect's attitude toward telling the truth.

The third distinction between interviews and interrogations is that interviews may be conducted at any point in an investigation; whereas interrogations are usually only conducted during the later stages of an investigation (Inbau *et al.*, 2001). Because the interview is an essential means by which information is gathered and investigations are conducted, interviews tend to occur at all stages of investigations. It is also common for a particular victim, witness, or suspect to be interviewed several times as an investigation proceeds. For example, a person found nearby a crime scene may be questioned about what they saw, and second interview of that same participant may be conducted to clarify earlier statements made by the participant or to address new information that has been discovered during the course of the investigation. An interrogation, on the other hand, is usually only conducted at the later stages of an investigation. This occurs for two reasons. The first is that the interrogator only wants to interrogate people that he or she is reasonably certain are guilty (Inbau *et al.*, 2001). A reasonable level of certainty is needed because interrogation is an uncomfortable process for the participant, and the interrogator does not want to needlessly cause stress to participants that he or she has no reason to believe are involved in criminal acts. A reasonable level of certainty can usually only be obtained at the later stages of an investigation. The second reason is that the more investigative information that is available, the more likely an interrogation is to succeed. In the realm of the polygraph, an interview to discuss the situation under investigation and develop test questions will always precede the testing process, and interrogation will usually only be conducted after the charts have been run and are analyzed as being deceptive (or possibly inconclusive).

The fourth distinction between interviews and interrogations is that interviews can be conducted in a variety of environments; whereas, interrogations should be conducted in privacy (Inbau *et al.*, 2001). Ideally, both interviews and interrogations would be conducted only in private as this type of environment is optimal for achieving the goals of both interviews and interrogations; however, the practical necessities of investigative work often make it difficult or impossible to interview people in a private place. For example, a police officer responding to an armed robbery scene may have to interview the victim on the street in order to get a description of the suspect out on the air as quickly as possible. It should, however, be noted that the polygraphing process will almost always provide the opportunity to interview the participant in private. While it is acceptable to interview participants in a variety of environments, participants should only be interrogated in private. One of the reasons for this is that it is already difficult for a person to admit his or her wrongdoing, and this difficulty will be enhanced if the participant is not interrogated in private (Inbau *et al.*, 2001). A second reason is that, because the interrogation process is accusatory in nature, the interrogator does not want to potentially commit slander by mistakenly accusing an innocent person in front of others.

The final distinction between interviews and interrogations is that note-taking is acceptable during all parts of an interview, but is discouraged during the first part of an interrogation (Inbau *et al.*, 2001). Because of the question and answer structure of the interview, there is often time to take notes about what was said or done; however, because the initial part of an interrogation is a monologue, an interrogator simply will not have time to take notes and maintain control of the monologue. Now that the distinctions between interviews and interrogations have been addressed, this chapter will proceed to discuss the interviewing process in depth.

INTERVIEWS

As was noted above, for the purposes of this chapter, interviewing will be defined as a non-accusatory dialogue conducted at any point during an investigation. It is also recommended that an interview precede an interrogation in almost all circumstances (Inbau *et al.*, 2001). This section of the chapter will proceed by discussing each of the goals of the interview process (gathering factual information; assessing credibility; and preparing the participant for interrogation) in some depth.

Gathering Factual Information

Many in the investigative community consider the gathering factual information process as a simple matter of asking people who, what, when, where, and why; however, the process is much more complex than that. Extracting information from people requires that their memory be accessed. It has been amply demonstrated that memory is not fixed, but rather memory is quite malleable. As such a person's memories can be altered, destroyed or even altogether fabricated if they are interviewed improperly. Indeed, one author has viewed information gathered from people as a form of trace evidence, and, as such, it can be contaminated, destroyed or simply missed altogether (Wells, 1995). The proper interviewing of participants has garnered a substantial amount of attention from academics, and an effective means of interviewing to avoid contaminating, destroying or simply missing information has been developed. This process is called the cognitive interview (Fisher & Geiselman, 1992). The cognitive interview was developed in two parts (the original cognitive interview and the enhanced cognitive interview) which the following sections will discuss.

The original cognitive interview A substantial amount of research has addressed how memories are created, stored and retrieved. Because police officers have little or no control over how the memory of a witness is created or stored, the focus of police interviewing research has been on how to facilitate a witness's or victim's ability to retrieve the information that he or she has encoded (Fisher & Geiselman, 1992). The original cognitive interview (OCI) is based upon two components of cognitive theory. These are the encoding specificity principle and the multi-component view of the memory trace (Köhnken *et al.*, 1999). The encoding specificity principle states that the effectiveness of a memory probe is related to the probe's similarity to the environment in which the memory was encoded. This principle suggests that if the context of the event is reinstated prior to the recall attempt, the attempt will be more successful. The multi-component view of memory contends that a memory is not stored as a single, complete representation of the original event; instead, the memory is stored as a multifaceted collection of features (Köhnken *et al.*, 1999). This principle suggests that different types of memory probes may be able to access different information about the same event.

From these basic principles, the four instructions of the OCI were developed. The first is the restatement of the physical and emotional context in which the event to be remembered occurred. This procedure first involves asking the participant to recall the physical environment of the event. For example, the participant might be asked to think about the location of the event, the time of day, what the area smelled like, and what noises he or she heard. Second, the participant is asked to remember how they felt when the event was occurring. This part of the technique is believed to enhance recall by activating the psychological state of the participant that was present at the time the memory was created. This, in turn, increases the likelihood that relevant information will be accessible. The second technique is to ask the participant to recall the event from different perspectives. For example, a witness may be asked to try and think about what the victim of a crime saw. The third technique involves asking the victim or witness to recall the events in a different time order. These two techniques represent separate memory probes that, under the multi-component memory trace principle, may allow the participant to access unique information about the event in question that was not accessible when other probes were used. The fourth technique is that the participant is asked to report anything, including things that they cannot completely remember. This is believed to enhance the information that is retrieved in two ways (Memon & Bull, 1991). The first is that, if the participant includes only the information that they think is relevant, information that is important to the investigation might be excluded. The second is that recalling partial details may lead to the recall of additional relevant information. In addition to the four basic techniques, other supplemental techniques may be used to elicit specific information regarding physical appearances, names, objects and conversations.

The enhanced cognitive interview Extensive laboratory and field research into the original cognitive interview revealed several problems with the general interviewing techniques that are used by many people. Among these was a tendency to interrupt the participant and use question and answer, rather than free recall type questions (Fisher *et al.*, 1987). This led Fisher and Geiselman to add some components to the original cognitive interview. The resulting interviewing technique is commonly referred to as the enhanced cognitive interview (ECI) (Fisher *et al.*, 1987). The first of the new components in the ECI is rapport-building. The interviewer is instructed to try and get to know the witness and his or her expectations. This is believed to make the participant more comfortable and thereby increase their ability to recall information. The second of the new components is a transfer of control to the participant. The participant is encouraged to take an active role in the interview. This means that the interviewer will allow the participant to take the time that he or she needs to retrieve information, and the interviewer will attempt to structure the interview in a way that matches the participant's recollection of the event rather than a report form. This also means that the interviewer will not interrupt the participant. The third new component is that the interviewer attempts to enhance recall by using focused memory techniques (such as focusing on only a person's face) and encourages extensive retrieval attempts (Memon & Bull, 1991).

Effectiveness

The most comprehensive meta-analysis to date examined 42 cognitive interviewing studies that involved almost 2500 interviewees (Köhnken *et al.*, 1999). This analysis indicated that the cognitive interview

(CI) allowed participants to recall significantly more correct details (d = .87) than other interviewing techniques, but participants who were interviewed using the CI also recalled more incorrect details (d = .28). Because the CI produces more information than other types of interviews, it is useful to consider the accuracy rate of the CI compared to other types of interviews. This rate is calculated by dividing the total number of correct details by the total number of details recalled. The Köhnken *et al.* (1999) meta-analysis found that the accuracy rate of the CI and other types of interviews were similar (85 % and 82 % respectively). Overall, these results suggested that the CI is effective at eliciting more information without decreasing the accuracy rate of the information that is recalled. As such, the CI appears to be an effective technique for meeting the interview goal of gathering investigative information.

Assessing Credibility

The assessment of credibility is the primary reason that a polygraph test is conducted. As such, assessing credibility during the pre-test interview often takes on less importance then it does during a normal investigative interview; yet, some research has suggested that polygraph examiners are more accurate at assessing truth or deception when they not only assess the charts, but also conduct the pre-test interview (Ginton *et al.*, 1982). This finding suggests that the pre-test interview may have some diagnostic value. This section of the chapter will therefore give a brief review of the literature regarding the detection of deception during interviews.

General ability A substantial amount of research has examined the ability of people to detect deception during interviews. A recent meta-analysis of this body of literature revealed that, on average, people are only slightly better than chance (54 %) at detecting deception (Bond & DePaulo, unpublished). Additional research has suggested that those with a special interest in detecting deception, such as law enforcement personnel, are in general not more accurate at detecting deception than the public (Ekman & O'Sullivan, 1991; Ekman, O'Sullivan & Frank, 1999). These findings suggest that people regardless of profession are not particularly skilled at detecting deception during interviews. It should, however, be noted that a small body of research, which has involved having people judge the interviews of actual criminal suspects, has reported much higher detection of deception accuracies than are found in the rest of the literature (Blair & McCamey, 2002; Horvath & Jayne, 1994; Mann, Vrij & Bull, 2004). It may be that deception is easier to detect in these high-stakes 'real-life' situations than it is during laboratory experiments. Indeed, there is ample reason to believe that several of the mechanisms that have been posited to cause behavioral differences between truth-tellers and liars are more likely to be activated, and activated to a greater degree, during actual criminal interviews than laboratory experiments. Additionally, investigators do not interview people without having a contextual background to which the participant's statements can be compared. In other words, an investigator always has case facts against which a participant's statements can be vetted. This comparison may provide investigators with an additional tool to detect deception that is not present in almost all laboratory experiments, and, thereby, increase detection of deception accuracies in actual criminal situations.

Cues to deception A large body of work has also addressed the behavioral cues that may indicate deception. A comprehensive meta-analysis has recently summarized this body of work (DePaulo *et al.*, 2003). This meta-analysis examined 158 possible cues to deception and found that very few of these cues reliably distinguished truth from deception. For the purpose of brevity, this section of the chapter will focus only on the results of a sub-analysis of this study. This sub-analysis examined only those studies in which a person committed a transgression. For the purposes of the meta-analysis, a transgression was generally described as a violation of a social norm that the participant considered to be serious or important. Examples of these transgressions included cheating on tests and stealing. This sub-analysis was chosen because it is the type of lie that is most likely to be related to the issue(s) under examination during a polygraph test. The sub-analysis revealed only four cues that reliably differentiated truth-tellers from liars across studies. Liars tended to speak faster than truth-tellers. Truth-tellers exhibited more foot and leg movements than liars. Liars blinked more than truth-tellers. Finally, liars were subjectively judged to be more nervous or tense than truth-tellers. This study also found that most of the behavioral differences between truth-tellers and liars were small or moderate in magnitude. This suggests that detecting deception on the basis of behavioral cues alone will be difficult to do. It should also be noted that the vast majority of studies included in the meta-analysis involved laboratory studies, and therefore, the behaviors of suspects during criminal interviews may vary substantially from the behaviors reported in the meta-analysis. It has also been suggested that the training of law enforcement officers in the detection of deception should only include those cues that have been validated through extensive research in the relevant contexts (Blair & Kooi, 2004).

Preparing the Suspect for Interrogation

The final goal of the interviewing process is to prepare a participant for interrogation should it become necessary to confront the participant at a later time. The first way that an interview helps to prepare the participant for a subsequent interrogation is through the development of rapport. A non-accusatory interview allows an investigator to achieve a higher level of rapport than can be achieved during an accusatory interrogation (Inbau *et al.*, 2001). This rapport should serve to increase the participant's liking of the interrogator, and liking has generally been demonstrated to increase the effectiveness of persuasive attempts (O'Keefe, 1990).

The second way that an interview prepares the participant for interrogation is by allowing the interviewer to identify and deal with areas of potential resistance before the interrogation. Part of this is accomplished simply by the interviewer laying out the expansive scope of the investigation during the interview. Often the participant is unaware of all of the effort that has already gone into an investigation. Laying out the general investigative process should help to enhance the credibility of both the interrogator and the investigation. Enhanced credibility has generally been found to increase the effects of persuasive arguments when the source of the message is attempting to change the valence (direction) of a receiver's attitude (O'Keefe, 1990). The process of laying out the investigation may also identify pieces of evidence with which the participant does not agree. This gives the investigator and participant a chance to discuss these areas of contention in a non-accusatory manner and may allow the two to reach an understanding regarding the evidence. If an understanding cannot be reached, then at least the investigator knows not to focus on the areas of contention during a subsequent interrogation. This should enhance the interrogation's chances of success. Because conducting an interview may enhance the chances of an interrogation succeeding, it has been recommended that an interview should almost always precede an interrogation (Inbau *et al.*, 2001). Now that the goals of interviewing have been discussed in some depth, interrogations will now be addressed.

INTERROGATIONS

As was mentioned in the first section of this chapter, an interrogation is an accusatory, persuasive monologue that is usually conducted during the later stages of an investigation. The goal of an interrogation is to get a participant who is believed to be withholding information to tell the truth. This section will proceed by identifying the general process of interrogations, reviewing the literature about the effectiveness of interrogations, and finally discussing interrogation errors.

The Process

Several interrogation manuals are currently in print (Aubry & Caputo, 1980; Hess, 1997; Holmes, 2002; Inbau *et al.*, 2001; Walters, 2002; Zulawski & Wicklander, 2001), and these manuals teach interrogation techniques that are remarkably similar to each other (Blair, 2005b). Based on these manuals, the interrogation process can be perceived as consisting of two parts. The first is acquiring the first admission of guilt and the second is developing the full confession. It is necessary to distinguish the two parts because the two parts use very different techniques and, as such, function differently from each other. The two parts will be discussed in detail. Additionally, the Inbau *et al.* (2001) manual will be used as a reference point as it is the most commonly cited manual in the literature.

Acquiring the first admission The acquiring the first admission phase of an interrogation is the first step, and may dominate a majority of the time that an interrogation takes. During this part, the interrogator uses a variety of persuasive tactics in an attempt to overcome the participant's resistance toward telling the truth. Before these tactics are discussed, it is necessary to first set out some basic guidelines that interrogations should follow. The first is that, while the interrogation is accusatory, it is not hostile in nature; rather, the interrogation is sympathetic in nature. The interrogator does not yell at and badger the participant into submission; instead, the interrogator empathizes with the participant and suggests that he simply wants to get the full story from the participant so that the case can be fairly evaluated. Additionally, the interrogation must meet legal guidelines. Because the applicable legal guidelines vary from jurisdiction to jurisdiction, only two general legal points will be made here. First, while the interrogation is persuasive and the statements that the interrogator uses may cause the participant to infer that the consequences will be less severe if the participant confesses or more severe if the participant does not confess, the interrogator must not make explicit threats of punishment or promises of leniency. Second, the interrogator should never use physical force to produce a confession. The three phases of the acquiring the first admission part of the interrogation process shall now be discussed. These are the opening, the body, and the acquisition of the admission.

Opening Because the interrogation is accusatory in nature, it often begins with a direct accusation of the participant's guilt (Inbau *et al.*, 2001). This may be something phrased something like, 'Our investigation clearly indicates that you did X', where X refers to the issue under investigation. In the polygraph context, this accusation may be a statement like, 'You are not passing.' After this accusation is made, it is commonly repeated to give the participant a chance to react (Inbau *et al.*, 2001). It is believed that innocent suspects will react strongly to this accusation by consistently denying involvement and not allowing the interrogation to proceed to the next phase; whereas, the guilty may not respond at all or offer weak denials that quickly cease (Inbau *et al.*, 2001). If the participant does not offer a strong denial, the interrogator then transitions into the next phase of this part of the interrogation. This transition may take the form of, 'What I want to do is sit down with you for a few minutes and see if we can't get this sorted out.'

Body The body of the interrogation consists of the interrogator using various persuasive or compliance-gaining strategies to get the participant to divulge the information that the interrogator believes that the participant is withholding. These strategies or statements are commonly referred to as themes, rationalizations or arguments in the interrogation training literature (Aubry & Caputo, 1980; Holmes, 2002; Inbau *et al.*, 2001; Walters, 2002; Zulawski & Wicklander, 2001). As was previously mentioned, these strategies are delivered in a monologue format. This portion of the interrogation is also likely to be the longest phase of the interrogation.

The strategies used by interrogators can be seen as utilizing one of two processes. The first is a rational actor process and the second is a negative state relief process. The rational actor process operates from the viewpoint that people are logical, and when presented with a choice between two options, they will chose the one that results in the most positive benefits while resulting in the least negative consequences. The participant is seen as engaging in a rational calculus wherein the costs and benefits of the available courses of action are evaluated, and the course of action with the best ratio of benefits to costs is chosen. This model of behavior has been used to describe behaviors in a variety of contexts and is especially popular in the field of economics. In the interrogation context, this point of view assumes that the participant of the interrogation carefully assesses the benefits and consequences of either confessing or not confessing and chooses the option with the best benefits/costs ratio (Ofshe & Leo, 1997). Since the participant has not already confessed, it can be assumed that the participant believes at the outset of the interrogation the costs of confession outweigh the benefits.

The job of the interrogator then is to alter the participant's perceptions, in a legal manner, so that the participant believes that confessing is a superior course of action to not confessing. It should also be noted that actual criminal justice system punishment is not the only cost or benefit that the participant might consider. Other possibilities might include what other people (friends, family, co-workers and the general public) might think about the participant, and the possibility of his or her work taking disciplinary action.

There are a variety of tactics that can be used to persuade the participant that confession is the best course of action. While a thorough discussion of the universe of possible tactics is beyond the scope of this manuscript, a few examples will be presented here for the benefit of the reader. The interrogator can attempt to make the crime under investigation seem less serious by contrasting it with a more serious crime. If the participant stole $1000, the interrogator can suggest that this is small compared to other cases that he or she has worked on, which involved tens of thousands of dollars. This makes the $1000 seem much less serious. The interrogator can also suggest that the crime was done for a reason that is more morally acceptable then other possible reasons. For example, the interrogator may suggest that the money might have been stolen to pay bills, which is different from using the money to pay for drugs. The interrogator might then suggest that it is important for people to know that the money was used for bills; because if they do not, they may assume the worst about the participant.

The second method that can be utilized to move a participant toward a confession is based on the negative state relief model (Baumann, Chialdini & Kendrick, 1981). This model proposes that negative emotions produce a negative state within the participant, and that, if this negative state becomes acute enough, the participant will take action to relieve this negative state. In the interrogation context, the dominant negative state for the guilty offender is probably guilt. This guilt is caused by the offender's knowledge that he or she has behaved non-normatively. It can be assumed that, at the outset of the interrogation, the guilt perceived by the offender is not yet severe enough to cause him or her to confess. Under this model then, the interrogator can move the participant toward confession by making his or her feelings of guilt more acute. A thorough discussion of all of the possible ways that this can be accomplished is again beyond the scope of this manuscript, but an example is given here for the benefit of the reader. In the case mentioned above, where the participant stole $1000, the interrogator might say something like, 'Look, you did something that was wrong and I am sure you feel bad about that. It is not too late to make things right. The only way that you can do that now is to be up front and tell the truth about taking the money. Otherwise, those bad feelings will get worse and worse.' Interrogation in and of itself is not a pleasant experience. It is possible that the anxiety caused by interrogation could also produce a negative state that then motivates the participant to confess. Tactics like moving into the participant's personal space or simply continuing the interrogation could serve to make this feeling of anxiety more acute and, thereby, produce a confession.

It should be noted that either or both routes (rational actor or negative state) could be operating to some degree during the interrogation. It is also common for interrogators to attempt to use both routes during an interrogation. In many cases, it may be the combined influence of both methods that produces confessions. In other words, the participant might confess both because he or she believes it is the best option from a benefits/costs perspective, and because his or her negative state is uncomfortable. Once the participant appears to be accepting the statements of the interrogator, the interrogation is ready to move into the next phase, the first admission of guilt.

The first admission of guilt The interrogation literature suggests that it is extremely difficult for a person to simply say, 'I did it,' to the interrogator; therefore, a method called the alternative question is often used to produce the first admission of guilt (Inbau *et al.*, 2001). The alternative question presents the suspect with a choice between two possible explanations for why the crime was committed. One of the choices is more psychologically attractive than the other. For example, in the theft case mentioned above, the suspect may be asked, 'Did you take the money because you needed it for bills or for drugs?' If the suspect accepts either alternative, this represents his or her first admission of guilt. The alternative question is often presented several times to the suspect with slight variations each time. For example, in the case above, the suspect could also be asked, 'You needed the money for bills, right? It wasn't for drugs. Was it? You just needed the money for bills. Didn't you?'

Once the participant makes his or her first admission, their resistance to telling the truth has generally been overcome. As a result, it is no longer necessary to continue using the persuasive monologue that is the hallmark of the first part of the interrogation; therefore, the second part of the interrogation is ready to commence.

Developing the full confession The first admission of guilt is an important step in the interrogation, but this admission does not represent a full confession. In order for an admission to be considered a full confession, it must include the details surrounding the participant's participation in the criminal act. Because the participant's resistance has been overcome and the goal of the interrogation is now to develop a complete and truthful account of the participant's involvement in the crime, this part of the interrogation comes to closely resemble the interviews that were discussed above. Indeed, it is often difficult to distinguish this part of the interrogation from an interview. The interrogation now uses a question and answer format like an interview. Also, the CI techniques that were discussed previously may be useful at this point in an interrogation. Now that the basic interrogation process has been discussed, this chapter will address the effectiveness of the above discussed techniques.

Effectiveness

Two aspects of the effectiveness of interrogations will be discussed in this portion of the chapter. These are the frequency of successful outcomes when participants are exposed to interrogations, and the impact of confessions on the court process.

Frequency of successful outcomes Only two studies have examined the frequency of successful interrogation outcomes in the last twenty years in the United States (Cassell & Hayman, 1996; Leo, 1996). In the United Kingdom, five studies have examined the frequency of successful outcomes during the same time frame (Irving & McKenzie, 1989; Moston & Stephenson, 1992; Moston, Stephenson & Williamson, 1992; Pearse *et al.*, 1998; Phillips & Brown, 1998). These studies have used a variety of methodologies ranging from direct observations of interrogations (Irving & McKenzie, 1989; Leo, 1996), to reviewing taped interrogations (Leo, 1996; Moston *et al.*, 1992; Pearse *et al.*, 1998) to questionnaires and reviewing police documents (Phillips & Brown, 1998) to observing case screening meetings between prosecutors and detectives (Cassell & Hayman, 1996). These studies also exhibited some variation in the way that interrogation outcomes were classified, but, in general, all of the studies recognized at least a confession, which involved an admission of substantial involvement in the criminal activity on the part of the suspect, and admissions, which involved the suspect giving information that tended to implicate him or her in the crime but fell short of an admission of substantial involvement. If the goal of the interrogation is seen as gaining any incriminating information, the success rate of interrogations in the above mentioned studies ranged from a low of 42% to a high of 65%.

The interrogation success rates in the American studies tended to be lower than in the UK studies. Four possible reasons for this difference have been proposed (Gudjonsson, 2003). First, the limited number of studies and the small sample sizes of the studies in the US may make generalization of these studies to the entire US unjustified. Second, Miranda may have a greater impact on interrogation success rates in the US than the PACE requirements have in the UK. Third, the English legal representatives may be relatively ineffective at protecting their clients. Forth, cultural differences in the two countries might produce the different success rates. Regardless of the reasons for the differences in the interrogation success rates of the two countries, interrogations appear to produce useful information in a large percentage of cases.

Impact of confessions on court proceedings Both Leo (1996) and Cassell and Hayman (1996) explored the impact of confessions on the processing of a case in the US. Leo (1996) found that suspects who provided incriminating information were more likely to be charged and to plead guilty or be found guilty at trial. Confessors also received longer sentences. Cassell and Hayman's findings were similar to Leo's. Cassell and Hayman (1996) found that suspects whose cases involved successful interrogations were more likely to have charges filed, and, either through plea-bargaining or trial, to result in the conviction of the suspect. Suspects who made some type of statement during an interrogation were also less likely to receive concessions during plea-bargaining. Research in the UK has produced similar results (Phillips & Brown, 1998).

Overall, these studies suggest that successful interrogations have a significant impact on subsequent court proceedings. Specifically, suspects who give at least some incriminating information during interrogation are more likely to be charged, convicted and receive longer sentences than those who do not. This holds with the common perceptions of police, prosecutors and academics, all of whom view a confession as a powerful piece of evidence. Because confessions appear to be such powerful pieces of evidence, interrogation errors are naturally a concern to both practitioners and academics.

Interrogation Errors

Two types of interrogation error are possible. A false positive occurs when a suspect confesses to a crime that they did not commit (false confession), and a false negative occurs when a suspect does not confess to a crime that they did commit (false denial). False confessions have received considerable attention. However, the problem of false denials has received relatively little attention. False positives will be discussed first.

False positives In wrongful conviction studies, false confessions are often cited as one of the major causes of wrongful convictions (Gudjonsson, 2003; Huff, 2002; Leo, 2001; Westervelt & Humphrey, 2001). In order to explore the scope of the false confession problem, several questions must be answered. These are: do false confessions occur?; how often do they occur?; and what is the role of interrogations in causing false confessions?

False confessions do occur. However, one of the major difficulties in attempting to classify a confession as true or false involves determining whether or not the suspect actually committed the crime. Contrary to what is portrayed in popular television shows, in many cases, the evidence suggesting the guilt or innocence of a suspect is circumstantial at best (Horvath & Meesig, 1996). It is rare that direct evidence, such as DNA or fingerprints, is available. However, enough cases of confessions that have been refuted by significant direct evidence of innocence have been reported in the literature that it appears extremely unlikely that all of the confessors in these cases were guilty in fact.

The next obvious question is how often do false confessions occur? This is an extremely difficult question to answer. In addition to the problem of identifying the actual guilt or innocence of the participant that was mentioned above, we do not know how many interrogations are conducted every year because this information is not reported to any central location. Additionally, most researchers have explored the rate of false confessions by looking at wrongful convictions that were produced at least in part by confessions. This adds the additional difficulty of attempting to determine how often wrongful convictions occur and what proportion of wrongful convictions are due to false confessions. This is no simple task, and because of the lack of data available to form accurate estimates, estimates are likely to contain a large amount of error. However, using estimates of interrogations, arrests, convictions and error rates, researchers have arrived at estimates of wrongful convictions resulting from false confessions that range from a low of 10 (.001% of all convictions) to a high of 840 (.04% of all convictions) per year in the United States (Cassell, 1998; Huff, Rattner & Sagarin, 1986).

Another methodology for attempting to determine the frequency of false confessions resulting from police interrogations is to select a random sample of cases and then look for false confessions in the sample. Cassell (1998) examined the sample from the Cassell and Hayman (1996) study and did not find evidence of any false confessions. Additionally, Leo (who is a known critic of police interrogation tactics and believes that modern interrogation tactics are likely to produce false confessions) did not report any false confessions in his 1996 study of

182 police interrogations. One would assume that if evidence of any false confessions had surfaced in his study, he would have reported it. A limitation of this methodology is that if false confessions occur at an extremely low rate (as was suggested by the estimates in the above paragraph), a very large sample would be needed to detect any false confessions.

As was mentioned before, it is difficult to determine how often false confessions occur, but the above data suggest that they are extremely rare. It should be noted that some authors have rejected the above methodologies and suggested that it is impossible to accurately determine the rate of false confessions for the methodological reasons that were mentioned above (Leo & Ofshe, 1998). However, Leo and Ofshe (1998) also stated that the problem of false confessions is severe enough that sweeping changes should be made in the United States judicial system. How they arrive at this conclusion when they state that the frequency of false confessions (and therefore scope of the problem) cannot be determined is unclear. Some of the changes that have been recommended in the US are similar to the changes that were implemented with the PACE legislation in the UK.

The final question that this section will attempt to answer is how interrogations might cause false confessions. It has been suggested that interrogations can cause two types of false confessions (Gudjonsson, 2003; Leo, 2001). The primary difference between these two types of false confession is whether or not the false confessor actually believes that he or she committed the act to which he or she confessed. When the false confessor believes that he or she actually committed a crime in which he or she had no involvement, the confession is commonly referred to as internalized (Gudjonsson, 2003; Kassin & Wrightsman, 1985; Ofshe & Leo, 1997). An internalized false confession is generally believed to follow a three-step process. First, the interrogator attacks the suspect's confidence in his or her memory. Next, the interrogator suggests that the suspect committed the crime and does not remember committing the crime due to some form of amnesia or blackout. Finally, after the suspect accepts that he or she must have committed the crime, the interrogator and suspect work together to produce a detailed confession (Gudjonsson, 2003; Leo, 2001). Gisli Gudjonsson has conducted extensive research into this type of false confession and has found some evidence that suggests that children, those with low IQs, and drug addicts may be particularly vulnerable to this type of false confession (see Gudjonsson, 2003 for a thorough review of internalized false confession research).

It has also been suggested that the use of false evidence can cause internalized false confessions to occur. Two studies have explored this possibility (Kassin & Kiechel, 1996; Redlich & Goodman, 2003). Both studies involved having the participant type on a keyboard after instructing them not to press a certain key, as this would cause the computer to crash. After a set period of time, the computer automatically crashed, and the researcher accused the suspect of pressing the prohibited key. With half of the participants in Kassin and Kiechel's (1996) experiment, a confederate claimed to have seen the participant pressing the prohibited key. This false evidence procedure produced significantly more internalized false confessions than the no false evidence procedure. In the Redlich & Goodman (2003) study, the experimenter presented the participant with a computer printout that showed that the participant had pressed the prohibited key in the false evidence conditions. This study did not find that false evidence significantly impacted internalization. This suggests that the Kassin and Kiechel (1996) false evidence effect may not be robust. Additional research is needed to resolve the question of whether or not, and under what conditions, the presentation of false evidence can cause internalized false confessions.

False confessions that occur when the suspect does not believe that she or he committed the crime are commonly referred to as a compliant false confessions (Gudjonsson, 2003; Inbau *et al.*, 2001; Kassin & Wrightsman, 1985; Ofshe & Leo, 1997). This type of confession is believed to occur because the suspect seeks some form of benefit as a result of the confession, to avoid some form or negative consequence if he or she does not confess, or both (Gudjonsson, 2003; Inbau *et al.*, 2001; Kassin & Wrightsman, 1985; Leo, 2001). It has been suggested that compliant false confessions are the result of a two-step process (Leo, 2001; Ofshe & Leo, 1997). The first step requires the interrogator to convince the suspect that his or her situation is hopeless. This hopelessness is primarily the result of the suspect's belief that negative consequences are unavoidable. The interrogator is able to convince the suspect of the unavoidability of consequences through repeated accusations of guilt, the presentation of real or fictitious evidence, and by stopping attempts to deny guilt. Proponents of this model believe that the use of false evidence is especially likely to lead to false confessions. Once a suspect is convinced that the situation is hopeless, the interrogator proceeds to step two.

During step two, suspects are presented with inducements to confess. These inducements are believed to move suspects to confess by convincing them that the benefits of confession outweigh the costs of a continued claim of innocence (Leo, 2001). These inducements generally fall into two categories (Kassin & McNall, 1991). The first is a 'hard sell' technique that is referred to as maximization. Maximizations attempt to increase the participant's perceptions of the negative consequences of continuing to deny committing the crime. Maximizations involve tactics such as exaggerating the seriousness of the offence and suggesting that others will think poorly of the suspect if he or she does not confess. The second category of interrogation tactics is a 'soft-sell' technique that is referred to as minimization. Minimizations seek to minimize the target's perceptions of the negative consequences of confessing. Common minimization tactics include offering face-saving excuses, blaming the victim or citing extenuating circumstances. The use of both types of tactics together is often referred to as the min/max technique (Kassin & McNall, 1991). Proponents of this model of false confessions believe that the statements commonly used by police officers to induce confessions communicate promises of leniency and threats of punishment to suspects that are similar to the explicit threats of punishment and promises of leniency that are not allowed under the law. It is, therefore, believed that the use of these inducements will cause both innocent and guilty suspects to confess because both perceive that they will receive fewer negative consequences if they confess and more negative consequences if they do not confess.

This area of false confessions is of great concern to interrogators because the process that is believed to cause these compliant false confessions is essentially the interrogation process that was discussed earlier in this manuscript. One study has provided limited support for the view that minimization or maximization techniques may alter perceptions of punishment (Kassin & McNall, 1991). This study involved having the participants read transcripts of interrogations that contained various interrogation tactics. The results revealed that minimizations or maximizations could alter the amount of punishment that the participants recommended in some, but not all, of the conditions. The authors suggest that this is evidence that the use of minimizations or maximizations can cause false confessions. However, this conclusion is hard to defend based on the design of the study. The participants were reporting how much punishment they thought that a hypothetical offender would receive; not how much punishment they thought that they would receive if they were involved in the situation. This would suggest that this inference would be extremely prone to error. Additionally, the participants did not indicate that they thought that the minimization or maximization technique would cause more people to falsely confess in the first part of the experiment. Why the participant's perceptions of punishment are widely considered valid, but their perceptions of confession rates are not, is unclear.

The results of the Kassin and McNall (1996) false evidence study are also often cited as proof that false evidence can cause compliant false confessions. This conclusion is unjustified because their study was designed specifically to look at internalized false confessions. Additionally, one study which attempted to examine the impact of false evidence on false confessions when the participants were certain that they had not committed the prohibited act failed to find a direct significant effect of false evidence on false confessions (Blair, 2004). Clearly additional research is needed before it can be definitively claimed that false evidence, minimizations or maximizations cause false confessions.

Other research that has looked at actual cases of false confessions has suggested that compliant false confessions are only likely to occur when coercive tactics (such as beatings or threats) are used, the participant is mentally handicapped and/or the suspect is a juvenile (Blair, 2005a). These findings, along with those of Gudjonsson (2003), suggest that it may be the interplay of vulnerable personalities and certain interrogation tactics which produces false confessions rather than the tactics themselves.

False negatives The problem of failing to gain incriminating information from a guilty suspect has received very little attention. To the author's knowledge only one person has addressed this issue (Cassell, 1998). Cassell suggested that the failure to obtain a confession could have two negative outcomes. The first is that the guilty may not be convicted. Recall that the studies on case processing suggested that suspects who gave at least some incriminating information were more likely to be charged and convicted than suspects who did not. This also suggests that cases that involve guilty suspects who do not give incriminating information are less likely to have charges filed, and, thus, these guilty suspects are less likely to receive a conviction.

The second negative outcome suggested by Cassell (1998) is that if the guilty suspect does not confess, an innocent person might be convicted of the crime. This contention is supported by the fact that in many wrongful conviction studies, numerous innocent suspects were later exonerated based upon the confession of the guilty party (Bedau & Radelet, 1987; Gross, 1996; Rattner, 1988). Cassell (1998) goes on to suggest that the danger of losing confessions by tightening restrictions on interrogations far outweighs the risks of convicting an innocent suspect due to a false confession.

Additionally, while the overall success rates reviewed earlier suggest that interrogations are successful somewhere between 42 % and 65 % of the time, full confessions occurred at substantially lower rates. If we assume that the majority of suspects that are interrogated are guilty, the low rates of full confession suggest that the false-negative rate is high.

Obviously there is still significant room for improvement in the effectiveness of police interrogation tactics. Future research should explore how the false-negative rate of interrogations can be reduced without increasing the false-positive rate.

REFERENCES

Aubry, A.S. & Caputo, R.R. (1980). *Criminal Interrogation* (3rd edn). Springfield, IL: Charles C. Thomas.

Baumann, D.J., Chialdini, R.B., & Kendrick, D.T. (1981). Altruism as hedonism: Helping and self-gratification as equivalent responses. *Journal of Personality and Social Psychology*, *40*, 1039–1046.

Bedau, H.A. & Radelet, M.L. (1987). Miscarriages of justice in potentially capital cases. *Stanford Law Review*, *40*, 21–179.

Blair, J.P. (2004). The roles of interrogation, perception, and personality in producing compliant false confessions. *Dissertation Abstracts International*, *65* (4), 1547 (UMI No. 3129461), *20*, 44–57.

Blair, J.P. (2005a). A test of the unusual false confession perspective using cases of proven false confessions. *Criminal Law Bulletin*, *41*, 127–144.

Blair, J.P. (2005b). What do we know about interrogation in the United States? *Journal of Police and Criminal Psychology, 20*, 44–57.

Blair, J.P. & Kooi, B. (2004). The gap between training and research in the detection of deception. *International Journal of Police Science and Management*, *6*, 77–83.

Blair, J.P. & McCamey, W.P. (2002). Detection of deception: An analysis of the behavioral analysis interview technique. *Illinois Law Enforcement Executive Forum*, *2*, 165–170.

Bond, C.F. & DePaulo, B.M. (2006). Accuracy of deception judgments. *Personality and Social Psychology Review, 10*, 214–234.

Cassell, P.G. (1998). Protecting the innocent from false confessions and lost confessions and from Miranda. *Journal of Criminal Law and Criminology*, 88, 497–556.

Cassell, P.G. & Hayman, B.S. (1996). Police interrogation in the 1990s: An empirical study of the effects of Miranda. *UCLA Law Review*, *43*, 839–931.

DePaulo, B.M., Lindsay, J.J., Malone, B.E. *et al.* (2003). Cues to Deception. *Psychological Bulletin*, *129*, 74–118.

Ekman, P. & O'Sullivan, M. (1991). Who can catch a liar? *American Psychologist*, *46*, 913–920.

Ekman, P., O'Sullivan, M., & Frank, M.G. (1999). A few can catch a liar. *Psychological Science*, *10*, 263–266.

Fisher, R.P. & Geiselman, R.E. (1992). *Memory-enhancing techniques for investigative interviewing: The cognitive interview*. Springfield, IL: Charles C. Thomas.

Fisher, R.P., Geiselman, R.E., Raymond, D.S. *et al.* (1987). Enhancing enhanced eyewitness memory: Refining the cognitive interview. *Journal of Police Science and Administration*, *15*, 291–297.

Ginton, A., Daie, N., Elaad, E., & Ben-Shakhar, G. (1982). A method for evaluating the use of the polygraph in a real-life situation. *Journal of Applied Psychology*, *67*, 131–137.

Gross, S.R. (1996). The risks of death: Why erroneous convictions are common in capital cases. *Buffalo Law Review*, *44*, 469–490.

Gudjonsson, G.H. (2003). *The psychology of interrogations and confessions: A handbook*. Hoboken, NJ: John Wiley & Sons, Inc.

Hess, J.E. (1997). *Interviewing and Interrogation for Law Enforcement*. Cincinnati, OH: Anderson Publishing.

Holmes, W.D. (2002). *Criminal Interrogation: A Modern Format for Interrogating Criminal Suspects Based on the Intellectual Approach*. Springfield, IL: Charles C. Thomas.

Horvath, F. & Meesig, R. (1996). The criminal investigation process and the role of forensic evidence: A review of empirical findings. *Journal of Forensic Science*, *41*, 963–969.

Horvath, F.S. & Jayne, B.P. (1994). Differentiation of truthful and deceptive criminal suspects in behavioral analysis interviews. *Journal of Forensic Sciences*, *39*, 793–807.

Huff, C.R. (2002). Wrongful conviction and public policy: The American Society of Criminology 2001 Presidential address. *Criminology*, *40*, 1–18.

Huff, C.R., Rattner, A., & Sagarin, E. (1986). Guilty until proven innocent: Wrongful conviction and public policy. *Crime and Delinquency*, *32*, 518–544.

Inbau, F.E., Reid, J.E., Buckley, J.P., & Jayne, B.C. (2001). *Criminal interrogation and confessions* (4th edn). Gaithersburg, MD: Aspen.

Irving, B. & McKenzie, I.K. (1989). *Police interrogation: The effects of the police and criminal evidence act*. London: Police Foundation of Great Britain.

Kassin, S.M. & Kiechel, K.L. (1996). The social psychology of false confessions: Compliance, internalization, and confabulation. *Psychological Science*, *7*, 125–128.

Kassin, S.M. & McNall, K. (1991). Police interrogations and confessions: Communicating threats and promises by pragmatic implication. *Law and Human Behavior*, *21*, 233–251.

Kassin, S.M. & Wrightsman, L. (1985). Confession Evidence. In S.M. Kassin & L. Wrightsman (Eds), *The psychology of evidence and trial procedure* (pp. 67–94). Beverly Hills, CA: Sage.

Köhnken, G., Milne, R., Memon, A., & Bull, R. (1999). The cognitive interview: A meta-analysis. *Psychology, Crime and Law*, *5*(1–2), 3–27.

Leo, R.A. (1996). Inside the interrogation room. *Journal of Criminal Law and Criminology*, *86*, 266–303.

Leo, R.A. (2001). False confessions: Causes, consequences, and solutions. In S.D. Westervelt & J.A. Humphrey (Eds), *Wrongly convicted: Perspectives on failed justice* (pp. 36–54). New Brunswick, NJ: Rutgers University Press.

Leo, R.A. & Ofshe, R.J. (1998). The consequences of false confessions: Deprivations of liberty and miscarriages of justice in the age of psychological interrogation. *Journal of Criminal Law and Criminology*, *88*, 429–496.

Mann, S., Vrij, A., & Bull, R. (2004). Detecting true lies: Police officers' ability to detect suspects' lies. *Journal of Applied Psychology*, *89*, 137–149.

Memon, A. & Bull, R. (1991). The cognitive interview: Its origins, empirical support, evaluation, and practical implications. *Journal of Community and Applied Social Psychology*, *1*, 291–307.

Moston, S.J. & Stephenson, G.M. (1992). Predictors of suspect and interviewer behaviour during police questioning. In F. Loesel, D. Bender & T. Bliesener (Eds), *Psychology and law: International perspectives* (pp. 212–218). Berlin: De Gruyter.

Moston, S., Stephenson, G.M., & Williamson, T.M. (1992). The effects of case characteristics on suspect behaviour during questioning. *British Journal of Criminology*, *32*, 23–40.
Ofshe, R.J. & Leo, R.A. (1997). The social psychology of interrogation: The theory and classification of true and false confessions. *Studies in Law, Politics, and Society*, *16*, 189–251.
Ofshe, R.J. & Leo, R.A. (1998). The decision to confess falsely: Rational choice and irrational action. *Denver University Law Review*, *74*, 979–1122.
O'Keefe, D. J. (1990). *Persuasion: Theory and research.* Thousand Oaks, CA: Sage.
Pearse, J., Gudjonsson, G.H., Clare, I.C.H., & Rutter, S. (1998). Police interviewing and psychological vulnerabilities: Predicting the likelihood of a confession. *Journal of Community and Applied Social Psychology*, *8*, 1–21.
Phillips, C. & Brown, D. (1998). *Entry into the criminal justice system: A survey of police arrests and their outcomes.* London: Home Office.
Rattner, A. (1988). Convicted but innocent: Wrongful conviction and the criminal justice system. *Law and Human Behavior*, *12*, 290–307.
Redlich, A.D. & Goodman, G.S. (2003). Taking responsibility for an act not committed: The influence of age and suggestability. *Law and Human Behavior*, *27*, 141–156.
Walters, S.B. (2002). *Principles of Kinesic Interview and Interrogation* (2nd edn). New York: CRC Press.
Wells, G.L. (1995). The scientific study of witness memory: Implications for public and legal policy. *Psychology, Public Policy, and Law*, *1*, 726–731.
Westervelt, S.D. & Humphrey, J.A. (Eds) (2001). *Wrongly convicted: Perspectives on failed justice.* New Brunswick, NJ: Rutgers University Press.
Zulawski, D.E. & Wicklander, D.E. (2001). *Practical Aspects of Interview and Interrogation* (2nd edn). New York: CRC Press.

CHAPTER 13

Alternate Technologies for the Detection of Deception

JENNIFER M.C. VENDEMIA, MICHAEL J. SCHILLACI, ROBERT F. BUZAN, ERIC P. GREEN AND SCOTT W. MEEK

NEW DIRECTIONS IN THE DETECTION OF DECEPTION

Future technologies will integrate with existing polygraph techniques in one of three ways: (1) they will provide another source of information within the standard polygraph-testing scenario, (2) they will provide an alternate methodology to existing exams, or (3) they will identify new theoretical information about deception. If it is the case that future technologies reveal something new about deception, all 'technological boats' will rise. In other words, the more we know about the processes of human deception, the better all forms of measurement will be. However, there is not one path to new knowledge about deception. Some researchers who study new measurement technologies choose to use polygraph-like scenarios (e.g., Kozel, Padgett & George, 2004; Rosenfeld *et al.*, 1991). Others choose to use alternate strategies such as the oddball task or tests of semantic incongruity (e.g., Allen, Iacono & Danielson, 1992; Boaz *et al.*, 1991; Janisse & Bradley, 1980). Still others choose to use theoretical modeling approaches (e.g., Dionisio *et al.*,

The Use of the Polygraph in Assessing, Treating and Supervising Sex Offenders: A Practitioner's Guide
Edited by Daniel T. Wilcox.

2001; Vendemia, 2003b; Vendemia & Buzan, 2004b; Vendemia, Buzan & Green, 2005).

At the present time, developing technologies such as thermal imaging, voice recognition, and pupillometry operate within the existing polygraph methodology. These measures, like the polygraph, assess peripheral nervous system (PNS) activity, which is reliably manipulated by the standard detection of deception exam. They rely on emotion-related change to detect differences between an individual's deceptive and truthful responses. In contrast, many alternative psychophysiological detection of deception (PDD) techniques, such as event-related brain potential (ERP), functional magnetic resonance imaging (*f*MRI), and positron emission tomography (PET), assess aspects of deception that are not dependent on emotion-related change. For example, there is evidence to suggest that the cognitive processes involved in deception, such as attention, workload, memory and question salience, can be valid and reliable measures of deception. This is an important realization because, unlike PNS indicators of deception used in the standard polygraph approach, these cognitive processes are thought to be outside of one's control, thus not able to be manipulated by, or dependent on, emotion-related change.

NEW TECHNOLOGIES WITHIN THE EXISTING POLYGRAPH METHODOLOGY

Voice

Thus far, the most disappointing of the 'future' technologies has been voice stress analysis (VSA). The simple theory behind this measure states that anxiety related to deception can be detected by slight fluctuations in vocal recordings. This theory has received little scientific support. Nonetheless, voice stress technology built around this theory has been embraced by the public; 'lie-detectors' based on this methodology have even been advertised in popular catalogs such as *The Sharper Image*. One of the reasons for the continued public support of VSA in light of scientific criticism may be that the concept of VSA appears to have high face validity. In other words, the measurement of voice stress seems to correspond to 'common-sense' perceptions of deceptive behavior (Myers & Hansen, 1997, p. 160).

Efforts to detect deception by examining voice patterns date back to at least 1971 (National Academy of Sciences, 1979). But these efforts have largely been the efforts of marketers and salesman, not scientists. Unfortunately for the American taxpayer, many earnest law enforcement agencies and legitimate government funding organizations, under intense pressure to find alternate means of detecting deception, have fallen victim to incredible marketing claims of success. Who would not want a magic wand that could instantly detect deception while a suspect spoke? Imagine the possibilities of being able to detect a lie from a tape of a person's voice or while they spoke on television. Political debates would never be the same! Unfortunately none of the claims of voice stress marketers have ever been substantiated.

The voice stress devices that have been marketed include the Psychological Stress Evaluator (PSE), the Hagoth, the Mark II VSA and the Computerized Voice Stress Analyzer (CVSA). The CVSA is the most recent of these devices and has been heralded as a new dawn in voice stress detection. However, the only difference between CVSA and earlier devices is that it presents recorded vocal stimuli on a computer screen rather than on paper. Of the 15 university-grade publications on voice stress, only one found any evidence that voice stress may be effective; an attempt to replicate that study was unsuccessful. Table 13.1 presents a summary of studies presented in a comprehensive review of the scientific merits of voice stress analysis (Krapohl, 2001). The basic conclusions of these studies are that voice detection of deception is not valid, is not reliable and clearly does not work.

Thermal Imaging

Thermal imaging technology measures changes in regional facial blood flow, particularly around the eyes (see Figure 13.1). Changes in facial blood flow are often quite obvious, such as when a person blushes. However, the goal of thermal imaging is to capture changes in blood flow related to the fright/flight response mediated by the sympathetic nervous system (Pavlidis, Eberhardt & Levine, 2002a, 2002b). The clear advantage of this system is that individuals can be tested for deception without their awareness because measurement takes place through a camera that is sensitive to changes in temperature. The major drawback of current thermal imaging technology is the processing demand: results from a camera are recorded on a computer, and those files must undergo substantial computer processing before they can be interpreted.

Very few studies of thermal imaging as a deception detection methodology have been published, but early results have been promising. For instance, Pollina and Ryan (2002) had participants commit a simulated murder and theft similar to Pavlidis *et al.* (2002). Thermal images of the participants' faces were recorded as they answered questions during a standard polygraph examination. Pollina and Ryan (2002) found

Table 13.1 Studies that evaluated voice stress in the detection of deception

Authors	Year	Device	Participants	Location	Result
Brenner, Branscomb & Schwartz (1979)	1979	PSE	(a) 20; (b) 16	Lab	–/+
Brown, Senter & Ryan (2003)	2003	Vericator	170	Lab	
Cestaro (1995)	1995	CVSA	42	Lab	–
Cestaro (1996)	1996	CVSA	120	Lab	–
Cestaro & Dollins (1994)	1994	Verbal pitch & spectral energy	44	Lab	–
Hollien, Geison & Hicks (1987)	1987	PSE	–	Lab Lab	– –
Horvath (1978)	1978	PSE	60	Lab	–
Horvath (1979)	1979	PSE	64	Lab	–
Janniro & Cestaro (1996)	1996	CVSA	109	Lab	–
Kubis (1973)	1973	PSE, VSA	174	Lab	–
Nachshon & Feldman (1980)	1980	(a) PSE (b) PSE	20 56	Lab Field	– –
Nachshon, Elaad & Amsel (1985)	1985	PSE	40	Field	–/+
O'Hair & Cody (1987)	1987	Mark II VSA	49	Lab	–/+
Palmatier (1996)	1996	CVSA	50	Field	–
Suzuki *et al.* (1973)	1973	Voice pitch, intensity, duration	3	Case/ Field	–
Timm (1983)	1983	PSE	6	Field	–

Note: Partially adapted from Krapohl (2001), *Tech talk: Voice Stress Analysis Research*, American Polygraph Association

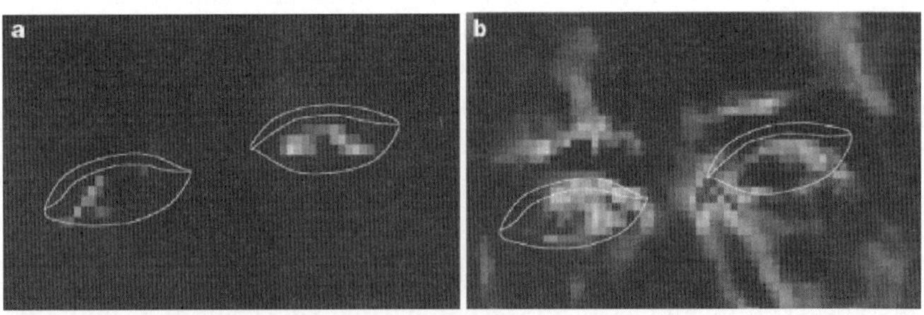

Figure 13.1 Periorbital thermal images of a participant before (a) and after (b) lying about a theft of which the participant was guilty. Reproduced from Pavlidis *et al.* (2002), with permission

that, although thermal imaging alone was unable to reliably detect deception, adding thermal imaging to the standard polygraph examination significantly increased their ability to differentiate deceivers from non-deceivers. Although this research is still in its infancy, preliminary findings suggest that thermal imaging remains a very promising deception detection technology.

Another scientific experiment, conducted at the Department of Defense Polygraph Institute (DoDPI), randomly assigned 20 volunteers to stab a mannequin and rob it. The participants were later instructed to assert their innocence during a thermal imaging exam. In the test, 83 % of the participants were correctly categorized as innocent or guilty (Pavlidis *et al.*, 2002b). However, the authors note that this technology is not quite ready for mass application; the high false-positive rate precludes the large-scale introduction of thermal imaging into security-screening applications (Pavlidis *et al.*, 2002a).

Pupillometry

Pupillometry, the study of changes in pupil size and movement, is not a modern technique. While pupillometry is best known for assessing attention and alertness, it was first studied in conjunction with deception in the 1940s (Berrien, 1942; Berrien & Huntington, 1943; Harney, 1943). These early studies suggested that deception was associated with a change in pupil size (see Figure 13.2). Study participants responded truthfully or deceptively to critical items presented among non-critical items. Berrien and Huntington (1943) measured pulse and pupil dilation and found a pupillary response related to the emotional effects of deception. Results showed that changes in pupil size occurred

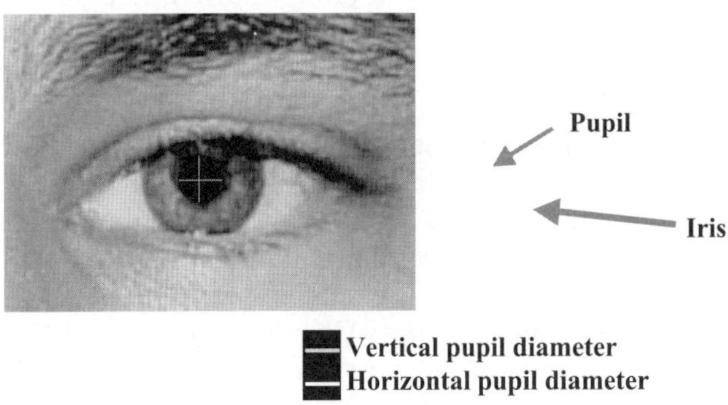

Figure 13.2 Illustration of vertical and horizontal pupil diameter utilized in pupillometry

whenever a crime-relevant question was asked, though the change was more pronounced when the participant intended to be deceptive. However, their data showed no improvement in deception detection for pupillary response over vascular changes.

Pupillometry is a robust measure of mental load that accurately reflects differences in processing demands between individuals, between tasks (such as lying and telling the truth) and within tasks (Bradley & Janisse, 1981a). When using this measure, variables such as environmental illumination level and psychosensory reflexes must be controlled (Tryon, 1975).

Pupillometry studies have identified a clear pattern of pupil dilation responses to mental workload (Simpson, 1969). Under increasing mental workload, pupil size increases until workload reaches asymptote (or overload) at which point dilations level off or decrease (Granholm, Asarnow & Sarkin, 1996; Peavler, 1974). Peavler (1974) argued that the cessation of pupil dilation following 'overload' results from the suspension of processing effort. This pair of responses, increase followed by asymptote, not only differentiates between levels of task difficulty, but also between individual differences in the ability to perform these tasks (Ahern & Beatty, 1979; Beatty, 1982; Peavler, 1974). Ahern and Beatty (1979) found that more intelligent participants (as measured by Scholastic Aptitude Tests) showed smaller evoked pupillary dilations than less intelligent students while performing tasks of the same difficulty; Peavler (1974) showed that differences in digit recall ability were associated with differences in pupil size.

The pattern of access into long-term memory has also been associated with differences in pupil dilation. (Headley, 1981; Krüger, Nuthmann & van der Meer, 2001). Headley (1981) was able to separate different patterns of memory retrieval from long-term semantic memory based on participants' unique patterns of pupil dilation. Krüger *et al.* (2001) used pupillometry to demonstrate that accessing items in memory by going sequentially backwards through time was more difficult than remembering past events forwards sequentially in time.

In studies of pupillometry and deception, such as concealed information (CI) paradigms, larger dilations were identified in 'guilt' than in 'innocent' participants (Bradley & Janisse, 1981b; Lubow & Fein, 1996). However, factors other than deception can influence pupil size. A participant's uncertainty about the test's outcome can cause greater relative changes in pupil size than certainty (Bradley & Janisse, 1979), and the more effective a participant believes the test to be (the bogus pipeline effect), the greater the change in pupillary response (Bradley & Janisse, 1981). The cognitive processes involved in deception can also influence pupillary dilation. Participants generate demonstrably greater pupil dilations when they respond deceptively to learned episodic or semantic information (Dionisio *et al.*, 2001), as well as to autobiographical information (Heilveil, 1976) than they do when responding truthfully.

Additionally, occulomotor measures can be used to assess and control for several variables known to affect ERPs, *f*MRI and polygraph measures of deception. In particular, saccade (a ballistic eye movement) velocity, pupil diameter, pupil constriction latency and pupil constriction amplitude have all successfully identified high and low arousal levels. These measures can be combined with behavioral measures to establish performance norms of the deceptive tests based on alertness, a variable that substantially influences the degree and latency to which respondents orient to salient stimuli.

New Technologies Outside of the Existing Polygraph Methodology

Brain wave. Event-related potentials (ERPs) have been used to detect deception for several decades (see Figure 13.3). In 1994, *Time* magazine named Larry Farwell *Inventor of the Year* for his work on the identification of brain waves associated with deception. However, intense debates on the theoretical and methodological approaches to using ERPs to identify deception continue. Like thermal imaging, ERPs measure

Figure 13.3 The control room during an ERP study showing clockwise from the top screen: the participant being recorded, a topographical map of the EEG, the question prompt in the study, and the initial crime scene footage (adapted from McCloskey and Zaragoza, 1985)

large quantities of data. Unlike thermal imaging, however, ERPs can be used to explore in depth the many underlying cognitive mechanisms associated with deception.

Conflicting theories of lying have been developed based on the brain processes known to elicit ERPs (Boaz *et al.*, 1991). Research suggests that the process of deception may involve attentional capture (Allen & Iacono, 1997), working memory load (Allen & Iacono, 1997; Dionisio *et al.*, 2001; Stelmack, Houlihan & Doucet, 1994a; Stelmack *et al.*, 1994b), or perceived conflict between question meaning and the examinee's memories (Boaz *et al.*, 1991).

Attentional capture refers to the directing of attention, generally toward a threat. For example, loud noises capture our attention because they could be threatening. For similar reasons, questions to which one is prepared to lie grab attention because of the threat of being caught. Working memory load refers to how many unique ideas an individual can attend to at one time. An individual telling the truth does not need to keep ideas in active awareness, but someone who is being deceptive must keep track of deceptive answers as well as truthful answers. Telling a lie is a far more cognitively complex activity than telling the truth.

Research has suggested that three waveforms are related to deception: the P3b, P3a and N4 (Allen & Iacono, 1997; Allen *et al.*, 1992; Bashore & Rapp, 1993; Boaz *et al.*, 1991; Pollina & Squires, 1998; Rosenfeld *et al.*, 1999; Vendemia & Buzan, 2005). These waves, illustrated in Figure 13.4, vary in the way they are generally produced and

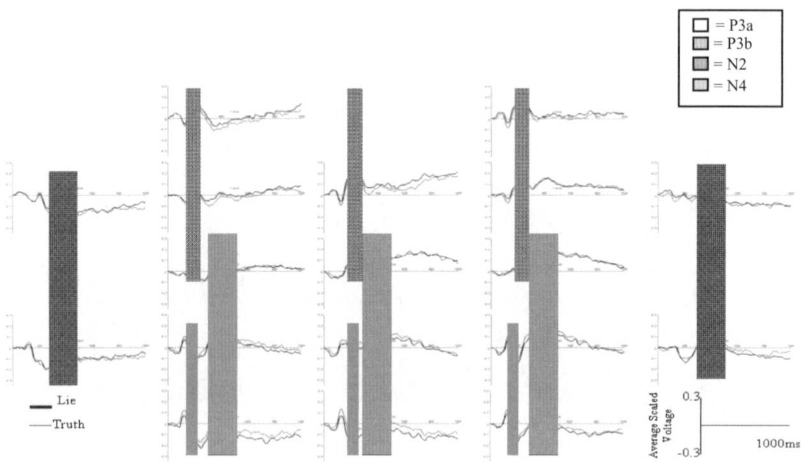

Figure 13.4 ERP waveforms of interest in the detection of deception

in the way they are studied in relation to deception. The P3b is by far the most frequently reported component of the three and is typically studied in the context of the CI (concealed information) oddball paradigm. An oddball paradigm presents an infrequently occurring stimulus within a sequence of frequently occurring stimuli. For example, a single high-pitched tone presented among a group of low-pitched tones would grab attention because it is different. This switch in attention is related to the P3b.

The 'oddball' stimulus produces a large positive ongoing peak with a latency of 350–600 ms and a distribution whose maximum amplitude occurs at parietal sites and whose minimum amplitude occurs at anterior sites (Verleger, 1997). Similar to the general oddball paradigm, the CI/oddball consists of low probability stimuli that involve guilty knowledge presented among a series of high probability stimuli that do not involve guilty knowledge. In this paradigm, the low probability guilty knowledge items elicit a larger P3b component than the non-targets (Allen *et al.*, 1992). Although researchers reporting ERPs from the CI/oddball in this area do not explicitly describe this waveform as a P3b, its spatio-temporal characteristics closely match those of the P3b (Rosenfeld *et al.*, 1999).

The CI/oddball effect has been demonstrated across multiple design permutations.

Across these studies, the P3 component of the ERP accurately and reliably indicated the presence of concealed knowledge (Allen & Iacono, 1997; Allen *et al.*, 1992; Bashore & Rapp, 1993; Ellwanger *et al.*, 1996; Farwell & Donchin, 1991; Rosenfeld, 1995, 2002; Rosenfeld *et al.*, 1996). However, the P3b is involved in many types of higher cortical functions, including stimulus evaluation (Gevins, Cutillo & Smith, 1995; Ruchkin *et al.*, 1990; Verleger, 1997), attention resource allocation (Comerchero & Polich, 1999), and updating of information held in working memory (Donchin & Coles, 1988; Ruchkin *et al.*, 1990). Thus, the precise cognitive sources for the effects of deception on the P3b remain unclear.

An often criticized confound of the CI/oddball task further obscures the findings (Allen & Iacono, 1997). Participation in an activity is not required to generate an ERP response to questions about that action; knowledge of the act is sufficient to bring about a measurable response. For example, a witness to a criminal episode will exhibit ERP responses to questions about the crime that are similar to ERP responses of the criminal. In the psychophysiological detection of deception field, therefore, the CI paradigm is now referred to as the concealed knowledge paradigm because central and peripheral nervous system responses are associated with the mere possession of knowledge, but not explicitly with guilt.

Two main theories of deception, the attention theory and the working memory load theory, suggest different patterns of response for the P3b based on the antagonistic effects of attention and workload (Kok, 2001). Attention theorists argue that attentional capture of the low frequency CI items increases the amplitude of the P3b, while working memory load theorists argue that the increased working memory demands required for deceptive processing suppress the P3b. Manipulating task demands can generate both of these effects. The P3b is larger in tasks with an attention grabbing concealed information item, while in tasks with no such oddball the P3b is suppressed. In order to examine the actual effects of deception, other waveforms must also be studied.

Like the P3b, the P3a is elicited by an oddball paradigm. In one variant of the oddball, the three-stimulus paradigm, the P3a occurs in response to novel-infrequent stimuli presented in addition to the 'typical' oddball stimuli. The P3a can be elicited by shifts in attention (Comerchero & Polich, 1999), switching from difficult to easy task demands (Comerchero & Polich, 1999; Harmony *et al.*, 2000), and alerting (Katayama & Polich, 1998). Across studies reporting the P3a in an oddball, it is alerting stimuli combined with initial attentional allocation that produce the phenomenon (Katayama & Polich, 1998). The term 'P3a' is applied to an assortment of early P3 components with anterior distributions, and the exact conditions necessary to evoke a P3a vary across paradigm and stimulus demands (Katayama & Polich, 1998). In general, the waveform is characterized as a positive going peak with an anterior distribution, and a post-stimulus latency of 250–350 ms (Comerchero & Polich, 1999; Harmony *et al.*, 2000; Spencer, Dien & Donchin, 1999).

Two ERP studies of deception reported an early positivity with spatiotemporal characteristics similar to the P3a (Matsuda *et al.*, 1990; Pollina & Squires, 1998). Neither of the reported studies involved the oddball paradigm: (a) Pollina and Squires (1998) employed graded judgments of true and false sentences and (b) Matsuda *et al.* (1990) used a two-stimulus target detection task in which the first stimulus involved participant-related information. Although the findings were mixed, Pollina and Squires (1998) suggested that the P3a occurred in probably true conditions.

Unlike P3b and P3a, the last component reported in studies of deception, the N4 component, is sensitive to semantic incongruity. Some researchers argue that deception represents an incongruity between internal truth and external response (Bashore & Rapp, 1993). The N4 is a large negative going peak occurring at around 400 ms post-stimulus with maximum amplitude in anterior and temporal regions (see Figure 13.5). It is produced by stimuli that are incongruent in relation

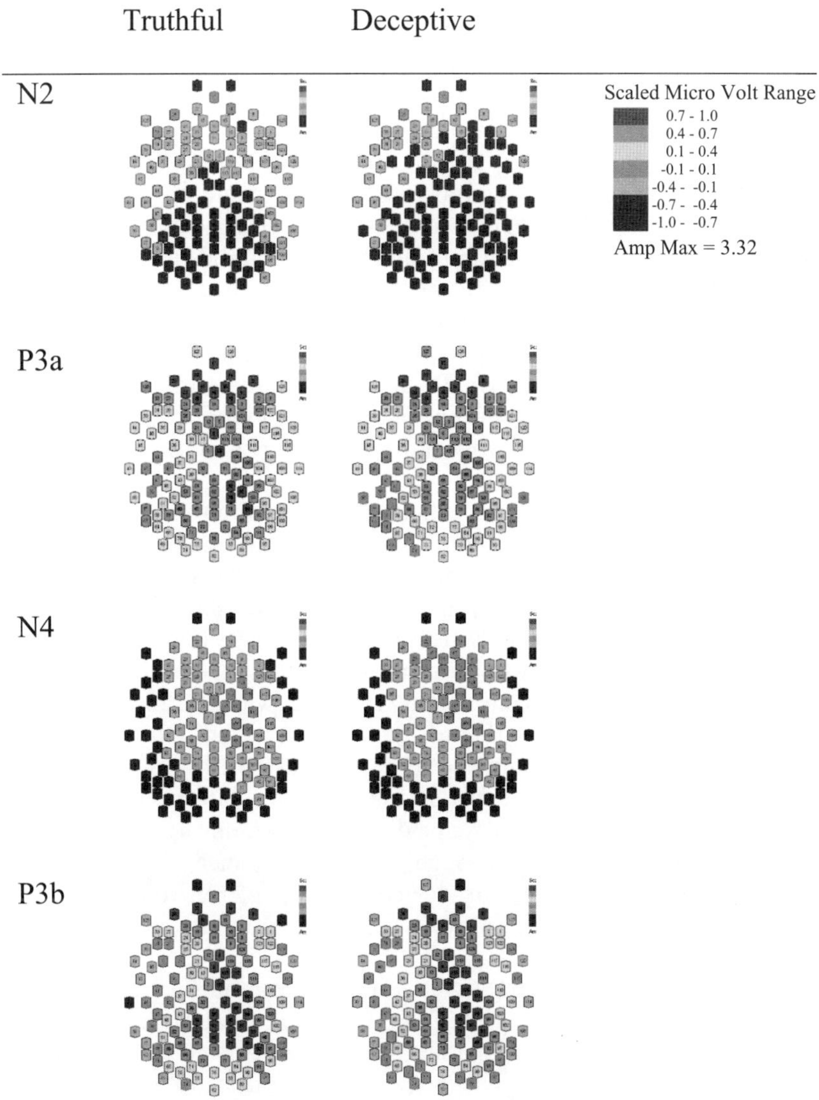

Figure 13.5 Topographical distributions of activity for ERP components of interest in the detection of deception

to the preceding context, and is predominantly limited to linguistic information.

The N4 component has also been elicited by the possession of concealed knowledge in sentence completion tasks involving false sentence completions (Boaz *et al.*, 1991) and in a two-stimulus target detection task (Stelmack *et al.*, 1994a, 1994b). Bashore and Rapp (1993) suggest that the N4 is reactive to anomalies in semantic and episodic memory as well as to inconsistencies in language semantics. A study that did not share language inconsistency, but did share anomalies in semantic and episodic memory, found no differences in N4 amplitude. In that study, participants made graded truth-value judgments that were sometimes inconsistent with memory, and these failed to alter N4 amplitude or latency (Pollina & Squires, 1998). In a two-stimulus task, the N4 was not found to be sensitive to deception, but was found to be sensitive to response congruity with the second stimulus (Stelmack *et al.*, 1994a, 1994b).

Research by Vendemia and colleagues (Vendemia & Buzan, 2005), discussed in detail in the 'Fusing Alternative Technologies' section of this chapter, has revealed a combination of the P3a, P3b, N2, N4, and late positive potential during deception. Figure 13.4 shows the P3a, P3b, N2 and N4 depicted as ERP waveforms, while Figure 13.5 shows the topographical distributions of these ERP components across the scalp. The early positive component, the P3a, was localized to the anterior cingulate gyrus, a region of the brain involved in attention. The P3b was associated with activity in many different brain regions, and seemed to be involved in decision-making. The late occurring negativity (N4) was predominantly localized to the inferior frontal gyrus, and seemed to be related to congruity of the response. Finally, the late positive complex was associated with regions of the temporal gyrus and anterior cingulate, and may be related to a final reanalysis of the response.

Detecting deception using event-related potentials is a young, but promising technique. Research evaluating the relationships between emotion, stress, individual personality variables, memory-modifying misinformation and psychopathology with deception are ongoing. While research to date suggests that the psychophysiological detection of deception approach reliably differentiates truthful and deceptive responses, it remains to be seen what role ERP-based detection of deception methods will serve in the future. Additional research may lead to less cumbersome technologies and measurement strategies that will make ERP the ideal choice for a variety of security settings. Alternatively, the addition of event-related potential channels to other scientifically tested methodologies, such as polygraph, thermal imaging, or functional magnetic resonance imaging, may further improve the ability of these methods to detect deception.

Functional Magnetic Resonance Imaging (*f*MRI)

When a human being engages in any cognitive activity, such as subtraction, reading, or lying, various parts of the brain become active. Increased activity in these areas increases the metabolism rate of the neurons, which therefore need more blood for nourishment. Brain mapping is achieved by setting up an MRI scanner in such a way that blood flow to the active areas of the human brain shows up superimposed on an MRI image.

In an *f*MRI experiment, a participant will lie in a magnet (see Figure 13.6) while performing an experimental task. In the earliest

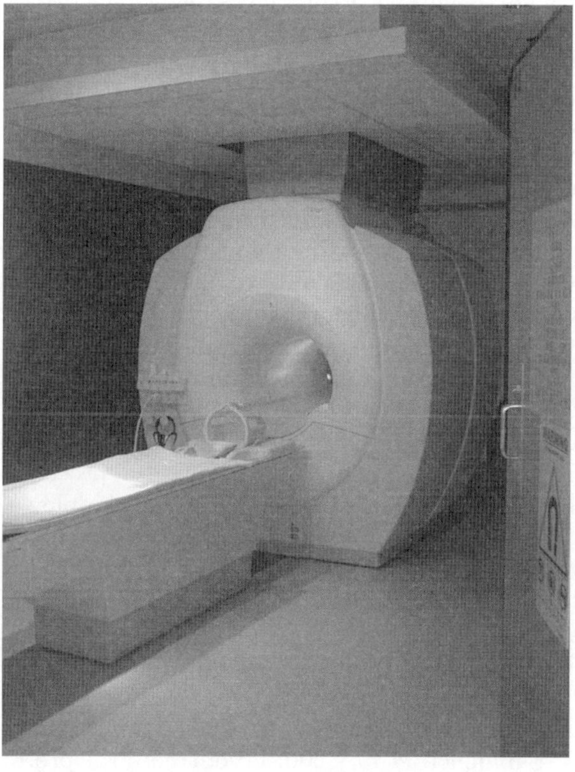

Figure 13.6 A typical *f*MRI machine. The participant lies prone on the table with his head facing the magnetic coil. The table is moved into the bore of the magnet during recording

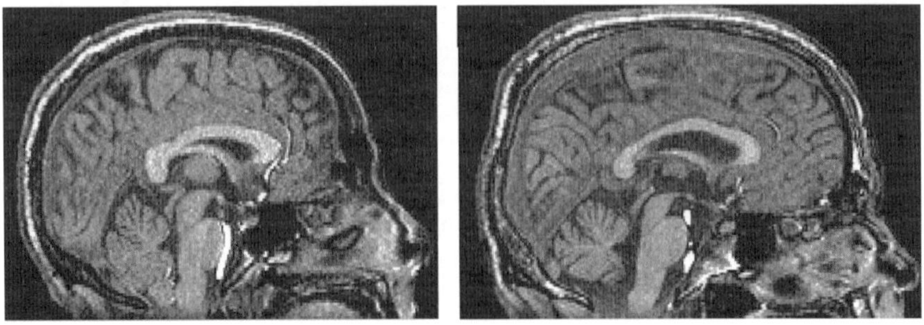

Figure 13.7 Midsagittal structural magnetic resonance images of left hemispheres from two people showing corpus callosum, cerebellum, brainstem and cortical regions

*f*MRI studies, participants watched patterns of grids, such as checkerboards, while scientists measured the output from the visual cortex. First, an MRI image is taken of the individual's brain, which, like a fingerprint, has its own unique shape and size (see Figure 13.7). Later, this image will serve as a template on which the images of brain activity will be overlaid.

Next, a series of low-resolution scans are taken over time, some during the task and some while the individual is not engaged in the task. For example, some scans might be taken while an individual is lying and others while an individual is telling the truth. The two sets of scans are later compared to see which is more active. Although it is possible to randomly present deceptive and truthful items with this technique, most *f*MRI research paradigms require that participants maintain the behavior of interest for an extended period of time. Thus, participants in *f*MRI-based deception research lie to a series of questions, then tell the truth to a series of questions, an experimental procedure known as a block design. Researchers using this technology employ a wide range of different paradigms, and for this reason and others the results across studies have not been consistent.

In block design *f*MRI studies, researchers have associated activations in the caudate (Lee *et al.*, 2002), cerebellum (Ganis *et al.*, 2003), cingulate (Faro *et al.*, 2004; Ganis *et al.*, 2003; Kozel *et al.*, 2004; Lee *et al.*, 2002), cuneus (Ganis *et al.*, 2003), fusiform/parahippocampal area (Ganis *et al.*, 2003; Kozel *et al.*, 2004), precental gyrus (Ganis *et al.*, 2003; Langleben *et al.*, 2002), ventrolateral prefrontal cortex (Faro *et al.*, 2004; Spence *et al.*, 2001), medial prefrontal cortex (Ganis *et al.*, 2003; Langleben *et al.*, 2002; Spence *et al.*, 2001), prefrontal cortex (Faro *et al.*, 2004; Ganis *et al.*, 2003; Kozel *et al.*, 2004; Lee *et al.*,

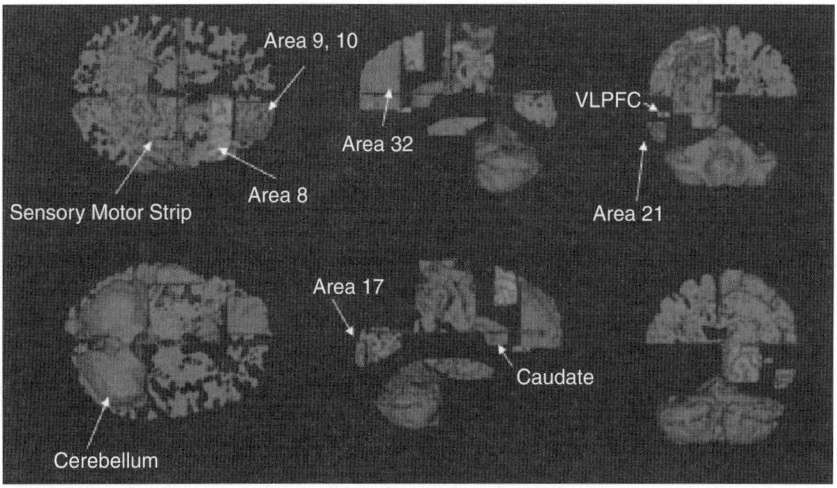

Figure 13.8 Cortical activation regions reported in Bhatt *et al.*'s review of *f*MRI deception studies (Bhatt *et al.*, under review)

2002), left frontal (Ganis *et al.*, 2003; Langleben *et al.*, 2002; Spence *et al.*, 2001), left inferior parietal (Langleben *et al.*, 2002; Lee *et al.*, 2002; Spence *et al.*, 2001), and temporal (Faro *et al.*, 2004; Kozel *et al.*, 2004; Lee *et al.*, 2002; Stelmack *et al.*, 1994b) regions with the act of deception. Bhatt, Fishbein and Zeffiro (under review) performed a meta-analysis of the brain regions activated in *f*MRI studies of deception. We have created a three-dimensional cortical map of their results, which are presented in Figure 13.8.

As is evident from Bhatt's review, the number of individual activations reported in these studies is quite varied, with activations from single participants ranging throughout the cortex (Figure 13.8). This tremendous variability in *f*MRI activations can be attributed to the large number of paradigmatic differences in these studies. Table 13.2 lists *f*MRI studies in which participants engaged in deceptive behavior or observed deceptive behavior, and the specifics of each paradigm. It is clear that these studies differ on how participants were 'motivated' to deceive, the types of lies they were asked to tell, the information about which they lied, and the type of polygraph scenario they attempted to parallel.

Even given these differences, activations in certain regions could be anticipated based on the underlying processes engaged in each study. For example, the studies by Kozel *et al.* (2004a, 2004b), and Langleben *et al.* (2002), utilized a risk-taking scenario in which participants would

Table 13.2 Studies reporting *f*MRI differences in deception, compiled from Bhatt *et al.* (under review)

Author	Paradigm Description	Lie Type
Ganis *et al.* (2003)	Recorded work/vacation scenarios, after 1 week delay generated alternate scenarios and memorized them.	1. Memorized 2. Spontaneous
German *et al.* (2004)	Observers indicated whether real or acted clips revealed completed acts.	Observation only
Grezes *et al.* (2004)	Observers indicated whether actors actually lifted heavy boxes or pretended to lift heavy boxes.	Observation only
Kozel *et al.* (2004a)	For a reward, participants lied and told the truth regarding objects under which 50 $ was hidden.	Concealed information
Kozel *et al.* (2004b)	For a reward, participants, lied and told the truth regarding an object under which 50 $ was hidden.	Concealed information
Lee *et al.* (2002)	For a reward, participants lied in a card playing scenario.	Concealed information
Lee *et al.* (2002)	For an imaginary reward, participants faked amnesia to digits and autobiographical information.	Simulated amnesia 1. digits 2. autobiographic memory
Spence *et al.* (2005)	Participants were told to lie and tell the truth to events that happened earlier in the day.	Directed lie to episodic memory

receive a monetary reward if they 'fooled' the examiner, but no reward if they failed to 'fool' the examiner. Given this condition, activation in the orbitofrontal cortex, a region of the frontal cortex that has been implicated in the integration of motivational stimuli when guiding response selection, could be anticipated. Only Kozel *et al.* (2004a, 2004b) identified activation in this region.

John Gabrieli and other *f*MRI researchers argued that the anterior prefrontal cortex, or Brodmann's Area 10 (see Figure 13.8), is involved in the act of deception (personal communication, July 14, 2005). Ramnani and Owen (2004) argued that this area is activated when an individual must make simultaneous considerations of multiple relations. When an individual deceives, these multiple relations may occur between situational context, goal-driven behavior, divergence of the deceptive information from truthful information, and a variety of internal states. Given the generalist nature of these 'simultaneous considerations', it is no surprise that several researchers have identified activation in this region during the act of deception (Faro *et al.*, 2004; Ganis *et al.*, 2003; Kozel *et al.*, 2004; Lee *et al.*, 2002; Vendemia, 2004a).

However, the most widely reported region of activation is the anterior cingulate (Faro *et al.*, 2004; Ganis *et al.*, 2003; Kozel *et al.*, 2004; Lee *et al.*, 2002; Spence *et al.*, 2001; Vendemia & Buzan 2004a). This activation is broken down into two main areas, the ventral anterior cingulate and the dorsal anterior cingulate. Some researchers believe that this area is involved in conflict resolution while others believe that it is involved in attention shifting and resource allocation processes. It may be likely that the more ventral region is involved in conflict resolution while the more dorsal area is involved in attention shifting; however, as it is theoretically possible that the act of deception involves both processes, it may be difficult to parcel out these anatomical correlates.

Fusing Alternative Technologies Together to Create a Model of Deception

The goal of testing deception using a modeling approach is to assess the cognitive processes that subserve the larger process of deception and to identify consistent patterns of activity in multiple measures of deception. The difference between utilizing testable models to develop a theory versus utilizing a data-driven approach is purely methodological and is not based on the type of dependent variable gathered. According to Keppel (1991), a testable model is, '... a fairly general statement about the assumed nature of the world that we translate into an experiment. Typically ... a research hypothesis asserts that the (variables) will produce an effect' (p. 24).

Work in our lab began with a model (Figure 13.9) based on literature from the fields of polygraphy and ERPs. Individual hypotheses derived from the model were then tested in a sequence of 13 individual experiments over a period of 5 years. These studies involved several dependent variables including behavioral measures (reaction time and errors), ERPs (N2b, P3a, P3b, N4 and LPC), and ERP combined with *f*MRI measures.

According to this model executive control monitors an ongoing dialogue with another person. The skill and degree to which this is applied depends on the type of coping mechanisms an individual uses and how skilled an individual is at cognitive control. When a question to which the individual intends to deceive arises, certain characteristics of that

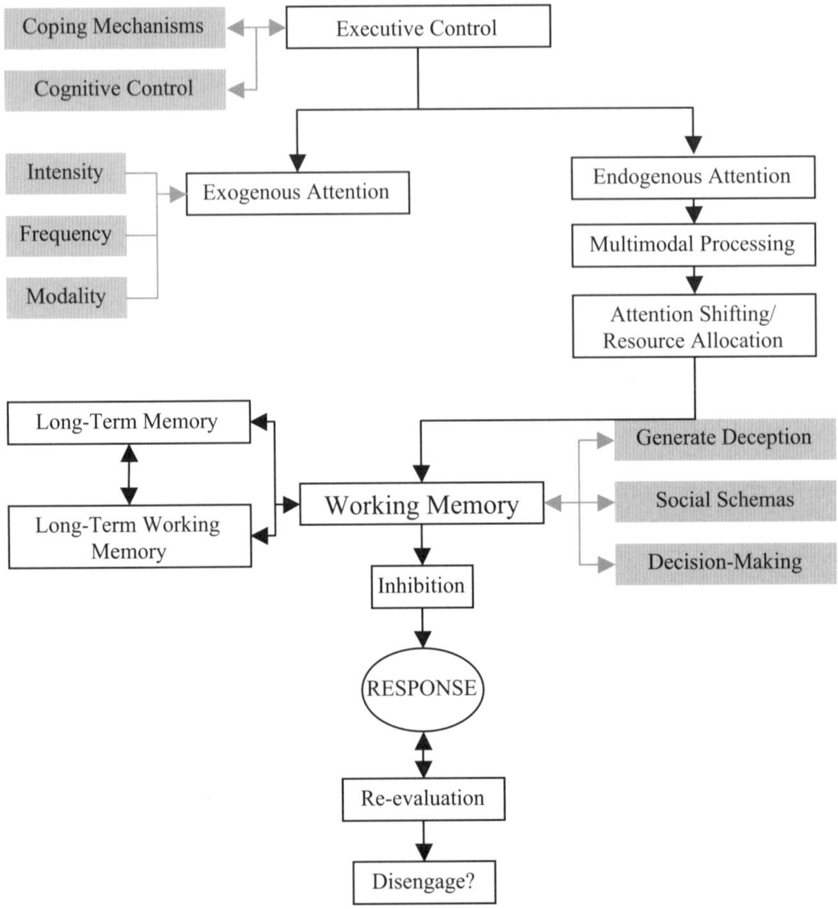

Figure 13.9 A working model of deceptive behavior

question, such as intensity (how strongly the question is asked), frequency (how often the question has been asked), and modality (is the question spoken or printed), attract their attention. The individual has no control over these demands on the exogenous attention system, but can control aspects of the endogenous attention system such as how the individual processes incoming stimuli and how they allocate resources to prepare the deception. These resources are then held in working memory, and the truthful information is pulled from long-term memory. In the case of individuals who have expert information or who have heavily practiced the deception, the information may be generated by a special type of memory called long-term working memory. Once the truthful information is held in working memory, the individual must generate a deception and make a decision based on the social demands and the risk-benefit ratio to be deceptive or truthful. After that decision is made the person inhibits the inappropriate response and delivers the situationally appropriate response. In certain individuals, this is followed by a re-evaluation of the response and a disengagement of the deceptive working memory.

This model depicts the complexity of the cognitive process of deception from which we can infer its measurable psychophysiological activations. When individuals are in an environment in which they feel they must be prepared to lie, they are likely to be in a state of heightened alertness in which they must be vigilant about their every action. Not only must they lie convincingly when required, they must tell the truth when appropriate. They must further maintain a coherent and cohesive story; any lies they tell must fit together within their deceptive 'storyline'. Such vigilance is controlled by what is commonly referred to as the 'central executive', which encompasses the 'executive functions'.

The executive functions include a vast array of cognitive activities associated with behavioral control and execution, many of which are tapped into by the deceptive act. When one is uncertain whether one must lie or tell the truth to the next question, the endogenous attentional system is strongly activated; the respondent must quickly assess the situation to determine which response is correct. Our theory suggests that doing so will increase activation in the occipital/parietal region of the brain, a higher-order multimodal association area that controls awareness of one's surroundings and self. As attention shifts from one stimulus to another (i.e., from one question to the next), we would expect more medial-frontal *f*MRI activations related to attentional resource reallocation or a P3a ERP waveform. Next, comparing the stimulus item with the internal representation of the event in question requires the interaction of working memory, long-term memory, and long-term working memory. Long-term memory access may be associated with a negative waveform at about 400 ms that is observed in the temporal regions. We would anticipate psychophysiological findings associated with the executive control of this problem-solving and response-selection process, such as in the dorsolateral prefrontal cortex (Brodmann's areas 9 and 10) or a P3b ERP waveform occurring between 350 and 600 ms post-stimulus associated with working memory.

Finally, to generate a deceptive response, the respondent must inhibit a prepotent but situationally inappropriate response (e.g., the 'truth') and answer the question. This activity will likely produce frontal activations associated with the executive inhibition of behavior, followed by precentral gyrus activity as the response is carried out. The motor activity will vary somewhat in location depending on response modality; verbal responses will activate a more ventral portion of the precentral gyrus than will manual responses. There is ERP evidence in the form of a late positive component (LPC) activation to support the notion of a re-evaluation after the response, which may serve to prepare respondents for upcoming questions.

In the initial studies testing this model, we had participants respond truthfully or deceptively to statements with a true or false base truth-value, such as the true statement 'Grass is green.' Similar to semantic verification tasks, participants evaluated these sentences and then made truthful or deceptive evaluations of the sentence's base truth-value. In order to examine the impact of long-term memory access, Study One (N = 42) used statements with semantic long-term information (general world knowledge), while Study Two (N = 45) used autobiographic long-term information statements (personal information such as, 'My name is [Name]' where [Name] is replaced by each participant's actual name) were used.

To begin formulating the specifics of the neuronal aspects of the theory, we undertook a post-hoc analysis of electrical current dipole sources (i.e., the sources of the electrical activity in the brain as measured from the scalp) on the data from Study One. Four ERP waveforms were affected by the experimental manipulations: an early positive component (P3a) in the cingulate gyrus, a subsequent centro-parietal positivity (P3b) with multiple cortical sources, a late occurring negativity (N4) in the inferior frontal gyrus, and a late positive complex in regions of the temporal gyrus and anterior cingulate (Vendemia, 2003b). The reaction time data showed that it took participants longer to deceive than to tell the truth, suggesting that deception is the more difficult task. With respect to long-term memory, participants took longer to respond to general world knowledge than to autobiographical knowledge. This phenomenon was additive with deception, suggesting that individuals retrieve information from long-term memory when deceiving (Vendemia, 2003b; Vendemia *et al.*, 2005a; Vendemia, Buzan & Simon-Dack, 2005b).

In the next sequence of studies, we (Vendemia *et al.*, 2005b) investigated the impact of preparedness to deceive on behavioral dependent variables (reaction time and errors). Three studies (N = 45, N = 44, N = 38, respectively) assessed reaction time in relation to deception, response congruity and preparedness to deceive. Each study provided less information preparing respondents to lie or tell the truth to each item than did the previous study. We found that deceptive responses generated longer reaction times than did truthful responses and that this relationship remained constant across response type (i.e., responding with 'agree' versus responding with 'disagree') and preparedness to deceive. Overall, participants took longer to respond when they were less prepared to deceive and when responding with 'disagree.' However, there was no interactive effect between preparedness to deceive and deception.

In the next sequence of studies (Vendemia *et al.*, 2006), we continued to examine and unite the various methodological approaches. Building upon the previous experiments, we derived hypotheses about the impact of preparedness to deceive on ERP waveforms associated with deception. Over three levels of preparedness ($N = 34$, $N = 27$, $N = 23$), we manipulated working memory load by utilizing truthful and deceptive response demands combined with congruent and incongruent response demands. Random presentation of response demands across trials in all three experiments required attention shifting within and between each trial, while preparedness to deceive was systematically decreased across the three studies. Four waveforms were identified through principal components analysis: an N2b occurring at 150–250 ms with an anterior maximum; a P3a occurring at 250–450 ms with an anterior maximum, an N4 occurring at 300–500 ms with anterior and temporal maxima, and a P3b occurring at 500–700 ms with a parietal maximum (see Figure 13.5).

The N2b, which had been identified in earlier studies, had not previously varied with experimental manipulations related to long-term memory or workload. In this study, however, we found it to vary systematically with preparedness; the more prepared an individual was to deceive, the shorter the latency of this waveform and the larger its amplitude. Classically, the N2b is elicited in 'attend' conditions, and is associated with transient arousal and the orienting response (Loveless, 1983; Loveless, 1986; Näätänen & Gaillard, 1983). Decreased N2b latency is indicative of decreased orienting toward task-related stimuli (Nordby *et al.*, 1999), while increased N2b latency is associated with the decline in attentional skill with age (Amenedo & Díaz, 1998). The N2b has also been associated with attention-switching tasks involving deception (Vendemia, 2003a; Vendemia & Buzan, 2005); individuals tend to orient to stimuli to which they must respond deceptively. As the tasks became more difficult and the response prompt became more relevant to the correct completion of the task, N2b latencies increased.

The next construct that we tested was practice. Theoretically, deception involves executive function with access into long-term working memory processes, which can be improved through practice. A three-session longitudinal study examined the effect of practice on RT in relation to deception and response congruity (Session One, $N = 43$; Session Two, $N = 36$; Session Three, $N = 25$). Participants evaluated self-referent sentences and responded truthfully or deceptively. Findings indicated that RT decreased with increasing practice, but that deceptive responding consistently generated longer RTs than truthful responding regardless of practice.

In addition to examining the impact of preparedness, working memory load and practice, our laboratory began to investigate the effect of incomplete or inaccurate memories on the process of deception. In order to conduct these studies, we utilized a misinformation paradigm. Researchers in the field of misinformation have disagreed on whether the experiments in this area are truly showing misinformation effects, whether they are representative of patterns of recognition, or perhaps are the result of a source conflict effect (McCloskey & Zaragoza, 1985). In order to better investigate the cognitive processes involved in the misinformation effect, we added a memory workload task using deception. A pilot study with 96 participants (72 females, 24 males) showed main effects of narrative content and deception and a significant interaction between narrative content and deception on reaction times. Two current studies in our laboratory seek to parse out the possible explanations for this effect. In order to investigate recency effects, we are conducting a study using a modified forced-choice paradigm with novel response items replacing the misinformation items. In order to investigate source conflict, we are also conducting a study with novel response items and misinformation items.

Other research in our lab also merges developing detection of deception technologies. Using ERP and *f*MRI techniques, we studied neocortical correlates of deception. Participants ($N = 15$) were measured on two testing days while they performed the same deception-related semantic verification task with autobiographical information: (1) while their ERPs were recorded, and (2) while *f*MRI measures were recorded. Data from the *f*MRI were used to seed dipole models of the event-related data to garner specific cortical sources underlying the event-related signal, providing a specific localization of deception processes in time and cortical space. The preliminary results from this study suggest that general aspects of the visual attention system are involved in the deceptive process and that both the exogenous and endogenous components of attention are invoked.

Additionally, we studied a novel analysis approach for high-density event-related scalp potential data within a quantum mechanical formalism wherein each channel is treated as an independent two-state system. Empirical voltage values obtained with a 128-channel EEG/ERP array during truthful and deceptive responses to questions regarding autobiographical information were used to define energy values at discrete time points; exact solutions for the probability amplitudes are written in terms of the Rabi formulae at resonance assuming a 'pure truth' start. We assessed cognitive activity levels over areas of the cortex by summing energy density contributions over neighboring channels and demonstrated that, while channel and response states remain independent, transitions among response states occur through population inversions induced by cutoff and revival of the time-dependent potential. A phase analysis of the transition rates for the truthful and deceptive channel states shows that after transitions cease, the states evolve independently, allowing for effective discrimination of the response state for 72% of the participant population. In addition, a time course analysis for extrema of the cognitive activity levels over posterior and anterior regions of the brain suggested that neocortical interactions may be responsible for differing workloads for executive and semantic processes such that attention-switching task demands take longer for the case of deception. These results suggest that the quantum approach presented may provide a useful tool for the analysis of higher cognitive functioning (Schillaci *et al.*, under review).

Through our work, we have determined that (a) both the exogenous and endogenous attentional systems play roles in the act of deception and that (b) communication of information in the endogenous attentional system from posterior to anterior regions is slower during deception. The exogenous system is impacted by a variety of factors related to stimulus presentation such as frequency, modality and intensity. Furthermore, we have shown that the reaction time of deceptive behavior is intimately related to the type of memory about which one is being deceptive. The faster the access to the memory, the faster is the overall reaction time. For example, individuals lie much more quickly to semantic-autobiographical information than to purely semantic information.

Additionally, we found strong support that both truthful and deceptive memories are held in working memory, and then one or the other is inhibited preceding a response. We have successfully developed a testable model of deception based on a review of existing theories in the literature and refined it with data from our initial research, systematically testing individual constructs from that model successfully over several years. With each study, individual aspects of this model were refined and additional testable hypotheses created. The next clear step in this process is to measure the impact of individual differences on the constructs within this model.

CONCLUSIONS

This chapter has reviewed a variety of technologies and techniques for detecting deception. Some of these techniques, such as voice stress analysis and pupillometry, have been used for a long time, while others such as thermal imaging, ERP and *f*MRI are still fairly young. The analysis strategies that support these technologies are also burgeoning. We have reached a point in time where the specificity and complexity of our measurement tools approximate the complexity of the process we are attempting to model.

Thermal imaging shows potential, with preliminary research findings suggesting high rates of accuracy in detecting deception. Pupillometry, more often studied than thermal imaging, has demonstrated an ability to detect deception. However, factors other than deception have been shown to affect pupil diameter, a fact which may cloud findings of deception-related pupillometry examinations. ERP and *f*MRI research, though still in development, show promise as countermeasure-resistant forms of deception detection. Conversely, research on Computerized Voice Stress Analysis (CVSA) has been quite disappointing. Having failed to produce replicable results in rigorous scientific inquiry, CVSA has been found to be a deception detection technology that is neither reliable nor valid.

In the current sociopolitical climate with terrorism an ongoing global threat, the further development and study of reliable instruments to detect deception is of growing importance. Security screenings and interrogations could be greatly facilitated by using deception detection technology. However, each technology, whether established or developing, may have a particular niche in the deception detection field. One technology may be too cumbersome for use in airplane passenger screening, while the accuracy of another may be too low to provide adequate security. Additional research is therefore necessary to determine the reliability, validity and accuracy of each instrument as well as the specific arenas in which each deception detection technology is most appropriately used.

REFERENCES

Ahern, S. & Beatty, J. (1979). Pupillary responses during information processing vary with scholastic aptitude test scores. *Science*, *205*, 1289–1292.

Allen, J.J. & Iacono, W.G. (1997). A comparison of methods for the analysis of event-related potentials in the deception detection. *Psychophysiology*, *34*, 234–240.

Allen, J.J., Iacono, W.G., & Danielson, K.D. (1992). The identification of concealed memories using the event-related potential and implicit behavioral measures: A methodology for prediction in the face of individual differences. *Psychophysiology*, *29*, 504–522.

Amenedo, E. & Díaz, F. (1998). Automatic and effortful processes in auditory memory reflected by event-related potentials: Age-related findings. *Electroencephalography and Clinical Neurophysiology: Evoked Potentials*, *108*, 361–369.

Bashore, T.R. & Rapp, P.E. (1993). Are there alternatives to traditional polygraph procedures? *Psychological Bulletin*, *113*, 3–22.

Beatty, J. (1982). Task-evoked pupillary responses, processing load, and the structure of processing resources. *Psychological Bulletin*, *91*, 276–292.

Berrien, R.E. (1942). Pupillary responses as indicators of deception. *Psychological Bulletin*, *39*, 504–505.

Berrien, R.E. & Huntington, G.H. (1943). An exploratory study of pupillary responses during deception. *Journal of Experimental Psychology*, *32*, 443–449.

Bhatt, S., Fishbein, D., & Zeffiro, T.A. (under review). A review of neural signatures of deception using functional neuroimaging. *JICRD*.

Boaz, T.L., Perry, N.W., Raney, G. *et al.* (1991). Detection of guilty knowledge with event-related potentials. *Journal of Applied Psychology*, *76*, 788–795.

Bradley, M.T. & Janisse, M.P. (1979). Pupil size and lie detection: The effect of certainty on detection. *Psychology: A Journal of Human Behavior*, *16*, 33–39.

Bradley, M.T. & Janisse, M.P. (1981a). Accuracy demonstration, threat, and the detection of deception: Cardiovascular, electrodermal, and pupillary measures. *Psychophysiology*, *18*, 307–315.

Bradley, M.T. & Janisse, M.P. (1981b). Extraversion and the detection of deception. *Personality and Individual Differences*, *2*, 99–103.

Brenner, M., Branscomb, H.H., & Schwartz, G.E. (1979). Psychological stress evaluator – two tests of a vocal measure. *Psychophysiology*, *16*, 351–357.

Brown, T.E., Senter, S.M., & Ryan, A.H. (2003). *Ability of the vericator to detect smugglers at a mock security checkpoint* (No. DoDPI03-R-0002). Fort Jackson, SC: Department of Defense Polygraph Institute.

Cestaro, V.L. (1995). *A comparison between decision accuracy rates obtained using the polygraph instrument and the computer voice stress analyzer (CVSA)* (No. DoDPI95-R-001). Fort McClellan, AL: Department of Defense Polygraph Institute.

Cestaro, V.L. (1996). *A comparison of accuracy rates between detection of deception examination using the polygraph and the computer voice stress analyzer in a mock crime scenario* (No. DoDPI95-R-0004). Fort McClellan, AL: Department of Defense Polygraph Institute.

Cestaro, V.L. & Dollins, A.B. (1994). *An analysis of voice responses for the detection of deception* (No. DoDPI94-R-0001). Fort McClellan, AL: Department of Defense Polygraph Institute.

Comerchero, M.D. & Polich, J. (1999). P3a and p3b from typical auditory and visual stimuli. *Clinical Neurophysiology*, *110*, 24–30.

Dionisio, D.P., Granholm, E., Hillix, W.A., & Perrine, W.F. (2001). Differentiation of deception using pupillary responses as an index of cognitive processing. *Psychophysiology*, *38*, 205–211.

Donchin, E. & Coles, M.G.H. (1988). Is the p300 a manifestation of context updating? *Behavioral and Brain Sciences*, *121*, 357–374.

Ellwanger, J., Rosenfeld, J.P., Sweet, J.J., & Bhatt, M. (1996). Detecting simulated amnesia for autobiographical and recently learned information using the p300 event-related potential. *International Journal of Psychophysiology*, *23*, 9–23.

Faro, S., Mohamed, F., Gordon, N. *et al.* (2004). *Functional MRI of deception and truth with polygraph correlation*. Paper presented at the Radiological Society of North America, Chicago, IL, November.

Farwell, L.A. & Donchin, E. (1991). The truth will out: Interrogative polygraph ('lie detection') with event-related potentials. *Psychophysiology*, *28*, 531–547.

Ganis, G., Kosslyn, S., Sotse, S. *et al.* (2003). Neural correlates of different types of deception: An *f*MRI investigation. *Cerebral Cortex*, *13*, 830–836.

Gevins, A., Cutillo, B., & Smith, M.E. (1995). Regional modulation of high resolution evoked potentials during verbal and non-verbal matching tasks. *Electroencephalography and Clinical Neurophysiology*, *94*, 129–147.

Granholm, E., Asarnow, R.F., & Sarkin, A.J. (1996). Pupillary responses index cognitive resource limitations. *Psychophysiology*, *33*, 457–461.

Harmony, T., Bernal, J., Fernández, T.T. *et al.* (2000). Primary task demands modulate p3 amplitude. *Cognitive Brain Research*, *9*, 53–60.

Harney, J.W. (1943). Pupillary responses during deception. *Journal of Criminal Law and Criminology*, *34*, 135–136.

Headley, D.B. (1981). Pupillometric assessment of retrieval operations in factual long-term memory. *Acta Psychologica*, *49*, 109–126.

Heilveil, I. (1976). Deception and pupil size. *Journal of Clinical Psychology*, *32*, 675–676.

Hollien, H., Geison, L., & Hicks, J.W., Jr. (1987). Voice stress analysis and lie detection. *Journal of Forensic Sciences*, *32*, 405–418.

Horvath, F. (1978). An experimental comparison of the psychological stress evaluator and the galvanic skin response in detection of deception. *Journal of Applied Psychology*, *63*, 338–344.

Horvath, F. (1979). Effect of different motivational instructions on detection of deception with the psychological stress evaluator and the galvanic skin response. *Journal of Applied Psychology*, *64*, 323–330.

Janisse, M.P. & Bradley, M.T. (1980). Deception, information and the pupillary response. *Perceptual and Motor Skills*, *50*, 748–750.

Janniro, M.J. & Cestaro, V.L. (1996). *Effectiveness of detection of deception examinations using the computer voice stress analyzer* (No. DoDPI95-P-0016). Fort McClellan, AL: Department of Defense Polygraph Institute.

Katayama, J. & Polich, J. (1998). Stimulus context determines p3a and p3b. *Psychophysiology*, *35*, 23–33.

Keppel, G. (1991). *Design and analysis: A researcher's handbook* (3rd edn). Englewood Cliffs, NJ: Prentice Hall.

Kok, A. (2001). On the utility of p3 amplitude as a measure of processing capacity. *Psychophysiology*, 39, 557–577.

Kozel, F.A., Revell, L.J., Lorberbaum, Z., & Jeffrey P. (2004a). A Pilot Study of Functional Magnetic Resonance Imaging Brain Correlates of Deception in Healthy Young Men. *Journal of Neuropsychiatry and Clinical Neurosciences*, *16*, 295–305.

Kozel, F., Padgett, T., & George, M. (2004b). A replication study of the neural correlates of deception. *Behavioral Neuroscience*, *118*, 852–856.

Krapohl, D. (2001). *Tech talk: Voice stress analysis research*. American Polygraph Association.

Krüger, F., Nuthmann, A., & van der Meer, E. (2001). Pupillometric indices of temporal order representation in semantic memory. *Zeitschrift für Psychologie*, *209*, 402–415.

Kubis, J.F. (1973). Comparison of voice analysis and polygraph as lie detection procedures (Technical Report No. Lwl-cr-03b70, Contract dad05-72-c-0217). Aberdeen Proving Ground, MD: US Army Land Warfare Laboratory.

Langleben, D., Schroeder, L., Maldjian, J. *et al.* (2002). Brain activity during simulated deception: An event-related functional magnetic resonance study. *Neuroimage*, *15*, 323–328.

Lee, T., Liu, H.-L., Chan, C. *et al.* (2002). Lie detection by functional magnetic resonance imaging. *Human Brain Mapping*, *15*, 157–164.

Loveless, N.E. (1983). The orienting response and evoked potentials in man. In D. Siddle (Ed.), *Orienting and habituation: Perspectives in human research*. New York: John Wiley & Sons, Inc.

Loveless, N.E. (1986). Potentials evoked by temporal deviance. *Biological Psychology*, *22*, 149–167.

Lubow, R.E. & Fein, O. (1996). Pupillary size in response to a visual guilty knowledge test. *Journal of Experimental Psychology: Applied*, *2*, 164–177.

Matsuda, T., Hira, S., Nakata, M., & Kakigi, S. (1990). The effect of one's own name upon event related potentials: Event related (P3 and CNV) as an index of deception. *Japanese Journal of Physiological Psychology and Psychophysiology*, *8*, 9–18.

McCloskey, M. & Zaragoza, M. (1985). Misleading post-event information and memory for events: Arguments and evidence against memory impairment hypotheses. *Journal of Experimental Psychology*, *114*, 1–16.

Myers, A. & Hansen, C.H. (1997). *Experimental Psychology*. Pacific Grove, CA: Brooks/Cole.

Näätänen, R. & Gaillard, A.W.K. (1983). The N2 deflection of ERP and the orienting reflex. In A.W.K. Gaillard & W. Ritter (Eds), *EEG correlates of information processing: Theoretical issues* (pp. 119–141). Amsterdam: North Holland.

Nachshon, I. & Feldman, B. (1980). Vocal indices of psychological stress – a validation study of the psychological stress evaluator. *Journal of Police Science and Administration*, *8*, 40–53.

Nachshon, I., Elaad, E., & Amsel, T. (1985). The validity of the psychological stress evaluator. *Journal of Police Science and Administration*, *13*, 275–282.

National Academy of Sciences. (1979). *On the theory and practice of voice identification*. Washington, DC: National Academies Press.

Nordby, H., Hugdahl, K., Jasiukaitis, P., & Spiegel, D. (1999). Effects of hypnotizability on performance of a stroop task and event-related potentials. *Perceptual and Motor Skills*, *88*, 819–830.

O'Hair, D. & Cody, M.J. (1987). Gender and vocal stress differences during truthful and deceptive information sequences. *Human Relations*, *40*, 1–14.

Palmatier, J. (1996). *The validity and comparative accuracy of voice stress analysis as measured by the CVSA: A field study conducted in a psychophysiological context*. A federally-funded study conducted by Dr John Palmatier in cooperation with the Michigan State Police.

Pavlidis, I., Eberhardt, N.I., & Levine, J.A. (2002a). Erratum: Seeing through the face of deception. *Nature*, *415*, 602.

Pavlidis, I., Eberhardt, N.I., & Levine, J.A. (2002b). Seeing through the face of deception: Thermal imaging offers a promising hands-off approach to mass security screening. *Nature*, *415*, 35.

Peavler, W.S. (1974). Pupil size, information overload, and performance differences. *Psychophysiology*, *11*, 559–566.

Pollina, D.A. & Ryan, A. (2001). *The relationship between facial skin surface temperature reactivity and traditional polygraph measures used in the psychophysiological detection of deception: A preliminary investigation* (Report No. DoDPI102-R-0007.) Fort Jackson, Columbia, SC: DoD Polygraph Institute.

Pollina, D.A. & Squires, N.K. (1998). Many-valued logic and event-related potentials. *Brain and Language*, *63*, 321–345.

Ramnani, N. & Owen, A.M. (2004). Anterior prefrontal cortex: Insights into function from anatomy and neuroimaging. *Nature Reviews Neuroscience*, *5*, 184–194.

Rosenfeld, J.P. (1995). Alternative views of Bashore and Rapp's (1993) alternatives to traditional polygraphy: A critique. *Psychological Bulletin*, *117*, 159–166.

Rosenfeld, J.P. (2002). Event-related potentials in detection of deception, malingering, and false memories. In M. Kleiner (Ed.), *Handbook of Polygraph Testing* (pp. 265–286). San Diego, CA: Academic Press.

Rosenfeld, J.P., Angell, A., Johnson, M., & Quan, J. (1991). An ERP-based, control-question lie detector analogue: Algorithms for discriminating effects within individuals' average waveforms. *Psychophysiology*, *28*, 319–335.

Rosenfeld, J.P., Ellwanger, J.W., Nolan, K. *et al.* (1999). P300 scalp amplitude distribution as an index of deception in a simulated cognitive deficit model. *International Journal of Psychophysiology*, *33*, 3–19.

Rosenfeld, J.P., Sweet, J.J., Chuang, J. *et al.* (1996). Detection of simulated malingering using forced choice recognition enhanced with event-related potential recording. *The Clinical Neuropsychologist*, *10*, 163–179.

Ruchkin, D.S., Johnson, R., Canoune, H.L., Ritter, W., & Hammer, M. (1990). Multiple sources of the p3b associated with different types of information. *Psychophysiology*, *27*, 157–176.

Schillaci, M., Vendemia, J.M.C., Buzan, R.F., & Green, E.P. (under review). Modeling deception as a two-state system. *IEEE Transactions on Biomedical Engineering*.

Simpson, H.M. (1969). Effects of a task-relevant response on pupil size. *Psychophysiology*, *6*, 115–121.

Spence, S.A., Farrow, T.F.D., Herford, A.E. *et al.* (2001). Behavioral and functional anatomical correlates of deception in humans. *Neuroreport: For Rapid Communication of Neuroscience Research*, *12*, 2849–2853.

Spencer, K.M., Dien, J., & Donchin, E. (1999). A componential analysis of the ERP elicited by novel events using a dense electrode array. *Psychophysiology*, *36*, 409–414.

Stelmack, R.M., Houlihan, M., & Doucet, C. (1994a). *Event-related potentials and the detection of deception: A two-stimulus paradigm* (No. NTIS AD-A318 987/5INZ.) Ottawa: University of Ottawa.

Stelmack, R.M., Houlihan, M., Doucet, C., & Belisle, M. (1994b). Event-related potentials and the detection of deception: A two-stimulus paradigm. *Psychophysiology*, *7*, s94.

Suzuki, A., Watanabe, S., Taheno, Y. *et al.* (1973). Possibility of detecting deception by voice analysis. *Reports of the National Institute of Police Science*, *26*, 62–66.

Timm, H.W. (1983). The efficacy of the psychological stress evaluator in detecting deception. *Journal of Police Science and Administration*, *11*, 62–68.

Tryon, W.W. (1975). Pupillometry: A survey of sources of variation. *Psychophysiology, 12*, 90–93.

Vendemia, J.M.C. (2003a). Detection of deception. *Polygraph, 32*, 97–106.

Vendemia, J.M.C. (2003b). *Neural mechanisms of deception and response congruity to general knowledge information and autobiographical information in visual two-stimulus paradigms with motor response* (No. DoDPI99-P-0010.)

Vendemia, J.M.C. & Buzan, R.F. (2004a). *Mapping the brain during deception: Extended studies of deception using HD-ERP and fMRI.* Paper presented at the Annual Meeting of the American Polygraph Association, Orlando, FL.

Vendemia, J.M.C. & Buzan, R.F. (2004b). Neural mechanisms of deception and response congruity in a visual two-stimulus paradigm involving autobiographical information. *Psychophysiology, 40*, S88.

Vendemia, J.M.C. & Buzan, R.F. (2005). Neural mechanisms of deception and response congruity in a visual two-stimulus paradigm with motor response. *Polygraph, 34*, 24–46.

Vendemia, J.M.C., Buzan, R.F., & Green, E.P. (2005c). Practice, work load, and reaction times in deception. *American Journal of Psychology, 118*, 413–430.

Vendemia, J.M.C., Buzan, R.F., & Simon-Dack, S.L. (2005b). Reaction time of motor responses in two-stimulus paradigms involving deception and congruity with varying levels of difficulty. *Behavioural Neurology, 16*, 25–36.

Vendemia, J.M.C., Buzan, R.F. , Green, E.P., & Schillaci, M.J. (2006). Neural mechanisms of deception and response congruity in a visual two-stimulus paradigm with motor response. *Journal of Neurotherapy: Special issue EEG and the Law, 9* (3), 45–70.

Verleger, R. (1997). On the utility of p3 latency as an index of mental chronometry. *Psychophysiology, 34*, 131–156.

CHAPTER 14

Forensic Assessment of Sexual Interest: A Review

E. KALMUS, ANTHONY R. BEECH AND B. WARBERG

INTRODUCTION

Over the past decade, the polygraph has increasingly been used to assess sex offenders and has become an accepted means of gaining information about this particular subgroup of offenders (Branaman & Gallagher, 2005). While the polygraph has demonstrated its utility in helping to gather more extensive information about the sexual history of offenders (Heil *et al.*, 2000; Wilcox *et al.*, 2005), for addressing denial (Wilcox, Sosnowski & Middleton, 1999) of sexual offences (Salter, 1997) and from monitoring (Wilcox & Sosnowski, 2002; Wilcox, Sosnowski & Middleton, 2000) current behavior for sexual risk (Grubin *et al.*, 2004), this tool is not specifically designed to assess sexual interest. This chapter discusses the predominant methods specifically involved in the assessment of sexual preference in sexual offenders, aside from polygraphy. Alongside descriptions of the techniques, some consideration will be given to their validities, reliabilities, strengths and weaknesses, as discussed within the published literature. Sexual preference assessments can be divided into three broad categories; physiological,

The Use of the Polygraph in Assessing, Treating and Supervising Sex Offenders: A Practitioner's Guide
Edited by Daniel T. Wilcox.

self-report and attentional. Physiological techniques attempt to discriminate various physical responses to visual and auditory stimuli and include measurements of penile tumescence and pupil dilation. Self-report measures rely upon the participant communicating their opinion or preference through questionnaires or card sorting tasks. Attentional methods essentially investigate the relative effect of differing sexual stimuli upon basic processing tasks. However, before progressing further it would be useful to briefly elaborate upon the human erotic response, of which sexual preference is clearly a mediating factor.

THE EROTIC RESPONSE

There are two distinguishable factors within the human erotic response, 'sexual arousal' and 'sexual desire' (Rempel & Serafini, 1995). Sexual arousal is a solely physiological response, which comprises of a range of autonomic reactions, best described in Masters and Johnson's book *Human Sexual Response* (1985). Sexual desire is a psychological process, which generally involves anticipation, motivation and cognitive imagery. Sexual arousal, itself, is mediated by erotic activity and the erotic stimulus present (Freund, 1978). In short, the level of sexual arousal experienced is primarily influenced by the degree to which the stimulus is experienced as sexually attractive, or sexually desired. Once a desired stimulus is present, arousal level is affected by behavioral response. Sexually compatible behaviors, whether physical (e.g., masturbation) or psychological (e.g., fantasy), will serve to increase arousal. Conversely, sexually neutral or incompatible behaviors (e.g., distraction, cold shower) would reduce sexual arousal.

Singer (1984) presented a useful model from which methods of measuring sexual interest can easily be conceptualized. Singer presented the human sexual response as three independent, but generally sequential components. The first stage, an *aesthetic response*, is an emotional reaction to noticing an attractive face or figure; it results in an increase in attention towards the object of attraction. Progressing from the first stage is the *approach response*. The approach response involves bodily movements towards the attractive object. The final stage recognizes that with both attention and closer proximity, physical reactions result in genital tumescence and was labeled the *genital response*, i.e., arousal. Singer, like many clinicians and researchers, recognizes that there is an array of autonomic responses, but argues that in measuring sexual responses the genital response, specifically genital tumescence, is the most reliable, convenient and obvious response to measure in males.

MEASURES OF PENILE TUMESCENCE

The measurement of penile tumescence (plethysmography) involves contrasting individuals' genital responses to differing sexual stimuli. A number of very detailed reviews concerning plethysmography have been published (Marshall & Fernandez, 2000; Murphy & Barbaree, 1994; O'Donohue & Letourneau, 1992; Quinsey, 1977).

The underlying assumption is that as genital response is indicative of sexual arousal, and sexual arousal is indicative of sexual desire (Rempel & Serafini, 1995), a consistent genital response to specific types of stimuli would indicate sexual preference. Despite the inherent association of sexual response to sexual preference, Amoroso and Brown (1973) opposed the assumption that physiological arousal is wholly synchronized to psychological arousal. Aside from impotence, Bancroft (1971) notes instances of reflexive penile arousal, where genital responses are evident, but contrary to psychological arousal or preference.

A further and potentially more problematic assumption is that relative penile responses indicate relative sexual preferences (Earls, 1983). Essentially, a consistent and relatively larger penile response to one type of stimuli (e.g., females) would indicate a sexual preference over another type of stimuli with a lesser response (e.g., males). The implications of this assumption will be discussed later.

There are two main methods of measuring penile response and both will be described. Volumetric phallometry was pioneered by Freund (1963) and measures the displacement of air produced by the penis being enclosed in an airtight glass cylinder. Circumferential plethysmography measures changes in penile girth through the variation of electrical resistance in a strain gauge (Barlow *et al.*, 1970), or rubber/mercury band (Fisher, Gross & Zuch, 1965) placed around the penis. Circumferential plethysmography was first developed in the 1940s and used as a binary indicator of arousal (Ohlmeyer, Brilmayer & Hullstrung, 1944, cited in Rosen & Keefe, 1978), but during the late 1960s it evolved to produce analogue measurements (Janssen *et al.*, 1997).

In general, comparison studies of the volumetric and circumferential devices indicate very high correlations. Still, the volumetric device is considered more sensitive (McConaghy, 1999; Murphy & Barbaree, 1994), but this sensitivity has been considered a shortcoming by Wheeler and Rubin (1987) who argued that observed variations between the two devices were often produced by the extraneous variable of the participant moving position, thus affecting the volumetric but not circumferential properties. A well-recognized criticism of circumferential devices is that they can fail to observe changes during the initial stage of penile engorgement in some individuals for whom an increase in penis length may occur without any increase, or even a reduction, in circumference (Earls & Marshall, 1982; Freund, Langevin & Barlow, 1974; Murphy, Haynes & Worley, 1991). In a more recent study, Kuban, Barbaree and Blanchard (1999) reported little agreement between simultaneous volumetric and circumferential methodologies for responses less than 10 % of full erection, but penile responses larger than 10 % of full erection reported a very high correlation ($r = .90$).

Due to its relative ease of use and commercial availability, the circumferential method has become more common. As a demonstration of the device's expediency, a discreet and portable circumferential plethysmograph was demonstrated by Rea, DeBriere, Butler and Saunders (1998). Despite advances in application, both techniques remain expensive and highly technical in interpretation (Abel *et al.*, 1998).

Stimulus Variance in Plethysmography

There are notable variations in the stimuli used across all the published studies. Variations in stimulus set can include format (how it is presented) and content (what is presented). Clinically, the stimulus content is the independent variable upon which the dependent variable, penile response, is measured. The common stimulus formats include video, pictures, audio descriptions (first, second and third person), written text and fantasy. Stimulus content varies on the length of exposure, type of activity portrayed, whether consenting or forced, the degree of explicitness and the age and sex of stimulus figure(s). Invariably to produce a sexual response, sexually explicit material is required, and so explicit stimuli are mostly used. Aside from the general use of explicit material, the remaining variations of stimulus sets, across studies, can make comparison between studies problematic as the content and format can influence response. Video is generally considered to produce the greatest responses (Abel, Blanchard & Barlow, 1981; Abel *et al.*, 1978; Julien & Over, 1988), but Gaither and Plaud (1997) noted that the studies did not always match the stimulus content in each format. Still, despite its effectiveness, Proulx (1989) noted that video is rarely used clinically as it often results in maximum responses across the conditions, or ceiling effect, and therefore prevents discrimination of preference.

Often, more than one stimuli type is used simultaneously, for example, pictures and audiotapes of aggressive and non-aggressive sexual activities, involving children or adults, have been used to discern rapists from pedophiles (Looman & Marshall, 2001). Proulx (1989) observed that pictures and audio descriptions are often combined. Generally, pictures are used to measure age and gender preference, and audiotapes to measure the activity preference.

There is a general acknowledgment of the need for standardization in the methodologies and stimulus sets used in plethysmography (Marshall & Fernandez, 2000; Murphy & Barbaree, 1994; Seto, 2001). Whilst stimulus sets are available on request from clinicians, legal and ethical issues concerning the production of explicit sexual and violent materials involving children and adults have prevented the commercial development of standardized stimulus sets.

Discriminative Validity

As the purpose of plethysmography is to discriminate sexual preferences, it is little surprise that much of the research has been placed upon discriminative validity. Despite methodological concerns, plethysmography remains the most accepted means of identifying sexual preference (Quinsey & Chaplin, 1988), and has been demonstrated to discriminate between non-offenders, offenders and different types of sexual offenders. In attempting to discriminate child sex offenders, a penile response to child stimuli is anticipated. In contrast, when attempting to discriminate rapists, clinicians investigate penile response to violent stimuli.

Plethysmographic comparisons of child sex offenders to non-offenders have produced significant differences (Barbaree & Marshall, 1989; Freund, 1965; Quinsey & Chaplin, 1988; Quinsey, Chaplin & Carrigan, 1979), and so have comparisons of rapists to non-offenders (Abel *et al.*, 1977; Abel *et al.*, 1978; Barbaree, Marshall & Lanthier, 1979; Earls & Proulx, 1986; Howes, 1998; Quinsey, Chaplin & Upfold, 1984; Seto & Kuban, 1996). However, generally the studies also exhibited a large proportion of wrongly classified participants (McConaghy, 1999).

Also, the difficulty in discriminating non-offenders and rapists is exacerbated by the observation that non-offenders can display sexual arousal to violent sexual stimuli (Blader & Marshall, 1984; Murphy *et al.*, 1985). Furthermore, studies comparing responses of child sex offenders to rapists also produce significant group differences, but again high discriminative error rates of between 23 % and 65 % are reported (Looman & Marshall, 2001).

Groth and Birnbaum (1978) presented a theory that sexual preference within child sex offenders was divided into preferences towards adults and children. Extra-familial offenders were suggested to prefer children and offended as a result of their predilection. Conversely, incestuous child sex offenders' primary preference was proposed to be towards adults, but interpersonal problems within the family, and a (recent) failure to attain sexual and/or emotional fulfillment with an existing adult partner resulted in offending. This theoretical distinction between incestuous and extra-familial child sex offenders has been empirically investigated, with significance generally demonstrable, but overlap still remained (Barbaree & Marshall, 1989; Barsetti *et al.*, 1998; Frenzel & Lang, 1989; Seto, Lalumière & Kuban, 1999; Studer *et al.*, 2002; Studer *et al.*, 2000). Whilst plethysmography is rarely cited as a legal methodology for indicating guilt, the apparent lack of sexual preference exclusivity within known offenders may also lead to reconsideration of the high level of clinical value afforded to sexual preference assessment.

Test-Retest Reliability and the Problem of Low Responding to Stimulus

Whilst the previous section identified concerns with plethysmographic research findings, the following sections explore some fundamental threats to its clinical implementation. Furthermore, a number of the concerns raised previously may result from these issues. Although much of the plethysmography literature is concerned with validity, few studies actually explore test-retest reliability (Marshall & Fernandez, 2000; Simon & Schouten, 1991). Of the studies reporting test-retest coefficients, scores have ranged from a very low r = .29 in non-offenders, r = .44 in rapists (Barbaree, Baxter & Marshall, 1989) to a low r = .53 overall reliability by combining a sample of pedophiles, rapists and non-sexual offenders (Wormith, 1986). To elaborate, these findings suggest that less than 30 % of the total variance from the first testing would be accounted for in the second. Where plethysmography has been used clinically as a pre/post-treatment outcome measure, poor test-retest findings raise questions concerning its appropriateness for this task.

As was described earlier, a participant would ideally demonstrate a large penile response to attractive stimulus content, and low penile response to unattractive stimulus content. A large effect would encourage confidence in the discrimination of sexual interests or preferences. Sadly, low responding participants, with penile responses of less than 10 to 20 % of full erection across all conditions, represent between 20 and 75 % of participants within published studies (Looman *et al.*, 1998). To avoid errors, many studies exclude low responders due to the noted inaccuracies of measuring low responses circumferentially. Unfortunately, by excluding low responders, research findings will still be distorted, as only high responders with greater variability are entered into analysis. Consequently, the significance of group differences becomes inflated (Murphy & Barbaree, 1994). Additionally, as results can only refer to high responders, generalizability is reduced (Murphy *et al.*, 1991). As an alternative to excluding low responders, ratio or ipsative transformations of raw data allow for a proportioning of specific responses relative to the participant's overall response (Furr, 1991; Harris *et al.*, 1992; Quinsey *et al.*, 1984). Essentially, the individual's raw data is transformed into z-scores, and responses are distinguished in terms of a standard deviation irrespective of the raw total variation. Consequently, sexual arousal and preferences are being discerned through differences of tumescence, whereby the total observed tumescence is less than 2mm. Currently, there are a number of dilemmas presented by low responders and there is little agreement concerning the use of their data (Marshall & Fernandez, 2000).

Faking and Other Extraneous Variables

Whilst assessments of sexual interest can be a defining factor in identifying a treatment pathway, findings also have a major impact upon perceptions of risk and dangerousness. Individuals producing consistently greater responses to more violent or deviant stimuli would be likely to raise more concern. Consequently, offenders wishing to avoid being labeled as dangerous or deviant may deliberately attempt to fake. Here, a number of studies have demonstrated that up to 80 % of participants can consciously suppress penile responses upon request (Farkas, Sine & Evans, 1979; Golde, Strassberg & Turner, 2000; Hall, Proctor & Nelson, 1988; Howes, 1998; Mahoney & Strassberg, 1991). Furthermore, a lesser but still significant number of participants were able to consciously increase their penile response on request (Abel *et al.*, 1978; Avery-Clark & Laws, 1984; Quinsey & Bergersen, 1976; Quinsey & Carrigan, 1978). Therefore an offender wishing to fake would suppress their response to deviant stimuli, whilst attempting to increase their response to non-deviant stimuli. (Castonguay *et al.*, 1993; Looman *et al.*,1998).

As was discussed at the start of this chapter, Freund's (1978) model of sexual arousal proposed that arousal level is mediated by the presence of compatible or incompatible behaviors. Accordingly, participants attempting to fake often use distraction to inhibit responses, and fantasy or muscle contractions to increase their response. Furthermore, practice is recognized to be an important variable as participants with more experience of plethysmographic testing were also able to fake more effectively (Freund, Watson & Rienzo, 1988). This effect of practice experience on faking may provide some explanation for the previously noted test-retest concerns.

Considering the frequencies at which participants have been reported to be able to fake, researchers have attempted to develop procedures to counter or interfere with faking techniques. As distraction is recognized to be the chief strategy, attempts have been made to prevent its use with mixed success. Henson and Rubin (1971) asked participants to simply provide a continuous commentary of the stimulus film, but found little change in responses. When participants were asked to continuously indicate whether a stimulus video was portraying violent or sexual scenes, effectively a semantic tracking task, penile responses were higher than in a no task condition (Proulx, Cote & Achille, 1993; Quinsey & Chaplin, 1988). Unfortunately, Golde *et al*. (2000) found that repeated testing would reduce the effectiveness of a similar semantic tracking task at preventing faking.

Another reported strategy to combat faking involved redefining how the stimulus was employed. By presenting the stimulus when the penis was observed to be at 50% of full erection, voluntary control was demonstrated to be impaired (Malcolm, Davidson & Marshall, 1985). In effect, rather than initiating the sexual arousal response, the stimulus was used as a sexually compatible or incompatible stimulus, and consequently its relative effect upon penile tumescence was considered to indicate preference. Unfortunately, this study has not as yet been replicated, nor has its concurrent validity been established.

Despite these developments, voluntary psychological methods of controlling penile tumescence (fantasy or distraction) are still acknowledged to be 'virtually impossible to prevent' (Marshall & Fernandez, 2000, p. 811), and perhaps even more worryingly they remain virtually impossible to detect. Still, physical methods of increasing response, involving muscle contractions, are recognized to produce a uniquely staggered profile and are easily identifiable (Freund *et al*., 1988; Keltner & Doyle, 1986).

Other variables observed to have a notable effect on penile responses include environmental features and anxiety. Hale and Strassberg (1990) observed that induced anxiety significantly inhibited penile response in non-offending participants. Conversely, Amoroso and Brown (1973) suggested that the plethysmographic apparatus itself might actually increase penile response. They found that non-offending participants rated sexual images to be significantly more stimulating when wearing the apparatus.

Plethysmography Summary

Plethysmography has been considered the most convenient and effective means of measuring sexual interests by a number of researchers and clinicians. Still, research findings raise concerns about its validity and reliability. Given the potential consequences of plethysmographic testing, the degree of discriminative inaccuracy and its susceptibility to faking is alarming. Consequently, the clinical utility of plethysmography, and the confidence with which it is regarded, has been questioned (Marshall & Fernandez, 2003). Interestingly, Travin, Cullen and Melella (1988) reported over half of their 107 offenders denying their offence would subsequently admit an interest in either forced or pedophiliac sexual activity, once confronted by their plethysmographic results.

OTHER PHYSIOLOGICAL MEASURES

In comparison to plethysmography, there is a relative paucity of literature examining the use of other physiological methods to measure sexual interest or arousal. Zuckerman's (1971) review of physiological methodologies remains probably the definitive overview (Kalmus & Beech, 2005), but while research continues there is little to challenge plethysmography's position. Moreover, much of the recent physiological research proceeds in conjunction with circumferential plethysmography, in an attempt to increase its reliability. This section will describe other physiological measures, initially still focused upon the penis, and then measures that observe other aspects of sexual arousal.

Thermistor or Temperature Measurements of Penile and Groin Temperature

Increased blood flow to the genital area produces a temperature change, which has been measured to identify arousal. Tests have demonstrated high correlations between thermistor, self-report and plethysmography data in non-offenders presented with sexual and non-sexual videos (Abramson *et al.*, 1981; Rubinsky *et al.*, 1985; Webster & Hammer, 1983). Comparatively, the thermistor device was slower to recognize the beginnings of penile detumescence than the plethysmograph, but hypothetically, a thermistor may be able to detect initial arousal, through temperature variations, in cases where early tumescence produces no circumferential increase. Due to concerns about the obvious invasiveness of plethysmography, measurements of abdominal temperature, as opposed to penile temperature, were investigated as an alternative. Unfortunately, there was little correlation with self-report and tumescence data (Beck, Barlow & Sakheim, 1983).

Photoelectric Surface Blood Volume Measurement

During arousal, the increase of blood flow to penile tissues also produces an increase in surface blood volume (Masters & Johnson, 1966), which can be measured. A comparison study of photoelectric surface blood volume measurement to self-report and plethysmography produced significant correlations in only 10 of 24 maximum-security hospital patients (Hinton, O'Neill & Webster, 1980). Researchers used explicit videos to discern arousal to heterosexual or homosexual, child or adult, and forced or consenting stimuli. In reviewing their findings, the researchers reported a high degree of defensiveness and inconsistent data in over two-thirds of the non-correlating participants. Whether measuring volume, circumference, temperature, or surface blood volume changes, it seems that all methods measuring penile arousal remain susceptible to attempts to suppress or increase penile response. The defensiveness and inconsistent data reported in the last study led to the suggestion that it was faking that confounded the outcome (Card & Farrall, 1990; Farrall & Card, 1988).

Pupillometry

Pupillometric assessment of sexual preference was first demonstrated by Hess and Polt (1960). They reported pupil dilation in participants presented with sexually preferred images, and pupil constriction if presented with non-preferred stimuli. The pupillary response could be a function of Singer's (1984) *aesthetic response* stage of the erotic response, dilation being a physiological consequence of the increased attention towards a preferred object. Unfortunately, Hess's research has been criticized for poor methodology, small sample size, statistical errors and inconsistent effects (Zuckerman, 1971). Stimulus luminescence, or the brightness of the visual stimuli, has also been shown to produce a more significant effect than the considered attractiveness of the images, especially when photographic slides were used (Garrett, Harrison & Kelly, 1989). Subsequent studies with heterosexual, homosexual, male and female non-offenders have shown pupillary responses to be consistent with preferred stimuli (Bernick, Kling & Borowitz, 1971; Hamel, 1974; Schnelle *et al.*, 1974), but inconsistencies have led to the conclusion that the technique could not discern preference reliably (Garrett *et al.*, 1989; Peavler & McLaughlin, 1967). Consequently there has been little further published research investigating pupillometrics and sexual preference.

Electro-Encephalographic (EEG) Measurement

During daily neural activity, nerves transmit information through electrical signals. These electrical signals can be detected and recorded by EEG measurement. To measure sexual interest, the EEG has been used to measure contingent negative variation (CNV), and has produced promising data. Rather than measuring an aspect of arousal produced by a stimulus, participants are made aware of the type of visual image with which they are about to be presented, and the technique identifies neurological effects of increased anticipation for pending preferred images. Howard, Longmore, Mason and Martin (1994) described two studies using CNV. The first compared heterosexual and homosexual men and women and found significant correlations with stated preference. The other study compared 34 child sex offenders to controls. Whilst the non-offending control group was observed to show a greater preference towards adult stimuli, the offenders as a group showed no significant difference between child and adult stimuli. When the offenders were divided into plethysmographically ascertained pedophilic and non-pedophilic child sex offender subgroups, the non-pedophilic offenders demonstrated a greater preference towards adult stimuli. The pedophilic offender group, again, produced an insignificant difference between child and adult stimuli. The authors were cautious about their findings, as there were individual discrepancies with plethysmographic data. Theoretically, though, due to the measured effect being situated at a neurophysiological level, it could be less influenced by conscious factors and faking than penile response. Unfortunately, no further research has been published about this potentially promising measure of sexual preference.

Summary of Physiological Assessments

Physiological assessment of sexual arousal is clearly an area overshadowed by plethysmography. Plethysmography is the measure of choice to which other methodologies are compared. Yet inconsistencies, and the raised concerns in interpreting plethysmographic data, suggest that the measure is not as robust as its use implies. Consequently, concurrent validity of alternative measures is likely to produce anomalous results due to potential inaccuracies produced by plethysmography. Perhaps, as a result of poor correlations, and the degree to which plethysmography is established and available, there has been little recent research investigating other physiological assessment of sexual arousal.

A number of factors including reliability, invasiveness, and the reliance on explicit imagery have led to concerns frequently being raised about the use of physiological measures. The invasiveness of physiological techniques, especially plethysmography, has been noted to prohibit the gathering of normative data with non-offenders, and can clinically prevent the evaluation of sexual preference in children and adolescents

(Harris *et al.*, 1996). The use of explicit imagery has historically caused a number of anecdotal legal scrapes for clinicians and researchers alike, but these stimuli are increasingly being considered exploitative and unethical, especially images of children (Abel *et al.*, 1998). Consequently, practical and ethical concerns have resulted in the development and clinical use of other methods to measure sexual interest.

NON-PHYSIOLOGICAL METHODS OF DISCRIMINATING SEXUAL INTEREST

In comparison to plethysmography, there are substantially fewer published studies investigating the range of non-physiological methods of discriminating sexual interest. These methods can be divided into two main categories: self-report techniques and attentional methodologies. Self-reports can include clinical interviewing, card sorting tasks and questionnaire techniques. Despite the clinical interview representing a central aspect of sex offender assessment (Craissati, 1998) this chapter will restrict its focus of self-reports to standardized card sorts, inventories and questionnaires. Discussion of these attentional methods will follow.

Card Sort

The card sort can use similar stimuli to plethysmography, but instead of objectively measuring a physiological response, the individual is simply asked to rate how arousing they find each stimulus card or rank them in order of attractiveness. The stimulus sets can be either pictorial or descriptive, but as a physiological response is not required they do not necessarily need to be explicit. In a comparison of a card-sorting task to plethysmography, Laws, Hanson, Osborn and Greenbaum (2000) observed the card sort to have a significantly higher accuracy in discriminating heterosexual and homosexual child sex offenders than plethysmography. A subsequent combining of the data from the two methodologies resulted in a perfect discriminative accuracy of 100 % for identifying female preference child sex offenders, and a 70 % accuracy for identifying male preference child sex offenders. Unfortunately, because all the offenders within the sample were previously known to be admitting of their deviant sexual preference, any generalizations concerning the efficacy of card sorts should be made cautiously.

An investigation of the reliability of the Sexual Interest Card Sort Questionnaire (Holland *et al.*, 2000), reported very high internal consistency and discriminative validity in a sample of those admitting paraphilias and child sex offenders. The Sexual Interest Card Sort Questionnaire uses descriptions of a range of paraphilias and fetishisms, and accurately identified paraphilic preference in many admitting participants. On a cautionary note, when the card sort was adapted and presented to less obliging adolescent offenders (Hunter, Becker & Kaplan, 1995), little correlation to phallometric data was observed. A greater concern was that despite the very poor discriminative effect, the measure demonstrated a high test-retest reliability and internal consistency within the study, and hence appeared robust.

Haywood and Grossman (1994) investigated sexual interest ratings of pictures of adults and children, using a scale of 0 to 100, with denying and admitting child sex offenders, and non-offenders. The deniers, as a group of 30 from 75 offenders, rated least interest in images of boys, girls and men (mean = 0–3.8), admitters rated highest on these items (mean = 13.3–15.6). Still, the admitters' ratings of children amounted to only 25 % of the amount that non-offenders rated images of adult women (mean = 62.9). These differences were reported as statistically significant. Additionally, deniers' ratings of women (mean = 38.2) were higher than the admitters' ratings (mean = 29) of women, but still relatively lower than non-offenders' ratings of women. While these response patterns may be interesting to study, they also highlight just how susceptible the card sort is to denial, or faking.

Standardized Inventories and Questionnaires

Holland *et al.* (2000) noted that many clinicians believe it is often easier for offenders to admit a deviant sexual preference using self-report questionnaires than in a clinical interview. Indeed, a number of questionnaire measures are available for assessing human sexuality, and an evaluation of non-forensic assessments for marital therapy can be obtained in Talmadge and Talmadge (1990). Reviews of general forensic inventories and questionnaires can be found in Hanson, Cox and Woszcsyna (1991), and Salter (1988). This section of the chapter will maintain its focus on measures of sexual interest and will provide an overview of three assessments that attempt to discern deviant sexual preference. These assessments are the Clarke Sexual History Questionnaire (Paitich *et al.*, 1977), the Thorne Sex Inventory (Thorne, 1966), and the Multiphasic Sex Inventory (Nichols & Molinder, 1984).[1]

[1]Another well-known questionnaire for assessing this area, the Wilson Sex Fantasy Questionnaire (Wilson, 1978; reprinted in Salter, 1988), has been omitted here due to an absence of journal-published data concerning its psychometric properties.

The Clarke Sexual History Questionnaire. The Clarke Sexual History Questionnaire- Revised (SHQ-R) (Langevin & Paitich, 2002) has been published in 5 versions over the past 30 years. The current version consists of 508 items relating to sexual history, dysfunction, age/gender interest, paraphilias, pornography and fantasy, and behaviors, including exhibitionism, rape, and heterosexual or homosexual pedophiliac activity. The SHQ-R's reliability has been demonstrated with a reported total sample of 899, although this figure has been reached through combining previous samples from previous versions where the scales are unchanged. The published figures for internal consistency were mostly considered to be high, but test-retest data was not provided. Despite in-house development there is little journal-published data on the SHQ. The first version's (SHQ, Paitich *et al.*, 1977) discriminative validity was reported to be poor at classifying participants to their offence-type or control group, but a higher discriminative effect was produced by comparing specific offender groups to non-offenders. As yet, there has been no published discriminative study of the SHQ-R.

The Thorne Sex Inventory. The Thorne Sex Inventory (TSI) (Thorne, 1966) is a 200-item true/false structured interview. It contains nine scales concerning sexual behavior that had been derived through factor analysis. The scales regarded to be most associated to sexual offending are 'Sexual Maladjustment and Frustration', 'Neurotic Conflict Associated to Sex', 'Sexual Fixations and Cathexes', and 'Loss of Sex Controls'. These scales were all reported to have high (between $r = .67$ and $r = .79$) test-retest reliability over a period of three months (Allen & Haupt, 1966), and also produced significantly different group profiles for a range of offenders and non-offenders (Haupt & Allen, 1966). Unfortunately the measure was not considered to discriminate offenders from non-offenders effectively enough. In relation to assessing sexual interest, the 'Sexual Fixations and Cathexes' scale was the most specific. This scale comprised of subscales pertaining to Children, Voyeurism, Exhibitionism, Fetishism, Sadism and Masochism. Many of the questions related to static factors including having been accused of child molesting, or were direct questions of preference. Unfortunately, each subscale was comprised of only a few items, for example, the 'Children' subscale had three items in total.

The TSI was developed to assess sex offenders, but similarly to the card sort methodology, it can be heavily influenced by denial or social desirability (Haupt & Allen, 1966). The TSI does have some items relating to denial, but only applied to the 'Homosexuality' scale. Today the TSI is rarely used clinically, but it has influenced the development of other measures and is a good source of robust questions (Hanson *et al.*, 1991).

The Multiphasic Sex Inventory. The Multiphasic Sex Inventory (MSI) is commonly employed in the assessment of sexual offenders (Beech, Fisher & Thornton, 2003; Kalichman *et al.*, 1992), and it has frequently been utilized in researching treatment prognosis and outcome (Beech, Fisher & Beckett, 1998; Geer *et al.*, 2001; Simkins *et al.*, 1989). The MSI is a comprehensive, 300-item, true/false self-report questionnaire. Individual MSI results are presented across 20 scales. The scales represent sexual offences, including 'Child Molest' and 'Rape' scales, and paraphilias, including 'Voyeurism' and 'Fetish' subscales. Additionally, the measure examines other factors including sexual knowledge, sexual functioning and aspects of denial. The inventory is well tested and has a good overall test-retest reliability, $r = .89$, over a three-week interval (Nichols & Molinder, 1984), and $r = .71$ over a three-month interval (Simkins *et al.*, 1989).

The 'Child Molest' scale is comprised of 39 items, four specific to incestuous offences. The manual specifies that this scale refers specifically to the child sex offender who invests time grooming the victim, rather than the spontaneous assault (Nichols & Molinder, 1984). Although the manual did not provide any reliability data for this scale, Kalichman *et al.* (1992), reported it to have strong internal consistency of $a = .90$ with rapists, but no internal consistency data was published on this scale using child sex offenders.

Despite the range of sexual behavior scales, growing evidence suggests that the MSI actually best measures levels of denial (Schlank, 1995). The elements of denial, including cognitive distortions, justifications and response desirability are all measured on separate subscales. All three scales have had good test-retest and internal consistency data reported (Kalichman *et al.*, 1992; Simkins *et al.*, 1989). A factor analysis of a large-scale evaluation of UK sex offender treatment programs, observed the MSI denial scales labeled as 'Justifications', 'Cognitive Distortion and Immaturity', and 'Social Sexual Desirability' related more to factors of pro-offending attitudes, self-pity or perceptions of oneself as the victim, and denial of offence (Beech *et al.*, 1998). Despite these more recent findings, the measure is robust and effective at accurately differentiating child sex offenders' level of denial (Clark & Grier, 1995). Simkins *et al.* (1989) observed that as denial scores decreased, the 'Child Molest' scale scores increased significantly. Also, whilst the 'Social Sexual Desirability' scale was not reported to change through treatment, 'Cognitive Distortion' and 'Justification' scales were noted to reduce (Miner *et al.*, 1990).

Overall, it seems that while denial and (reversed item) lie scales are intrinsic to the MSI, like any self-report measure it remains vulnerable to faking. The MSI's strength is that it is very good at recognizing when it is being faked. Therefore, despite attempting to assess sexual interest, the MSI is most effective in discerning offender presentation, for example, level of denial, rather than type of offender.

Summary of Self-Report Measures

Self-report measures have been demonstrated to be very effective and reliable in facilitating the admitting offender to present their sexual interests and preferences. Both card-sort tasks and questionnaires are relatively easy and cheap to use. Unfortunately, they can also be easily faked. Of the questionnaires, it seems that only the MSI is commonly used today. The MSI has a good evidence base, reporting very good psychometric properties, but as was noted, its demonstrated strength is in its ability to identify faking and denial in offenders. Therefore, a combination of a card sort and MSI may represent a strong pairing of self-report assessment measures. The card sort would examine an offender's sexual interests and the MSI could act as a reliability check, identifying the likelihood of their faking on the card sort.

Attentional Methodologies

There are currently two methods of assessing sexual interest through attention. One is by measuring viewing time, and the other is by investigating information processing. Singer's (1984) *aesthetic response* stage of sexual arousal acknowledged that an individual will attend more to an attractive object. Therefore, the simplest method of measurement is to covertly measure the viewing times of a range of visual stimuli and compare. The inherent assumption is that the images with the longest viewing time would be likely to represent what is attractive to the person. The other technique of attentional assessment discriminates the effect of increased attention upon information-processing tasks. Essentially, a simple information-processing task would be impaired by the effect of the increased attention given to the attractive image. Therefore, the discrimination of sexual interest would be through identifying conditions in which the greatest relative impairment occurred.

Viewing time. Rosenzweig (1942) first noted differences in the viewing times of sexual images related to sexual interest. Zamansky (1956) observed that homosexual men viewed images of naked men for longer than images of naked women and heterosexual men viewed images of naked women longer. In a review of viewing time methodology, it was observed that the correlation between viewing time and ratings of attractiveness across four independent samples was very high (Quinsey *et al.*, 1996). Recent studies using explicit stimulus sets to combine phallometry with measurements of viewing time, found viewing time to correlate well with measurements of sexual arousal, and to produce strong test-retest reliabilities (Abel *et al.*, 1998; Harris *et al.*, 1996). Again, the notable distinction from physiological methods is that the *aesthetic response* (Singer, 1984) can be produced by just seeing an attractive object or face. Consequently, assessments of viewing time response do not require explicit or naked imagery.

The 'Abel Assessment for Sexual Interest' (AASI) (Abel *et al.*, 1998; Abel *et al.*, 2001), uses entirely non-nude images of children and adults. Sexual interest is measured through covert measures of viewing time, alongside a self-report sexual history and interest questionnaire. The individual's complete response set is compared to offending models derived from groups of admitting offenders perpetrating against girls or boys and a group of denying participants 'believed by therapists to be actual child molesters' (Abel *et al.*, 2001, p. 712). Consequently, by comparing viewing time interest and the questionnaire responses to these groups, the AASI produces a probability statistic of sexual offending. Despite the measure's reported accuracy, the authors point out that probability does not ensure certainty. The authors state that the sensitivity level used produced a differentiation accuracy of between 73 % and 86 %, thus a discriminative inaccuracy of between 14 % and 27 % still remains.

Viewing time measures have also been developed for use within the intellectually disabled offender population specifically a measure called Affinity[2] (Glasgow, Osbourne & Croxen, 2003). Affinity also uses a wholly non-explicit stimulus set of images that have been independently sorted by five judges to unanimously fit into one of four age categories. The individual rates the attractiveness of images, whilst viewing time is covertly measured before and after each rating, until they push the 'next' button. There is no normative data, and the measure relies on individual sex and age-group viewing time discrepancies to identify potential interest. Consequently, supporting evidence is presented in terms of five single cases, which demonstrate the pre-task measure's ability to discriminate sexual preference. Unfortunately, the post-task measure was found to be inconsistent, and some learning disabled offenders were noted to find the assessment difficult to understand.

[2]Available from David Glasgow at <dvglasgow@aol.com>

Despite viewing time measurement never being disclosed, the test is potentially transparent and thus vulnerable to faking, perhaps just by counting. There has been some investigation into viewing time vulnerability to faking. Research into the 'Abel Assessment for Interest in Paraphilias' (Abel *et al.*, 1998) involved participants being tested twice and instructed to attempt to obscure their responses in one test. Initial findings suggested internally consistent results and trends across the two conditions, despite changes in the overall scores. Still, concerns were raised that only a subset of categories were analyzed and little data was published (Fischer & Smith, 1999).

Due to Abel's paraphilia assessment findings concerning faking, and the use of a 'liar/denier' model and questionnaire, the AASI could be considered less vulnerable to faking. Still, faking remains a foremost and pervasive threat to the assessment of sexual interest, with intrinsic implications for its reliability. Consequently, there is a need to develop a measure of sexual interest that is more resilient to faking.

Information processing. Wright and Adams (1994) were the first to demonstrate the effect of increased attention to arousing images on a choice-reaction task, in a non-forensic assessment of sexual preference interference. Eighty participants comprised of heterosexual, and homosexual, males and females were presented with naked images of men and women. Each image had one clearly visible dot placed in either a corner or in the centre. Participants held a pad and were required to press a button corresponding to the placement of the dot being viewed on the image. A significant increase in the timed latency of button pushing was observed across all groups for preferred-sex images, at the $p = .05$ level. The study demonstrated that increased visual attention, associated with Singer's (1984) first stage of sexual arousal, *aesthetic response*, observably interfered with cognitive performance on a simple reaction task. Despite viewing time remaining the dependent variable in this study, the distinction from viewing time tests was that the latency was a product of the degree of interference that each image produced, and not the length of time the participant chose to look at the picture. Unfortunately there has been no further published research using this methodology.

Beech *et al.* (2008) demonstrated, with the rapid presentation of images in sequence, the effect of sexual interest on attention blink to differentiate 36 child sex offenders and 20 non-offending controls. Within each sequence of 10 images there were 2 sets of target images. The first target image was either a non-sexualized child or an animal, and was closely followed by a second target image of either a chair or a train.

Participants were required to identify both sets of target images, and a significantly greater error rate was observed for the offender group in sequences when the second target image followed an image of a child, rather than an animal. The results from the offender group were also significantly different from the non-offenders who displayed a slight non-significant error trend towards the opposite direction. Using Receiver Operating Characteristics analysis, the Area Under the Curve was found to be .77 ($p = .001$) with an overall effect size of $d = 1.16$. Additionally, the use of cutoff scores was shown to discriminate offenders and non-offenders with very encouraging accuracy. The research was a very successful pilot experiment, but the paradigm requires further study to investigate its concurrent validity and test-retest reliability.

Summary of Attentional Methodologies

Attentional techniques have attempted to circumvent the vulnerabilities that other methods of discriminating sexual preference experience. Covert measures of viewing latencies could be effective, but once it was known that viewing time was being measured the test could easily be faked. Due to the effect occurring at a higher level than other techniques, information-processing methods seem to promise fewer opportunities for successful faking. Still, there has been limited research in this area.

CONCLUSIONS

The range of forensic assessments discussed in this chapter can contribute to a much more comprehensive understanding of sexual interests in offenders. These tools can be used in alignment with polygraph and broader efforts to assess and effectively manage offenders, providing an increasingly refined framework for effectively working with sex offenders. In terms of future developments of sexual interest assessment methods described in this chapter, information-processing paradigms currently seem to offer most promise. Whilst using information processing to measure sexual interest has a strong face-validity and resilience to faking, its validity, reliability and utility remain to be fully demonstrated. Further physiological research involving plethysmography will continue to attempt to improve its reliability, standardization and vulnerability to faking. Further comparisons of these methodologies can be found in Kalmus and Beech (2005).

REFERENCES

Abel, G.G., Blanchard, E.B., & Barlow, D.H. (1981). Measurement of sexual arousal in several paraphilias: The effects of stimulus modality, instructional set and stimulus content on the objective. *Behavior Research and Therapy, 19*, 25–33.

Abel, G.G., Barlow, D.H., Blanchard, E.B., & Guild, D. (1977). The components of rapists' sexual arousal. *Archives of General Psychiatry*, *34*, 895–903.

Abel, G.G., Blanchard, E.B., Becker, J.V., & Djenderedjian, A. (1978). Differentiating sexual aggressiveness with penile measures. *Criminal Justice and Behavior*, *5*, 315–332.

Abel, G.G., Huffman, J., Warberg, B., & Holland, C.L. (1998). Visual reaction time and plethysmography as measures of sexual interest in child molesters. *Sexual Abuse: A Journal of Research and Treatment*, *10*, 81–95.

Abel, G.G., Jordan, A., Hand, C.G. *et al.* (2001). Classification models of child molesters utilizing the Abel Assessment for Sexual Interest. *Child Abuse and Neglect*, *25*, 703–718.

Abramson, P.R., Perry, L.B., Seeley, T.T. *et al.* (1981). Thermographic measurement of sexual arousal: A discriminant validity analysis. *Archives of Sexual Behavior*, *10*, 171–176.

Allen, R.M. & Haupt, T.D. (1966). The Sex Inventory: Test-retest reliabilities of scale scores and items. *Journal of Clinical Psychology*, *22*, 375–378.

Amoroso, D.M. & Brown, M. (1973). Problems in studying the effects of erotic material. *Journal of Sex Research*, *9*, 187–195.

Avery-Clark, C.A. & Laws, D.R. (1984). Differential erection response patterns of sexual child abusers to stimuli describing activities with children. *Behavior Therapy*, *15*, 71–83.

Bancroft, J. (1971). The application of psychophysiological measures to the assessment and modification of sexual behavior. *Behavior Research and Therapy*, *9*, 119–130.

Barbaree, H.E. & Marshall, W.L. (1989). Erectile responses amongst heterosexual child molesters, father-daughter incest offenders and matched nonoffenders: Five distinct age preference profiles. *Canadian Journal of Behavioural Science*, *21*, 70–87.

Barbaree, H.E., Baxter, D.J., & Marshall, W.L. (1989). The reliability of the rape index in a small sample of rapists and non-rapists. *Violence and Victims*, *4*, 299–206.

Barbaree, H.E., Marshall, W.L., & Lanthier, R.D. (1979). Deviant sexual arousal in rapists. *Behavior Research and Therapy*, *17*, 215–222.

Barlow, E.H., Becker, R., Leitenberg, H., & Agras, W.S. (1970). A mechanical strain gauge for recording penile circumference change. *Journal of Applied Behavior Analysis*, *3*, 73–76.

Barsetti, I., Earls, C.M., Lalumière, M.L., & Belanger, N. (1998). The differentiation of intrafamilial and extrafamilial heterosexual child molesters. *Journal of Interpersonal Violence*, *13*, 275–286.

Beck, J.G., Barlow, D.H., & Sakheim, D.K. (1983). Abdominal temperature changes during male sexual arousal. *Psychophysiology*, *20*, 715–717.

Beech, A.R., Fisher, D., & Beckett, R. (1998). *Step 3: An evaluation of the Prison Sex Offender Treatment Programme* (UK Home Office Occasional Report). London: HMSO. Available electronically from www.homeoffice.gov.uk/rds/pdfs/occ-step3.pdf.

Beech, A.R., Fisher, D., & Thornton, D. (2003). Risk assessment of sex offenders. *Professional Psychology: Research and Practice*, *34*, 339–352.

Beech, A.R., Kalmus, E., Tipper S.P., Jean-Yves Baudouin, Flak, V., & Humphreys, G.W. (2008). Children induce an enhanced attentional blink in child molesters. *Psychological Assessment, 20*, 397–402.

Bernick, N., Kling, A., & Borowitz, G. (1971). Physiologic differentiation of sexual arousal and anxiety. *Psychosomatic Medicine*, *33*, 341–352.

Blader, J.C. & Marshall, W.L. (1984). The relationship between cognitive and erectile measures of sexual arousal in non-rapist males as a function of depicted aggression. *Behavior Research and Therapy*, *22*, 623–630.

Branaman, T.F. & Gallagher, S.N. (2005). Polygraph testing in sex offender treatment: A review of limitations. *American Journal of Forensic Psychology*, *23*, 45–64.

Card, R.D. & Farrall, W. (1990). Detecting faked penile responses to erotic stimuli: A comparison of stimulus conditions and response measures. *Annals of Sex Research*, *3*, 381–396.

Castonguay, L.G., Proulx, J., Aubut, J., McKibben, A., & Campbell, M. (1993). Sexual preference assessment of sexual aggressors: Predictors of penile response magnitude. *Archives of Sexual Behavior*, *22*, 325–334.

Clark, M. & Grier, P. (1995). Using the Multiphasic Sex Inventory with child molesters. *Psychological Reports*, *77*, 623–625.

Craissati, J. (1998). *Child sexual abusers: A community treatment approach*. Hove: Psychology Press.

Earls, C.M. (1983). Some issues in the assessment of sexual deviance. *International Journal of Law and Psychiatry*, *6*, 431–441.

Earls, C.M. & Marshall, W.L. (1982). The simultaneous and independent measurement of penile circumference and length. *Behavior Research Methods and Instrumentation*, *14*, 447–450.

Earls, C.M. & Proulx, J. (1986). The Differentiation of Francophone Rapists and Non-rapists Using Penile Circumferential Measures. *Criminal Justice and Behavior*, *13*(4), 419–429.

Farkas, G.M., Sine, L.F., & Evans, I.M. (1979). The effects of distraction, performance demand, stimulus explicitness and personality on objective and subjective measures of male sexual arousal. *Behavior Research and Therapy*, *17*, 25–32.

Farrall, W.R. & Card, R.D. (1988). Advancements in physiological evaluation of assessment and treatment of the sexual aggressor. *Annals of the New York Academy of Sciences*, *528*, 261–273.

Fischer, L. & Smith, G. (1999). Statistical adequacy of the Abel Assessment for Interest in Paraphilias. *Sexual Abuse: A Journal of Research and Treatment*, *11*, 195–205.

Fisher, C., Gross, J., & Zuch, J. (1965). Cycle of penile erection synchronous with dreaming (REM) sleep. *Archives of General Psychiatry*, *12*, 27–45.

Frenzel, R.R. & Lang, R.A. (1989). Identifying sexual preferences in intrafamilial and extrafamilial child sexual abusers. *Annals of Sex Research*, *2*, 255–275.

Freund, K. (1963). A laboratory method for diagnosing predominance of homo- and hetero- erotic interest in the male. *Behavior Research and Therapy*, *1*, 85–93.

Freund, K. (1965). Diagnosing heterosexual pedophilia by means of a test for sexual interest. *Behavior Research and Therapy*, *3*, 229–234.

Freund, K. (1978). A conceptual framework for the study of anomalous erotic preferences. *Journal of Sex and Marital Therapy*, *4*, 3–10.
Freund, K., Langevin, R., & Barlow, D. (1974). Comparison of two penile measures of erotic arousal. *Behavior Research and Therapy*, *12*, 355–359.
Freund, K., Watson, R., & Rienzo, D. (1988). Signs of feigning in the phallometric test. *Behavior Research and Therapy*, *26*, 105–112.
Furr, K.D. (1991). Penis size and magnitude of erectile change as spurious factors in estimating sexual arousal. *Annals of Sex Research*, *4*, 265–279.
Gaither, G.A. & Plaud, J.J. (1997). The effects of secondary stimulus characteristics on men's sexual arousal. *Journal of Sex Research*, *34*, 231–236.
Garrett, J.C., Harrison, D.W., & Kelly, P.L. (1989). Pupillometric assessment of arousal to sexual stimuli: Novelty effects or preference? *Archives of Sexual Behavior*, *18*, 191–201.
Geer, T.M., Becker, J.V., Gray, S.R., & Krauss, D. (2001). Predictors of treatment completion in a correctional sex offender treatment program. *International Journal of Offender Therapy and Comparative Criminology*, *45*, 302–313.
Glasgow, D.V., Osbourne, A., & Croxen, J. (2003). An assessment tool for investigating paedophile sexual interest using viewing time: An application of single case research methodology. *British Journal of Learning Disabilities*, *31*, 96–102.
Golde, J.A., Strassberg, D.S., & Turner, C.M. (2000). Psychophysiologic assessment of erectile response and its suppression as a function of stimulus media and previous experience with plethysmography. *Journal of Sex Research*, *37*, 53–59.
Groth, A.N. & Birnbaum, H.J. (1978). Adult sexual orientation and attraction to underage persons. *Archives of Sexual Behavior*, *7*, 175–181.
Grubin, D., Madsen, L., Parsons, S. *et al.* (2004). A prospective study of the impact of polygraphy on high risk behaviors in adult sex offenders. *Sexual Abuse: A Journal of Research and Treatment*, *16*, 209–222.
Hale, V.E. & Strassberg, D.S. (1990). The role of anxiety on sexual arousal. *Archives of Sexual Behavior*, *19*, 569–581.
Hall, G.C.N., Proctor, W.C., & Nelson, G.M. (1988). Validity of physiological measures of pedophilic sexual arousal in a sexual offender population. *Journal of Consulting and Clinical Psychology*, *56*, 118–122.
Hamel, R.F. (1974). Female subjective and pupillary reaction to nude male and female figures. *Journal of Psychology*, *87*, 171–175.
Hanson, R.K., Cox, B., & Woszcsyna, C. (1991). *Sexuality, personality and attitude questionnaires for sexual offenders: A review*. Working paper available from the Ministry of the Solicitor General of Canada.
Harris, G.T., Rice, M.E., Quinsey, V.L., & Chaplin, T.C. (1996). Viewing time as a measure of sexual interest among child molesters and normal heterosexual men. *Behavior Research and Therapy*, *34*, 389–394.
Harris, G.T., Rice, M.E., Quinsey, V.L. *et al.* (1992). Maximizing the discriminant validity of phallometric assessment data. *Psychological Assessment*, *4*, 502–511.
Haupt, T.D. & Allen, R.M. (1966). A multivariate analysis of variance of scale scores on the Sex Inventory, Male Form. *Journal of Clinical Psychology*, *22*, 387–395.
Haywood, T.W. & Grossman, L.S. (1994). Denial of deviant sexual arousal and psychopathology in child molesters. *Behavior Therapy*, *25*, 327–340.

Heil, P., Ahlmeyer, S., McCullar, B., & McKee, B. (2000). Integration of polygraph testing with sexual offenders in the Colorado department of corrections. *Polygraph*, *29*, 26–30.

Henson, D.E. & Rubin, H.B. (1971). Voluntary control of eroticism. *Journal of Applied Behavioral Analysis*, *4*, 37–44.

Hess, E.H. & Polt, J.M. (1960). Pupil size as related to the interest value of visual stimuli. *Science*, *132*, 349–350.

Hinton, J.W., O'Neill, M.T., & Webster, S. (1980). Psychophysiological assessment of sex offenders in a security hospital. *Archives of Sexual Behavior*, *9*, 205–216.

Holland, L.A., Zolondek, S.C., Abel, G.G. *et al.* (2000). Psychometric analysis of the Sexual Interest Card Sort Questionnaire. *Sexual Abuse: Journal of Research and Treatment*, *12*, 107–122.

Howard, R.C., Longmore, F.J., Mason, P.A., & Martin, J.L. (1994). Contingent negative variation (CNV). and erotic preference in self-declared homosexuals and in child sex offenders. *Biological Psychology*, *38*, 169–181.

Howes, R.J. (1998). Plethysmographic assessment of incarcerated non-sexual offenders: A comparison with rapists. *Sexual Abuse: Journal of Research and Treatment*, *10*, 183–194.

Hunter, J.A., Becker, J.V., & Kaplan, M.S. (1995). The Adolescent Sexual Interest Card Sort: Test-retest reliability and concurrent validity in relation to phallometric assessment. *Archives of Sexual Behavior*, *24*, 555–561.

Janssen, E., Vissenberg, M., Visser, S., & Everaerd, W. (1997). An in vivo comparison of two circumferential penile strain gauges: The introduction of a new calibration method. *Psychophysiology*, *34*, 717–720.

Julien, E. & Over, R. (1988). Male sexual arousal across five modes of erotic stimulation. *Archives of Sexual Behavior*, *17*, 131–143.

Kalichman, S.C., Henderson, M.C., Shealy, L.S., & Dwyer, M. (1992). Psychometric properties of the Multiphasic Sex Inventory in assessing sex offenders. *Criminal Justice and Behavior*, *19*, 384–396.

Kalmus, E. & Beech, A.R. (2005). Forensic assessment of sexual interest. A review. *Aggression and Violent Behavior*, *10*, 193–217.

Keltner, A.A. & Doyle, C.L. (1986). Alcohol-state-dependent penile tumescence measurements in the assessment of a sexually aggressive man. *Criminal Justice and Behavior*, *13*, 223–236.

Kuban, M., Barbaree, H.E., & Blanchard, R. (1999). A comparison of volume and circumference phallometry: Response magnitude and method agreement. *Archives of Sexual Behavior*, *28*, 345–359.

Langevin, R. & Paitich, D. (2002). *The Clarke Sexual History Questionnaire-Revised: Technical Manual*. Available from Multi-Health Systems Inc.

Laws, D.R., Hanson, R.K., Osborn, C.A., & Greenbaum, P.E. (2000). Classification of child molesters by plethysmographic assessment of sexual arousal and a self-report measure of sexual preference. *Journal of Interpersonal Violence*, *15*, 1297–1312.

Looman, J. & Marshall, W.L. (2001). Phallometric assessments designed to detect arousal to children: The responses of rapists and child molesters. *Sexual Abuse: A Journal of Research and Treatment*, *13*, 3–13.

Looman, J., Abracen, J., Maillet, G., & DiFazio, R. (1998). Phallometric nonresponding in sexual offendercs. *Sexual Abuse: A Journal of Research and Treatment*, *10*, 325–336.

Mahoney, J.M. & Strassberg, D.S. (1991). Voluntary control of male sexual arousal. *Archives of Sexual Behavior, 20,* 1–16.

Malcolm, P.B., Davidson, P.R., & Marshall, W.L. (1985). Control of penile tumescence: The effects of arousal level and stimulus content. *Behavior Research and Therapy, 23,* 273–280.

Marshall, W.L. & Fernandez, Y.M. (2000). Phallometric testing with sexual offenders: Limits to its value. *Clinical Psychology Review, 20,* 807–822.

Marshall, W.L. & Fernandez, Y.M. (2003). Sexual preferences: Are they useful in the assessment and treatment of sexual offenders? *Aggression and Violent Behavior, 8,* 131–143.

Masters, W.H. & Johnson, V.E. (1966). *Human sexual response.* Boston: Little, Brown and Co.

McConaghy, N. (1999). Unresolved issues in scientific sexology. *Archives of Sexual Behavior, 28,* 285–318.

Miner, M.H., Marques, J.K., Day, D.M., & Nelson, C. (1990). Impact of relapse prevention in treating sex offenders: Preliminary findings. *Annals of Sex Research, 3,* 165–185.

Murphy, W.D. & Barbaree, H.E. (1994). *Assessments of sex offenders by measures of erectile response: Psychometric properties and decision making.* Victoria: Safer Society Press.

Murphy, W.D., Haynes, M.R., & Worley, P.J. (1991). Assessment of adult sexual interest. In C.R. Hollin & K. Howells (Eds), *Clinical approaches to sex offenders and their victims* (pp.77–92). Chichester, UK: John Wiley & Sons, Ltd.

Murphy, W.D., Haynes, M.R., Coleman, E.M., & Flanagan, B. (1985). Sexual responding of 'nonrapists' to aggressive sexual themes: Normative data. *Journal of Psychopathology and Behavioral Assessment, 7,* 37–47.

Nichols, H. & Molinder, I. (1984). *Manual for the Multiphasic Sex Inventory.* Available from Nicholls & Molinder, 437 Bowes Drive, Tacoma, WA 98466, USA.

O'Donohue, W.T. & Letourneau E. (1992). The psychometric properties of the penile tumescence assessment of child molesters. *Journal of Psychopathology and Behavioral Assessment, 14,* 123–174.

Ohlmeyer, P., Brilmayer, H., & Hullstrong, H. (1944). Periodische organge imschlaf II. *Pfluengers. Archiv fuer die Gesamta Physiologic, 249,* 50–55.

Paitich, D., Langevin, R., Freeman, R. *et al.* (1977). The Clarke Sexual History Questionnaire: A clinical sex history questionnaire for males. *Archives of Sexual Behavior, 6,* 421–435.

Peavler, W.S. & McLaughlin, J.P. (1967). The question of stimulus content and pupil size. *Psychonomic Science, 8,* 505–506.

Proulx, J. (1989). Sexual preference assessment of sexual aggressors. *International Journal of Law and Psychiatry, 12,* 275–280.

Proulx, J., Cote, G., & Achille, P.A. (1993). Prevention of voluntary control of penile response in homosexual paedophiles during phallometric testing. *Journal of Sex Research, 30,* 140–147.

Quinsey, V.L. (1977). The assessment and treatment of child molesters: A review. *Canadian Psychological Review, 18,* 204–220.

Quinsey, V.L. & Bergersen, S.G. (1976). Instructional control of penile circumference in assessments of sexual preference. *Behavior Therapy, 7,* 489–493.

Quinsey, V.L. & Carrigan, W.F. (1978). Penile responses to visual stimuli: Instructional control with and without auditory sexual fantasy correlates. *Criminal Justice and Behavior*, *5*, 333–342.

Quinsey, V.L. & Chaplin T.C. (1988). Preventing faking in phallometric assessments of sexual preference. *Annals of the New York Academy of Sciences*, *528*, 49–58.

Quinsey, V.L., Chaplin T.C., & Carrigan, W.F. (1979). Sexual preferences among incestuous and non-incestuous child molesters. *Behavior Therapy*, *10*, 562–565.

Quinsey, V.L., Chaplin T.C., & Upfold, D. (1984). Sexual arousal to nonsexual violence and sadomasochistic themes among rapists and non-sex offenders. *Journal of Consulting and Clinical Psychology*, *52*, 651–657.

Quinsey, V.L., Ketsetzis, M., Earls, C. & Karamanoukian, A. (1996). Viewing time as a measure of sexual interest. *Ethology and Sociobiology*, *17*, 341–354.

Rea, J.A., DeBriere, T., Butler, K., & Saunders, K.J. (1998). An analysis of four sexual offenders' arousal in the natural environment through the use of a portable penile plethysmograph. *Sexual Abuse: A Journal of Research and Treatment*, *10*, 239–255.

Rempel, J. & Serafini, T. (1995). Factors influencing the activities that people experience as sexually arousing: A theoretical model. *Canadian Journal of Human Sexuality*, *4*, 3–14.

Rosen, R.C. & Keefe, F.J. (1978). The measurement of human penile tumescence. *Psychophysiology*, *15*, 366–376.

Rosenzweig, S. (1942). The photoscope as an objective device for evaluating sexual interest. *Psychosomatic Medicine*, *4*, 150–157.

Rubinsky, H.J., Hoon, P.W., Eckerman, D.A., & Amberson, J.I. (1985). Groin skin temperature: Testing the validity of a relatively unobtrusive physiological measure of psychosexual arousal. *Psychophysiology*, *22*, 488–492.

Salter, A.C. (1988). *Treating child sex offenders and their victims*. London: Sage.

Salter, A. (1997). *Sex offender assessment and risk management issues*. National Organisation for the Treatment of Abusers (NOTA) Annual Conference. Southampton, England.

Schlank, A.M. (1995). The utility of the MMPI and the MSI for identifying a sexual offender typology. *Sexual Abuse: A Journal of Research and Treatment*, *7*, 185–194.

Schnelle, J.F., Kennedy, M., Rutledge, A.W., & Golden, S.B. (1974). Pupillary response as indication of sexual preference in a juvenile correctional institution. *Journal of Clinical Psychology*, *30*, 146–150.

Seto, M.C. (2001). The value of phallometry in the assessment of male sex offenders. *Journal of Forensic Psychology Practice*, *1*, 65–75.

Seto, M.C. & Kuban, M. (1996). Criterion-related validity of a phallometric test for paraphilic rape and sadism. *Behavior Research and Therapy*, *34*, 175–183.

Seto, M.C., Lalumière, M.L., Kuban, M. (1999). The sexual preferences of incest offenders. *Journal of Abnormal Psychology*, *108*, 267–272.

Simkins, L., Ward, W., Bowman, S., & Rinck, C.M. (1989). The Multiphasic Sex Inventory: Diagnosis and prediction of treatment response in child sexual abusers. *Annals of Sex Research*, *2*, 205–226.

Simon, W.T. & Schouten, P.G. (1991). Plethysmography in the assessment and treatment of sexual deviance: An overview. *Archives of Sexual Behavior*, *20*, 75–91.

Singer, B. (1984). Conceptualising sexual arousal and attraction. *The Journal of Sex Research*, *20*, 230–240.

Studer, L.H., Aylwin, A.S., Clelland, S.R. *et al.* (2002). Primary erotic preference in a group of child molesters. *International Journal of Law and Psychiatry*, *25*, 173–180.

Studer, L.H., Clelland, S.R., Aylwin, A.S. *et al.* (2000). Re-thinking risk assessment for incest offenders. *International Journal of Law and Psychiatry*, *23*, 15–22.

Talmadge, L.D. & Talmadge, W.C. (1990). Sexuality assessment measures for clinical use: A review. *American Journal of Family Therapy*, *18*, 80–105.

Thorne, F.C. (1966). *The Sex Inventory. Journal of Clinical Psychology*, *22*, 367–374.

Travin, S., Cullen, K., & Melella, J.T. (1988). The use and abuse of erection measurements: A forensic perspective. *Bulletin of the American Academy of Psychiatry and the Law*, *16*, 235–250.

Webster, J.S. & Hammer, D. (1983). Thermistor measurement of male sexual arousal. *Psychophysiology*, *20*, 111–115.

Wheeler, D. & Rubin, H.B. (1987). A comparison of volumetric and circumferential measures of penile erection. *Archives of Sexual Behavior*, *16*, 289–299.

Wilcox, D.T. & Sosnowski, D. (2002). Polygraph testing sex offenders. Probation in Europe, Conférence Permanente Européenne de la Probation, No. 26.

Wilcox, D.T., Sosnowski, D. & Middleton, D. (1999). Sex offenders, probation and the polygraph. *NOTA (National Organisation for the Treatment of Abusers) News*, *32*, 18–23.

Wilcox, D.T., Sosnowski, D. & Middleton, D. (2000). Polygraph and the community management of sex offenders. *Forensic Update* (Bulletin of the British Psychological Society), *61*, 20–25.

Wilcox, D.T., Sosnowski, D., Warberg, B., & Beech, A.R. (2005). Sexual history disclosure using the polygraph in a sample of British sex offenders in treatment. *Polygraph Journal*, *34*, 171–181.

Wormith, J.S. (1986). Assessing deviant sexual arousal: Physiological and cognitive aspects. *Advances in Behavior Research and Therapy*, *8*, 101–137.

Wright, L.W. & Adams H.E. (1994). Assessment of sexual preference using a choice reaction time task. *Journal of Psychopathology and Behavioral Assessment*, *16*, 221–231.

Zamansky, H.S. (1956). A technique for measuring homosexual tendencies. *Journal of Personality*, *24*, 436–448.

Zuckerman, M. (1971). Physiological measures of sexual arousal in the human. *Psychological Bulletin*, *75*, 297–329.

Index

Abel Assessment for Sexual Interest (AASI) 313, 314
Abrams, S. 42, 55, 71, 75, 123, 169, 182, 185–6
accuracy 34–5, 38, 39, 41, 155–6, 197–8
  common errors reducing 78–9
    inaccurate interpretation of results 85–8
    insufficient preparation 79–80
    poorly developed questions 80–5
  factors improving
    consequences for test results 200–1
    offender preparation 200
    question construction 199–200
    repeat testing 202–3
  impact of examiner skills 199
  statistical concepts 156–8
  studies evaluating
    example of good accuracy study 167–8
    field studies 163–5
    laboratory studies 166–7
    post-conviction 60–1, 158–62
    pre-conviction 162–3
  surveys of expert opinion 168–9
  unpublished evidence 169–70
  versus utility 198–9
'acquaintance' test 69
actuarial risk assessment 132–3, 198
acute-dynamic risk factors 143–6
additional information, disclosure of
  advantages for offenders 208–10
  increase in following polygraph testing 52–5
  negative effects on professionals 211–12
  value to professionals 210–11
admissions of prior offences
  increase in following polygraph testing 52–5
  US methods of responding to 195–6
  see also confessions
Affinity, viewing time measure 313
age crossover 140, 203, 204
Ahlmeyer, S. 53, 54, 188, 200–1, 203
alternative technologies 267–8
  event-related potential (ERP) studies 273–9
  functional MRI (fMRI) studies 279–83
  model of deception 283–9
  pupillometry 271–3
  thermal imaging 269–71
  voice stress analysis (VSA) 268–9, 270
American Polygraph Association (APA) 71–2
  standards 43, 67, 113, 174, 189
  training course 36, 43, 67
Ames, Aldrich, Russian spy 40–1
anecdotal evidence 169–70
anxiety
  detected by voice stress analysis 268
  during interrogation 255
  in polygraphees 69, 83–4, 146

Association for the Treatment of Sexual Abusers (ATSA)
  guidelines for polygraph use 42–3, 49, 218
  polygraphy overcoming reliance on self-reports 218
attentional methodologies 312
  information processing 314–15
  viewing time measures 312–14

Backster, Cleve 37
base rates, impact of 161–2, 163, 208
battering
  interventions 232
  precursors to 233–4
Beatty, Judge 71
Beech, A. R. 53, 133–8, 141, 143, 145–6, 314–15
behavioral confirmation effect 173–4
Ben-Shakhar, G. 167, 173
biases, examiner 172–4
bogus pipeline effect 58, 142–3
brain activation during deception 279–83
brain waves, measurement of 273–9, 285–7

card sort 308–9
case studies 97–9
  denial breakdown 99–103
  disclosure of new information 103–10
child pornography
  case studies 101–3, 105–6, 108–10
  see also internet offenders
child sexual offending, possible link to image downloading 114–15
civil investigations, use of polygraph for 66–7
Clarke Sexual History Questionnaire 310
clinical application of polygraph 88–9
cognitive behavioral therapy (CBT) 224
  Relapse Prevention Model 225, 229
cognitive confirmation effect 172–3
cognitive interview (CI) 246
  effectiveness of 248–9
  enhanced cognitive interview (ECI) 248
  original cognitive interview (OCI) 246–8
community supervision/treatment 11–12, 16, 50–1, 130, 147, 183
Comparison Question Test (CQT) 32, 37
  accuracy of
    countermeasures reducing 170–1
    examiner bias affecting 172–3
    expert opinion of 168–9
    field studies 165
    impact of socialization 174–5
    laboratory studies 166–7
  use in SHDE exam 117–18
comparison questions 36–7, 69, 84, 170–1
compliant false confessions 260, 261–2
Computerized Voice Stress Analyzer (CVSA) 269
concealed knowledge paradigm 275
confessions
  impact on court proceedings 257
  interrogation techniques
    acquiring first admission 252–3
    developing full confession 255–6
  psychological aspects of 59–60
  see also false confessions
consequences of test results
  improving accuracy 200–1
  pre- and post-conviction differences 86–7
construct validity 156
containment approach 16, 24–5, 42, 78
  aspects of 191
  criminal justice incentive for compliance 194–5
  effectiveness of 196–7
  handling offences disclosed 195–6
  polygraph testing as one tool of 193–4
  in prison environment 193
  team approach 191–3
contingent negative variation (CNV) 307

Control Question Test (CQT) *see* Comparison Question Test (CQT)
controversy surrounding polygraphy 2, 25, 31, 43, 50, 181
Coors, William 38
countermeasures used by offenders 170–1, 206, 208
criminal investigations, use of polygraph in 38–9
Criminal Justice and Courts Service Act (2000), UK 11
criterion validity 156
crossover sexual offending 1–2
  characteristics 139
    age of victim 140, 203, 204
    relationship to victim 140–1, 203, 205
    sex of victim 139–40, 206, 207
  disclosure of 54
'cybersex' 115

deceptive behavior model 284–9
'defensive lying' 59
'demand characteristics' of pre- and post-conviction testing 85, 88
denial 21–2, 51
  breaking down, case studies 99–103, 111
  four types of 72–3
  and monitoring exam 77–8
  MSI questionnaire measuring levels of 311–12
  pre- and post-conviction differences 87–8
  problems of false 257–62
  and self-reports 115, 116, 119–20
  shame maintaining 21
  SHDE revealing 124
  specific issue testing 44, 51–2, 72–4, 79, 82, 227–8
developmental factors, etiological model 134, 135
DI (Deception Indicated) result 37
  consequences of 86–7
disclosure
  advantages for offenders 208–10
  case studies 103–10
  false confessions 148–9
  of high-risk behaviors 56–7, 144–5
  increase in following polygraph testing 52–5
  minimization of 133–4
  of sexual history 74–6, 115–16
  versus change 147–8
domestic abuse 231
  consequences of 223
  link with stalking 237
  new legislation, UK 224
  non-reporting of 222
    reasons for 223
  polygraph history exam 227
  prevalence in the UK 221, 222
  treatment programs 224–5, 231–3
    use of polygraph 233–4
drug abuse
  accuracy study 160–2
  reduced following polygraph testing 58, 71
dynamic risk assessment 133–4

Earle, J. H. 110–11
Elaad, E. 167, 173
electro-encephalographic (EEG) measurements of arousal 306–7
Employee Polygraph Protection Act (1988), US 40
employee screening 37–9, 40, 41, 67, 172–3
England and Wales
  case studies in polygraph utility 97–111
  other post-conviction applications of polygraphy 217–40
English, K. 42, 53, 54–5, 71, 97, 111, 140, 145, 182, 203, 205–7
enhanced cognitive interview (ECI) 248
errors in polygraphy 45, 78–88
  consequences of 212
  influence of base rates 208
  see also accuracy
ethical issues 38, 67, 81–2, 146–7, 301, 307–8
Ethical Standards and Principles for the Management of Sexual Abusers (ATSA) 42–3

etiological model of risk 134, 135
  developmental factors 134
  vulnerability factors 136–7
etiology of sex offending, link to risk factors 12–13
event-related potentials (ERPs) 273–9
examiners
  examiner bias 172–4
  preparation 79–80
  skills, impact on accuracy 45, 80–4, 199
  training 4, 43, 67, 68–9, 85, 182, 189
  see also therapists
executive functions 285
expectations of examiner, effect on polygraph outcomes 172–4
experimentally controlled studies, importance of 54, 55, 143, 158
expert opinion surveys 168–9
expressive violence 235
external validity 158

faking 170–1, 228–9, 303–4, 312, 314, 315
false confessions 59–60, 148–9, 258
  chances of making 202–3
  false evidence producing internalized 259–60, 261–2
  frequency of 258–9
  as a result of polygraph testing 202–3
  role of interrogation 259–62
  see also false positives
false evidence, producing internalized false confessions 259–60, 261–2
false negatives 156, 157
  influence of high base rates 208
  negative outcomes of 262
  rates of 158–60, 165, 166, 167, 174, 202–3
  reducing 68–9
false positives 68, 85, 156, 157, 257
  and false confessions 258–62
  rates of 158, 159, 165–7, 174, 198
  reducing by 'trial run' 69
  and repeat testing 202–3, 208
Farwell, Larry 273
Fay, Floyd Buzz 40
field studies 160–1, 162, 163–5, 175
forensic assessment of sexual interest 297–8
  human erotic response 298
  non-physiological methods 308
    attentional methodologies 312–15
    card sort 308–9
    issues with self-report measures 312
    standardized questionnaires 309–12
  physiological measures
    electro-encephalography (EEG) 306–7
    ethical and practical issues 307–8
    photoelectric surface blood volume 305–6
    plethysmography 299–305
    pupillometry 306
    thermistor measurements 305
frame of reference (TOR) 85–6
Frye, James 33–4
'Frye test' 34
functional magnetic resonance imaging (fMRI) 279–83
functional risk assessment 131–2

galvanic skin response (GSR) 35, 66
Gannon, T. A. 142–3
gender crossover 139–40, 206, 207
Ginton, A. 167–8, 173
Grubin, D. 3, 18, 56–7, 59, 61, 144, 158–61, 185, 228
guidelines
  for interrogations 252
  for post-conviction testing 3–4, 22, 34, 42–3, 189
  Sex Offender Management Board, Colorado 192
guilt 21, 34, 35
  acquiring first admission of 252–5
  and socialization 174–5
  see also confessions

Hanson, R. K. 14–15, 20, 133, 228–9, 232, 308, 309
Harway, M. 232–4
Heil, P. 53, 140, 200–1, 203, 205

high-risk behaviors 50
  deterrent effect of polygraph 185–6
  disclosure of 56–7, 144–5
  effect of maintenance testing 185, 188–9, 190
  SHDE revealing true level of 123
  towards children 121, 124
historical risk factors 136, 138–42
history examination
  for domestic abusers 226–7, 233
  sexual history 74–6, 115–16
history of polygraph 65–7
  post-conviction use 41–5, 70–2
  pre-conviction use of 32–41
  in the United States 182–4
Holden, E. J. 45, 68–9
honesty, polygraph facilitating 227–9
human rights violation issues 146–7

immunity from prosecution 74–5, 195
incest, relationship crossover 203, 204
information processing, effect of sexual arousal 314–15
information revealed by polygraph tests 186–9
  see also additional information, disclosure of
instrumental violence 234–5
interagency/interdisciplinary team approach 191–7
internal validity 158
internalized false confessions 259–60, 261–2
internet offenders 113–14
  denial of high-risk behavior 124
  downloaders of child pornography 114–15
  sexual behavior checklist 127–8
  sexual history disclosure polygraph exam (SHDE) 115–16
    lying, definition of 116
    studies using 116–23
interrogations 243, 251–2
  differentiating from interviews 244–6
  effectiveness of 256–7
  errors 257
    false negatives 262
    false positives 258–62
  general process 252–6
interviews 243
  assessing credibility 249–50
  differentiating from interrogations 244–6
  gathering factual information 246–9
  preparing suspect for interrogation 251
irrelevant questions 34, 36

job recruitment 37–8
juvenile testing 183

Keeler, Leonarde 35–6

laboratory studies 166–7, 175
Lafayette, polygraph manufacturer 118, 172
Larson, John 34–5
learning disabled offenders, assessment of sexual arousal 313
legislation 2–3, 10–12, 40, 43, 237–8
'lie detectors' 33, 38, 49, 58, 66, 67–8, 169
lying
  conflicting theories of 274
  'defensive' 59
  definition of 116–17
  history of polygraph 32–3, 35
  see also false negatives; false positives
Lykken, D. T., critic of polygraph 38–9, 42, 168–9

Madsen, L. 56, 57–8, 59, 61, 145, 148, 158–61
Magical X effect 139
maintenance polygraph examinations 52, 72, 76–7
  case studies 102–3, 109
  facilitating treatment 228–9
  helping to monitor offender behavior in the community 340
  identification of persistent risk 188–9

maintenance polygraph examinations (*Continued*)
  for monitoring treatment progress 185
  pre-test interview questions
    domestic abusers 233–4
    stalkers 239–40
    violent offenders 236
Maletzky, B. M. 51
Marston, William 33–4
masturbation
  case studies 100–3, 105, 106–7
  to child pornography 118–21
  to deviant fantasies, risk factor 56, 57–8, 77, 190
  questions about 92, 127–8
Matte, J. A. 45
maximizations and minimizations, interrogation tactics 260–1
McKee, B. 53
Meet the Folks (BBC1 television program) 32–3
Megan's Law 11, 12
memory
  effect of inaccurate 288
  model of deception 284–5, 287–8, 289
  retrieval using cognitive interviews 246–8
  working memory load theory 274, 276
Mentally Disordered Sex Offender Statutes (MDSOs) 11
min/max technique 261
misdiagnosis *see* false negatives; false positives
misinformation paradigm 288
monitoring polygraph examinations
  other offending populations 228–9, 230, 231, 233
  sex offenders 44, 55–7, 71–2, 77–8
multidisciplinary approaches 78, 191–4, 237
Multiphasic Sex Inventory (MSI) 311–12
multiple issue test 197–8
Munsterberg, Hugo 33

NDI (No Deception Indicated) result 37, 118
  consequences of 86–7
    improving accuracy 200–1
negative predictive power 156–7
  impact of base rates 162
negative state relief model, interrogation tactic 254–5
Nicholson, Harold, Russian spy 40

O'Connell, M. A. 52, 203, 204
oddball paradigm 275–6
Offender Management Act (2007), UK 2, 3
offenders
  advantages of disclosure 208–10
  gaps in treatment/supervision of 218–19
  human rights of 146–7
  minimizing disclosure 133–4
  over-reliance on self-reports of 218
  reasons for non-reporting of offences 219
  see also sex offenders
offending behavior
  role of polygraph in managing
    assessment 225–7
    monitoring and supervision 229–30
    treatment 227–9
  using polygraph to validate change in 219–20
  see also sexual offending
Ogard, E. 55, 71, 185–6
onset age of offenders 24, 141, 187–8
original cognitive interview (OCI) 246–8

paraphilias
  Abel's assessment of 313, 314
  arrest rates 184
  crossover studies 203–7
  and history of non-sexual offending 23–4
PCSOT (post-conviction sex offender testing) 32, 43–4, 113, 158–62
Peak of Tension Test (POT) 35
penile tumescence, measures of 299–305
periodic polygraph testing, deterrent effect of 3, 41, 42, 55, 57–8, 71
personality disorders and false confessors 59–60

personality, impact on accuracy of polygraph 161, 174–5
photoelectric surface blood volume measurements 305–6
physical factors affecting accuracy of test results 85
physiological correlates of countermeasures 171–2
physiological reactivity 66
  establishing normal range 70
plethysmography 23, 299–300
  concerns about 304–5
  discriminative validity 301–2
  faking 303–4
  problem of low responders 303
  stimulus variance 300–1
  test-retest reliability 302–3
polygraphy
  conventional use of 66–7
  effect on professionals 210–12
  first scientific evaluation of 38
  scientific principles underlying 66
  standards for use of 42–3, 67
  training in 4, 43, 67, 68–9, 85, 182, 189
  working principles 67–70
pornography *see* child pornography
positive predictive power 156–7
  impact of base rates 162
'positive therapist style' 15–16
post-conviction polygraphy 16–19
  application to non-sex offender populations 220–4
    domestic abuse 221
    general violence 222
    stalking 221–2
  caveats to the use of 22–5
  empirical evidence 52–5
  guidelines and standards 3–4, 42–3
  history of 41–5, 70–2
  implications for practice 19–22
  UK legislation providing for 2–3
post-conviction sex offender testing (PCSOT) 43, 44–5
  accuracy of
    errors reducing 78–88
    studies 158–62
  background and history 65–7, 70–2
  examinations 44
    maintenance 76–7
    monitoring 77–8
    sexual history disclosure 74–6
    special issue denial testing 72–4
  standards 42–3, 67, 113, 189
  treatment and supervision of sex offenders 49–50
  see also containment approach
practice effect 287–8
'practice' polygraph examinations 82–3
pre-conviction polygraph testing
  accuracy, research evidence for 162–3
  background 32–3
  controversy surrounding 31, 43, 50
  criticisms of 31, 67
  demand characteristics 85, 88
  denial issues 87
  emotional impact of exam on polygraphee 86
  'investigative-type' uses 43, 66–7
  'practice' examinations 82–3
  time of reference and frame of reference 85–6
predictive accuracy, estimate of 132–3
prevalence rates
  non-sexual offences 220, 221, 222
  sex offending 9–10
privacy invasions 147
probation, use of maintenance exam during 76–7
professionals, effect of polygraph information on 210–12
psychological dispositions, causal role of 136
'psychological set', establishing 67–8, 82–3, 88
psychopaths, polygraph effectiveness with 45, 175, 201
publication bias 170
pupillometry 271–3, 306
'Pygmalion effect' 172

questionnaire studies
  on accuracy of polygraph tests 158–60
  on value of polygraph testing 57–8
questionnaires
  MOLEST 142–3
  sexual history 76, 92–5
  sexual interest 309–12, 313, 314

questions
  comparison 36–7, 69, 84, 170–1
  denial-related 74
  impact of poorly developed 80–4, 199–200
  non-judgmental 76
  relevant and irrelevant 34, 36, 37, 69–70, 117–18

rapists, adult-child crossover 203, 204
rational actor process, interrogation strategy 253–4, 255
Reagan, Ronald 39, 40
Receiver Operating Characteristic (ROC) curve 157
  Area Under Curve Analysis (AUC) 132–3
recidivism
  domestic abusers 232
  in sexual offenders 9, 55, 140
    predictors of 14, 19–20, 114
      polygraph identifying 186
    probability of 132–3, 198
    reduction of 18–19
      containment model 78, 196
      by periodic polygraph exams 55, 71, 77–8
      relapse prevention model 13, 15, 22, 144–5, 229
regulation of polygraphy, lack of 67
rehabilitation principles 14
Reid, J. E. 36–7
relapse prevention (RP) model 13, 50, 224–5
  with cognitive behavioral therapy 14–15
  effectiveness of 15, 225
  pre-offence build-up phase of 229
  treatment stages 50
relationship crossover 140–1, 203, 205
Relevant-Irrelevant Test (RIT) 34, 35, 36
'relevant' questions 36, 37, 69–70, 117–18
reoffending *see* recidivism
repeat polygraph testing
  deterrent effect of 41, 42, 55, 57–8, 71
  improving accuracy 202–3
results of polygraph testing
  inaccurate interpretation of 85–8
  physical factors affecting 85
risk assessment 129–31
  current methods 131
    actuarial assessment 132–3
    dynamic assessment 133–4
    functional assessment 131–2
  dynamic risk factors linked to recidivism 14
  etiological model 134
    developmental factors 134–5
    vulnerability factors 136–7
  future directions 149
  polygraph-assisted 137–8
    assessing psychological traits 142–3
    crossover offences 139–41
    dilemmas of 146–9
    eliciting historical/static profiles 138–42
    monitoring acute-dynamic risk factors 143–6

Salter, Anna 3, 42, 73
scoring systems, initial polygraph 37
self-reports
  over-reliance upon 218
  validation of 219–20, 238–40
sensitivity 156, 158
sex offenders
  assessment of using polygraph 52–5
  monitoring of using polygraph 55–7
  motivation to change 147–8
  onset age of 24, 141, 187–8
  relationship to victim 140–1
  underestimation of past histories 184–5
Sex Offenders Act (1997), UK 11
sexual fantasies, risk factor 20–1
sexual history disclosure polygraph examination (SHDE) 51, 74–6, 115–16
  future directions 123–4
  studies using 116–23
sexual history questionnaire 92–5
  completing prior to examination 75–6
Sexual Interest Card Sort Questionnaire 308–9

sexual interest, measurement of *see* forensic assessment of sexual interest
sexual offending
  costs to community 10
  etiology and risk factors 12–13
  management strategies 10–12
  prevalence of 9–10
  treatment outcome 14–15
  treatment style 15–16
  under-identification of 186–7
  under-reporting of 184
Sexually Violent Predator Statutes (SVP) 11
shame 21
SHDE (sexual history disclosure polygraph examination) 74–6, 115–16
Simons, D. 54, 200–1, 206
skin conduction (perspiration) 66, 142–3
SONAR (Sex Offender Need Assessment Rating) 133
Sosnowski, D. 17, 53, 56, 97, 98
specific issue (denial) testing 44, 51–2, 72–4, 77–8, 79, 82, 227–8
specificity 156, 158
spies tested with the polygraph 40–1
stable-dynamic risk 136, 142–3
stalking
  current treatment/supervision 237
  gaps in the system 237–8
  polygraph application 238–40
  prevalence of 221–2
  stalker behaviors 239–40
  types of stalkers 236–7
  victim profile 237
standards 3–4, 43, 67, 113, 189
state factors, etiological model 135, 136–7
Static-99, actuarial instrument 132–3
static risk factors 136, 138–42
statistical concepts 156–8
substance abuse, risk factor 98, 133, 235, 237
'successive hurdles' approach 198
supervision
  community 11, 16, 50–1, 130
  criminal justice 194–5
  gaps in the system 218–19, 232–3, 237–8
  non-sexual offenders 231, 235, 237
  use of polygraph 41–2, 44, 51–2, 55–7, 61
  see also maintenance polygraph examinations
surveys of expert opinion 168–9

'tagging' of offenders 51, 218
temperature measurements
  of sexual arousal 305
  thermal imaging 269–71
test-retest reliability 302–3
Teuscher, T. 41–2
therapists
  attitude, effect on accuracy 201
  impact of information on 210–12
  style, effect on treatment outcome 15–16, 21, 24
  see also examiners
thermal imaging 269–71
thermistor device, detection of sexual arousal 305
Thorne Sex Inventory (TSI) 310–11
threat(s)
  attentional capture 274
  automatic response to perception of 66, 68
  consistent correlate of violence 238
  as inducement to confess 261
time of reference (TOR) 85–6
training 4, 43, 67, 68–9, 85, 182, 189
treatment
  cognitive behavioral therapy (CBT) 224
  domestic abuse 231–4
  general violence 235–6
  polygraph facilitating honesty 227–9
  of sex offenders 13
    containment approach 191–7
    difficulty monitoring progress 185
    outcome and management 14–16
    relapse prevention approach 50–1
  stalking 237–40

triggering risk factors, etiological model 135, 137
Tuttle, Judge 71

under-reporting
  by offenders 140, 147
  by victims 184, 222, 223
United Kingdom (UK)
  case studies of convicted sex offenders 97–111
  legislation 2–3, 11
  need for standards 3–4
  other post-conviction applications of polygraphy 217–40
United States
  accuracy issues in use of polygraph 197–201
  countermeasures used by offenders 206, 208
  crossover studies 203–6, 207
  effect of polygraph information on professionals 210–12
  history of polygraph 32–41
  legislation 10–11, 40, 43
  polygraph in the context of a containment team 191–4
    admissions of prior offences 195–6
    criminal justice incentives for compliance 194–5
  post-conviction sex offender testing 41–5
  US Congress Office of Technology Assessment (OTA) report 39–40
unpublished evidence of polygraph accuracy 169–70
utility of polygraph, case studies illustrating 97–111
utility versus accuracy debate 198–9

validation of offenders' self-reports 219–20, 238–40
validity, concepts of 156–8
Vendemia, J. M. C. 278, 286–7
victim crossover characteristics 139–41
viewing time measures 312–14
violent behavior/crimes 222
  consequences of 222–3
  current treatment/supervision 235
  expressive and instrumental 234–5
  polygraph application 235–6
  under-reporting of 222, 223
voice stress analysis (VSA) 268–9
  studies evaluating 270
vulnerability factors, etiological model 135, 136–7

Warberg, B. 53, 56
Ward, T. 21, 134, 136–8, 141, 143, 145–6
working memory
  load theory 274, 276
  model of deception 284–5, 287–8, 289